Crisis and Reform
in Latin America

Crisis and Reform in Latin America

FROM DESPAIR TO HOPE

Sebastian Edwards

Published for the World Bank

OXFORD UNIVERSITY PRESS

Oxford University Press

OXFORD NEW YORK TORONTO
DELHI BOMBAY CALCUTTA MADRAS KARACHI
KUALA LUMPUR SINGAPORE HONG KONG TOKYO
NAIROBI DAR ES SALAAM CAPE TOWN
MELBOURNE AUCKLAND
and associated companies in
BERLIN IBADAN

Published by Oxford University Press, Inc.
200 Madison Avenue, New York, N.Y. 10016

Oxford is a registered trademark of Oxford University Press.

Manufactured in the United States of America
First printing August 1995

The findings, interpretations, and conclusions expressed in this study are entirely
those of the author and should not be attributed in any manner to the World Bank,
to its affiliated organizations, or to members of its Board of Executive Directors
or the countries they represent.

Library of Congress Cataloging-in-Publication Data

Edwards, Sebastian, 1953–
  Crisis and reform in Latin America : from despair to hope /
Sebastian Edwards.
    p. cm.
  Includes bibliographical references and index.
  ISBN 0-19-521105-7
    1. Structural adjustment (Economic policy)—Latin America.
  2. Economic stabilization—Latin America. 3. Latin America—
  Economic policy. 4. Latin America—Economic conditions—1982–
  I. Title.
  HC125.E39   1995
  338.98—dc20   95-6551
                                                            CIP

Contents

===

PREFACE   *vii*

1. INTRODUCTION: THE LAUNCHING OF THE REFORMS   *1*
   The Reforms, 1982–93: A Brief Overview   *6*
   Plan of the Book   *10*

PART I. THE DEBT CRISIS AND EARLY ADJUSTMENT: 1982–87   *15*

2. MUDDLING THROUGH: ADJUSTMENT FROM 1982 TO 1987   *17*
   Was the Debt Crisis Anticipated?   *18*
   External and Domestic Origins of the Crisis   *22*
   The Adjustment   *23*
   Heterodox Stabilization Attempts in the Mid-1980s   *33*
   Fiscal Control and Incomes Policies: The Mexican Pacto   *39*

3. THE EMERGENCE OF A NEW LATIN AMERICAN CONSENSUS   *41*
   The Crisis of Traditional Economic Thinking in Latin America:
      An Overview   *43*
   Factors behind the Emerging Consensus   *48*
   How Broad is the Emerging Consensus?   *58*

PART II. AN ERA OF ADJUSTMENT AND REFORM: 1987–93   *67*

4. MACROECONOMIC ADJUSTMENT AS A PRIORITY   *69*
   Debt Restructuring, Debt Relief, and Macroeconomic Adjustment   *71*
   Fiscal Policy and Macroeconomic Equilibrium   *83*
   Exchange Rates, Inflation, and Disinflation   *99*
   Summary and Conclusions   *105*
   Appendix 4-1: Debt and Debt Service Reduction Agreements   *106*
   Appendix 4-2: Inflationary Inertia and Nominal Exchange
      Rate Anchors   *107*

v

5. The Opening of Latin America   *115*
   From Protectionism to Liberalization: Some Analytical Aspects   *117*
   Recent Trade Liberalization Reforms in Latin America
     and the Caribbean   *124*
   Effects of Trade Liberalization   *129*
   Real Exchange Rate Behavior, Capital Inflows, and the Future
     of Trade Reforms in Latin America   *137*
   Regional Trading Blocs in Latin America   *142*
   Appendix 5-1: Productivity Growth and Openness:
     An Econometric Analysis   *164*

6. Privatization and Deregulation   *170*
   Privatization and Deregulation: Analytical Issues
     and Policy Options   *171*
   Privatization Programs in Chile, Mexico, and Argentina   *183*

7. Capital Market Deregulation, Savings, and Investment   *200*
   Financial Repression in Latin America: Historical Background   *203*
   Financial Deregulation in Latin America: Regional Trends
     and Selected Experiences   *208*
   Savings and Investment   *224*
   Appendix 7-1: Financial Development and Productivity Growth   *249*

8. Poverty, Income Distribution, and Human Resources   *252*
   Poverty and Income Distribution   *256*
   Education, Human Capital Formation, and Social Conditions   *273*
   Labor Market Regulations in Latin America   *277*
   Addressing the Social Agenda: Policy Options and Priorities   *286*

Part III. Looking toward the Future   *293*

9. The Mexican Crisis of 1994 and the Future
   of the Latin American Reforms   *295*
   The Mexican Peso Crisis of 1994 and Its Lessons   *296*
   Latin America after Mexico   *303*
   Conclusions   *313*
   Appendix 9-1: The Simple Economics of Current Account
     Sustainability   *314*

Notes   *319*

References   *331*

Index   *353*

Preface

DURING THE PAST FEW YEARS, THE LATIN AMERICAN COUNTRIES HAVE
gone through major economic reforms that have greatly changed the region's
economic landscape. What started as an isolated and slow process—Chile was
the sole reformer in the 1970s—has become a sweeping movement affecting
virtually every country in the region. The economic system that had emerged
in the 1930s, based on heavy government intervention, protectionism, and
broad regulations, has given way to one based on market orientation, openness, and competition. Perhaps the greatest sign of change is the eagerness
with which most nations in the region have pursued free trade agreements
with the industrial world. This contrasts sharply with the economic isolation-
ism and autarkic attitude of only a decade or so ago. What makes the current
reform process particularly attractive is that it has taken place at a time when
democratic rule has returned to virtually every country, Cuba being the glaring
exception.

This book deals with the history of the Latin American economic reforms.
It analyzes the economic developments in the region from 1982 to 1994. The
starting point is the debt crisis of 1982, and the discussion then focuses on the
heterodox plans of the mid-1980s, the stabilization programs of the late
1980s, the opening to international trade, the privatization and deregulation
process, and social security reforms. Finally, the book describes the circumstances that led to the Mexican peso crisis of December 1994. Throughout,
the discussion emphasizes the evolution of social conditions in the region,
including poverty and inequality.

The analysis addresses a number of important conceptual issues that have
preoccupied economists for a long time. Among other topics, it deals with the
sequencing of reform, the speed of trade liberalization, the role of ideas in the
launching of a reform process, alternative modes of privatizing state-owned
enterprises, the effectiveness of exchange rates as nominal anchors, and the

use of emergency social funds as a way of providing a social safety net during the transition. An important conclusion of the analysis is that many of the lessons from the Latin American countries will be useful to other nations embarked on reform processes, including Asian and Eastern European countries.

The book ends with an analysis of the eruption of the Mexican crisis of 1994 and an evaluation of Latin America's challenges for the future. In the last chapter, I argue that there is an urgent need to reduce the region's legendary degree of poverty. Social unrest in a number of countries has recently reminded regional leaders that a significant number of people, more than 110 million by some counts, still live in abject poverty. Simply put, this means that if Latin America is to achieve social peace and stability, and if the market-oriented reforms are to be consolidated, the political coalition that supports the modernization process will have to be expanded. This, in turn, means that the rate of economic growth will have to accelerate significantly and the fruits of progress will have to be distributed more evenly.

I started working on this book in July 1992, when I was at UCLA's Anderson Graduate School of Management. S. Shahid Husain and Marcelo Selowsky, then vice president and chief economist, respectively, of the World Bank's Latin America and the Caribbean Region, persuaded me that the time was ripe for evaluating the Latin American structural adjustment program. In March 1993, I finished a draft that was circulated broadly and discussed extensively in numerous seminars at the World Bank, research institutions, and universities. I am grateful to many colleagues for their comments, suggestions, and criticisms. They helped to improve the manuscript greatly. In September 1993, a revised and shortened version of the original manuscript was circulated at the World Bank Annual Meetings under the title "Latin America and the Caribbean a Decade after the Debt Crisis."

In revising the manuscript, I especially benefited from long and detailed comments by Andres Bianchi, Albert Fishlow, Arnold Harberger, and Francisco Gil Díaz. Fernando Losada assisted me diligently, and almost always with a good sense of humor, throughout the many stages of this project. The finished book is the product of a team of capable professionals, led by Alfred Imhoff, that included Vicki Chamlee, Gaudencio Dizon, Elizabeth Forsyth, Audrey Heiligman, and Cindy Stock. I am particularly grateful to Jennifer Abner, who not only typed the final version efficiently but has made my life manageable since I came to the World Bank.

Sebastian Edwards
Washington, D.C.
August 1995

CHAPTER 1

Introduction:
The Launching of the Reforms

LATIN AMERICA ENTERED THE POST–WORLD WAR II ERA WITH GREAT optimism. International reserves were at record levels, an incipient manufacturing sector was developing vigorously, and faith in the ability of government policies to secure growth and cure social ills was almost unlimited. Moreover, the creation of the Bretton Woods institutions generated expectations of a stable international economic environment, free of the financial and payments crises that had afflicted the region for many decades. Starting in the mid-1940s, most Latin American countries followed a development strategy based on a high degree of protectionism, government-led industrialization, and broad involvement of the state in economic activities. For some time it seemed that this approach was working and that early promises of growth and prosperity would materialize, allowing the Latin American countries to move gradually into the ranks of the more industrialized nations.

Between 1950 and 1980, Latin America grew at an annual average rate of almost 6 percent, significantly faster than the industrial nations and only marginally slower than the East Asian economies.[1] However, this rapid growth was accompanied by disturbing developments that steadily undermined the long-term sustainability of the regional strategy. First, excessive protectionism and generalized government controls greatly encouraged rent-seeking activities and created a rigid economic structure unable to react rapidly to changing world economic conditions. Second, in many countries the combination of increasing burdens on public sector budgets and inefficient tax systems reduced government's ability to provide social services efficiently and generated an increasing degree of inequality. By the late 1970s, the region had, by far, the most unequal distribution of income in the world. Third, as a result of weak public finance structures, more and more countries were forced to rely on inflationary financing as a way to bridge government expenditures and reve-

Table 1-1. Evolution of Foreign Indebtedness in Selected Countries of Latin America, 1975–92

Country	Ratio of debt to GDP[a]					Net transfers on public and publicly guaranteed debt (millions of dollars)				
	1975	1980	1983	1987	1992	1975	1980	1983	1987	1992
Early reformers										
Bolivia (1985)	0.50	0.88	1.40	1.35	0.81	90	151	–138	92	169
Chile (1975)	0.66	0.44	0.91	1.13	0.47	–219	–517	876	–627	–768
Mexico (1985–86)	0.17	0.30	0.62	0.78	0.35	2,493	1,241	–4,238	–1,707	–8,503
Second–wave reformers										
Costa Rica (1988)	0.35	0.57	1.33	1.04	0.61	88	229	–176	–65	–272
Jamaica (1987–88)	0.56	0.71	1.06	1.57	1.31	129	122	205	–78	–286
Trinidad and Tobago (1987–88)	0.06	0.13	0.18	0.38	0.42	–16	137	7	–252	–112
Uruguay (1987–88)	0.22	0.17	0.65	0.58	0.46	56	95	198	–139	80
Third–wave reformers										
Argentina (1990–91)	0.15	0.35	0.44	0.54	0.30	315	852	114	–1,643	–2,311
Brazil (1991)	0.19	0.30	0.48	0.42	0.31	2,073	199	573	–5,413	–4,142
Colombia (1990–91)	0.21	0.21	0.29	0.47	0.35	147	487	443	–1,159	–2,003
El Salvador (1989–90)	0.23	0.26	0.48	0.45	0.33	13	68	221	–61	–95
Guatemala (1992)	0.07	0.15	0.20	0.39	0.26	18	93	167	–212	–258
Guyana (1989)	0.61	1.34	2.47	4.83	5.01	88	44	8	20	–37

Honduras (1990)	0.34	0.58	0.69	0.79	1.09	82	167	118	5	20
Nicaragua (1990)	0.39	1.05	1.47	1.68	6.02	105	180	231	478	219
Panama (1992)	0.43	0.84	1.00	1.06	1.14	173	-62	-61	-218	-466
Paraguay (1991–92)	0.15	0.21	0.25	0.68	0.27	20	79	186	5	-486
Peru (1991)	0.31	0.45	0.59	0.63	0.92	666	-258	1,005	198	-322
Venezuela (1989)	0.05	0.42	0.47	0.72	0.61	-310	-85	-260	-2,384	-559
Nonreformers										
Dominican Republic	0.19	0.30	0.43	0.77	0.60	40	261	14	-21	-139
Ecuador	0.16	0.51	0.72	1.00	0.97	109	408	-256	92	-461
Haiti	0.10	0.21	0.35	0.39	0.29	10	27	28	67	1
Latin America and the Caribbean										
Average	0.19	0.32	0.54	0.61	0.38	n.a.	n.a.	n.a.	n.a.	n.a.
Total	n.a.	n.a.	n.a.	n.a.	n.a.	5,539	3,934	n.a.	-12,918	-20,815

n.a. Not applicable.

Note: The years in parentheses following the country names represent the approximate starting date of reforms. Nonreformers of course do not have dates.

a. Stock of total external debt, outstanding and disbursed, at the end of the period.

Source: Data base of the World Bank, International Economics Department.

nues. And fourth, as a consequence of the inward-looking strategy, exports were greatly discouraged, barely growing between 1960 and 1980.

After the first oil shock of 1973, the mode of development followed by Latin America became increasingly unsustainable, as a growing percentage of capital accumulation was financed with foreign borrowing. The aggregate current account deficit for Latin America and the Caribbean more than doubled between 1972 and 1982, rising from 2.2 to 5.5 percent of gross domestic product (GDP). Also, after 1973, the state enterprise sector grew at a fast pace, crowding out private initiatives. Moreover, as a consequence of the maze of regulations and distortions accumulated during the decades of heavy government intervention, the return on physical investment was relatively low. This development strategy was clearly unsustainable, as reflected by the region's ratio of foreign debt to GDP, which grew rapidly from 0.19 in 1975 to 0.46 in 1982, and by the slowdown in economic growth (see table 1-1).

The policies followed by Latin America since World War II contrasted sharply with those adopted by a group of economies in East Asia—Hong Kong, Republic of Korea, and Singapore, among others—since the mid-1960s. While the majority of the Latin American governments encouraged inward-looking growth and underestimated the importance of macroeconomic stability, the East Asian economies implemented policies that actively and vigorously encouraged exports and preserved macroeconomic equilibria. Additionally, domestic savings in East Asia increased to a point where the need to rely on foreign borrowing was significantly reduced (see World Bank

Table 1-2. Economic Performance in East Asia and Latin America, 1965–80
(percentage)

Indicator	Latin America and the Caribbean	East Asia
Annual rate of growth of real GDP	6.0	7.2
Annual rate of growth of manufacturing	7.0	10.6
Annual rate of inflation	31.5	9.3
Annual rate of growth of exports	−1.0	10.0
Ratio of gross national savings to GDP		
1965	0.19	0.23
1980	0.20	0.29
Ratio of debt to GDP, 1980	0.35	0.17
Share of income received by lower 20 percent of population, approximately 1980	2.9	6.2

Note: GDP, gross domestic product. Inflation is measured as the percentage change in the consumer price index. Growth of exports refers to the evolution of the volume of exports.

Source: World Bank, *World Development Report,* various years.

1993a for a detailed discussion of the East Asian "miracle" economies). The data in table 1-2 capture in an eloquent way the main historical differences in economic performance in these two regions in the 1965–80 period. In addition to growth differentials, four facts stand out. First, East Asia's vigorous export growth of 10 percent a year contrasted sharply with the decline of Latin America's exports at the rate of 1 percent a year. Second, the average rate of inflation was three times higher in Latin America than in East Asia.[2] Third, the saving rate was substantially higher in East Asia than in Latin America. In fact, the differential in saving rates between the two regions increased significantly between 1965 and 1980. And fourth, income was distributed in a more unequal fashion in Latin America than in East Asia.[3]

The debt crisis unleashed in 1982 and the failure of early policies implemented in some countries to deal with it—the Austral Plan in Argentina, the Cruzado Plan in Brazil, and the APRA Plan in Peru—played an important role in reshaping policy views in Latin America. It became increasingly apparent that relying heavily on the state to run the economy did not generate the expected results. Instead of *protecting* the public from major external shocks, the overexpanded state greatly weakened the ability of these economies to react to foreign disturbances. Politicians and policymakers began to sense— slowly at first and then more rapidly—that the inward-oriented policies followed by the majority of countries in the region since World War II were no longer sustainable. The differences in performance between Latin America and East Asia became particularly startling when the East Asian economies rapidly recovered from the debt crisis. As the 1980s unfolded, economists dealing with Latin America, including the staffs of the World Bank, the International Monetary Fund, and other multilateral institutions, recommended with increasing insistence that the region shift its development strategy toward market-based policies. At the end of the 1980s, a growing number of political leaders began to adopt a new vision of economic policy based on market forces, international competition, and a limited role for the state in economic affairs. After 1989, an intensification and generalization of this reform process occurred, with more and more countries opening to international trade and embarking on ambitious privatization programs. In the early 1990s, there was a clear sense in many countries that, although the reform agenda was moving forward, the social sectors were lagging behind. As a result, policymakers in many nations began to supplement the modernization reforms with social programs focused toward reducing inequalities and eradicating poverty. Social upheaval in some countries—Santiago del Estero and Jujuy provinces in Argentina and Chiapas state in Mexico, for example— suggested that the increased emphasis on social programs not only constituted good economics but also made eminent political sense.

The purpose of this book is to provide a history of Latin America's experience with adjustment and market-oriented reforms during 1982–93 and to discuss some of the policy lessons—successes as well as failures—of this period.[4] The point of departure is the 1982 debt crisis, and the main focus is the reform process that rapidly spread across the region. In many cases, the reforms are too recent to draw firm conclusions on their outcomes. In these cases, there is a need to be guarded when offering preliminary results. The main emphasis is the analysis of the reforms themselves, including some aspects of the political economy of change. In addition to documenting the reform process over the 1982–92 decade, the book discusses some of the most important unresolved issues that Latin America will have to face as it enters the new millennium. A particularly important issue addressed in this book refers to the *sustainability* of the Latin American reforms, specifically whether the reforms are likely to be durable or whether, on the contrary, they are likely to be reversed, plunging Latin America back into dirigisme, populism, and inequality. This issue has become particularly pressing in the aftermath of the Mexican peso crisis of December 1994 (see chapter 9 for further details).

The Reforms, 1982–93: A Brief Overview

The Latin American reforms of the 1980s and early 1990s are impressive.[5] Most countries opened up their economies to international competition, implemented major stabilization programs, and privatized a large number of state-owned firms. Toward mid-1993, analysts and the international financial media were hailing the market-oriented reforms as a success and proclaiming that some Latin American countries were on the way to becoming a new generation of "tigers." Foreign investors rapidly moved into the region, and consultants and academics scrambled to analyze the Chilean, Mexican, and Argentine experiences in order to learn firsthand how these countries, which only a few years ago seemed hopeless, had become highly attractive for international business. Also, policymakers and politicians in Eastern Europe turned to Latin America for lessons on how to move toward a market-oriented economic system.

By 1992, the reforms were beginning to bear fruit, as more and more countries began to recover and to experience higher rates of growth (see table 1-3). Also, macroeconomic equilibrium had been achieved in most countries, exports were expanding, and productivity had grown substantially. Additionally, starting in 1991 private foreign capital entered the region at a pace that surprised even the most optimistic observers.[6]

In spite of this progress, a decade after the crisis a number of problems persisted. Physical infrastructure had deteriorated severely, and in many countries the extent of poverty had increased. Despite spectacular progress, inflation continued to be high, refusing, even in some of the best cases, to drop back to single digits. Moreover, in some countries, the economic reforms were not accompanied by the modernization of political institutions. This created

Table 1-3. Selected Macroeconomic Indicators in Latin America and the Caribbean, 1982–92

Country	Growth in per capita GDP as a percentage of constant prices				Annual inflation rate (percentage)[a]		
	Average 1982–86	Average 1987–92	1991	1992	1982–86	Average 1987–92	Average 1992
Early reformers							
Bolivia	−5.0	0.7	1.7	1.3	776.5	15.8	12.1
Chile	−2.0	5.2	4.3	8.7	21.2	19.1	15.4
Mexico	−2.6	1.0	1.7	0.5	73.2	48.4	15.5
Average	−3.2	2.3	2.5	3.5	290.3	27.8	14.3
Weighted average	−2.6	1.4	1.9	1.3	79.1	45.1	15.4
Second-wave reformers							
Costa Rica	−1.0	2.0	−0.1	4.9	29.4	20.6	21.8
Jamaica	−1.2	2.3	0.0	1.3	17.1	28.9	68.1
Trinidad and Tobago	−0.6	−2.0	1.7	−0.9	11.1	8.5	6.5
Uruguay	−3.0	2.7	2.2	6.8	53.0	80.5	68.5
Average	−1.5	1.3	0.9	3.0	27.6	34.6	41.2
Weighted average	−1.8	1.5	1.2	4.0	33.5	43.9	45.6
Third-wave reformers							
Argentina	−0.9	0.6	7.6	7.5	316.5	446.7	24.9
Brazil	1.3	−1.3	−0.3	−2.5	157.9	850.8	1,157.0
Colombia	0.8	2.0	1.2	1.1	20.6	27.3	27.0
El Salvador	−1.2	1.0	1.5	2.5	17.9	18.5	11.2
Guatemala	−4.0	0.8	0.3	1.6	12.0	19.2	10.0
Guyana	−4.3	−0.2	5.6	6.8	16.7	57.4	14.2
Honduras	−2.1	0.7	0.1	1.3	5.9	13.3	8.8
Nicaragua	−3.4	−4.9	−3.5	−2.4	123.1	2,151.3	20.3
Panama	0.5	−1.1	7.2	5.5	1.8	0.9	1.8
Paraguay	−3.1	1.0	−0.3	−1.0	19.2	24.5	15.1
Peru	−1.7	−4.9	1.2	−4.8	102.7	733.1	73.5
Venezuela	−2.3	1.6	7.8	5.1	10.2	40.2	31.4
Average	−1.7	−0.4	2.4	1.7	67.0	363.0	116.8
Weighted average	0.3	−0.6	2.0	0.3	159.5	623.8	695.7
Nonreformers							
Dominican Republic	−1.0	0.4	−2.6	5.7	16.7	35.7	4.5
Ecuador	−0.7	0.0	2.1	1.5	29.0	51.9	54.6
Haiti	−2.2	−4.1	−4.8	−6.7	7.6	8.2	25.2
Average	−1.3	−1.3	−1.8	0.2	17.7	31.9	28.0
Weighted average	−1.0	−0.4	−0.3	1.9	22.2	41.1	34.2
Latin America and the Caribbean							
Average	−1.8	0.2	1.6	2.0	83.6	212.4	77.2
Weighted average	−0.7	0.1	1.9	0.8	129.2	421.7	459.3

Note: GDP, gross domestic product.

a. Average growth in consumer price index for the period; compound growth rates.

Source: Data base of the World Bank, International Economics Department, supplemented by staff estimates.

tensions, and in some cases political unrest, including serious crises in Brazil, Guatemala, Haiti, Peru, and Venezuela. Additionally, in many countries—Mexico and Argentina, in particular—large capital inflows financed large and growing current account deficits and generated sizable pressures toward appreciation of the real exchange rate, and increased the vulnerability of the external sector. The uprising of the Zapatistas in Chiapas, Mexico, in early 1994 reminded analysts, in a brutal way, that Latin America's modernization process was far from over. By early 1994, Latin America still faced tremendous challenges, including maintaining prudent macroeconomic policy, effectively managing capital infows, alleviating poverty, reducing inequality, significantly increasing domestic savings, and creating solid economic, social, and political institutional foundations for long-term growth and development.

Even though it is difficult to date exactly the beginning of the reforms in each country, it is possible to argue that they only acquired full and generalized force in the late 1980s and early 1990s, after attempts to use traditional structuralist-inspired policies to solve the crisis had failed. At the time the reforms were initiated, different countries in the region experienced very different initial conditions. Some faced rapid inflation and highly distorted incentive systems; others faced relatively mild inflation and moderate distortions. The economic role of the state, including the importance of state-owned enterprises, also varied, as did the historical experiences with growth. While Brazil and Mexico, for example, grew rapidly between 1960 and 1975, growth performance in the Southern Cone—Argentina, Chile, and Uruguay—was dismal during the same period.

Although the intensity and scope of the reforms differed across countries, it is possible to classify them into four broad groups according to the approximate time of initiation of the reforms: early reformers, second-wave reformers, third-wave reformers, and nonreformers (table 1-3). Generally speaking, early reformers moved more rapidly in the transformation, having made progress in many areas. Chile represents a case on its own, having initiated the reforms in 1975, almost a decade before anyone else. The Chilean reforms are advanced and have touched almost every aspect of economic life. Mexico initiated the reforms in 1985 and moved broadly and deeply, building new institutions that have helped create the bases of a new economic system. The social development in Chiapas in early 1994 and the assassination of presidential candidate Luis Donaldo Colosio, however, introduced some doubts on the exact direction in which the Mexican reforms will move in the years to come. The second- and third-wave reformers started the transformation process in the late 1980s and early 1990s, and vary in the intensity and scope of reforms. Some countries, such as Argentina, rapidly and simultaneously dealt with many sectors, while others moved timidly and selectively on structural reforms or were reluctant until mid-1994 to enact credible and sustainable macroeconomic stabilization programs (Brazil).

Table 1-3 also contains data on macroeconomic indicators for twenty-four countries for 1982–92. Four features stand out. First, in almost every country the years immediately following the debt crisis (1982–86) resulted in severe declines in GDP per capita. Second, starting in 1987, GDP per capita began to recover in many countries. Growth was stronger among advanced reformers than among countries that delayed the adjustment process.[7] With a few exceptions, most countries experienced respectable to strong growth in 1992. Third, after accelerating in the second half of the 1980s, inflation declined substantially throughout the region. Once again, advanced reformers, as a group, made the greatest progress in this area. In the rest of this book, I investigate in great detail the post-reform evolution of other important variables, including savings, investment, income distribution, poverty, productivity, exports, capital flows, and exchange rates.

In analyzing the Latin American reforms, it is important to consider, at least, three broad stages: initiation, implementation, and consolidation of the reforms (Haggard and Kaufman 1992). By early 1993, most countries had initiated some of the reforms and entered the implementation process. A growing literature tries to explain why the reforms were initiated. There is little doubt that the magnitude of the 1982 crisis generated profound disappointment with traditional economic policies and political practices. This helped the emergence of new options on economic policy and opened the door to a return to democratic rule. Economic crises usually help economic reform because, in times of crisis, the costs of gridlock and disagreement are high and the risks of trying new policies are low (see Alesina and Drazen 1991; Hirschman 1987). The policies of the international institutions—the World Bank and the International Monetary Fund (IMF)—and the example of the East Asian economies also helped to launch the reform effort.

The implementation phase includes both stabilization policies aimed at attaining fiscal balance and macroeconomic equilibrium as well as policies geared toward eliminating microeconomic distortions and privatizing large portions of the state enterprise sector. By late 1992, this phase was very advanced in some countries—Chile, Mexico, and to some extent Argentina—where reforms were implemented in many areas. Moreover, in Chile and Argentina, the reforms are already bearing fruit in the form of accelerated growth, rapid improvements in productivity, and higher wages. Other countries—Ecuador, Nicaragua, and Peru—however, only initiated the implementation stage in the early 1990s, while a small group, of which Brazil is the most prominent case, had barely taken the first steps on the reform path by early 1993.

The third broad stage is characterized by the political and institutional consolidation of the reforms and a new understanding of the role of the public sector. This mature phase is attained when there is a generalized recognition that the reforms are generating sustainable and solid results and when new institutions are created that increase the transparency of the economic and political processes and shield the economy from the short-run effects of the political cycle. In most cases, this means that the reformist government has succeeded in forming broad and stable political coalitions and has convinced a large proportion of the population of the merits of the new economic order (Haggard and Kaufman 1992). In spite of the progress made in the implementation of the reforms in a large number of countries, only one of them—Chile—had reached mature consolidation by 1993. In this country there has been a second-generation reformist government, and the new administration, inaugurated in 1994, will continue to support the modernization process. More significant, in Chile the reduction of poverty through effective and focused programming acquired great importance in the last few years. Moreover, the country is well on the way toward creating new institutions that will help sustain the new economic structures through time. Until the Chiapas uprising, on January 1, 1994, most analysts thought that the reforms in Mexico were also in the process of consolidation. At the time of this writing, however, it is not possible to know how these developments will affect the future path of reforms.* In most other countries, it is too early to know whether the market-based programs will be sustained and succeed in generating Latin America's definitive takeoff. Moving from the implementation to the consolidation phase will, indeed, be one of the most difficult challenges facing most countries in the region during the next few years. This move toward consolidation will clearly require addressing issues related to poverty and inequality. If this is not done, there is a real danger that the reforms will stall and even that nostalgic voters will once again favor old populist-style programs.

One of the greatest difficulties in addressing the economic problems of Latin America is the extreme diversity of the region, whose countries have as many differences as similarities. For example, Brazil, with 150 million people and great regional disparities in income and development, contrasts sharply with small and relatively homogeneous Costa Rica. However, in spite of the obvious individual features of each country or region, it is still possible (and useful) to analyze the recent Latin American reforms from a broad and general perspective. This approach allows the extraction of general lessons that, it is hoped, will be valuable to other areas engaged in reform efforts. A second difficulty in discussing the evolution of the region as a whole is the poor quality of much of the available data. This forces the analyst to be cautious and, at times, to offer only preliminary conclusions.

Plan of the Book

The book is divided into three parts that roughly follow the chronology of economic development in Latin America during 1982–94. Part I, which includes chapters 2 and 3, deals with the years immediately following the debt crisis—1982–87. This period was characterized by an emergency adjustment

---

*Naturally, the peso crisis of December 1994 has created considerable doubts as to the short-term prospects of the Mexican economy (see chapter 9).

process in which countries had to improvise in an effort to generate rapid, massive transfers of resources to the industrial world. The specific aspects of these early adjustment packages are analyzed in chapter 2. During these early years, a number of countries—Argentina, Brazil, and Peru—experimented with heterodox plans aimed at reducing inflation. These programs were the last massive adjustment effort based on the traditional Latin American structuralist approach to economic development. Their failure ignited a process of deep soul-searching among political leaders and intellectuals in the region.

Chapter 3 deals with the change in policy views in Latin America, from protection and intervention to openness and competition, and summarizes the main elements of the reform programs (see Iglesias 1992 for an analysis of the evolution of economic thinking in Latin America). In this chapter, two aspects of the emergence of the new economic convergence in Latin America are addressed. First, which were the most important forces behind the emergence of this new vision? And, second, which are the specific components of the new broad consensual reform programs?

Part II of the book—chapters 4 through 8—covers mostly the period 1987–93. It concentrates on the recent reforms and, subject to data availability, on their outcomes. Throughout this discussion, a clear distinction is made between macroeconomic stabilization policies and microeconomic structural reforms. Chapter 4 concentrates on macroeconomic stabilization. The efforts made to deal with the debt-overhang problem are highlighted, and the fiscal reforms undertaken by most countries in the region are discussed. Some policy questions related to sequencing and speed are also addressed: should macro-adjustment precede the structural reforms, or can both types of policy be undertaken simultaneously? Should gradual stabilization be attempted, or are abrupt policies more appropriate? This chapter also deals with the role of nominal exchange rate anchors in anti-inflationary policies, evaluating their credibility and (potential) contribution to the overvaluation of the real exchange rate during the transition toward low inflation.[8]

Chapter 5 deals with the trade liberalization reforms that opened Latin America to international competition and, perhaps, constitute the most profound aspect of the transformation process. The policies implemented are documented, and their impact on productivity growth, expansion of exports, and economic performance is assessed. Recent efforts to create, or revitalize, regional trading blocs—MERCOSUR, the Andean Pact, the Central American Common Market, and Caribbean Community (CARICOM)—are discussed and their prospects evaluated. This chapter highlights the crucial role of real exchange rates in determining the success of trade reforms. The pressure that massive capital flows recently exerted on real exchange rates throughout the region is analyzed in some detail.

Chapter 6 discusses issues related to privatization and deregulation. One of the salient features of the recent Latin American reforms, and one that distinguishes them from past efforts at stabilizing and reducing the extent of distortions, is the emphasis on reducing the size of the state through massive privatizations. The role of foreign firms in the privatization process and the creation of new regulatory frameworks are addressed.

Chapter 7 concentrates on the deregulation of financial markets and on savings and investment. For years, the majority of the Latin American countries severely controlled capital markets, quantitatively allocating credit and keeping interest rates below ongoing rates of inflation (the ratio of loanable funds to GDP was significantly lower in Latin America than in Asia during 1960–85; see McKinnon 1991). The deregulation of the financial sector was an important component of most reforms. Interest rates were freed, and the creation of new financial institutions was encouraged. This chapter addresses policy issues related to the optimal timing of financial reform, the role of capital market supervision, and the opening of the capital account. It also discusses the interaction between public and private investment—especially the role of infrastructure investment—and the role of direct foreign investment in the process of capital accumulation. In this chapter, it is argued that, in spite of the reforms of capital markets, investment and savings remain at levels so low as to threaten future growth in the region.

Chapter 8 deals with recent developments in income distribution and human resources. The analysis focuses on the evolution of income inequality and on poverty and social indicators such as health, nutrition, and education. It shows that many aspects of human development deteriorated after the debt crisis erupted and that economic growth and education are the main vehicles for reducing poverty in the long run. However, because these two channels take a long time to change human conditions, in the short run programs aimed at directly and rapidly dealing with poverty should be implemented. It is argued that in order to avoid a return to populist practices, it is necessary to tackle social problems in an urgent, effective way and to develop new institutional settings that ensure stability and protect the economy from short-term and myopic political impulses. This type of reform not only will help maintain the path toward growth and prosperity but also is likely to strengthen the region's nascent democracies. Failure to act aggressively in this area will exacerbate distributive conflicts, is likely to prompt discontent, and, in some cases, may even create the bases for a return to populism, dirigisme, and eventually chaos. Aggressive targeted programs funded with reduced waste, higher tax compliance, and in some cases, higher taxes should be a central component of the region's crusade against poverty. In the years to come, an increase in the coverage and quality of education should be a fundamental policy priority throughout the region. Moreover, Latin America faces an urgent need to deregulate labor relations and to create modern labor market institutions consistent with the newly developed market-oriented economies. In most countries, labor market duality continues to exist, and labor relations are highly regulated. From an efficiency perspective, the arguments for reforming labor markets early in the transformation process are compelling.

The third part of the book is comprised of a solo chapter (chapter 9), which deals with future prospects for the region in the light of the Mexican crisis of December 1994. The main question asked is whether the market-oriented reforms will be sustained. It argues that the most pressing problems facing the region in the years to come refer to the need to consolidate the reform process. Policy reversals are common in Latin America's history and often result in frustration and skepticism. The Mexican crisis has generated great concern about short-run (and mainly macroeconomic) issues regarding the strength of the Latin American reforms. However, when analyzing the future of the region, it is important not to lose track of basic institutional and microeconomic issues. To consolidate the reforms, it is necessary to build strong and stable economic, judicial, and social institutions. It is necessary to design new legal structures to improve the civil service and strengthen tax systems and tax administration. Moreover, to avoid a return to populist practices, it is necessary to tackle social problems, especially income inequality, in an effective way and to develop new institutional settings that ensure stability and protect the economy from short-term and myopic political impulses. Consolidation of the new economic system in Latin America will require prudent macroeconomic management, a deepening of the structural and institutional reforms, and decisive poverty-alleviation programs. The "hostility" of the external environment after the Mexican crisis suggests that the challenges faced by the Latin American nations will be more daunting than what many analysts had envisaged.

The book ends with a score of questions for the future. This is the way it should be, because Latin America is rapidly moving into untested waters. As political leaders plunge forward, they will uncover new terrain and forge new lessons that, it is hoped, will be useful to other poor nations embarked on the difficult and pressing search for prosperity and social fairness.

PART I

*The Debt Crisis
and Early Adjustment: 1982–87*

CHAPTER 2

Muddling Through:
Adjustment from 1982 to 1987

In mid-August 1982, a group of highly ranked Mexican officials flew to Washington, D.C., to inform the U.S. secretary of the treasury that Mexico could no longer meet its international financial obligations. This announcement marked the beginning of the worst international financial crisis since the world depression in the 1930s. What was first thought to be a temporary illiquidity problem soon spread to many parts of the developing world (the World Bank's *World Development Report*, 1983, p. 3, stated that the "debt problems of most major developing countries are caused by illiquidity, not by insolvency"). After enjoying ample foreign financing for many years, Latin America suddenly faced an almost complete cut in commercial bank credit and was forced to transfer large amounts of financial resources to the industrial countries (CEPAL 1989).

During the late 1970s and early 1980s, most developing nations, and especially those in Latin America, embarked on a binge of foreign borrowing. Between 1975 and 1982, Latin America's long-term foreign debt quadrupled, growing from $45.2 billion to $176.4 billion.[1] In 1982 the region's total debt, including short-term debt and the use of credit from the IMF, stood at $333 billion. This huge increase in indebtedness was made possible by the liberal way the international financial community and, in particular, commercial banks provided funds to the developing world after the first oil shock in 1973. The pace at which Latin American countries were accumulating debt in the late 1970s and early 1980s—with increases of more than 20 percent a year— was not sustainable in the medium to longer run. Some type of adjustment was inevitable.[2] The world was shocked, however, by the severity of the crisis. Instead of seeing an orderly and slow reduction in the flow of borrowing, net capital flows came to a virtual halt in 1982 (many good pieces have been written on the debt crisis; see, for example, Sachs 1987).

The causes behind the rapid growth in borrowing varied. In Brazil, the accumulation of external debt was the result of a deliberate development policy based on heavy foreign borrowing to finance major import-substitution projects. In Mexico, the populist governments of Luis Echeverría Alvarez and José López Portillo borrowed heavily to finance spectacular growth in public expenditures. The discovery of additional oil reserves generated a wave of optimism that fueled the Mexican binge of borrowing. About half the Mexican debt accumulated as a result of the capital flight financed during the López Portillo administration (Buffie and Sangines 1988). In Chile, public borrowing played no role in the crisis. During 1975–82, the government's external debt barely increased, with most new foreign debt contracted by the private sector with no public guarantees. The opening of the Chilean economy, as part of the overall project of economic liberalization started in 1974–75, allowed the private sector to finance large increases in consumption, especially of durables, with money borrowed from abroad (Edwards and Edwards 1991).

This chapter analyzes the policies in Latin America in the five years following the eruption of the debt crisis. These years (1982–87) were characterized in most countries by emergency adjustment programs geared to generate very large trade surpluses in short periods. Given the sudden halt in external financing after 1982, the countries of Latin America had little choice but to use every possible tool to achieve the needed turnaround in their trade accounts. This resulted in a costly and disorderly adjustment, with drastic declines in real income, profound increases in unemployment, and rapid accelerations in inflation. As the crisis dragged on, in the mid-1980s, several countries experimented with so-called unorthodox adjustment policies that emphasized exchange and price controls and deemphasized demand management and fiscal discipline. The Austral and Cruzado plans in Argentina and Brazil and the APRA Plan in Peru were the clearest attempts at economic heterodoxy. These programs soon faltered, however, and after some months were abandoned. Their failure provided impetus for the emergence of a new consensus on development strategies in most Latin American countries (see chapter 3).

Was the Debt Crisis Anticipated?

In retrospect, it is difficult to believe that neither multilateral institutions nor independent policy analysts anticipated a crisis of such magnitude. And yet, it is hard to find serious warnings about the crisis in the literature of the time. For example, although the 1982 issue of the World Bank's *World Development Report* recognized that many developing countries were having difficulty repaying some of their debts, it did not even hint at the possibility of a generalized debt crisis that would give rise to a "lost decade" in Latin America. Similarly, in mid-1981, barely a year before the crisis erupted, Jeffrey Sachs argued that "much of the growth of LDC [less-developed country] debt reflects investment and should not pose a problem of repayment" (Sachs 1981, p. 243). Along similar lines, the IMF's 1982 *World Economic Outlook*, published in April of that year, suggested that, despite some payment problems, most Latin American economies would recover during that year and would continue to borrow strongly from the international financial community.

The existing evidence, then, suggests that as late as the first quarter of 1982, many prominent analysts did not expect a major crisis. Quite the contrary, at the time the common view was that toward the end of 1982 most countries in the region would begin to recover from the recession (IMF, *World Economic Outlook*, 1982). An important question, however, is whether, as the year unfolded, the international financial community began to sense that things were not going as well as predicted and that a major catastrophe was looming on the horizon. Several authors contend that the evolution of bond yields in the international secondary market reflects the (informed) public perception of the sovereign risk associated with a particular country's sovereign debt (Folkerts-Landau 1985; Sachs and Cohen 1986). According to this view, increases in the probability of debt default are reflected in increases in the premium on sovereign bonds over "risk-free" bonds of similar characteristics.[3]

In this section, data on yields on Mexican and Brazilian bonds in the secondary market are used to analyze the evolution of the perceived degree of riskiness of these two economies in the period surrounding the debt crisis. In particular, this analysis tries to determine the extent to which financial markets anticipated the crisis. Figure 2-1 presents monthly data on the spread between a Mexican government bond and a World Bank comparable bond and between a Brazilian bond and the same World Bank bond for the period October 1980 through March 1985. World Bank bonds are close to being risk free, and, thus, these spreads are good proxies for sovereign risk premiums.[4]

An interesting feature of this figure is that the spread of bond yields varied significantly during this period. For both countries, it was slightly negative or close to zero from October 1980 through mid-1982. It then jumped, reaching peaks of more than 800 basis points for Mexico and 600 basis points for Brazil. In late 1984 and early 1985, the spread declined markedly for both bonds. Also, this figure suggests that the market anticipated by only a few weeks— and only partially—the Mexican debt crisis of August 1982. As late as July 1982, the spread was slightly negative and not significantly different from the average for the preceding eighteen months. Gutentag and Herring (1985), however, argue that the market anticipated the crisis by approximately a full year. Clearly, that contention is not reflected in the data presented in figure 2-1.

The first major increase in the spread took place in early August 1982, just prior to Mexico's official announcement that it was facing serious problems in paying its debt. This jump in the spread, which for Mexico was equal to 319 basis points, took place only thirty days after Mexico obtained a jumbo loan for $2.5 billion under convenient conditions. The relative tranquility observed

Figure 2-1. Spreads on Mexican and Brazilian Bonds, October 1980–March 1985

Relative yield (percentage)

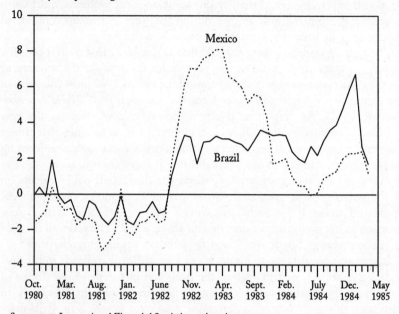

Oct. 1980 | Mar. 1981 | Aug. 1981 | Jan. 1982 | June 1982 | Nov. 1982 | Apr. 1983 | Sept. 1983 | Feb. 1984 | July 1984 | Dec. 1984 | May 1985

Source: IMF, *International Financial Statistics*, various issues.

in the spread's behavior until July 1982 is somewhat puzzling. Between the third quarter of 1981 and June of 1982, the international media carried a number of stories suggesting that both the Mexican and Brazilian economies were facing serious problems. For example, between July 1981 and mid-August 1982, the *New York Times* published twelve stories that stressed the sharp weakening of Mexico's external position. These stories included the Alfa Group's announcement that it could not pay its foreign debt (May 10, 1982), Minister Silva Herzog's forecast of zero growth for 1982 (May 13, 1982), and Mexico's request for an IMF team to visit the country (August 17, 1982). During the same period, the *New York Times* published four stories related to Brazil's external sector. A possible interpretation of the apparently normal behavior of the spread is that, as pointed out above, until July 1982 most analysts believed that these countries were going through temporary cash flow problems but that their solvency was not seriously at stake.[5]

During September 1982, new developments affected the Mexican economy negatively. On September 1, President López Portillo nationalized the banks; on September 7, the government announced that all principal payments on the foreign debt would be suspended until the end of 1984. On the positive side, the IMF announced that it expected to offer Mexico a $5 billion package by late 1982. The market reacted to this news by further discounting the value of Mexico's debt: in October 1982, the spread reached 612 basis points.

Between July and October 1982, no major events affected the Brazilian economy negatively. In spite of this, between July and October, the Brazilian spread increased 418 basis points. There is little doubt that the market was reacting to the Mexican and, to a lesser extent, Argentine situations and was in fact anticipating Brazil's formal acknowledgment that it could not make payments on its debt. Between October 1982 and April 1983, while the Mexican spread continued to climb, the Brazilian spread stabilized around 280 to 300 basis points. The fact that Brazil reached an early tentative agreement—in February 1983—with its creditors was reflected in the relatively lower and stable spread on its bonds.

Until December 1982, the behavior of the Mexican spread reflected the chaos that characterized the last few months of the López Portillo administration. In December of that year, President Miguel de la Madrid was sworn in, and strict austerity measures were announced. On December 22, the IMF gave final approval to a $4 billion loan to Mexico. Between December 1982 and April 1983, the Mexican government continued to negotiate with banks and to implement corrective measures. In May 1983, the IMF announced that Mexico's economic performance during the first quarter was in line with their agreement. In that month, the Mexican spread, for the first time in ten months, declined significantly: 152 basis points. For the next thirteen months, the Mexican spread continued to decline, as the economy's conditions improved somewhat. On August 27, 1983, an agreement to reschedule Mexico's debt was signed. After further reductions, in June 1984, the spread reached its lowest value since mid-1982. In July 1984, it began to climb once again. A possible explanation is that during the second half of 1984 the market was unsure whether the Mexican government was also going to reschedule its bond debt. In late 1984, however, Mexico officially announced that neither bonds nor debt to international agencies would be rescheduled, and the spread, once again, declined.

Throughout this period—April 1983 to June 1984—the Brazilian authorities continued to make progress in negotiations with the IMF and with banks. In July 1983, a new agreement with the IMF was reached, and disbursement of the $5.4 billion standby loan continued. At the same time, the political system was going through important reforms, as Brazil prepared for its first civilian president in twenty years. Between April 1983 and January 1985—the month when the new president was supposed to be chosen—the Brazilian spread increased steeply, climbing more than 390 basis points. The behavior of the spread during this period reflected, basically, political uncertainty. These months were characterized by political turmoil, as the issue of whether the next president should be elected by direct popular vote was actively, and sometimes violently, discussed. On January 15, 1985, Tancredo Neves was elected without major incident. That month the government reported that it had made important progress in negotiations to reschedule $50 billion of its debt. During March and April, the Brazilian spread dropped dramatically to its June 1982–June 1984 levels.[6]

External and Domestic Origins of the Crisis

The behavior of the world economy during the early 1980s—particularly the sluggish growth of industrial countries, the increase of world real interest rates, and the decline in commodity prices—was important in determining the timing and magnitude of the debt crisis. For Latin American nations, the deterioration of unit prices of non-oil exports and the hike in world interest rates explain almost half of the increase in the region's current account deficit in 1981 and 1982 (Bianchi, Devlin, and Ramos 1987).

The external shocks can be better understood by analyzing the evolution of the real international interest rate for these countries, computed as nominal LIBOR (London interbank offered rate) deflated by the rate of inflation for the region's exports. This real interest rate combines in one indicator the effects of both the higher international nominal interest rates and of the lower commodity export prices. For Latin America, it jumped from an average of –3.4 percent between 1970 and 1980 to 19.9 percent in 1981, 27.5 percent in 1982, and 17.4 percent in 1983. As a consequence of these changing conditions in the world economy, even countries with a large percentage of their debt contracted at fixed concessionary terms saw dramatic increases in their interest bill (for greater details, see Edwards 1986a).

In many countries, domestic policies also contributed to the crisis, with inadequate management of the exchange rate as perhaps the most important direct cause. Most countries that eventually ran into payments difficulties allowed their real exchange rates to become seriously overvalued in the late 1970s and early 1980s. This tendency toward overvaluation was in most cases the result of nominal exchange rate policies that were inconsistent with an overly expansive fiscal stance.

Argentina and Uruguay are prime examples. Both adopted a declining pre-announced rate of nominal devaluation as a way to reduce inflation, without first controlling the fiscal finances. The result was a substantial overvaluation of the real exchange rate and a steady loss of credibility in the sustainability of the stabilization and liberalization programs in the second half of the 1970s (Calvo 1986; Corbo, de Melo, and Tybout 1986). The major fiscal expansions in Mexico in the late 1970s also generated a serious overvaluation of the real exchange rate. The Mexican exchange rate crisis of February 1982 was a clear preview of the debt moratorium to come later that year.

Chile, too, had a severe appreciation of the real exchange rate in the years preceding the debt crisis. The cause, however, was not the inability to control fiscal accounts. It was rather the result of a combination of factors, including a wage rate policy that was inconsistent with the overall macroeconomic strategy. To reverse a stubborn inflationary process, the Chilean currency was fixed to the dollar in June 1979 just as wages were indexed to past inflation and capital controls were relaxed. The real exchange rate appreciated more than 30 percent between 1979 and 1981, provoking significant deprotection of

Table 2-1. Capital Flight from Selected Countries of Latin America, 1979–84
(billions of U.S. dollars)

Country	1979	1980	1981	1982	1983	1984
Argentina	2.2	3.5	4.5	7.6	1.3	−3.4
Brazil	1.3	2.0	−1.4	1.8	0.5	4.0
Mexico	−1.1	2.2	2.6	4.7	9.3	2.6
Venezuela	3.0	4.8	5.4	3.2	3.1	4.0

Source: Cumby and Levich 1987.

domestic tradables and encouraging a current account deficit of 14 percent of GDP in 1981. Additionally, very large inflows of capital during 1980 and 1981 generated significant pressure toward appreciation of the real exchange rate in Chile.[7]

The countries of Central America also had overvalued real exchange rates during 1973–81. The commodity export boom of 1975 allowed them to implement expansionary policies without immediate consequences for international reserves. But by the early 1980s, world economic conditions had changed, generating a sharp decline in their terms of trade. The overvaluation became painful as international reserves were rapidly depleted (Edwards 1986c).

Perhaps most devastating, the general tendency toward overvaluation fueled massive capital flight out of the region. In country after country, the public speculated against the central bank by acquiring foreign exchange and moving it abroad. Official data on capital flight are difficult to find, but many estimates suggest that in most Latin American countries capital outflows increased significantly in the years around the debt crisis and that overvaluation was closely related to capital flight (Cuddington 1986; see table 2-1).[8]

The Adjustment

In August 1982, just after Mexico's formal announcement that it was facing serious financial difficulties, commercial banks drastically reduced the flow of new funds to the developing world and to Latin America, in particular. Even countries that did not face payments problems and that had avoided macroeconomic disequilibria, such as Colombia, were affected by this reduction in foreign lending (Ocampo 1989; Thomas 1988). The reduction of foreign funds was brutal: almost 40 percent between 1981 and 1983. Moreover, the major debtors were forced to close their current account deficit in less than three years. The Latin American countries engineered a major turnaround in their trade balance by going from an aggregate deficit of almost $2 billion in 1981 to a surplus of more than $39 billion in 1984!

Latin America was severely hit by the sudden drying up of commercial bank loans. Starting in 1982, the net transfer of resources turned negative, and between 1982 and 1986 the annual net transfer averaged –$26.4 billion, compared with a positive average net transfer of more than $12 billion a year between 1976 and 1981 (see table 2-2). In real 1983 dollars, the net turnaround of resource transfers exceeded $70 billion in the three short years between 1980 and 1983.

During this early phase, very rapid adjustments in the current account and trade balance were achieved by contractions in imports and in investment. The real value of imports in Latin America and the Caribbean declined almost 25 percent between 1982 and 1987 (see table 2-3). In most countries, this compression was concentrated on imports of capital goods and intermediate inputs, seriously affecting future growth. A deterioration in the terms of trade of 20 percent between 1981 and 1986 made the Latin American adjustment tougher: countries needed even larger increases in exports to finance their resource transfers to the rest of the world. Because of the early emergency adjustment, investment in the region plummeted from an average of 23 percent of GDP in 1973–77 to 17 percent in 1983–86. For the major debtors—Argentina, Brazil, Chile, Colombia, Mexico, and Venezuela—it dropped from 19 percent of GDP to 16 percent.[9] In most countries, public investment, including that for infrastructure, and investment in construction were severely curtailed.

To reverse the net transfers, countries resorted to a combination of expenditure-reducing and expenditure-switching policies, including devaluations, multiple

Table 2-2. Capital Inflows and Net Resource Transfers, Latin America and the Caribbean, 1975–87
(billions of U.S. dollars)

Year	Net capital inflows	Net interest payments	Net transfer of resources
1975	14.3	5.6	8.7
1976	17.9	6.8	11.1
1977	17.2	8.2	9.0
1978	26.2	10.2	16.0
1979	29.1	13.7	15.4
1980	32.0	18.9	13.1
1981	39.8	28.5	11.3
1982	20.1	38.8	–18.7
1983	2.9	34.5	–31.6
1984	10.4	37.3	–26.9
1985	3.0	35.3	–32.3
1986	9.9	32.6	–22.7
1987	15.4	31.4	–16.0

Source: CEPAL, *Economic Survey of Latin America,* 1991.

Table 2-3. Selected Macroeconomic Indicators in Latin America and the Caribbean during the "Muddling Through" Period, Various Years, 1975–87

Country	Annual inflation, 1982–87	Ratio of central government fiscal deficit to GDP		Ratio of investment to GDP		Change in imports, 1981–87[b]	Change in exports, 1981–87[b]
		1982	1987	1975–82[a]	1982–87[a]		
Early reformers							
Bolivia	2,222.2	0.16	−0.01	0.22	0.10	−18.5	5.2
Chile	21.2	0.01	0.00	0.16	0.13	−28.1	43.7
Mexico	80.1	0.15	0.14	0.24	0.20	−50.5	62.8
Second-wave reformers							
Costa Rica	29.8	0.01	0.03	0.25	0.25	53.8	25.0
Jamaica	19.4	0.15	—	0.18	0.22	54.8	53.5
Trinidad and Tobago	1.7	0.12	0.06	0.28	0.23	23.2	56.3
Uruguay	57.7	0.09	0.01	0.22	0.14	−12.4	10.0
Third-wave reformers							
Argentina	346.1	0.07	0.04	0.23	0.13	−36.0	17.5
Brazil	173.3	0.03	0.12	0.23	0.19	−5.9	44.5
Colombia	24.2	0.05	0.01	0.19	0.19	−3.5	60.1
El Salvador	17.7	0.08	−0.01	0.18	0.12	−11.2	−10.8
Guatemala	14.0	0.05	0.01	0.18	0.12	−25.4	−25.7
Guyana	20.1	—	—	0.30	0.30	−41.8	−24.7
Honduras	4.5	—	—	0.22	0.15	0.1	5.4
Nicaragua	173.1	0.20	0.17	0.17	0.20	−25.2	−43.9
Panama	2.7	0.11	0.04	0.28	0.19	−6.4	10.6
Paraguay	22.3	0.00	0.00	0.28	0.24	3.3	41.0
Peru	101.8	0.03	0.06	0.25	0.23	−25.7	−9.7
Venezuela	12.6	0.04	0.04	0.33	0.20	−11.5	8.3
Nonreformers							
Dominican Republic	15.7	0.03	0.02	0.23	0.21	7.0	8.0
Ecuador	30.9	0.04	0.02	0.26	0.20	−2.8	11.7
Haiti	7.2	0.03	—	0.17	0.14	−14.5	−3.1
Latin America and the Caribbean	110.9	0.07	0.06	0.23	0.19	−24.7	33.5

— Not available.

a. Average.

b. Accumulated percentage.

Sources: World Bank, *World Debt Tables*, various years; IMF, *Government Financial Statistics*, various years.

exchange rates, capital controls, and import quotas. The adjustment required a boost in real interest rates and major changes in relative prices or real devaluations. The policy packages were designed for effectiveness in the short run, not for efficiency, income distribution, or welfare considerations. So, there were tradeoffs between different objectives, including improvements in the current account, reductions in inflation, and efficiency-enhancing structural reforms. By the mid-1980s, the Latin American countries were searching for methods to reduce their debt. Initially, these efforts were channeled through the secondary market. Only in 1989, with the Brady Plan, was an official framework for reducing the foreign debt developed. The main features of market-based and officially sponsored debt-reduction schemes are discussed in some detail in chapter 4.

Expenditure-Reducing Policies

During the emergency adjustment period, expenditure-reducing policies centered on efforts to cut public expenditure, especially public investment and government wages. Ecuador, Mexico, Uruguay, and Venezuela cut public expenditure more than 20 percent in real terms during 1982–86 (CEPAL 1988). Despite such efforts, government interest obligations on domestic and foreign debt rose significantly as a result of real devaluations, which increased the domestic currency cost of foreign debt, and of higher domestic and international interest rates. These higher obligations were particularly important for Argentina, Mexico, and Peru, where interest payments on the public sector's foreign debt were about 20 percent of government outlays.

The exchange rate practices, especially the reliance on multiple exchange rates, also pushed up government expenditures for several countries. In Argentina, the need to cover exchange rate guarantees after abandoning the preannounced nominal exchange rate (the *tablita*) generated staggering fiscal outlays. And Chile and Venezuela adopted preferential (lower) exchange rates for foreign currency debtors and implicit subsidies that absorbed public resources (Calvo 1986; Edwards and Edwards 1991).

Despite relatively successful efforts to reduce public spending, fiscal deficits in many countries were higher than before the crisis, due mainly to the decline in tax revenues as a result of the drop in economic activity. This problem was compounded, in almost every nation, by low tax compliance and very inefficient tax administrations that fostered evasion.

The debt crisis changed the sources of financing fiscal deficits. As foreign funds dried up, local governments turned to the inflation tax and issued additional domestic public debt. The need to rely on inflationary financing put pressure on monetary and domestic credit policies, which became significantly more expansive than what the IMF and the World Bank felt they should be. Contrary to previous experience with IMF-sponsored stabilization programs,

Table 2-4. Evolution of Real Average Wages in Selected Countries of Latin America, 1981–87
(1980 = 100)

Country	1981	1982	1983	1984	1985	1986	1987
Early reformers							
Chile	109	109	97	97	94	95	95
Mexico	104	104	81	75	77	72	73
Second-wave reformers							
Costa Rica	88	71	79	85	92	98	89
Uruguay	108	107	85	77	88	94	99
Third-wave reformers							
Argentina	89	80	101	127	108	110	103
Brazil	109	122	113	105	113	122	102
Colombia	101	105	110	119	115	120	120
Peru	98	101	84	70	60	76	80
Venezuela	86	79	77	76	91	90	92

Source: CEPAL, *Economic Survey of Latin America,* various years.

many of the early adjustment efforts were characterized by an acceleration in monetary growth, persistently high fiscal deficits, and very high inflation (Edwards 1989a; Sachs 1989a).

The restraint of wage increases was, in most countries, another major component of the expenditure-reducing package, and with few exceptions, the countries of the region experienced significant declines in real wages between 1981 and 1985 (see table 2-4). These reductions were attained mainly by severely controlling increases in public sector wages despite rapid inflation.

The adjustment also relied, in many countries, on tight domestic credit policies, with much of the burden during the early years falling on the private sector. Most governments reacted to the sudden cut in foreign funds by borrowing heavily from the domestic banking system, crowding out private borrowing. In many countries, private sector credit as a percentage of total credit to the banking sector declined substantially during 1982–87 (see table 2-5).[10] As a result, real interest rates increased sharply, keeping expenditure, particularly investment, in check. In some countries, however, the rise in real interest rates began before the debt crisis was officially unleashed in August 1982. In the Southern Cone (Argentina, Chile, and Uruguay), real interest rates climbed rapidly in mid-1981 as these economies overheated. Higher interest rates were an early sign that the need for adjustment was approaching rapidly. In Argentina, the annual real lending rate reached 19.3 percent in 1981, much higher than the average of 1.5 percent during 1978–80. As the

Table 2-5. Change in Real Domestic Credit in Selected Countries of Latin America and the Caribbean, 1975–87
(percentages)

Country	Accumulated change, 1982–87		Private sector as a percentage of domestic credit	
	Total	Private sector	1975–81	1982–87
Early reformers				
Chile	118.37	26.73	0.64	0.71
Mexico	−10.07	−38.69	0.41	0.30
Second-wave reformers				
Costa Rica	−1.29	7.64	0.63	0.47
Jamaica	−23.52	39.08	0.43	0.42
Uruguay	37.05	−6.77	0.80	0.62
Third-wave reformers				
Argentina	—	−24.15	0.76	—
Brazil	193.28	33.66	0.89	0.56
Colombia	64.64	31.84	0.70	0.68
El Salvador	−38.00	−39.36	0.84	0.58
Guatemala	−15.54	−0.34	0.79	0.59
Guyana	63.97	35.23	0.19	0.11
Honduras	65.10	57.47	0.73	0.56
Panama	20.55	11.41	0.81	0.78
Paraguay	14.26	−18.23	0.93	0.71
Peru	6.15	−31.19	0.36	0.46
Venezuela	29.57	27.33	1.59	0.89
Nonreformers				
Dominican Republic	1.25	18.64	0.61	0.49
Ecuador	53.57	7.81	0.87	0.79
Average for Latin America and the Caribbean	101.64	6.29	0.74	0.52

— Not available.

Source: IMF, *International Financial Statistics,* various years.

effects of the debt crisis were being felt in 1982 and 1983, the real lending interest rates remained high (around 12 percent a year) but not as high as in 1981. Likewise in Chile, the annual real interest rate reached 58.1 percent in 1981, much higher than the 8.5 percent average for the two preceding years. During 1982 and 1983, the real lending rate declined to the still remarkable level of 16 percent (Ramos 1986).

In the Southern Cone, the debt problems further shocked already weakened financial sectors. In Chile, the halt of capital inflows was partially responsible for a serious financial crisis in late 1982 and 1983. By the end of 1982, the foreign debt of the Chilean banking system exceeded $6.6 billion, a remarkable figure when compared with a mere $0.6 billion in 1978. These funds were obtained without government guarantee, mainly to finance the operations of large private conglomerates—the *grupos*. By mid-1982, many of these loans went bad as the *grupos* ran into difficult financial times due to the real overvaluation of the peso, among other factors. During 1982, the foreign funds available to Chilean banks declined more than 75 percent, a severe blow to the troubled financial sector. In January 1983, the government stepped in, liquidating two banks and nationalizing others. Responding to pressure from its foreign creditors, the Chilean government took over the foreign debt of these banks, guaranteeing its payment (Edwards and Edwards 1991; Harberger 1985b).

Expenditure–Switching Policies

After August 1982, most countries also relied on expenditure switching to improve their current account balances. In most cases, they used a combination of nominal devaluations and, at least initially, major escalations in import restrictions through higher tariffs, broader coverage of nontariff barriers, and multiple exchange rates (Bianchi, Devlin, and Ramos 1987).

Most countries experienced large depreciations in the real exchange rate during 1982–87, with an average accumulated real devaluation of 23 percent (see table 2-6). In many countries, the real devaluation was substantial, exceeding 40 percent and in some cases even surpassing 70 percent, as in Chile, the Dominican Republic, Ecuador, and Uruguay. To achieve such sizable adjustments in the real exchange rate, these countries had to implement very large nominal devaluations, but their effectiveness was in most cases rather low for two reasons.[11] First, the accompanying fiscal policies were not always tight, and, as pointed out earlier, in some countries the fiscal deficit even increased after the debt crisis erupted. Second, after the initial devaluations, most countries adopted a crawling peg regime for the nominal exchange rate. Although avoiding the erosion of international competitiveness in most countries, the frequent devaluations added fuel to the inflation and generated inflationary inertia (the relationship between a crawling peg regime and inflationary inertia is addressed in some detail in chapter 4).

Multiple exchange rates, another important feature of the early exchange rate policies in many countries, served three purposes. First, by implementing different exchange rates for capital and current account transactions—as in Venezuela—the authorities hoped to separate real transactions from volatile capital movements. More important, however, by imposing a free-floating exchange rate on capital flows, Venezuela tried to discourage capital flight

Table 2-6. *Nominal and Real Devaluation in Selected Countries of Latin America and the Caribbean, 1982–87*
(percentages)

Country	Accumulated nominal devaluation	Accumulated real devaluation	Effectiveness index[a]
Early reformers			
Bolivia	5,118,010.0	6.7	0.00
Chile	511.0	96.0	0.19
Mexico	4,756.0	24.1	0.01
Second–wave reformers			
Costa Rica	94.0	–32.5	–0.35
Jamaica	209.0	37.4	0.18
Trinidad and Tobago	50.0	–11.1	–0.22
Uruguay	2,241.0	70.3	0.03
Third–wave reformers			
Argentina	323,874.0	33.1	0.00
Brazil	48,649.0	26.9	0.00
Colombia	329.0	51.6	0.16
El Salvador	100.0	–26.5	–0.27
Guatemala	150.0	29.3	0.20
Guyana	233.0	30.0	0.13
Honduras	0.0	–19.5	—
Nicaragua	597.0	–99.0	–0.17
Panama	0.0	–2.7	—
Paraguay	337.0	46.0	0.14
Peru	5,637.0	–4.1	0.00
Venezuela	238.0	60.1	0.25
Nonreformers			
Dominican Republic	396.0	100.1	0.25
Ecuador	786.0	96.5	0.12
Haiti	0.0	–13.5	—
Average	250,327.1	22.7	0.00
Average excluding Argentina and Bolivia	3,266.0	23.0	0.01

— Not available.

a. Ratio of accumulated real devaluation to accumulated nominal devaluation. This index measures how much the real exchange rate was depreciated for every 1 percentage point of nominal devaluation. A value of 1 for the index means that the nominal exchange rate adjustment was highly effective, fully translated into a real devaluation. A low value, by contrast, means that the nominal devaluation had little success, with its real effect seriously eroded by high domestic inflation. Worse yet, a negative value of the effectiveness index means that, despite the nominal devaluation, the real exchange rate continued to appreciate.

Source: IMF, *International Financial Statistics,* various years.

without hurting the current account. This strategy failed because the lack of policy coherence encouraged even greater speculation and capital flight. Second, multiple exchange rates supplemented the system of protection. Indeed, when different exchange rates are applied to different commercial transactions, the outcome is the same as that of a differentiated tariff schedule (Dornbusch 1986). This practice was again used by Venezuela, as well as by the Dominican Republic, Honduras, and Mexico. Third, some countries, including Chile, Mexico, and Venezuela, applied a lower preferential exchange rate to the private sector's repayment of foreign debt. The reason was to avoid a general bankruptcy of the private sector, which had borrowed heavily from foreign banks at the previously fixed nominal exchange rate.

In addition to the multiple exchange rates, many major debtors supplemented their devaluation policies with trade restrictions, hiking import tariffs at least temporarily (Bianchi, Devlin, and Ramos 1987). Nontariff barriers were also increased substantially in an effort to accelerate the compression of imports and the turnaround of the trade account (see table 2-7). An important question is whether the use of quantitative restrictions during the initial

Table 2-7. Emergency Adjustment and Inefficient Allocations in Selected Countries of Latin America, 1982–87

Country and year	Examples of trade restrictions
Argentina	
1984	Decree 4070 enacted, requiring all imports to have a permit; all imports competing with local production subjected to authorization (with consultations to domestic producers' associations)
1985	Imposed tariff surcharges of 10 percent for imports and 9 percent for exports
Chile	
1982	Import surcharges ranging from 4 to 28 percent imposed on more than thirty items; also, a two-tier exchange rate established
1983	Import tariffs raised from 10 percent to a uniform 20 percent
1984	Import tariffs temporarily hiked to 35 percent
1985	The uniform import duty system stabilized at 20 percent (from the earlier uniform 10 percent)
Mexico	
1982	Quantitative restrictions imposed on all imports (during the 1970s, quantitative restrictions only affected 60 percent of imports)
Venezuela	
1983	Foreign exchange controls and a two-tier official exchange rate system imposed; quantitative restrictions placed on 70 percent of final consumption goods

Source: World Bank, several country-specific reports.

phases of the adjustment—instead of tariffs or more substantial devaluations—introduced unduly high costs for growth and efficiency. A well-known proposition in international trade theory is that, from a welfare perspective, tariffs are superior to quotas as a means to restrict trade. For a small country that faces given foreign currency prices for its imports, however, quotas effectively keep the value of imports below a certain target level. As long as countries need to establish credibility for their willingness to adjust—and this credibility is related to the ability to cut imports rapidly—quantitative restrictions might be justified in the (very) short run. From the perspectives of efficiency, fiscal performance, and income distribution, the maintenance of quantitative restrictions in the medium or longer run has well-known undesirable effects. For example, the generalized use of quantitative restrictions in Mexico in 1982–84 resulted in a very large reduction in imports of intermediate inputs, hurting the Mexican economy by reducing the level of activity and the prospects for future growth (Buffie and Sangines 1988). Naturally, to reduce the efficiency costs of the quota, it is recommended that their rights be auctioned. This was not done, however, during the early years of emergency adjustment operations.

Toward 1985–86, some countries began to relax their trade restrictions. Chile reduced tariffs to a uniform 20 percent in 1986. Starting in early 1986, Mexico began reducing the coverage of licenses. Bolivia, by contrast, fully abolished quotas and drastically reduced tariffs in 1985 as part of the stabilization program aimed at stopping hyperinflation. The process of trade liberalization is analyzed in chapter 5.

Despite the early adjustment efforts—and the costs—trade surpluses systematically fell short of interest payments. In 1986, the interest bill for the region amounted to 5.3 percent, and the trade surplus to 2.3 percent, of GDP. During the early years, the financing gap was closed, usually after long and protracted negotiations, by packages of funds from commercial banks and multilateral institutions.

Early on, some studies suggested that for the great majority of the highly indebted countries it was not possible in the short run to generate trade surpluses large enough to cover interest payments without significantly reducing real consumption (Selowsky and van der Tak 1986). A typical major debtor needed financing in the form of new money for about five years to experience some recovery in real consumption (2 percent a year) and in real income (4 percent a year). Once growth resumed, the indebted countries would be in a stronger position to service their obligations. Moreover, to the extent that the new money supported structural reforms, the recovery would be faster, generating robust and sustainable growth. This view—calling for substantial debt restructuring and even debt reduction—slowly gained acceptance among the creditor nations. It became part of the official debt strategy in March 1989, when the United States unveiled the Brady Plan for adjustment packages that combined debt relief and market-oriented reforms.

Heterodox Stabilization Attempts in the Mid-1980s

An important consequence of the early emergency adjustment programs was a rapid acceleration in inflation, particularly in Argentina, Bolivia, Brazil, Mexico, and Peru, where inflation reached or surpassed triple digits. In the mid-1980s, and as the debt crisis dragged on, Argentina, Brazil, and Peru experimented with anti-inflationary policies that emphasized exchange and price controls and deemphasized, in the design or implementation stages, demand management and fiscal discipline. At the core of these attempts was the belief that inflationary inertia had become a permanent feature of these economies. When indexation and inertia become ingrained, it was argued, inflation takes on a life of its own, and monetary authorities have little choice but to validate it (for detailed analyses of the heterodox programs, see Ocampo 1987). According to this view, the most important element in a stabilization program is breaking inertia. The Austral and Cruzado plans tried to do this by combining monetary reforms and incomes policies. Although the two plans were correct in pointing out the important role of indexation and inertia, they erred in not enforcing the necessary, and politically more difficult, policies for managing aggregate demand. By failing to attain fiscal equilibrium, these plans collapsed without reducing inflation.

The Peruvian stabilization program under President Alán García differed from both the Austral and Cruzado plans. Disregarding history and basic principles of economic theory, it consisted of a price freeze, a pegged exchange rate, wage increases, tax cuts, reduced payments on foreign debt interest, and increases in government spending. Repeating some of the most serious mistakes of previous populist regimes in Latin America, the plan resulted in an outburst of inflation, a reduction in real income, and a dramatic decline in real wages.

Although the immediate objective was to defeat inflation, all three programs were part of broader economic strategies that sought, one way or another, to strengthen the role of government. At the time, these plans, especially the Austral and Cruzado plans, were seen as alternatives to orthodox adjustment programs based on fiscal restraint and market-oriented reforms. Some observers even saw them as a final attempt to implement a development strategy based on a dominant government role (Taylor 1989 provides the analytical underpinnings of the neostructuralist position). This section analyzes the most important features of these stabilization programs (see table 2-8 and figure 2-2). In all cases, inflation declined in the short term but after a few months returned to its original (or even higher) level.

Argentina's Austral Plan

The Austral Plan initiated in June 1985 was the best designed of the so-called heterodox programs (there is an abundance of literature on the subject; see, for

Table 2-8. Main Features of Heterodox Plans in Latin America, 1985–86

Country and period	Exchange rate regime	Price controls	Wage controls	Initial devaluation	Fiscal adjustment	Monetary reform	Trade policy reform
Argentina, June 1985– December 1986	Fixed	Selective	Mainly public	40.2 percent	Initial, transitory	Yes	No
Brazil, February 1986– December 1986	Fixed	Selective	No	No	No	Yes	No
Peru, August 1985–August 1986	Fixed	Across-the-board	Across-the-board	12.0 percent	No	No	No

Sources: For Argentina, Instituto Nacional de Estadísticas y Censos, Fundación de Investigaciones Económicas Latinoamericanas, and the Banco Central de la República Argentina; for Brazil, the Bureau of Foreign Trade (CACEX), Banco Central de Brasil, and Instituto Brasileiro General de Estadística; and for Peru, the Instituto Nacional de Estadísticas and the Banco Central de Reserva de Perú.

example, Frenkel and Fanelli 1987; Kiguel 1991; and Ocampo 1987). It was based on three fundamental elements:

(1) *Prices, wages, and exchange rate management.* As a way of breaking inflationary expectations, a price freeze was decreed in June 1985. A fundamental element of this strategy was the control of public service prices. In addition, public wages were frozen, and the exchange rate was fixed. It was thought that the combination of these measures would put an immediate break on the inertial forces.

(2) *Fiscal adjustment.* By late 1984, the Argentine fiscal finances were completely out of hand, with the fiscal deficit bordering 15 percent of GDP. The architects of the Austral Plan tackled this problem by enacting a series of revenue-increasing measures, including higher prices for public services, higher import tariffs, and a forced savings scheme for workers. There also was great hope that the reduction of inflation alone would result in higher real revenues through a reversed Olivera-Tanzi effect (which is the erosion of government revenues in times of inflation due to lags in the collection of taxes). These policies quickly reduced the deficit to 2 to 3 percent of GDP by late 1985. But this success was short-lived, with the fiscal deficit surpassing 7 percent of GDP by late 1986. Why the resurgence? Public service prices, which had been fixed as a way to provide a nominal anchor, declined rapidly in

real terms, contributing to the deficit of state-owned enterprises. Also, the effect of lower inflation on tax revenues was small and short-lived.

(3) *Monetary reform.* The peso was replaced by a new currency, the austral, and a comprehensive and ingenious system was devised for transforming contracts signed in old pesos into australes—the *desagio*. This procedure, based on a sliding scale for exchanging pesos and australes, was designed to avoid serious income redistribution as a result of the decline in inflation. For monetary policy, the program aimed to remonetize the economy through increases in domestic credit.

The initial results of the Austral Plan were spectacular. Inflation dropped from 350 percent in the first half of 1985 to slightly more than 20 percent in the second half. This early success was greeted with euphoria. Some observers claimed early victory, and interest groups pressured the authorities to relax their fiscal stance. But by the end of 1985, the economy was already showing signs of stress. Since inflation had not disappeared, some key relative prices started to get out of hand. Because of the persistence of inflation, the real exchange rate became increasingly overvalued and the external accounts

Figure 2-2. Monthly Inflation Rates under the Heterodox Plans in Argentina, Brazil, and Peru, 1984–88

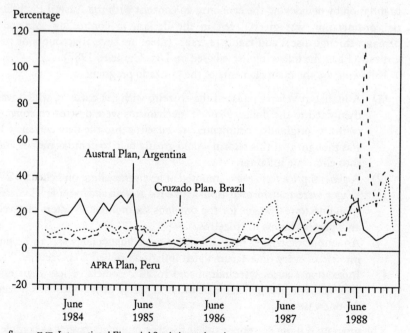

Source: IMF, *International Financial Statistics*, various issues.

showed alarming deficits. In addition, public service prices rapidly lagged in real terms.

In April 1986, the main anchors of the program—the exchange rate, public sector wages, and public service prices—were given up as the government announced a period of "price flexibilization." A crawling peg system was adopted, wages and prices were increased, and it was announced that future adjustments would be allowed "if justified." At that point, the magic was broken, and the credibility of the program dissipated. By late 1986, the fiscal deficit climbed to 7.2 percent of GDP, and inflation once again gained momentum. Despite new efforts to introduce controls, it was increasingly apparent, even to some of the original plan's authors, that price controls without major and sustained fiscal adjustments were doomed to failure. In 1988, as inflation was accelerating, the Alfonsín administration took the first steps toward trade liberalization reform (see chapter 5 for details).

Brazil's Cruzado Plan

In February 1986, the Brazilian government of President José Sarney unveiled a bold stabilization plan to address the rapid acceleration of inflation, which had surpassed an annual rate of 450 percent during the first two months of the year. As in Argentina, the program was based on the belief that indexation was the most important cause of inflation, so the key objective was to put an end to inflation by deindexing the economy. In contrast with the Austral Plan, little consideration was given, even in the design, to controlling aggregate demand through fiscal and credit restraint (there are several accounts of the Cruzado Plan; the following list is based on Dias Carneiro 1987).

Following are the main elements of the Cruzado program:

(1) A monetary reform replaced the cruzeiro with the cruzado, which was then fixed to the dollar. Explicit mechanisms were devised to convert contracts originally documented in cruzeiros into the new currency. It was thought that this reform would greatly help to deindex money and thus eliminate inflation.

(2) A general price freeze was imposed at levels prevailing on February 28.

(3) Wages were transformed from cruzeiros to cruzados at a level corresponding to real wages for the previous six months. Workers received an 8 percent bonus in cruzeiros.

(4) An automatic trigger mechanism for wage adjustments was to be put into effect every time accumulated inflation reached 20 percent.

(5) Indexation clauses were eliminated in all contracts of less than one year, and the nominal value of indexed public debt bonds was frozen for one year.

The program did not consider explicit fiscal or monetary targets as complements to the price freezes and deindexation measures. The architects of the program thought that the fiscal package implemented in December 1985 had already solved the fiscal problem. This premise was based not on serious analyses of the fiscal accounts, which have always been distorted and unreliable in Brazil, but on wishful thinking. And it was thought that an expansive monetary policy would be required to remonetize the economy once inflation declined (see Cardoso and Dornbusch 1987; for the Cruzado Plan in a broad historical setting, see Rabello de Castro and Ronci 1991).

Inflation dropped rapidly from 60 percent in the first quarter of 1986 to 8.3 percent in the second quarter and 2.1 percent in the third quarter. This success was short-lived, however. In the first quarter of 1987, and mostly as a result of the inability to control the fiscal and credit sides, inflation rebounded to 44 percent, and by the second quarter it was a staggering 95 percent!

During the middle of 1986, aggregate demand increased at a rate inconsistent with the price freeze. Contrary to what the authorities thought, the fiscal deficit was far from balanced. Moreover, the 8 percent increase in wages decreed in February put significant pressure on prices, as did the rapid rate of money creation—200 percent between February and July. An added problem was that in February 1986 many prices were fixed at disequilibrium levels, generating all sorts of reactions, including shortages, large losses in state-owned enterprises, and lobbying for relaxing the price freeze in some sectors.

In July 1986, the government attempted a new plan to control demand, but it was too little, too late. Fiscal imbalances continued to put pressure on prices, and in September 1986 the fixed nominal exchange rate was abandoned. By January 1987, the automatic wage adjustment was triggered, the crawling peg system based on mini-devaluations was fully reestablished, and indexation was once again in full swing. Instead of reducing inflation to zero, as its designers had promised, the Cruzado Plan left Brazil a legacy of frustration, skepticism, and even higher inflation.

Peru's APRA Plan

In August 1985, Alán García assumed the presidency, facing accelerating inflation, heavy foreign debt, and a stagnant economy. His government program called for a drastic reduction in inflation and a deep process of economic transformation aimed at improving income distribution and reactivating growth. Although this episode differs in many aspects from the Austral and Cruzado experiences, it, too, was based on extensive price controls and a disregard for fiscal balance. The main objectives of the APRA government were clearly summarized in the Plan Nacional de Desarrollo:

> The new economic policy seeks to pass from an economy of conflict and speculation to one of production and consensus. In this economy it is possible to make compatible stability, growth, distribution, and development in a context of national planning that finds concrete expression in dialogue and social and economic concertation.

Planning of economic development will be full, decentralized, and participatory, and concertation will center on the effort to make compatible the generation of savings and productive investment with attention paid to the undelayable priority of attending to social needs. We need to reconcile economic efficiency with social equity in a productive dynamic that is fundamentally sustained by domestic resources. [Presidencia de la República del Perú 1986]

The APRA program was based on four fundamental policy measures:

(1) Rapid expansion of effective demand through real wage increases, which, for the public sector, were financed by money creation
(2) Devaluation of 12 percent followed by a fixed nominal exchange rate, which put an end to the policy of frequent exchange rate adjustment (a crawling peg) in effect since 1978
(3) Reduction of nominal interest rate ceilings, as a way of providing financial relief to firms
(4) Imposition of price freezes for many industrial and agricultural products.

As in the Cruzado Plan, there was no concern for fiscal adjustment. The designers of the APRA economic blueprint believed that fiscal deficits in Peru were not necessarily expansionary and argued that, if there was unused capacity, it was possible to finance fiscal imbalances through money creation without creating inflationary pressure. They pointed out that firms, by increasing their scale of operation, would be able to *lower* prices (Presidencia de la República del Perú 1986).

In the short term, the Peruvian heterodox program was highly successful. Inflation fell sharply, employment increased, and the real wage rose substantially. In the last quarter of 1987, the real wage stood 52 percent above the level of 1985. Growth, too, was substantial. The economy grew 9.5 percent in 1986 and another 6.9 percent in 1987. By early 1987, the program was at the peak of its success: real GDP had grown cumulatively more than 20 percent since the third quarter of 1985, while inflation had fallen from 188 to 75 percent. Despite the success, the strain was starting to appear in rising cost pressures and a growing loss of foreign exchange. Although the constraints tightened only gradually and bottlenecks emerged in only a few places during the remainder of 1987, the continuation of expansionary policies could no longer be defended after July or August. The García government did not see it this way, however, and continued to push reckless expansion policies.

The massive increase in the budget deficit contributed to the acceleration of inflation. The deficit's increase was a consequence of a massive policy of subsidies and an extraordinary decline in real tax collection. In 1975–86, tax collection averaged more than 12 percent of GDP. By 1988, and as a result of a sharp decline in compliance, it had fallen to only 7.5 percent of GDP. The central bank's policy of multiple exchange rates—buying foreign exchange at a high price from exporters and selling it at a low or subsidized price to importers—also contributed to the deficit, generating losses equal to 2 percent of gross national product (GNP).

In late 1987, price controls had to be freed. Open inflation emerged, real wages declined sharply, and real output dropped rapidly. By the end of the García administration, Peru was approaching hyperinflation, social conflict had escalated, and the prospects for rapid recovery looked grim (for details on García's populist policies, see Dornbusch and Edwards 1990).

Fiscal Control and Incomes Policies: The Mexican Pacto

In the mid-1980s, the de la Madrid administration in Mexico implemented a broad stabilization plan that combined fiscal and credit constraint with an exchange rate anchor and incomes policies. This program was largely successful: after hitting 159 percent in 1987, inflation was reduced to 8.6 percent in 1993. The incomes policies became official in December 1987, when a three-party agreement, the Pacto de Solidaridad Social, was signed by government, the largest labor union, and representatives of the private sector.

In spite of the central role played by incomes policies, the Mexican program differed from the previously discussed heterodox programs in several respects. First, the cornerstone of the Mexican program was a major fiscal reform that turned a primary fiscal deficit of 12 percent of GDP in 1982 into a surplus equal to 6 percent of GDP by 1987! The Brazilian and Peruvian programs did not even consider fiscal adjustment in their design. Additionally, the policy sequencing was very different from that suggested in the Austral Plan. In Mexico, fiscal finances were brought under control before the incomes policies were put into effect. By 1986, a full year before the Pacto de Solidaridad, the fiscal deficit was virtually under control. This contrasts with the Austral Plan, where incomes policies were implemented at the same time as measures that attempted to cut the deficit.

A second important difference between the Mexican program and the Austral and Cruzado plans is that in Mexico the nominal exchange rate was not fixed rigidly. Instead, the Mexican authorities implemented a massive devaluation, which was followed by a brief interlude with a fixed rate and then by a system of preannounced daily devaluations. By combining these three elements—a large devaluation up front, a brief period of fixed rates, followed by a sliding adjustment—Mexico avoided, during the early period, the overvaluation of the real exchange rate that characterized the Austral episode.[*]

Third, contrary to the Austral and Cruzado plans, the Mexican stabilization program was but one component of a broader program to modernize,

---

[*]The overvaluation of the Mexican peso did not occur until 1993.

deregulate, and open the economy. Brazil and Peru, by contrast, made no efforts to reform the structure of the economy by increasing the role of markets and the private sector. To the contrary, an increase in government control was an important part of their heterodox plans. When Argentina initiated the opening of its external sector in 1988, the Austral Plan had already come to an effective end, failing to defeat inflation.

A fourth important difference is that in Mexico the incomes policies were the result of a concerted social agreement. In Argentina and Brazil, by contrast, the price and wage freezes were imposed by decree, without clear support from organized labor or the private producers' associations.

The failure of the heterodox programs of the mid-1980s resulted in a new round of frustration and disillusionment. As a result of these experiences, a growing number of regional leaders began to seek alternative economic strategies to solve the crisis. Toward the late 1980s, an increasing number of politicians, analysts, and intellectuals began to argue that the debt crisis reflected deep problems that went beyond the purely financial spheres. Out of this frustration emerged a deep revision of traditional economic thinking in the region, and by the early 1990s, a new consensus based on the need to foster market orientation and openness was gaining force (Iglesias 1992). The emergence of this new consensus is the subject of the next chapter.

CHAPTER 3

The Emergence of a New Latin American Consensus

DURING THE 1980S AND EARLY 1990S, THERE WAS A MARKED transformation in economic thinking in Latin America. The once-dominant view based on heavy state interventionism, inward orientation, and disregard for macroeconomic balance slowly gave way to a new paradigm based on competition, market orientation, and openness. In 1992 the United Nations Economic Commission for Latin America and the Caribbean (CEPAL), a historical supporter of inward-looking and government-led development, recognized that the most appropriate course was now to emphasize openness, market forces, macroeconomic balance, and social programs targeted to the poorest sectors of society (see CEPAL 1992a, the blueprint for the 1990s).

A consensus on the need to redefine the role of the state also emerged. Most analysts agreed that the ever-growing presence of the state in the 1950–80 period eventually stiffled efficiency and growth. By focusing on their role as producers, Latin American states tended to deemphasize the provision of effective social programs aimed at reducing inequality and poverty. In most of the region, and with the support of multilateral institutions, a process of massive privatization geared to reducing severely the state's economic presence in production was set in motion in the late 1980s. Moreover, increasingly it was recognized that traditional government programs, such as price controls, generalized subsidies, and minimum wages, did not reach the poorest groups of society and helped to maintain a very unequal distribution of income throughout most of the region (on inequality and poverty, see chapter 8).

In the late 1980s, many political leaders who had before favored populist policies began to support radical reforms that included fiscal discipline, the opening of international trade, financial liberalization, and privatization. Presidents Carlos Andrés Pérez in Venezuela and Carlos Menem in Argentina are perhaps the clearest examples of how the region's political leaders embraced new ideas and policy prescriptions. The market-oriented policies pursued by their governments—with various degrees of political success—were very different from those advocated by their political parties until the mid-1980s. Presidents César Gaviria of Colombia and Alberto Fujimori of Peru also supported strong market-based reforms, and the new democratic government of President Patricio Aylwin Azócar in Chile adopted a development path based on competition, privatization, and markets. The degree of doctrinal convergence in that part of Latin America was remarkable.

This transformation in economic views was the result of a combination of factors, including the failure of the heterodox programs in Argentina, Brazil, and Peru in the mid-1980s and the sense that the state-based development strategy of the previous decades had run out of steam. Many observers and political leaders considered the heterodox plans as a final opportunity for programs based on heavy government intervention to show that their policies would work in the new era of a global economy (many of the leaders of the heterodox plans called themselves neostructuralists; see Ocampo 1989 for a synthesis of that line of thought). When those policies failed, politicians turned elsewhere for guidance. The stellar performance of the East Asian economies provided an example worth considering and even emulating. Latin American leaders were especially impressed by East Asia's rapid recovery after the minor slowdown during the early debt crisis. The multilateral institutions, through their advice and programs, also played an important role in shaping the Latin American convergence and launching the reform process.

The emergence of a large group of professional economists also helped generate a convergence in doctrinal positions. As these individuals acquired prestige and gained influence, they developed new programs and helped ease the dialogue between the region's governments and the multilateral institutions. These professional economists—Domingo Cavallo in Argentina and Pedro Aspe in Mexico, for example—became the core of technocratic reform teams that, from within the national bureaucracies, engineered the practical aspects of the transformation process (on the role of reform teams in the political economy of the reform process, see, for example, Haggard and Kaufman 1992). The largely successful Chilean experience became a role model for many Latin American countries, as did the experience of Felipe González's Spain with competition, markets, and modernization. Finally, the collapse of the U.S.S.R. greatly affected those who, from the Marxist perspective, had long advocated replacing market mechanisms with dirigisme and central planning.[1] Despite the broad convergence of opinion about some of the most important elements of economic policy, by 1993 some important areas of discussion still had to be resolved. In particular, in designing modernization programs, policymakers in many countries were still unsure how far the state should retreat from active involvement in the economy.

Moreover, the Mexican crisis of 1994 and its sequels created additional doubts in some quarters as to the benefits of a dramatic opening of the Latin economies. Slowly, during the late 1980s and early 1990s, a new view emphasized the need to build an efficient state able to provide social programs targeted to the poor, to facilitate the accumulation of human capital, and to provide investment in key infrastructure programs. However, the extent to which social programs along these lines were actually implemented varied significantly across countries.

From a historical perspective, the convergence of views was a remarkable event, comparable only to the changes that took place in Eastern Europe in the late 1980s. This chapter deals with the changing economic paradigm in Latin America and documents the slow emergence of a broad consensual synthesis based on competition, openness, and targeted social programs. The first section provides a historical background and reviews the evolution of Latin American economic thinking in the 1950–80 period. The second deals with some of the reasons for the new policy perspective. It focuses on the role of the East Asian experience, on the advice and programs of multilateral agencies, and on Chile's pioneering experiences with market-oriented structural reforms. The final section analyzes the most important elements of the new approach to economic development, discusses some of the policy debates that emerged, and broadly summarizes the state of reforms in a large number of Latin American countries as of mid-1994.

The Crisis of Traditional Economic Thinking in Latin America: An Overview

The Great Depression of 1929–30 had a fundamental impact on the Latin American economies. Terms of trade plummeted—in Brazil, Chile, and Colombia, for example, by almost 50 percent—capital inflows stopped, and real income was severely reduced. The effects of the decline in worldwide demand for raw materials in 1929–30 were compounded by the adoption of protectionist policies in the United States and Europe, including the Smoot-Hawley Tariff of 1930 and the British Abnormal Importations Act of 1931.

Most Latin American countries reacted to these events by abandoning convertibility, devaluing their currencies, and imposing tariff barriers. Díaz-Alejandro (1981, p. 340) describes these policies as follows: "Exchange rate devaluations were not the only measures undertaken. . . . There were also increased tariffs, import and exchange controls, bilateral clearing agreements, and . . . multiple exchange rates" (see also Bianchi and Nohara 1988; Furtado 1969).

It is generally thought that sustained protectionism became dominant throughout Latin America in the early 1930s, if not earlier (see Leff 1968 on Brazil; Bianchi and Nohara 1988 on this issue for Latin America as a whole). However, Thorp (1992) argues convincingly that, in the middle to late 1930s, a number of countries, especially Argentina, Brazil, and Chile, implemented substantial trade liberalization policies aimed at encouraging openness and outward orientation and that export expansion played a key role in the Latin

American recovery toward the end of the 1930s. The eruption of World War II put an end to this episode of export-led growth, and once again the Latin American countries reacted to adverse world shocks by resorting to protectionism and inward-looking policies. This time, however, the end of the foreign disturbances was not followed by a period of openness and reinsertion into the world trade economic system. By the late 1940s and early 1950s, protectionist policies based on import substitution were well entrenched and constituted, by far, the dominant perspective (Díaz-Alejandro 1981).

The creation of CEPAL provided an intellectual underpinning for the protectionist position. In particular, the writings of Raúl Prebisch (1950) and Hans Singer (1950) lent respectability to import-substitution policies.[2] These authors' thinking was based on two fundamental premises: (1) a secular deterioration in the international price of raw materials and commodities would result, in the absence of industrialization in the developing countries, in an ever-widening gap between rich and poor countries, and (2) in order to industrialize, the smaller countries required (temporary) assistance in the form of protection for the newly emerging manufacturing sector. This reasoning was closely related to the infant industry argument for industrialization (see Balassa 1982; Little, Scitovsky, and Scott 1970). Between the 1950s and 1970s, many development economists embraced the inward-oriented view and devoted enormous energy to designing planning models that relied heavily on the import-substitution idea. This view became clearly dominant and was taught in most Latin American universities with great zeal.[3]

Prebisch's position developed as a criticism of outward orientation, which he considered to be incapable of permitting the full development of the Latin American countries. He argued that development required industrialization through import substitution and that this could be "stimulated by moderate and selective protection policy" (Prebisch 1984, p. 179). Eventually, however, the degree of protection extended to the incipient industries was anything but moderate, as more and more sectors required additional tariffs and other types of government support to continue facing foreign competition (Balassa 1982; Little, Scitovsky, and Scott 1970).

During the early years of import substitution, important heavy industries were created in the larger countries, and the basis for the development of a domestic manufacturing sector was set. During the 1950s, the industrial sector grew at rapid real rates, topping in some cases—Brazil and Mexico, for example—the 8 percent annual mark (Elías 1992). With the industrialization process, however, an array of restrictions, controls, and often contradictory regulations evolved. In most countries, lobbying developed as a way to secure the rents created by the maze of controls. It was, in fact, because of import restrictions that many of the domestic industries were able to survive. As a consequence, many of the industries created under the import-substitution strategy were quite inefficient. This inward-looking strategy generated rampant rent-seeking activities and resulted in the use of highly capital-intensive techniques, which hampered the creation of employment throughout the region (Balassa 1982; Krueger 1981; see chapter 5 for further elaboration).

In most countries, starting in the late 1940s, import substitution was accompanied by an acutely overvalued domestic currency that precluded the development of a vigorous nontraditional export sector.[4] The agricultural sector was particularly harmed by overvaluation of the real exchange rate. The lagging of agriculture became one of the most noticeable symptoms of many countries' economic problems of the 1950s and 1960s. Overvaluation of the real exchange rate played an important political role during this period, since it kept down prices of imported goods consumed by urban dwellers (the discrimination against agriculture during this period contrasts sharply with the case of East Asia, where serious efforts were made to avoid harming that sector; see World Bank 1993a).

In many countries, especially in Argentina, Brazil, Chile, Colombia, Peru, Uruguay, and Venezuela, fiscal imbalances became a staple of government policies (see Sunkel 1960 for a classic piece on the structuralist view of inflation; Dornbusch and Edwards 1990 examine these issues from the more extreme populist perspective). The inflationary problem became particularly serious in Chile, where the rate of increase of consumer prices averaged 36 percent a year during the 1950s, reaching a peak of 84 percent in 1955. Successive stabilization attempts failed as the authorities were unable to keep public finances in check.

After an auspicious beginning, the import-substitution strategy ran into difficulties during the late 1950s and early 1960s. At that time, most of the obvious substitutions of imported goods had already taken place, and the process was rapidly becoming less dynamic (Hirschman 1968). For example, during the 1960s total real industrial production grew in most countries at half the annual rate of the previous decade (Elías 1992). During the 1960s, more and more politicians and economists agreed that Latin America was facing long-run economic problems. It was generally recognized that the easy phase of the import-substitution process had ended and that inflation and the recurrent crises of the external and agricultural sectors had become serious obstacles for reassuming growth. Further, the increasingly unequal distribution of income and the unemployment problem posed serious challenges to any new economic program. Although most experts pointed out that low rates of domestic savings and investment constituted an important obstacle for growth, they differed markedly on other aspects of their diagnosis and on the policy packages proposed to take the country out of its relative stagnation (CEPAL played an important role in developing this diagnosis). At this time, the simple import-substitution policies came under attack from two flanks. On the one hand, a small number of economists, sometimes associated with the monetarist position, argued for orthodox-type stabilization programs based on fiscal restraint and a greater reliance on market forces (no serious recommendations were made, however, to introduce deep structural changes, such as privatizing government-owned firms). On the other hand, a growing number of intellectuals in the Marxist tradition, including the group known as *dependencistas,* argued that there was too little government presence in economic decisions and postulated a massive move toward full-fledged planning in the Eastern European style.[5]

Facing this two-pronged attack, the structuralist thinkers eventually concluded that their policies had to be reformed. Fishlow (1985) notes that the dominant economic view in Latin America experienced two important developments during the 1960s. First, import substitution was expanded from the country sphere to the regional level, and several attempts were made to create regional trading agreements. Perhaps the most comprehensive of these was the Andean Pact created in 1969, which grouped Bolivia, Chile, Colombia, Ecuador, Peru, and, later, Venezuela. However, the proposed regional arrangements did not tackle the high levels of protection and distortions imposed in the previous twenty years. In fact, the common external tariff proposed in the Andean Pact was extremely high and uneven, representing the expansion of the traditional structuralist thinking to a supranational level (see Edwards and Savastano 1988). The second development was the recognition of the importance of capital inflows as a way to supplement domestic savings and finance higher rates of capital accumulation. However, this option was centered around official flows of capital through multilateral institutions and did not give private flows a significant role. Also, no specific recommendations were made to alter the basic incentives structure of the economy or to provide market forces a greater role in long-run development strategies.

In the late 1960s and 1970s, the structuralist view continued to evolve, as it became evident that the degree of dynamism of most Latin American economies was in rapid decline. In particular, the expansion of exports became an important component of otherwise traditional economic programs in a number of countries. Active export-promotion programs were implemented in Brazil, Colombia, and Mexico.

Brazil provides the clearest example of a strategy based on expanding manufacturing exports with the aid of aggressive government policies, including export subsidies and an active crawling peg exchange rate system aimed at avoiding overvaluation of the real exchange rate (see Rodrik 1993 for a comparative analysis of Brazil's export-promotion scheme; see Rabello de Castro and Ronci 1991 for a critical view of sixty years of development policy in Brazil). Although this policy resulted in very rapid rates of growth of GDP and manufacturing exports, Brazil's economic base remained rigid and fragile (Coes 1991 evaluates Brazil's attempts to encourage exports during the 1970s). As Fishlow (1991b) argues, after decades of an industrialization strategy based on protective policies, Latin America, and especially Brazil, had relatively high wages and its exports could not become the "engine of growth," as occurred in East Asia. In spite of expanding at a rapid pace, exports still failed to relax the required foreign exchange constraint that for years had affected most countries. Moreover, the implementation of industry-specific subsidies aimed at "picking winners" generated large and growing lobbying activities.[6] As a consequence of these limitations, and as it is documented in chapter 2, during the 1970s virtually every country in the region, including Brazil, resorted to heavy foreign borrowing in order to obtain foreign exchange. The rapid accumulation of debt made these economies particularly vulnerable, as the region painfully learned in 1982.

The election of Salvador Allende Gossens to the presidency of Chile in 1970 gave left-wing critics—*dependencistas* and Marxists—an opportunity to implement a socialist-leaning strategy. The Unidad Popular's macroeconomic program was based on substantial fiscal expansions and massive increases in wages. It was thought that these policies would generate a higher degree of capacity utilization, without generating higher inflation; in fact, there was a belief that these policies could actually reduce inflation. This macroeconomic policy was supplemented by a deep structural program aimed at nationalizing banks, foreign trade, agriculture, and industry. After a short-lived economic recovery in 1971, the Chilean economy spiraled into chaos. Output declined, inflation soared, real wages dropped dramatically, and a severe balance of payments crisis ensued (for recent accounts, see Dornbusch and Edwards 1990; Larraín and Meller 1991). More than twenty years after the election of President Allende in Chile, García's administration in Peru experimented with very similar macroeconomic policies. Not surprisingly, the results were similar, plunging the Peruvian economy into a deep crisis (see Dornbusch and Edwards 1990; Lago 1991).

Between the late 1950s and 1970s, isolated attempts were made to reduce the role of government intervention and to introduce a greater reliance on market forces. The Chilean reforms of 1958–61 under President Jorge Alessandri, the Brazilian attempt in the mid-1960s under Minister Roberto Campos, the Uruguayan reforms of the 1970s led by Minister Alejandro Vegh Villegas, and the Argentine stabilization programs under Adalberto Krieger Vasena in 1967 and José Martínez de Hoz in the late 1970s are good examples of programs geared to reforming these economies. By and large, however, these were rather timid efforts that barely dented the predominant role of the state or the traditional Latin American distrust of markets. In particular, none of these efforts contemplated a serious process of privatization of government-owned firms.

In most countries, however, the role of the state in economic affairs expanded during the 1970s. The state-owned enterprises sector grew very fast, and controls and regulations became generalized. In a number of cases, especially Brazil, this trend was a deliberate response to the 1973 oil shock. It was thought that, by strengthening government intervention, the consequences of external shocks could be avoided in the future (Fishlow 1989). The events of the 1980s, however, showed that this notion of the state as an efficient social insurer was seriously flawed. Instead of reducing risks, the state distributed additional rents to interest groups and became increasingly unable to perform its duties as provider of social services. Income distribution became more unequal, as the Latin American economies became more vulnerable to foreign shocks.

By 1985–86, most of Latin America was at a crossroads. First, it was evident that, in spite of early pronouncements by the multilateral institutions, the debt crisis was more than a short-run liquidity problem. Second, and more serious, it was clear that, in spite of early accomplishments, the structuralist policies had run out of steam and, ultimately, that neostructuralism could not solve the region's ailments. What was, perhaps, more disappointing was that income inequality continued to worsen in most countries and the extent of poverty stood at extremely high levels. At this point, more and more Latin American leaders began to adopt a policy view based on openness, freer markets, deregulation, and privatization. By the early 1990s, many political leaders considered this view to be the only alternative for modernizing Latin America and for reducing the inequalities that had characterized the region for many decades. Enrique Iglesias refers to this phenomenon as the emergence of a "trend toward convergence" and identifies four fundamental components: (a) macroeconomic stability, (b) trade openness, (c) poverty alleviation, and (d) a reduced role for government (Iglesias 1992, pp. 80–81).

By late 1986 and early 1987, some senior members of CEPAL began to advocate publicly a rapid change in Latin America's course. For instance, in a highly influential document, Bianchi, Devlin, and Ramos (1987, p. 213) stated that "the debt problem requires a structural transformation of the economy in at least two senses: the growth strategy needs to be *outward oriented* and largely based on a domestic effort to raise savings and productivity" (emphasis added). The rest of this chapter discusses the way in which this convergence emerged and analyzes the major components of this new synthesis.

Factors behind the Emerging Consensus

In the mid-1980s, there was a broad perception that the development model followed after the 1940s had entered a deep and generalized crisis. Slowly, a new view began to emerge, propelled by the failure of the so-called heterodox programs in Argentina, Brazil, and Peru; the experience of the East Asian economies; the advice of the multilateral institutions; and the example of Chile (Haggard and Kaufman 1992 divide the causes behind the initiation of the reforms into externally centered explanations and state-centered explanations). In this section, the East Asian example, Chile's reforms, and the role of multilateral institutions are discussed in some detail.

East Asian Experience

For decades, the majority of economists in Latin America ignored the developments in East Asia. All interest in comparative economics was centered on Europe and the socialist countries, including China.[7] However, in the middle to late 1980s, and as a result of the debt crisis and of the region's stagnation, this began to change. As the debt crisis unfolded, a series of comparative studies, including some early ones sponsored by CEPAL and reports published by the World Bank, contrasted the experiences of the economies of Latin America with those of East Asia in an attempt to understand why economic performance, and especially growth, was stronger in the latter. These analyses unveiled four fundamental policy differences between these two groups. First, East Asia avoided excessive and variable protectionist policies. Second, and perhaps more important, after the mid-1960s, East Asian economies stayed away from overvalued exchange rates and real exchange rate volatility. Third, contrary to the Latin American countries, East Asian economies maintained a stable macroeconomic environment with low and steady rates of inflation. And fourth, they had significantly fewer regulations in almost every sphere of economic life (see Balassa 1988; Bianchi and Nohara 1988; Lin 1988; World Bank 1993a).

Although during 1965–80, the two regions had similar rates of growth—Latin America with a 6 percent average and East Asia with 7 percent—their export performance was very different. While real exports grew at an average of 10 percent a year in East Asia, they *declined* at a pace of 1 percent a year in Latin America and the Caribbean (see table 1-3 in chapter 1). Moreover, while income inequality declined in East Asia, it increased in Latin America during this period.

The marked difference in export behavior across the two regions was possibly what impressed Latin American leaders the most. In particular, the rapid expansion of exports in the Republic of Korea after the 1960s—a country that during the 1950s did not perform significantly differently than the Latin American nations—became a source of keen interest. Lin (1988) reports that during 1949–60 real export earnings grew slower in Korea (3.9 percent a year) than in Chile (4.3 percent). During that period, real GDP grew in Korea at the rather modest rate of 3.8 percent a year, not significantly different from Argentina's average of 3.6 percent. However, starting in the mid-1960s, the situation changed dramatically: between 1963 and 1990, Korea's merchandise exports grew, in terms of real U.S. dollars, at an annual rate of 23 percent. This stellar performance is often mentioned as a premier example of the positive results of outward-oriented policies (Krueger 1990).

However, Korea was not always an open economy. In fact, throughout most of 1950–63, Korea's external sector was highly distorted. Import-substitution policies were followed with great zeal during this period: most imports were subject to licensing, tariff rates were high (exceeding 50 percent in 1959–60), and a system of multiple exchange rates was in effect (Balassa 1988). With the exception of 1961–62, the classic National Bureau of Economic Research project on trade regimes classified Korea as a "highly repressed" economy throughout these years (Bhagwati 1978; Krueger 1978).

A major change in policy took place in 1964, when exchange rates were unified, a major devaluation was implemented, and a systematic process of outward orientation was started. At the same time, the accumulation of human capital, through an improvement in the coverage and quality of education, was encouraged, and basic infrastructure projects were pursued. Gradually, import tariffs were reduced, the coverage of import licenses was eased, and import prohibitions were eliminated. Massive programs aimed at encouraging exports were implemented as well. By the end of the 1980s, Korea's average import tariffs had been reduced to approximately 10 percent, and import licenses had been virtually eliminated (see Edwards 1993c). The transformation of Korea's external sector not only accelerated the growth of exports but also affected their composition. While in 1962 manufactured goods amounted to a mere 17 percent of total exports, by 1980 their share had climbed to 75 percent (Kim 1991).

Supporting exchange rate and export-promotion policies accompanied the Korean trade liberalization throughout 1964–93. After the devaluation of 1964, the Korean authorities made a concerted effort to maintain a highly depreciated—that is, competitive—real exchange rate. This contrasts sharply with the Latin American countries, where overvaluation of the exchange rate was the norm and real exchange rate volatility was rampant (Edwards 1989b; see Arellano 1990 for a comparison of exchange rate policy in Latin America and East Asia). In 1980, Korea pegged its nominal exchange rate to a basket of currencies, allowing periodic adjustments that reflected the development of a series of domestic and external factors. This system allowed Korean exports to remain highly competitive in the world economy but also generated accusations of unfair trade practices by the United States.[8]

Starting in the 1960s, an aggressive export-promotion scheme became an important complement to the Korean trade liberalization strategy. Throughout the years, exports were subsidized through a number of channels, including direct cash subsidies (until 1964), direct tax reductions (until 1973), interest rate preferences, indirect tax reductions on intermediate inputs, and tariff exemptions for imported intermediate materials. Kim (1991) calculates that these subsidies were reduced from 23 to 0 percent between 1963 and 1983. He argues, as others do, that export subsidies played an important role during the early years of the Korean export boom (the effectiveness of export subsidies in Latin America is a subject of controversy; see, for example, Nogués 1990).

A recent massive study undertaken by the World Bank (1993a) explores with great detail the causes behind the East Asian export success. It argues that in most cases the government organized contests among private firms, with export performance as the main criteria for determining winners. Those firms with a strong export record were rewarded with access to preferential credit and other types of special treatment. According to this study, the most important element of East Asia's success was that the export-promotion policies were strictly oriented toward results. If a particular scheme did not generate results in the form of higher exports in a relatively short period of time, it was promptly canceled. More important, the implementation of selective industrial policies that introduced distortions within the export sector did *not* play an important role in East Asia's success. The study reached this conclusion on the basis of three related pieces of evidence. First, when compared with an international benchmark, sectors that were heavily promoted—for instance, chemicals and basic metals in Korea—were no bigger than labor-intensive sectors that were not promoted (World Bank 1993a, pp. 312–13). Second, growth of total factor productivity was no faster in promoted sectors than in nonpromoted ones (World Bank 1993a, p. 316). And third, the failure of Korea's effort to develop the heavy and chemical industries in the 1980s provides evidence of the failure of selective policies. In the introduction to a group of country studies that provided background information for the World Bank book *The East Asian Miracle*, Leipziger and Thomas (1993) point out:

At the core of . . . success in East Asia has been pragmatic policymaking. . . . Policies have been reversed swiftly if experience showed them ineffective. Examples include . . . Korea's curtailment of the heavy and chemical industry drive in 1970–80. [p. 4]

And in a more revealing passage, they argue that

Korean intervention differed from the policy pronouncements in Brazil and India and many other import-substituting countries. Success was measured by export performance, and eventually all subsidies were expected to be withdrawn. [p. 15][9]

Lin (1988) compares trade policies in Argentina, Korea, and Taiwan (China). In the 1970s, the overall rate of effective protection was 10 percent in Korea, 5 percent in Taiwan (China), and 47 percent in Argentina. The contrast was even bigger in the manufacturing sector, where the effective rates of protection were -1 percent in Korea, 19 percent in Taiwan (China), and almost 100 percent in Argentina. These differences in protective rates affected relative incentives, generating a substantial bias against exports in Argentina. Modern theories of economic growth link openness with growth in productivity: more-open economies tend to engage in technological innovation faster, exhibiting more rapid improvements in productivity. According to Lin (1988), labor productivity increased 8.7 percent a year in Korea during 1973–85 and only 0.5 percent a year in Argentina. The vigorous growth experienced by other East Asian economies—including the second-generation "miracle" countries of Indonesia, Malaysia, and Thailand—since the late 1980s added impetus to the idea that a development path based on openness and market orientation can be extremely rewarding. More and more Latin American leaders are turning toward East Asia for inspiration and economic partnership.

The conduct of macroeconomic policy constitutes a second crucial difference between East Asia and Latin America (Sachs 1987). As documented in chapter 1, inflation was significantly higher in Latin America than in East Asia. Moreover, Latin America's inflation was more variable, whereas its real exchange rates were more volatile. The greatest advantage of a stable macroeconomic environment is that it reduces uncertainty, encouraging investment. Moreover, to the extent that the real exchange rate is stable, investment in the tradables sector will increase, as will exports. Sachs (1988) and Fischer (1988), among others, point out that in the adjustment-cum-reform process, the achievement of macroeconomic stability should *precede* the liberalization of trade in developing countries. Based on the experiences of Korea, Taiwan (China), and Japan, Sachs (1988) argues that massive and deep reductions in tariffs should only take place after macro-stabilization is firmly in place.[10]

In a series of papers, Sachs (1987, 1989b) hypothesizes that politics and income distribution played an important role in explaining the differences in macroeconomic policies in Latin America and East Asia. In particular, management of the exchange rate, especially devaluations, had very different political consequences in the two regions. While in East Asia overvaluation of the real exchange rate (and delayed corrective measures) negatively affected a relatively large number of producers of tradable goods in the rural sector, in Latin America it only affected a relatively small number of large, often absentee landowners (*latifundistas*). Thus, while in East Asia macroeconomic mismanagement had high political costs because it offended many small landowners, in Latin America it had relatively few political consequences. In fact, by allowing artificially low prices on food and other tradables, overvaluation of the real exchange rate in Latin America benefited the politically powerful urban working class.

The increased interest among senior CEPAL staff members in exploring differences between East Asia and Latin America during the middle and late 1980s played an important role in the development of the new consensus. In a way, this was like "Nixon in China." When the one institution that had for decades defended inward orientation expressed doubts about its validity and recognized that there were lessons to be learned from the East Asian experience with outward-oriented policies, it was difficult to dismiss those doubts as purely neoliberal propaganda. In that regard, the joint project undertaken in 1987 by CEPAL and the Institute of Developing Economies in Tokyo on the comparative experiences of the two regions was a pivotal event (the results from this study were published the following year as Bianchi and Nohara 1988). Also, a major study conducted during that same year by Fernando Fajnzylber, one of CEPAL's most respected theoreticians, and later published

(Fajnzylber 1990) was highly influential in pointing out the differences in performance in the two regions and the need to undertake major changes in the direction of Latin America's economic policies. This document later became the core of the innovative and "convergent" CEPAL blueprint for the 1990s, which emphasizes the need for combining market-oriented structural reforms with policies targeted toward the poor (CEPAL 1992a).[11]

Chile as a Role Model

In the late 1980s and early 1990s, Latin American political leaders and their economic advisers began to look closely at Chile's experience in an effort to gain insights and inspiration. The Chilean experiment gained in stature as a role model once it became apparent that the new democratic government of President Patricio Aylwin had embraced, and furthered, some of the main elements of the market reforms first implemented during the military regime. In the early 1990s, Chile as well as Mexico became role models throughout the region. Political leaders and policymakers increasingly turned to these countries for guidance on how to move in the reform front.

In the mid-1970s, when the Augusto Pinochet government first launched the reforms, the program was not popular among regional observers. In fact, most of Latin America's economists expressed great skepticism on the viability of this enterprise (during the 1970s, Argentina and Uruguay also embarked on market-oriented reforms, but they were not as intense as those in Chile; for a comparative study, see Ramos 1986). By the early 1980s, the experiment had acquired significant momentum and was being hailed by the international financial media as a big success. However, the debt crisis and some serious mistakes in macroeconomic management, including fixing the nominal exchange rate while maintaining backward-looking wage indexation, plunged the Chilean economy into a deep crisis in 1982. At that point, many analysts dismissed the experiment, arguing that a small country in the cone of South America could not indulge in market-oriented transformations (on the early years of the Chilean experiment, see, for example, Corbo, Condon, and de Melo 1985; Edwards 1985; Edwards and Edwards 1991; Harberger 1982; and the collection in Walton 1985).

Criticism of the market reforms was particularly severe inside Chile, with prominent economists grouped in the opposition think tank CIEPLAN launching a series of attacks against the program.[12] It was mainly criticized on three accounts: its excessive reliance on free prices and market forces, the reduced role of the government in economic matters, and the opening of international trade and financial transactions to foreign competition. Valdés (1989) provides a remarkably acute criticism of the overall program. His main point is that the implementation of market-oriented policies in Chile—initially through the influence of the University of Chicago–Catholic University program—responded to a deliberate effort to introduce "foreign" ideologies into the country. However, he fails to recognize that the introduction of market-based principles into Latin America followed the same pattern as that observed in the transmission of ideas at other times and other parts of the world (see, for example, Albert Hirschman's fascinating account of how Keynesian ideas were spread from the United States after World War II; Hirschman 1989).

The opening of the Chilean economy, which reduced tariffs to a uniform level of 10 percent, gave rise to the most abundant attacks. Critics argued that Chile should abandon the experiment and move rapidly toward a program in which the state would play a major role in supporting key industries through higher tariffs and other forms of subsidies. For instance, in a 1983 collection published by CIEPLAN, Foxley (1983a, pp. 42–44) argues:

> The State should articulate a "vision" about the country's productive future. . . The idea is to pick and develop "winners" . . . [To this effect] the State would use every instrument available . . . , including special credit lines, subsidies, import tariffs, and tax exemptions.[13]

Starting in 1985, the Chilean economy began to recover vigorously. And, by 1989, it had accumulated a very strong record of growth, which surprised most analysts, including domestic critics. As the presidential elections of 1989 approached, it became clear that the criticism of a market-based development path had subsided. In fact, the three presidential candidates presented remarkably similar economic proposals that shared many important elements. What was particularly significant was that (future president) Patricio Aylwin's program, drafted mostly by the CIEPLAN group, pledged to continue the most critical market-oriented policies. The program argued for "low import tariffs" and for ensuring that the economy had "positive real interest rates that maintain some relation with productivity" (see Edwards and Edwards 1991 for a discussion of the Aylwin program). By early 1990, it was clear to perceptive analysts that the incoming government was not going to fiddle with the main elements of the market reforms. If anything, the new authorities were ready to move even further in some areas, such as opening the economy and reducing import tariffs.[14] In fact, an early and highly significant decision was to slash import tariffs by one-third.[15]

The Aylwin government's decision to maintain the main aspects of the market reforms was clearly stated by Minister of Finance Alejandro Foxley (*Newsweek*, March 26, 1990) in a 1990 interview:

> Preserving the former government achievements means maintaining an open economy fully integrated into world markets, dynamic growth in exports, with a private sector fully committed to the task of [economic] development.

Although once in power, the leaders of the new democratic Chilean government firmly supported some of the most fundamental market reforms of the

1970s and 1980s, they still disagreed with the former rulers regarding the role of social-oriented and redistributive policies. In that regard, Foxley was equally clear:

> Remedying the former government shortcomings means recapturing the balance between economic growth and the deteriorated conditions of the middle and, above all, the lower classes.

What is particularly important, however, is that in seeking funding for social programs, the new Chilean government strongly and decisively rejected traditional formulas based on inflationary finance. Quite the contrary, the new administration made it clear from day one that the only way to increase social spending without generating unsustainable macroeconomic pressures was to find solid sources of government revenues. Additionally, the new government continued to focus social programs on the poor and avoided the blanket subsidies that had historically benefited the middle and upper classes. In short, the populist policies of yesteryear had no role in the new Chilean government.

An important political decision was to address head-on, during the first year of the administration, two critical economic reforms: a tax package aimed at funding the new social programs and a reform of the labor law that had been criticized by union leaders and some political commentators. Government officials were careful to explain that these two pieces of legislation constituted the *only* important changes to the economic model of Pinochet. In this way, and especially by tackling these issues immediately, the government sought to minimize possible negative effects that an uncertain policy could have on private investment. This strategy is clearly discussed in a perceptive document by Minister of the Presidency Edgardo Boeninger (1991, pp. 35–36):

> The administration first undertook the task of implementing reforms producing either uncertainty or cost increases in the economy (tax reform and changes in labor legislation). These have now [March 1991] been mostly completed, enabling the government to guarantee full stability of the rules of the economic game for the rest of its term, thus facilitating dynamic behavior by business.

The Role of the Multilateral Institutions

Several authors suggest that the new approach toward development policy in Latin America was imposed from the outside, especially by the U.S. Treasury, the World Bank, and the International Monetary Fund, the so-called Washington Consensus. Although these institutions obviously had a role to play in forging the new views, they do not deserve central billing in this process. An interpretation closer to history would give a fundamental role to the soul-searching that began in Latin America in the early 1980s. The two most important elements within this process were the failure of the heterodox programs and the reinterpretation of the Chilean experience. Although the multilateral institutions played a less central role than sometimes argued, they influenced the new convergence of doctrinal views in Latin America through empirical research, economic and sector analysis, lending practices, policy dialogue, and conditionality.

Perhaps the multilaterals' greatest intellectual influence in shaping the reform process was the central role they gave to trade liberalization. Several economic studies undertaken at the World Bank support empirically the position that less-distorted economies outperformed economies that impeded the development of markets. Early studies by Balassa (1982, 1985) and Feder (1983) suggest countries that pursued outward-oriented policies that encouraged exports grew faster than countries that followed protectionist strategies (see Fishlow 1991b and Edwards 1993c for methodological criticisms of these studies). Agarwala (1983), in a comprehensive work, presents data supporting the view that, in addition to trade protectionism, other distortions also slowed growth. Moreover, a series of World Bank studies point out that the (careful) deregulation of the financial sector generally results in a more efficient allocation of investment and eventually in more rapid growth (see, for example, Hanson and Neal 1985).

Studies sponsored by the World Bank also investigate the link between distortions—in particular trade restrictions—and the creation of employment. For example, Balassa (1982) addresses the long-term employment consequences of different trade regimes. In summarizing the experiences of eleven countries, Balassa points out that, because primary activities and manufacturing for exports are more labor intensive, "reducing tariffs will tend to benefit employment" (p. 65). In the most ambitious study on the labor market effects of trade liberalization reforms, Michaely, Choksi, and Papageorgiou (1991) argue that in most successful structural reforms the medium-run net effects on employment have been positive. This finding had an important role in the recent acceleration of trade liberalization reforms in a number of countries, including Argentina, Colombia, and Nicaragua. As political leaders became aware that the political costs of reforms (in the form of unemployment) were not as high as it was once thought, they were willing to move more swiftly.

Brazil provides an interesting example of how the multilateral institutions were able to influence trade policy through economic work and policy dialogue. In 1987, the government of Brazil announced its intention to implement a gradual trade reform that did not contemplate reducing nontariff barriers in an aggressive fashion. The World Bank staff considered the program to be too timid and discussed its concerns with the authorities. Additionally, in order to increase the awareness of the Brazilian public of the benefits of opening the economy, the Bank organized a series of seminars and conferences. This exchange of ideas generated several reports that were discussed with Brazilian officials and intellectuals for a period of several months. As a result of this process, the Collor de Melo government was in a position to act rapidly on the reform front in 1990, when most nontariff barriers were eliminated and the tariff reduction program was instituted (see Hicks 1992a).

The multilateral institutions also played an important role in shaping economic reforms in Central America. Through a series of reports, meetings, conferences, and discussions, a new generation of political leaders was persuaded of the need to move away from the old interventionist policies of the past and toward market-based reforms. For example, the early involvement of the World Bank and IMF in Costa Rica helped set the basis for reforms and paved the way for an early deal with private banks on debt reduction in that country. Also, the World Bank and the IMF were intimately involved in launching the Nicaraguan stabilization program of April 1991, which put an end to that country's hyperinflation.

The multilateral institutions also exerted influence through their lending programs. In particular, by conditioning the release of funds on the implementation of basic reforms, the multilateral institutions forced the Latin American authorities to develop comprehensive and consistent reform programs. Table 3-1 provides an overview of the conditionality content of IMF and World Bank programs during the early years of the debt crisis (see Sachs 1989b for a critical discussion of the role of conditionality in the adjustment and reform process). As can be seen, these conditions covered highly diverse areas, including trade reform, privatization, and financial liberalization. In some nations, there was initial resistance to some of the conditions, but as time passed and adjustment proceeded, many countries moved even more rapidly than was required by the multilateral agencies. For example, Mexico's privatization program greatly exceeded the original World Bank goals. Likewise, the extent and speed of trade liberalization reform in Colombia went beyond what the multilaterals had originally considered.

Table 3-1. Conditionality Contents of IMF and World Bank Programs
(percentage of programs with particular conditions)

Condition	IMF[a]	World Bank[b]
Trade liberalization	35	79
Exchange rate action	79	45
Tax reform	59	67[c]
Financial reform	44	51
Public enterprises reform and privatization	59	65

a. All high-conditionality programs during 1983–85.

b. All adjustment loans (mostly structural and sector adjustment loans) during 1982–89.

c. General fiscal policy actions.

Sources: For IMF high-conditionality programs, see Edwards 1989c; for adjustment loans, see World Bank 1990.

The World Bank made a significant effort to influence policies related to the human resources and social sectors. Although it is not possible to know with certainty whether the Bank's advice was critical, several countries implemented "emergency" social investment funds geared at funding community-based projects that simultaneously provide work to the unemployed and solve basic infrastructure problems. Those projects worked successfully in Bolivia and Jamaica and are now being implemented in Nicaragua. The World Bank's support helped make Mexico's Pacto de Solidaridad an effective instrument for dealing with social problems. Also, the Bank's position on the importance of nutritional programs directed at children has come to be accepted by most political leaders in the region and is a frequent component of social programs (see, for example, Psacharopoulos 1992; see also chapter 8 of this volume).

How Broad Is the Emerging Consensus?

Although there are still some important, and often deep, differences of opinion among Latin American leaders, the region is enjoying a degree of agreement on basic economic strategy not seen in the post–World War II period. What are the basic elements of this emerging consensus? Which are the components of the plans for action that belong to (almost) every blueprint for the next century? Initially, the new consensus focused on three broad economic areas. First, there was growing awareness of the need to generate macroeconomic stability through the control of public sector deficits. This was articulated recently by a broad group of political leaders from very different political persuasions in the following way: "Government spending must be kept in line with tax revenues and inflation must be controlled. Anti-poverty initiatives are invariably undermined by high inflation."[16] The second broad element of the emerging consensus refers to the importance of opening the external sector to foreign competition. This includes a growing feeling that regional economic integration, within the context of liberalized trade with the rest of the world, should play a key role in the region's future. For example, in a clear revision of its historical position, CEPAL (1992a, p. 21) recently expressed that "in the long term an internationally competitive orientation . . . promises to be more efficient and equitable, since . . . additional exports are usually more labor intensive than . . . import substitution."[17] The Mexican crisis of 1994 underscored the need to avoid real exchange rate overvaluation in the period immediately following a major trade liberalization reform. The third basic component is the need to reduce the role of the state in the productive process through major privatizations and deregulation programs. This process does not imply creating weak state institutions. Quite the contrary, the new consensus argues that a new and stronger modern state should be built. New institutions able to monitor economic activity, prevent abuses, and guarantee political stability should be developed in order to ensure the continuity of a regime that is based on competition and generates growth and employment.

Initially, one of the implicit premises of the newly emerging consensus was that traditional development strategies in Latin America had failed to generate sustained growth and reduce poverty. However, most of the early reform programs did not articulate explicitly the need to develop aggressive social programs conducive to tackling the poverty issue. For example, in his summary of a 1989 conference on Latin America's adjustment, Williamson (1990, p. 401) deliberately excludes poverty-reduction programs from his list of ten policies that comprise what he calls the Washington Consensus. He argues that, during the 1980s, concern for social issues was starkly absent from the U.S. agenda for the developing world, as well as from that of the majority of Latin American nations. As time passed, however, it became clear that the debt crisis, and especially the resulting decline in GDP in most countries, had substantially increased the level of poverty and inequality. The newly elected democratic leaders began to understand that it was urgently necessary to supplement the economic reforms with effective programs aimed at dealing with social issues. By the early 1990s, the Latin American Consensus had been broadened to include, as its fourth element, the implementation of poverty-reducing policies. A decade after the debt crisis, the authorities in most countries understood that expanded social programs not only made economic sense but also were politically essential to maintaining democracy and consolidating the reforms. As documented in chapter 8, however, the degree of progress made in advancing the social agenda varied substantially across countries. What is now clear, however, is that tackling the social problems and addressing the problems of poverty and inequality are essential to consolidating the reforms.

The emergence of this new economic convergence, and the fact that political groups of different persuasions began to move the region in broadly the same direction, generated a sense of hope in the future of Latin America. In spite of this guarded optimism, many difficult challenges lie ahead, including the creation of new institutions that will help modernize the political and economic structure. Additionally, the recent political turmoil in Brazil, Guatemala, Haiti, Mexico, and Venezuela indicates that the reforms need to be undertaken—and be perceived as being undertaken—with complete transparency. The suspicion—and, worse, the confirmation—of impropriety or corruption is one of the worst enemies of successful reforms.

To provide a panoramic view of how much progress was made until late 1993, table 3-2 contains a brief summary of five areas—fiscal adjustment, trade liberalization, financial market reform, labor market deregulation, and privatization—for a group of nineteen Latin American countries.

The second part of this book—chapters 4 through 8—analyzes in detail the ways in which different countries in the region attempted to put the elements

(Text continues on page 65.)

Table 3-2. Overview of Structural Reforms in Selected Countries of Latin America

Country	Fiscal reform	Trade reform	Financial market reform	Labor market reform	Privatization
Argentina	Reform in 1990; tax administration improved; tax simplification implemented; expenditures somewhat under control	Significant since 1990; export taxes eliminated; very limited quantitative restrictions; tariffs reduced to 0–22 percent range	Free currency convertibility; provincial banks not yet privatized; reserve requirements still high	New wage and employment bargaining system; new dispute-resolution mechanism; new employment act makes labor market more flexible; social security weak spot	Aggressive since 1991; 140 business units already sold; regulatory agencies need to be strengthened
Bolivia	Major reform, 1985; tax structure greatly simplified; tax administration improved	Significant in 1985; limited use of quantitative restrictions; import tariffs reduced to 5–15 percent range	Some action taken; state-owned banks still weak; supervisory framework weak	Some distortions still remain	Started in 1992
Brazil	No action taken	Timid; tariffs reduced gradually, all nontariff barriers removed in 1990	Little action	No reform; highly distorted	Important steps taken; process slowed in 1993
Chile	Tax reform, 1975; budget balanced; tax rates increased; 1980 tax laws to be changed in 1993	Major reform in 1975–79; quantitative restrictions eliminated; uniform import tariffs of 11 percent imposed	Major in 1975–79; interest rates deregulated; no credit allocation; capital account semi-open	Major reforms in 1979; labor laws reformed in 1990	Major; all but fifty state-owned enterprises sold; full participation of private sector in public utilities (except water)

Colombia	Fiscal adjustment initiated, 1985–86; two tax reforms in 1991 and 1992	Greatly accelerated in 1991; average tariff reduced from 83 percent in 1985 to 7 percent in 1992	Interest rates deregulated; credit allocation maintained; barriers to entry imposed	Reform of labor code in 1990; some distortions remain	Small number of state–owned enterprises; no significant action; tariffs redefined in terms of cost-based considerations
Costa Rica	Reform undertaken in 1987; tax simplification under way; tax administration reformed in 1992; weak control of expenditures	Started in 1986; average tariff reduced to 20 percent; some reduction in coverage of quantitative restrictions; export subsidies being phased out	Limited; interest rates freed in 1990; some remaining credit allocation; state banks given monopoly of demand of short-term deposits	No major action; some rationalization of minimum wage legislation; program of relocation of public sector workers	Very limited progress; new program to improve regulation of public utilities
Ecuador	No significant adjustment as of 1992	Very timid; 5–25 percent tariff range announced in 1992; 50 percent tariff on motor vehicles imposed	First steps in 1993	No action	Process to start in 1993
El Salvador	Tax reform in progress since 1989; weak tax administration; control of expenditures very fragile	Significant since 1989; all nontariff barriers eliminated; tariffs reduced to 5–20 percent range	Major; bank privatization well under way; free interest rates; reduced credit allocation	None	New program to improve financial and economic efficiency of public utilities

(Table continues on the following page.)

Table 3-2 (continued)

Country	Fiscal reform	Trade reform	Financial market reform	Labor market reform	Privatization
Guatemala	Tax reform 1992; coverage of value added tax broadened; exemptions eliminated; tax administration reform in progress	In progress since 1987; tariff range reduced to 5–30 percent; programmed to 5–20 percent; coverage of nontariff barriers reduced	Interest rates freed in 1989; credit allocation eliminated; capital account partially open	No significant action	No action
Guyana	Major tax reform; partial fiscal adjustment; primary current account surplus of 32 percent of GDP in 1992; initiation of tax and customs administration reform	Exchange rate liberalization in 1991; adoption of CARICOM's revised common external tariff in 1991, with a range of 0–45 percent; agreement to reduce tariffs to 0–20 percent by 1997; drastic reduction in trade licensing requirements; no other nontariff barriers	Introduction of market-determined interest rates in 1991; weak supervision; domination by state-owned financial institutions	No significant action	Initiation of comprehensive privatization programs; fourteen public enterprises divested; twenty companies still state-owned
Honduras	Partial fiscal adjustment in 1990–92; tax administration still weak; public sector deficit 3.5 percent of GDP	Reduced tariff range since 1992, 5–20 percent; exchange rate unification in 1990; nontariff barriers eliminated in 1992	Interest rates freed in 1992; some credit allocation remains; supervisory problems remain	No action	Almost no action; only privatization of payments' collection in electricity

Jamaica	Continuing fiscal adjustment to meet IMF targets for surplus 1992–93; tax administration weak, but major reform beginning	Tariffs reduced in April 1993 to 5–30 percent range (40 percent for agricultural products) as part of CARICOM agreement, which will bring all rates to 5–20 percent range by January 1998	Interest rates free; reserve requirements to be brought down; open to foreign banks	No action	Major privatization program under way, supported by public sector adjustment loan; private participation in the provision of energy
Mexico	Fiscal adjustment since 1985; tax reforms; improved tax administration	Major since 1985; coverage of nontariff barriers reduced from 90 to 17 percent; tariff range 0–20 percent; tariff average 13 percent	Since 1986; capital account open; no credit allocation; banks already privatized	Minor	Major; 100 state-owned enterprises already sold; forty to be privatized through 1996
Nicaragua	Major reform, 1991; weak administration; currently balanced budget (including grants)	Significant in 1992; trade privatized; tariffs reduced to 10–40 percent range; greatly reduced quantitative restrictions	Private banks allowed; free interest rates; state banks still dominate	New labor code to be assessed by National Assembly by mid-1994; social security reform pending, highly distorted labor market	Significant, but still very serious property problems; privatization of water, electricity, and communications projected
Paraguay	Tax reform in progress; poor tax administration; expenditures under control	Recently undertaken; major tariff reduction; maximum tariff halved	Project of new central bank act sent to Congress; new commercial bank act in effect; new capital market act; fairly open capital account	No action	Limited action; constitutional problems encountered; new government to implement privatization program

(Table continues on the following page.)

Table 3-2 (continued)

Country	Fiscal reform	Trade reform	Financial market reform	Labor market reform	Privatization
Peru	No tax reform; tax administration improved; substantial control of expenditures	Significant starting in 1990, deepened in March 1991; limited quantitative restrictions; tariff range 5–15 percent; export taxes abolished; customs system reform	In progress; state banks still very important; free interest rates; some credit allocation; capital account open	New Constitution of December 1993 makes labor market more flexible, abolishing employment stability clauses	Major action since 1992; 30 percent of state-owned enterprises already privatized (including Hierro Perú Iron Company)
Trinidad and Tobago	Fiscal adjustment, 1989–93; value added tax (15 percent) introduced in 1989; public sector deficit 9.5 percent of GDP in 1986 and 1 percent in 1991	Last quantitative restrictions on manufactured imports eliminated in 1992; CARICOM common external tariff adopted; tariff range to be narrowed gradually to 5–20 percent by 1988	Financial sector relatively undistorted; major divestment of two state-owned banks in 1991–92; exchange rate floated; restrictions on foreign exchange transactions eliminated	No significant action; youth training program in operation	Major divestment program under way; twenty-three state-owned enterprises targeted for divestment; Fertrin and T&T Urea Company sold in April 1993
Uruguay	Tax reform in progress; social security is major fiscal burden	Mild reform; reference prices important; quantitative restrictions abolished	Major reform completed; two bankrupt banks; capital account already open	No reform; indexed public sector wages	Very slow; plebiscite held in November 1992 against massive privatization policy
Venezuela	No tax reform; limited fiscal adjustment since 1990	Significant; coverage of quantitative restrictions reduced in 1991; tariff range reduced to 0–25 percent	Little action taken	No action	Some action; seventy-seven state-owned enterprises already sold

Note: CARICOM, Caribbean Community; GDP, gross domestic product; IMF, International Monetary Fund.

of this emerging consensus in place. Chapter 4 deals with the efforts to achieve macroeconomic equilibrium; chapter 5 discusses the process of international trade reform; chapter 6 concentrates on privatization and deregulation; chapter 7 focuses on capital markets, savings, and investments; and chapter 8 deals with the evolution of inequality and social conditions. The analysis unearths lessons and documents similarities as well as differences across countries. The most important conclusions, and some reflections on future challenges, are offered in chapter 9.

PART II

*An Era of Adjustment
and Reform: 1987–93*

CHAPTER 4

Macroeconomic Adjustment as a Priority

THE DEBT CRISIS OF 1982 GENERATED SERIOUS MACROECONOMIC dislocations throughout Latin America. Balance of payments deficits soared, and in most countries, the burden of foreign debt virtually paralyzed investment. In spite of early signs that the macroeconomic disequilibria had become extremely serious, many analysts argued that the crisis was merely a short-run liquidity problem, which would be solved through (minor) debt restructuring, new monies, and some reforms. Early on, both the World Bank and the IMF argued that the Latin American countries could grow out of the problem, without any need to implement debt-reduction programs.

As time passed, however, the lack of progress in solving the major disequilibria proved that this was more than a short-term liquidity crunch. By 1987, both creditors and debtors began to acknowledge the structural nature of the problems and the need to implement deep measures, including tax reforms, foreign debt relief, and institutional changes, to regain macroeconomic equilibrium. In particular, as it was discussed in chapter 3, a rapidly growing number of Latin American leaders realized that achieving sustainable growth would require stable macroeconomic conditions, an open external sector, and a market-oriented incentives structure.

In the mid-1980s, most of the Latin American nations faced three fundamental and related macroeconomic problems. First, there was a need to reduce, permanently and efficiently, the gap between aggregate expenditures and income. Second, inflation, which had jumped dramatically after 1982, had to be lowered to reasonable levels (determining what is a reasonable level for inflation was, and continues to be, a matter of some controversy). And third, it was necessary to generate a stable macroeconomic environment conducive to the resumption of growth.

The failure of the so-called heterodox programs in Argentina, Brazil, and Peru convinced policymakers that solving these macroeconomic problems required decisive fiscal adjustments, including major tax reforms. However, debt payments represented such a large percentage of exports—in some cases, almost 100 percent of marginal exports—that the political incentives to engage in fiscal corrections or other reforms were limited (Krugman 1988). Many Latin American countries faced a debt-overhang problem: since political leaders did not perceive direct short-term gains for their countries from the macroeconomic and structural reforms, they often made only timid efforts to undertake them. Without profound reforms, however, the external accounts did not improve enough to solve the crisis. In many countries, this circular problem stood in the way of aggressive and decisive early action toward adjustment.

The macroeconomic stabilization programs implemented in Latin America during the late 1980s dealt with four basic and related issues. First, most countries designed programs aimed at reducing the burden of the foreign debt. This was required to break the vicious circle generated by the debt-overhang problem and to smooth the transition toward market-oriented systems. To do this, countries used various channels, including debt-equity swaps, debt-conversion schemes, debt restructuring, and, after the Brady Plan was introduced in 1989, voluntary debt-reduction agreements with commercial banks. Second, most countries implemented fiscal adjustment programs aimed at reducing the public sector deficit. This was done through a number of initiatives, including tax reforms, expenditure cuts, and, in several countries, the sale of state-owned enterprises to both domestic and foreign parties. In many countries, privatizations were linked to debt-equity swaps, where foreigners exchanged outstanding debt for stakes in state-owned enterprises. Third, the macroeconomic adjustment packages required countries to implement consistent domestic credit policies that, at the same time, relieved the pressures on aggregate demand and avoided crowding out the private sector. And, fourth, countries designed exchange rate policies consistent with the anti-inflationary effort. As will be seen in this chapter, this was particularly difficult since, under most circumstances, a tradeoff exists between using the exchange rate to guide inflation downward—that is, as a nominal anchor— and using it to maintain a competitive real exchange rate. In addition to tackling these four problems, the Latin American countries had to build credibility for their programs, both to achieve macroeconomic equilibrium at a reduced cost and to ensure that the reforms would be sustained through time.

During the early phases of the crisis, the sequencing of macroeconomic stabilization and structural reform became an important policy issue. Policymakers asked whether fiscal reform should precede structural reform or whether both types of policies should be implemented simultaneously. By the late 1980s, most analysts began to agree that in countries with serious macroeconomic imbalances and very high inflation the most appropriate sequencing entails early and decisive action on the macroeconomic front, including solving the debt-overhang problem (see Edwards 1992a for an account of the sequencing debates; for early discussions, see Edwards 1984 and Fischer 1985; see also McKinnon 1991). This sequencing is appropriate because the uncertainty associated with very high inflation, including high variability of relative prices, reduces the effectiveness of market-oriented structural reforms. In countries with mild macroeconomic disequilibrium, such as Colombia and most of the Caribbean nations, macroeconomic and structural reforms cannot always be implemented simultaneously, but they tend to reinforce each other (for a detailed discussion of the sequencing of stabilization and structural reform, see Edwards 1984, 1992b). Increasingly, however, policy analysts are coming to the conclusion that sequencing is mostly a political issue. Reformers should try to make progress on whatever front they can (Klaus 1990).

Table 4-1 contains data on the evolution of inflation in Latin America between 1984 and 1993. Although it had declined since 1989, inflation in 1993 was still high from both a historical and an international comparative perspective. With a few exceptions, most countries failed to achieve one-digit inflation rates. In Brazil, moreover, inflation failed to subside largely because opposing factions of society reached a stalemate and were unable to agree on how to distribute the costs of disinflation.[1]

This chapter analyzes some of the most important aspects of the macroeconomic adjustment process in Latin America. The analysis concentrates on the 1986–93 period. (A discussion of the macroeconomic challenges that the region faces as a result of the Mexican crisis is presented in chapter 9.) The chapter is organized in four parts. The first deals with the restructuring of debt overhang and discusses efforts to reduce the debt based on the secondary market for foreign debt and programs sponsored under the Brady initiative after 1989. The second deals with fiscal adjustment and stabilization, highlighting the efforts made to implement tax reforms and to reduce expenditures as well as salient aspects of credit policy. The relationship among exchange rate policy, inflation, and disinflation is addressed in the third section, which analyzes two central issues: (1) the connection between management of the nominal exchange rate and inflationary inertia and (2) the desirability of adopting a fixed exchange rate in the longer run as a way to anchor prices. The final section summarizes the discussion and the macroeconomic policy problems facing the region. The chapter has two appendixes: appendix 4-1 defines some of the more technical terms used in the discussion of debt-reduction schemes; appendix 4-2 presents technical issues related to the use of exchange rates as anchors in stabilization programs.

Debt Restructuring, Debt Relief, and Macroeconomic Adjustment

As a result of the sudden halt of foreign capital flows in 1982, every country in Latin America had to generate very large trade surpluses to finance debt payments. The initial reaction by the creditor countries was that the debt crisis represented a temporary liquidity problem that could be solved with a combination of macroeconomic adjustment, debt-rescheduling agreements, and structural reforms. This approach was pushed by the U.S. government and, in

Table 4-1. Annual Inflation Rates in Selected Countries of Latin America and the Caribbean, 1984–93
(percentages)

Country	1984	1985	1986	1987	1988	1989	1990	1991	1992	1993
Argentina	688.0	385.4	81.9	174.8	387.7	4,923.6	1,343.9	84.0	18.6	8.0
Bolivia	2,177.2	8,170.5	66.0	10.7	21.5	16.6	18.0	14.5	11.4	9.8
Brazil	209.1	239.0	59.2	394.7	992.7	1,861.6	1,584.6	475.8	1,131.5	2,500.0
Chile	23.2	26.2	17.4	21.4	12.7	21.5	27.3	18.7	14.0	13.0
Colombia	18.4	22.4	21.0	24.0	28.2	26.1	32.4	26.8	25.7	22.6
Costa Rica	17.3	10.9	15.4	16.4	25.3	10.0	27.3	25.3	18.1	9.5
Dominican Republic	40.9	28.3	6.5	25.0	57.6	41.2	100.7	4.0	5.9	4.0
Ecuador	25.1	24.4	27.3	32.5	85.7	54.2	49.5	49.0	66.0	31.0
El Salvador	9.1	31.9	30.3	19.6	18.2	23.5	19.3	9.8	16.8	12.0
Guatemala	7.2	27.9	21.4	9.3	12.3	20.2	59.6	10.2	11.6	12.5
Haiti	5.4	17.4	−11.4	−4.1	8.6	10.9	26.1	6.6	17.5	n.a.
Honduras	2.7	4.2	3.2	2.9	6.6	11.5	36.4	21.4	5.4	12.5
Jamaica	31.2	23.3	10.4	8.4	8.9	17.2	29.7	76.8	13.7	23.0
Mexico	59.2	63.7	105.7	159.2	51.7	19.7	29.9	18.8	12.9	8.0
Nicaragua	47.3	334.3	747.4	1,347.2	33,547.6	1,689.1	13,490.2	775.4	2.2	22.0
Panama	0.9	0.4	0.4	0.9	0.3	−0.2	1.2	1.1	1.2	0.7
Paraguay	29.8	23.1	24.1	32.0	16.9	28.5	44.1	11.8	17.0	18.0
Peru	111.5	158.3	62.9	114.5	1,722.6	2,775.3	7,649.6	139.2	56.6	46.0
Trinidad and Tobago	14.1	6.5	9.9	8.3	12.1	9.3	9.5	2.3	7.7	9.4
Uruguay	66.0	83.2	70.6	57.3	69.0	89.2	129.0	81.5	58.6	51.0
Venezuela	18.3	7.3	12.7	40.3	33.5	81.0	36.5	31.0	33.4	46.0
Average for Latin America and the Caribbean	188.3	280.1	64.1	208.9	773.5	1,205.0	1,185.0	198.7	410.7	826.6

n.a. Not available.
Sources: CEPAL, *Economic Survey of Latin America,* various years; IMF, *International Financial Statistics,* various years.

practice, was coordinated by the IMF and the World Bank. The official approach called for lending new monies (up to $20 billion) to those countries that indeed engaged in structural reforms. Not surprisingly, the banking community endorsed this view, although it argued for shifting the burden of new financing to the multilateral and official institutions: "Realism demands an increased share of new money to be furnished by official sources during the next several years" (Morgan Guaranty and Trust Company 1987, p. 2). Debt-restructuring operations, IMF-sponsored programs, and World Bank structural adjustment loans were the most important elements of the official strategy. Between 1983 and 1988, the Latin American nations engaged in twenty-nine debt-restructuring operations with the private banks.

The 1984 issues of the International Monetary Fund's *World Economic Outlook* and of the World Bank's *World Development Report* included optimistic projections, predicting a steady decline of the debt to export ratio in Latin American countries until 1990. Things, however, did not work as expected, and in the following years more and more analysts recognized that the magnitude of the problem had been seriously underestimated (see the 1986 issue of the IMF's *World Economic Outlook*).

By 1987, the debt burden had clearly reduced the incentives for reforming the region's economies and was seriously affecting the ability of the debtor nations to grow (see Sachs 1987). In March 1989, a fundamental breakthrough in the official approach toward the debt crisis took place when the creditor nations and the multilateral institutions recognized that, in many cases, providing (some) debt forgiveness was in everyone's interest. For countries facing a very high implicit marginal tax on foreign exchange earnings, partial forgiveness of the debt would be equivalent to lowering the implicit tax and, thus, would encourage the type of reform conducive to higher exports and faster growth.[2] These ideas were put into practice through the Brady Plan, which encouraged creditors to enter into voluntary debt-reduction agreements with the debtor countries.

Since 1989, the official approach combined two basic mechanisms for alleviating the debt burden. First, the use of debt-reduction schemes based on secondary market operations was actively encouraged. Although this technique had been used since the mid-1980s, it acquired special momentum after 1988, when, in a number of countries, debt-equity swaps became an important mode for privatizing state-owned enterprises. Second, direct debt-reduction agreements between creditors (commercial banks) and individual countries became more common after the introduction of the Brady Plan. Between 1989 and 1992, Argentina, Brazil, Costa Rica, Mexico, Uruguay, and Venezuela reached agreements with their creditors to reduce their debt burdens. The rest of this section analyzes in some detail both mechanisms for reducing the burden of the debt: secondary markets and debt-forgiveness agreements. Additionally, it discusses the role of the multilateral institutions, especially the World Bank and the IMF, in providing resources to the Latin American countries during the early phases of the crisis.

Secondary Market–Based Programs

The secondary market for Latin American debt emerged in 1982 and by 1988 had a volume of $45 billion. In 1990, it reached $65 billion, and in some countries it became an important mechanism for reducing foreign indebtedness. In Chile, for example, more than $11 billion of foreign debt were retired through a variety of secondary market mechanisms. The merits of this approach have been widely debated in academic and policy-related circles (see, for example, Bulow and Rogoff 1988). Case studies on Bolivia, Chile, and Mexico provide three important attempts to use the secondary market to reduce the debt burden. Appendix 4-1 defines some of the more technical terms used in the discussion presented in this and the next section.

The Bolivian Buyback Scheme. In 1985, the new government of President Paz Estenssoro inherited an economy crippled by stagnation and inflation. The main objective of the new administration was to defeat hyperinflation and to put the country back on a path of growth. In September of that year, a drastic stabilization program was enacted. The main components were a severe reduction (elimination) of fiscal imbalances and the opening up of the economy via the dismantling of trade restrictions (see Morales 1987). The program was highly successful, reducing annual inflation from more than 8,000 percent in 1985 to 60 percent in 1986 and 10 percent in 1987. However, in early 1987, the Bolivian economy was still in a weak position, with a high rate of unemployment and a depressed level of economic activity. Thinking that servicing the debt would greatly impair the chances of recovery and growth, authorities sought innovative solutions to the debt problem.

In early 1987, Bolivia reached an agreement with its official creditors to reschedule its $3.4 billion of official debt. At that point, the possibility of a buyback scheme financed with donations and foreign aid from the industrial countries was contemplated (the Bolivian debt with private banks amounted to $670 million). In July 1987, Bolivia's 131 creditor banks agreed, in principle, to participate in a debt-reduction operation, and in November a special trust account was opened at the IMF to receive donations to finance the buyback scheme (see Lamdany 1988 for a detailed analysis of the Bolivian and Mexican schemes). The buyback plan was approved under the following conditions: (1) Bolivia's international reserves could *not* be used, and only donations from other countries could finance the operation; (2) if not enough funds were donated to buy all the debt offered, the buyback would take place on prorated terms; (3) offers had to be uniform across banks; and (4) unused funds would be returned to donors. Bolivia, for its part, established that participating banks would have to renounce any claims on arrears.

In addition, a debt-conversion scheme was implemented whereby bank debt could be exchanged for twenty-five-year, zero-coupon bonds denominated in bolivianos. The bonds were indexed to the dollar and were collateralized with AAA/Aaa twenty-five-year U.S. dollar–denominated bonds. These investment bonds were offered at 11 cents to the dollar. Before the buyback was considered, the average price for Bolivian debt in the secondary market was 6 cents per dollar in 1986; it increased sharply, however, as soon as the possibility of the scheme began to be discussed. It reached 13 cents to the dollar in late 1987, when the fund at the IMF was established and the buyback period was opened. In January 1988, Bolivia announced that the buyback price was 11 cents to the dollar. In March, the results of the offer were made public: fifty-three banks had offered $340 million, or about 40 percent of Bolivia's debt with private banks. The cost of the operation was $28 million.

Was this deal in the interests of Bolivia? The answer depends on the opportunity cost (if any) of the funds used. If these funds did not crowd out other aid, there are good reasons to think that the operation had a positive return from Bolivia's perspective. If, however, the buyback crowded out alternative sources of funds, the answer is not so clear. Bulow and Rogoff (1988) contend that a partial buyback rarely benefits the debtor country for two reasons. First, the creditor pays the average (or market) price of the debt, while the reduction in the stock of debt is only marginal. Second, in the sovereign case, a buyback does not reduce the debtor's collateral (for an opposite view, see Sachs 1989c). Also, some authors argue that unilateral attempts to reduce the debt burden, including the Bolivian scheme, do not benefit debtor countries, whereas concerted approaches that consider a group of debtors do (Diwan and Rodrik 1992).

Chile's Debt-Conversion Schemes. Among the major debtors, Chile was the most aggressive in using the secondary market to reduce the debt. By early 1993, the Chilean debt had been reduced more than $11 billion—more than 30 percent of Chile's long-term bank debt—through diverse procedures based on the secondary market (see table 4-2). This was done through two mechanisms: (a) a debt-conversion program known as Chapter 18 and (b) a debt-equity-swap program known as Chapter 19.[3] These mechanisms were discontinued in January 1993, when Chile's standing in world financial markets was greatly improved and voluntary lending to the country had resumed.

The Chapter 18 mechanism allowed (private) domestic debtors to buy indirectly their own foreign liabilities in the secondary market. Foreign exchange for these operations was not provided by the Central Bank of Chile at the official rate; it had to be obtained in the parallel market. To avoid negative macroeconomic consequences from this procedure—including increased money creation and excessive pressure on the parallel market for foreign exchange—the authorities tightly controlled access to the Chapter 18 mechanism by auctioning licenses (see Larraín and Velasco 1990 for a description of the actual mechanics of Chapter 18 operations).

An important aspect of Chapter 18 operations is that Chilean residents captured most of the secondary market discount, which at some points bordered 50 percent. The discount was shared by (1) the central bank, (2) the

Table 4-2. Debt Conversion in Chile as of February 1993

Operation	Millions of U.S. dollars
Chapter 18	3,280
Chapter 19	3,600
Capitalization DL 600	304
Portfolio adjustments	156
Other operations	3,984
Total	11,323

Source: Banco Central de Chile, *Boletín Mensual,* March 1993.

suppliers of foreign exchange in the parallel market, and (3) various interme-diaries. Larraín (1988) calculates that in 1987 the average discount on Chapter 18 operations amounted to 35.7 percent. Of these, the central bank got the lion's share, capturing 20.5 percentage points; suppliers to the parallel market for foreign exchange got 3.3 points; and the rest corresponded to different fees (these computations refer to all operations that used Chapter 18, not only those of the private sector).

A debt-equity swap or a debt-capitalization scheme, known as Chapter 19, was also used. This mechanism allowed foreign investors to buy Chilean private debt at a discount in the secondary market and to convert it into internal debt. This debt was then sold in the domestic secondary market, and the proceeds were used to acquire domestic productive assets, including state-owned enterprises being privatized by the government, or to finance domestic investment projects. Participants could not repatriate profits for the first four years, and the principal could only be repatriated after ten years. Chapter 19 operations were not subject to quota allocation and were approved on a case-by-case basis by the central bank in order to identify bona fide investors and avoid round-tripping operations. From a practical point of view, this scheme amounted to providing a (very) large subsidy to foreign investors.

In evaluating the merits of the Chapter 19 program, it is necessary to address the possibility that it crowds out foreign investment (Dornbusch 1989b raises this issue within the general context of debt-equity swaps). The question is whether participants in the program would have invested in Chile anyway or, more important, whether they would have invested in the country even if offered a significantly lower subsidy. If they would have participated under both conditions, the program crowded out other investments, and its benefits were negligible or even negative. Alternatively, the program may have generated additionality, attracting new foreign investors. Larraín (1988) asserts that since foreign banks opted to participate in these schemes, even though equity investment is not their main line of business, there was at least some additionality, and the scheme as a whole was beneficial for Chile.[4]

The Mexican 2008 Bond. During the early years of the debt crisis, Mexico tried a number of market-based mechanisms to reduce its debt burden. From a legal standpoint, the Mexican debt restructuring of March 1985 opened the door to innovative debt-conversion schemes. This agreement established that Mexico could engage in both debt-equity swaps as well as in debt-exchange operations without being subject to the sharing provisions. Under these terms, the consent of only 51 percent of Mexico's creditor banks was required to waive the negative pledge clauses. The critical level of waivers was obtained in February 1988 (see Lamdany 1988).

In December 1987, Mexico announced that it was willing to exchange $10 billion of its debt for twenty-year collateralized bonds that carried a spread over LIBOR of 1⅝ percent. This spread was approximately twice as high as the spread paid on rescheduled debt. The bonds would be amortized in one payment on maturity and collateralized with nonmarketable twenty-year and zero-coupon U.S. treasury bonds (however, a provision allowed Mexico to make early amortization). The acquisition of the collateral was to be financed with international reserves.

On January 18, 1988, Mexico invited creditor banks to present bids that included the amount of the bid and a bid ratio that determined how much of the debt they would tender for each dollar of face value of bonds. The Mexican authorities publicly expected to obtain an approximate discount of 50 percent. Most independent analysts, however, thought that this was highly unlikely. Since the secondary market value of the Mexican debt was around that mark at the time, this would have meant that banks considered the 2008 bonds as cash. Mexico received 320 bids from 139 banks for a total of $6.7 billion. The bids ranged from 60 to 75 cents, significantly higher than what the Mexican authorities expected. Mexico accepted bids from ninety-five banks that amounted to $3.7 billion and used $430 million in international reserves to buy the collateral. The average conversion ratio was 1.43, and the Mexican debt was reduced only $1.1 billion (see Gil Díaz 1988).

The Mexican 2008 bond poses, at least, two important analytical and policy questions. Why did the bids of the participating banks differ so much from Mexican expectations? Banks considered two elements—the principal and the flow of interest payments—when pricing the bonds (Lamdany 1988). The principal was collateralized, considered a safe component, and priced accordingly. Interest payments, however, carried the risk associated with other Mexican debt and were therefore discounted. The second question is whether the 2008 bond operation was beneficial for Mexico. Although initially most analysts answered this question in the affirmative, the unveiling of events showed that this was not exactly the case. In effect, in 1989 and under the auspices of the Brady Plan, Mexico was able to obtain a more convenient deal in which $48 billion of its foreign debt became eligible to be exchanged under more favorable conditions than the 2008 bond operation of the previous year. Under the Brady agreement, Mexico's debt was exchanged at 65 cents to the dollar for thirty-year, zero-coupon bonds.

The Early Debt Crisis and the Multilateral Institutions

Even though the multilateral institutions failed to grasp the magnitude of the debt crisis during its early years, they contributed voluminous resources to the Latin American countries. In this way, the debtor nations reduced the magnitude of the resource transfer to the rest of the world. For example, between 1980 and 1986, the World Bank more than doubled its net disbursements to Latin America, from $1.2 billion to $2.8 billion. During the same period, the net resource transfer from the Bank—a measure that subtracts the interest payments from net disbursements—increased from $600 million to almost $1.1 billion. The International Monetary Fund channeled very large amounts of resources toward the region immediately after the crisis erupted. The IMF's net transfers to Latin America and the Caribbean were negative in 1980 (–$173 million) and reached almost $6 billion in 1983.

From the early stages of the crisis, the World Bank was concerned with helping engineer a smooth and sustainable adjustment that would simultaneously accomplish three objectives: (a) reduce macroeconomic instability; (b) restore growth, including a minimum increase in consumption; and (c) reduce the degree of debt overhang. Within this framework, ensuring some growth of consumption during the transition was considered to be crucially important from both economic and political points of view. Without that minimum expansion of consumption, countries would lack the will to undertake the reforms and would stagnate.

Selowsky and van der Tak (1986) argue that this type of adjustment could not be achieved overnight and that in some countries it would require a significant amount of time. Additionally, in order to exploit optimally the intertemporal tradeoffs between the different objectives of the adjustment process, the debtor countries needed to receive, during the early stages, additional foreign resources. In this way, they could gain time to implement the domestic reforms required to accelerate growth and reduce the debt burden. A crucial aspect of the Selowsky–van der Tak analysis is that, under some circumstances, the initial conditions are so severe that the only way to restore a viable debt to output ratio is for the creditors to forgive some of the debt. This argument was made before the Bank officially supported programs based on (partial) debt forgiveness. Analytical work undertaken at the IMF's Research Department, under the leadership of Jacob Frenkel, also explored the merits of debt-forgiveness programs. In the late 1980s, this line of argument made headway among officials of the creditor countries. It became increasingly evident that, under a number of circumstances, some debt reduction could be beneficial to both debtors and creditors.

The Brady Plan and Debt-Reduction Programs

The disappointing outcome of the Mexican 2008 bond and the lack of progress made in solving the crisis with the two other large debtors—Argentina and Brazil—prompted a change in the official debt strategy in early 1989. In March of that year, U.S. Secretary of the Treasury Nicholas Brady announced a new initiative based on voluntary debt reduction. He proposed exchanging old debt for new long-term debt with a lower face value. The exact conversion ratios, and the detailed characteristics of the new instruments, were to be negotiated between the debtor countries and their creditors. To make this new approach feasible and attractive to creditor banks, the industrial nations and multilateral institutions devoted a substantial amount of resources— on the order of $30 billion—to guarantee the new concessional bonds. Typically, principal payments on these new securities were backed by thirty-year, zero-coupon U.S. treasury bills, and interest payments were subject to rolling three-year guarantees (see, for example, Cline 1989 for a discussion of the genesis of the Brady Plan).

To be eligible for Brady Plan negotiations, countries had to show willingness—plus some prior action—to engage in serious economic reform. From an incentives point of view, this new initiative was intended to have two effects: first, to reward countries truly committed to implementing modernization reforms and, second, to lift the debt-overhang burdens associated with extremely high payments. In 1989, Mexico and Costa Rica were the first countries that, within the Brady Plan framework, reached broad agreements with their creditors to reduce the value of their debt. Venezuela and Uruguay followed in 1990 and 1991, and Argentina and Brazil signed draft agreements in 1992.

Table 4-3 contains summary information on the six broad debt-reduction deals signed as of March 1994.[5] The first column contains the total value of the debt covered by each of the agreements. In Argentina and Costa Rica, it includes both principal and arrears. As can be seen from these data, the volume of debt subject to each arrangement was quite large. For example, in Mexico, more than $48 billion were exchanged for concessional bonds, a figure substantially higher than the $3.7 billion converted under the Mexican 2008 bond scheme discussed above.

The next three columns present the amount of debt eligible for conversion under three different options. The first is a debt-buyback option, where the old debt obligation is canceled by a cash payment at a fraction of the original liability. For instance, in Costa Rica $159 million were used to retire old debt for a face value of $991 million. This operation, then, carried a discount of 84 percent: each dollar of old debt was exchanged for 16 cents in cash. The second option consists of using discounted bonds to retire the original debt. Creditors receive long-term—usually thirty-year—bonds in exchange for the

Table 4-3. Debt Reduction in Selected Countries of Latin America, Various Years, 1989–93
(millions of U.S. dollars, unless otherwise noted)

Country and date of agreement	Face value of eligible debt	Buyback[a]	Discounted bonds[a]	Par bonds[b]	New money[b]	Total debt, December 1991[c]
Argentina, 1993	23,160[d]	n.d.	n.d. (35)	n.d. (35)	0 (4–6)[e]	56,273
Brazil, 1993	44,000[f]	0	n.d. (35)	n.d[g]	n.d.[g]	118,148
Costa Rica, 1989	1,602[f]	991 (84)	0	579 (6.5)	0	3,966
Mexico, 1989	48,089	0	20,851 (35)	22,427 (6.25)	4,387 (LIBOR +13/16)	98,263
Uruguay, 1991	1,610	633 (44)	530	0	448 (LIBOR +1)	3,049
Venezuela, 1990	19,098	1,411 (55)	1,794 (30)	10,333 (6.75)	6,060 (LIBOR +7/8)	34,081

n.d. Not yet determined (subject to banks' choice).

a. Numbers in parentheses are the percentage discount.

b. Numbers in parentheses are the interest rate.

c. Includes IMF and net short-term debt.

d. Estimated. In addition there are $8.6 billion in arrears, including imputed interest.

e. Interest rate increases from 4 percent in the first year to 6 percent in the seventh year; 6 percent from then on.

f. Estimated. In addition there are $6 billion in arrears, including imputed interest.

g. Several par bonds are offered, with different maturities/grace periods, interest rates, and collateral: option A, 30/30 years, rate is 4 to 6 percent in the first seven years, 6 percent from then on, full collateral principal, twelve-month interest; option B, 15/9 years, rate is 4 to 5 percent in the first six years, LIBOR + 13/16 from then on, twelve-month interest collateral for six years; option C, 20/10 years, LIBOR + 13/16, but interest above the rate in bond B is capitalized, no collateral; option D, 20/10 years, 8 percent and interest above the rate in bond B is capitalized, no collateral; option E, 18/10 years, LIBOR + 7/8, no collateral; under option E, new money is equivalent to 18.18 percent of debt tendered for debt-conversion bonds.

h. Includes past-due interest.

Source: World Bank, several country-specific reports.

original debt instruments. Although the new bonds carry a market interest rate, the exchange between old debt and new bonds takes place at a ratio below one to one. The actual conversion ratio is negotiated individually and varies from country to country. Argentina, Brazil, and Mexico negotiated a 35 percent discount, while Venezuela obtained only a 30 percent discount. The principal on the new bonds is usually guaranteed by U.S. zero-coupon bonds.

The third option for reducing the debt burden consists of exchanging old debt for new bonds with the same face value—the so-called par bonds—and a below-market interest rate. The collateral on the principal and the guarantee on interest payments are similar to those on the discounted bonds discussed above. The recent Argentine and Brazilian agreements included several types of par bonds.

In most cases, the debt-reduction packages included the provision of new money to the debtor countries. These fresh resources were necessary to help cover interest payments on the converted debt during the early years and to help smooth the transition toward more-open, market-oriented economic systems. Generally, improving the quality of the adjustment, including the implementation of fiscal reforms, is a time-intensive activity. Because it takes time to reduce macroeconomic imbalances efficiently, it is important to have foreign financing during the transition. There is a strong complementarity between a stabilization effort based on efficient fiscal measures and external financing (Selowsky and van der Tak 1986). The amounts of the new resources provided by the Brady Plan agreements appear in column six of table 4-3. Finally, the last column in this table contains information on the total value of the debt in each of these countries by the end of 1991.

There is little doubt that the Brady-endorsed debt-reduction packages helped these countries by reducing their debt burdens and allowing them to implement the reforms required to move toward sustainable growth. In Mexico, for example, the World Bank estimated that the debt-relief deal reduced the net transfer to creditors by $4 billion a year between 1989 and 1994, a figure close to 2 percent of GDP. Moreover, the 1989 debt-reduction agreement allowed Mexico to grow, on average, at a rate 2 percentage points above what would have been attained in the absence of the agreement (see van Wijnbergen 1990). Nevertheless, several countries—most notably Chile and Colombia—have declined to participate in the Brady Plan. Their authorities argue that the strategies followed until now—a combination of support from multilateral agencies, economic reform, and market-based debt reduction—have worked well and efficiently for them.

The urgency of the years immediately following the eruption of the debt crisis has subsided. Nevertheless, most countries in the region still suffer the consequences of the debt explosion of the 1970s and early 1980s. In particular, interest payments on the foreign debt still represent high percentages of

GDP—in Colombia, for example, almost 3 percent and in Brazil almost 2 percent. In a few countries—Nicaragua being the premier example—the magnitude of the debt is so large (more than three times GDP) that massive debt-reduction agreements would be required to achieve a longer-run solution.

After almost ten years of negative net resource transfers, Latin America experienced positive transfers from the rest of the world in 1991. The magnitude of net capital inflows into the country increased drastically in 1992 and 1993, surpassing $20 billion.

Figure 4-1 exhibits the remarkable recovery of the prices of Latin American debt certificates in secondary markets since 1990 for four largest debtors. This fact indicates the renewed confidence in the region that the international financial community showed in the early 1990s. Argentina, for instance, which was recovering from the hyperinflation of 1989, enjoyed a fourfold increase in the price of its debt from 1990 to 1993, a clear signal of easier access to international financing.

Paradoxically, the increase in capital flows into Latin America after 1991 generated serious problems related to the behavior of the real exchange rate. As capital flowed into these countries, foreign exchange became too abundant, pressuring the real exchange rate toward appreciation. This resulted in real exchange rate overvaluation, a loss of international competitiveness, and political pressures on behalf of exporters to implement compensating policies. In

Figure 4-1. Prices of Debt in the Secondary Market in Selected Countries of Latin America, 1990–93

Percentage of face value

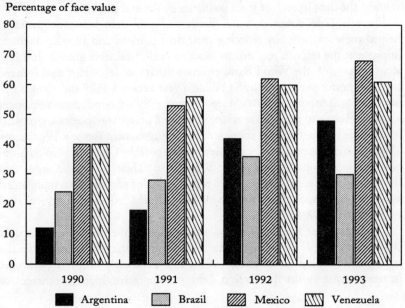

Source: World Bank, *Financial Flows to Developing Countries*, 1993.

Table 4-4. Inflation and Seigniorage in Selected Countries of Latin America and the Caribbean, Annual Averages for 1971–82
(percentage)

Country	Inflation	Seigniorage
Bolivia	30.3	21.6
Brazil	47.4	17.7
Chile	147.6	17.5
Colombia	22.0	17.1
Dominican Republic	10.0	6.7
Ecuador	13.2	14.4
El Salvador	11.2	11.4
Honduras	8.3	5.8
Jamaica	17.0	4.7
Mexico	21.2	23.9
Nicaragua	16.8	8.8
Paraguay	12.8	15.4
Peru	38.2	20.7
Venezuela	9.2	5.7

Note: Inflation is defined as the rate of change in the consumer price index and seigniorage as the change in base money relative to total government revenue.
Source: Edwards and Tabellini 1991.

the case of Mexico, the reliance on foreign inflows and the overvaluation of the real exchange rate were at the center of the new crisis that erupted in December of 1994. This issue is addressed in detail in chapters 5 and 9.

Fiscal Policy and Macroeconomic Equilibrium

Fiscal imbalances traditionally have been at the heart of Latin America's macroeconomic disequilibrium. The inability, or unwillingness, of governments to raise sufficient tax revenues to cover expenditures has forced them to rely on money creation, or seigniorage, to finance the public sector deficit.[6] Table 4-4 contains data on annual average inflation and seigniorage in selected Latin American countries for 1971–82. Inflation is defined as the percentage change in the consumer price index; seigniorage is the change in base money relative to total government revenues. As can be seen, in some countries money creation accounted, on average, for almost one-fourth of government revenues during this period.

In recent analyses, more and more authors emphasize the political economy dimensions of the macroeconomic and inflationary problem (see, for example, Alesina 1988; Alesina and Drazen 1991). They argue that relying on seigniorage to finance the public deficit is highly influenced by the political conditions of the country. Very often, politicians behave strategically, trying to constrain their opponents' policy options. This type of behavior tends to produce political gridlock, inefficient tax systems, and, thus, inflation. In some circumstances, political polarization can be so intense that the government operates on the wrong side of the seigniorage Laffer curve (see Bruno 1991; Dornbusch and Fischer 1993; Edwards and Tabellini 1991).

An important feature of the political economy approach to inflation is that macroeconomic disequilibrium, including the use of seigniorage to finance public expenditures, is directly related to the government's inability to commit itself credibly to a certain line of action. Politically motivated governments face large incentives to renege on their promises and to run public deficits above what they have promised. To implement a credible and lasting reduction in macroeconomic imbalances, fiscal corrections must be accompanied by institutional reforms that allow the authorities to commit themselves to certain courses of action in the future (on credibility, see Calvo 1978; Persson and Tabellini 1990).

The fundamental policy implication of this discussion is that the credible reduction (or elimination) of the public sector deficit should be at the center of stabilization programs. Although in many successful anti-inflationary episodes, fiscal action is supplemented by other measures, including incomes policies, the effort to correct public sector finances is invariably the most important component of those (successful) programs. This is pointed out in chapter 2, where the Mexican stabilization program is compared with the heterodox episodes in Argentina, Brazil, and Peru. What distinguishes the Mexican experience from the heterodox efforts is that Mexico only implemented incomes policies once fiscal finances were fully under control.

In the presence of a significant debt burden, the need to reduce fiscal imbalances efficiently becomes particularly pressing. In this case, it is necessary not only to reduce the gap between traditional expenditures and noninflationary revenues but also to generate sufficient funds to finance the transfer of resources to the rest of the world. However, an efficient restructuring of fiscal finances—that is, a restructuring that replaces antiquated tax systems with new and modern ones and that redefines priorities for expenditures—takes significant effort and time. In the meantime, while these reforms are being implemented, temporary sources of financing have to be found. In most cases of debt restructuring, the multilateral organizations and debt-relief plans sponsored by the Brady Plan provided the resources needed to finance the adjustments.

This section deals with some of the most important aspects of fiscal and credit adjustment in Latin America in the late 1980s and early 1990s. The discussion deals, first, with general regional trends and then discusses in greater detail three case studies—Chile, Mexico, and Argentina.

Fiscal Austerity in the Late 1980s

During the late 1980s and early 1990s, most countries in the region sought to reduce their public sector imbalances as a way to restore macroeconomic equilibrium and foster economic growth. Their efforts to do so were based on a combination of revenue-increasing policies—including tax reforms, privatization of public firms, and improved tax administration—and expenditure cuts. Tables 4-5 through 4-8 provide a broad summary of the magnitude of the adjustment programs in a selected group of countries.

Table 4-5 deals with the bottom line and contains data on the evolution of the consolidated public sector deficit as a percentage of GDP for thirteen countries. An advantage of these data is that they refer to the public sector, including government-owned enterprises, provinces, and municipalities, and not to the narrower concept of central government. In most cases, public finances improved markedly between 1986 and 1991; with the exception of Costa Rica and Brazil, in 1991, every country in the table drastically reduced its public sector deficit after the mid-1980s (in some countries, these figures are affected by revenues obtained from the sale of public enterprises).

Mexico and Nicaragua are two cases, in which substantial—and in the case of Nicaragua, truly gigantic—deficits were transformed into large surpluses. Nicaragua's adjustment after 1990 was part of the Chamorro administration's successful battle against hyperinflation. The control of public finances, coupled with measures such as fixing the nominal exchange rate and reprivatizing a number of enterprises, reduced the rate of inflation from 13,490 percent in 1990 to a mere 2.2 percent in 1992. In Mexico, the turnaround in the fiscal

Table 4-5. Public Sector Balance as a Percentage of GDP in Selected Countries of Latin America and the Caribbean, 1986–91

Country	1986	1987	1988	1989	1990	1991
Argentina	−4.1	−6.5	−7.0	−21.8	−3.3	−1.8
Brazil[a]	−3.7	−5.7	−4.8	−6.9	1.3	−3.0
Chile	—	−4.3	−0.7	3.5	1.6	0.3
Colombia[b]	−0.3	−2.0	−2.2	−2.9	−0.8	−0.1
Costa Rica[b]	—	−0.3	−0.3	−2.8	−2.9	—
Ecuador	−5.1	−9.6	−5.1	−0.9	0.4	—
Jamaica	−5.6	−5.4	−12.8	−6.3	−2.9	−0.4
Mexico	—	—	—	−1.6	1.2	3.5
Nicaragua	—	—	−36.7	−18.4	−17.8	4.0
Peru	—	—	—	−10.7	−6.5	−3.2
Trinidad and Tobago[c]	−9.5	−7.7	−6.5	−4.4	−1.4	−0.9
Uruguay	−5.2	−4.2	−5.0	−7.6	−3.6	—
Venezuela[d]	—	−5.4	−9.3	−1.3	—	−3.0

— Not available.

Note: A positive number is a surplus; a negative number is a deficit.

a. Operational nonfinancial deficit, including net interest payments.

b. Nonfinancial public sector.

c. Overall balance of the nonfinancial public sector.

d. So-called reduced public sector.

Sources: IMF, *Government Financial Statistics*, various years; World Bank, *World Tables*, 1992; individual country reports.

deficit was the central component of a stabilization program aimed at recovering the country's historical macroeconomic stability and achieving rates of inflation consistent with those prevailing in its partners in the North American Free Trade Agreement.*

Chile is another interesting case of fiscal management. In the mid-1980s, and as a result of the debt crisis and the failure of several financial institutions, Chile developed large public sector deficits. These, however, were eliminated in 1988–89 through reduced expenditures and a new tax reform. The generation of positive government savings became an important component of the government strategy to accelerate growth; by 1989, a comfortable public sector surplus had been achieved (for a discussion of the government's macroeconomic strategy during this period, see Fontaine 1989). This surplus allowed the new administration of President Aylwin to finance an increase in social expenditures aimed at reducing poverty and improving income distribution in the early 1990s.

Contrasting stories can be found in Brazil and Argentina. Between 1986 and 1988, both countries experienced significant fiscal disequilibria that were closely related to the failure of the heterodox experiments. Public sector finances deteriorated rapidly in Argentina until, in early 1989, the country suffered a complete breakdown of macroeconomic management and succumbed to hyperinflation. In late 1989, the new administration of President Carlos Menem embarked on a stabilization program that drastically reduced the government deficit. Brazil followed a divergent path. After a brief interlude with fiscal austerity during the early years of the Collor de Mello administration, the country slipped back into increasingly large public imbalances that fed a voracious inflation, which reached 1,132 percent in 1992 (in 1994, a new stabilization plan, which recognized the importance of fiscal discipline, was implemented).

In most countries, the improvement in the public sector accounts was accomplished through a combination of higher revenues and lower expenditures. On the revenue side, most programs included (a) tax reforms aimed at improving the efficiency and effectiveness of the tax system; (b) improvements in tax administration, including efforts to reduce evasion; (c) increases in the price of public services to cover costs; and (d) sales of state-owned enterprises.

As pointed out in chapter 3, World Bank and IMF conditionality focused, among other things, on the need to implement significant tax reforms throughout Latin America. These reforms had several objectives, including the reduction of distortions, the simplification of the tax system, and an increase in tax revenues. Table 4-6 presents data on tax rates for individuals, local corporations, and foreign companies before and after the reform period in a number of countries. Table 4-7 contains data on the evolution of the value

---

*During 1993–94, however, Mexico's public sector surplus was substantially reduced. This reduction was particularly important during 1994 in the wake of the presidential elections.

added tax. Several interesting facts emerge from these tables. First, the majority of the countries (eleven out of eighteen with relevant data) reduced the top income tax rate, increased the minimum rate, and raised the exemption level for the personal income tax. For the region as a whole, the average exemption increased from approximately one GDP per capita in 1985 to almost two in 1991 (Shome 1994). The combination of these two measures was expected to increase the efficiency of the tax system while reducing its (traditional) degree of regressiveness. Second, the maximum marginal rates on the corporate income tax, in general, were reduced, as was the number of corporate tax rates. An important aspect of these tax reforms is that they eliminated the uncertainty that traditionally surrounded the taxation of capital gains. Most countries decided to treat capital gains as ordinary income. And third, most countries reduced the withholding rate on foreign remittances in an effort to encourage foreign investment.

Table 4-6. Tax Rates in the Periods before and after Reform in Selected Countries of Latin America and the Caribbean, Various Years, 1985–93
(percentage)

Country	Personal income tax		Corporate income tax		Withholding taxes on foreign remittances[a]	
	1985–86	1991	1986	1992	1986	1993
Argentina	16.5–4.5	6–30	0–33	20	23	17
Bolivia	...–30	13	0–30	0	25	13
Brazil	0–60	10–25	29–50	25–40	25	22
Chile	0–57	5–50	10–37	15–35	40	38
Colombia	...–49	5–30	40	30	40	12
Costa Rica	5–50	10–25	0–50	30	15	18
Dominican Republic	2–73	3–70	0–49.3	0–49.3	20	30
Ecuador	19–40	10–25	0–59	0–44.4	40	36
El Salvador	3–60	10–50	0–30	0–25	22	20
Guatemala	11–48	4–34	0–42	12–34	16	17
Honduras	3–40	3–40	0–55	0–40.2	10	18
Mexico	3–55	3–55	5–42	0–35	37	22
Nicaragua	15–50	6–50	0–45	0–35.5	20	30
Panama	13–56	2.5–56	0–50	2.5–45	30	22
Paraguay	5–30	0	0–30	0–30	23	25
Peru	2–56	5–56	0–40	0–30	42	19
Uruguay	0	0	0–30	0–30	30	—
Venezuela	12–45	4.5–45	18–67.7	20–67.7	20	15
Regional average	5–36	7–47	3.4–46.3	8.6–36.5	27	22

... Negligible.
— Not available.
a. Simple average.
Source: Shome 1994.

Table 4-7. Value Added Tax in Selected Countries of Latin America and the Caribbean, Various Years, 1967–94

Country	Date introduced or proposed	Rate at introduction	Rate as of January 1994
Argentina	January 1975	16	18, 26, 27[a]
Bolivia	October 1973	5, 10, 15	14.92[b]
Brazil[c]	January 1967	15	9, 11
Brazil[d]	January 1967	15	17
Chile	March 1975	8, 20	18
Colombia	January 1975	4, 6, 10	8, 14, 20, 35, 45
Costa Rica	January 1975	10	8
Dominican Republic	January 1983	6	6
Ecuador	July 1970	4, 10	10
El Salvador	September 1992	10	10
Guatemala	August 1983	7	7
Haiti	November 1982	7	10
Honduras	January 1976	3	7, 10
Jamaica	October 1991	10	12.5
Mexico	January 1980	10	10
Nicaragua	January 1975	6	5, 6, 10
Panama	March 1977	5	5, 10
Paraguay	July 1993	12	10
Peru	July 1976	3, 20, 40	18
Venezuela	October 1993	10	10

a. Supplementary value added tax rates of 8 and 9 percent on imports of noncapital goods: through catch-up, these can revert to 18 percent retail.

b. Effective rate (legislated tax-inclusive rate is 13 percent).

c. On interstate transactions depending on region.

d. On interstate transactions.

Source: Shome 1994.

Perhaps the most important effect of the reforms in the area of taxation is that by the end of 1993, most Latin American countries had adopted a value added tax system. Additionally, most had sought to make the value added tax more efficient by reducing the number of rates and broadening its base. Most countries that were able to increase their ratio of tax revenue to GDP significantly did so by increasing the contribution of the value added tax to total revenues.

In every country, except Costa Rica and Jamaica, tax revenues were higher in 1991 than in 1988 (see table 4-8). Given the tax rates and coverage, however, the region's total revenues continued to be low, largely because tax compliance was still unsatisfactory and tax administration did not improve sufficiently.

In every country, with the exception of Venezuela, total public sector expenditures were lower in 1991 than in 1987 (see table 4-9). Comparing the evolution of tax revenues and expenditures shows clearly that the reduction in expenditures made the greatest contribution to the attainment of fiscal equilibrium. In many countries, expenditures were reduced across-the-board, affecting social programs. Many countries tackled this problem by trying to increase the efficiency of social programs, targeting social expenditures, and designing emergency social trends.

A second feature of the expenditure adjustment programs is that, in almost every country, capital expenditures were reduced drastically. In four out of the eight countries with available data, capital expenditures in 1991 were more than 25 percent lower than the already depressed levels of 1987. The nature of these cuts varied from country to country. In some cases, large and inefficient government projects were canceled or postponed; in others, public investment in infrastructure was cut, generating serious shortcomings in the provision of transportation and power. According to World Bank estimates, in order to solve the infrastructure deficit, Latin America would have to invest $50 billion a year between 1994 and 2000.

In some countries, including Argentina, Chile, and Mexico capital expenditures that were traditionally made by the government were shifted to the private sector. For example, in Mexico, allowing the private sector to charge tolls on newly constructed highways increased the construction of roads. However, very high tolls for using these highways resulted in a somewhat low degree of use. Also, the Mexican government actively encouraged private sector involvement in the provision and treatment of water, the collection of garbage, and the generation of electrical power—activities that were traditionally reserved for government-owned companies.

Table 4-8. Tax Revenues as a Percentage of GDP in Selected Countries of Latin America and the Caribbean, 1987–91

Country	1987	1988	1989	1990	1991
Argentina[a]	17.8	16.2	14.9	19.1	20.0
Brazil	18.1	17.8	18.4	23.9	21.2
Colombia	14.9	14.4	14.4	14.4	15.8
Costa Rica	22.4	22.0	22.7	22.2	22.2
Guyana	32.8	39.7	38.7	40.7	40.2
Jamaica[b]	28.6	26.7	27.4	25.8	27.2
Mexico	8.6	9.6	10.2	10.5	10.7
Nicaragua	—	20.9	24.6	16.6	24.0
Trinidad and Tobago[c]	27.6	25.3	24.6	25.1	29.7

— Not available.

a. Includes national administration plus social security taxes.

b. Central government; includes bauxite levy.

c. Central government.

Sources: IMF, *Government Financial Statistics*, various years; World Bank, *World Tables*, 1992; individual country reports.

Table 4-9. Total and Capital Expenditures of the Public Sector as a Percentage of GDP in Selected Countries of Latin America and the Caribbean, 1987, 1989, and 1991

Country	1987		1989		1991	
	Total expend- iture	Capital expend- iture	Total expend- iture	Capital expend- iture	Total expend- iture	Capital expend- iture
Argentina	22.3	3.8	19.0	2.8	21.6	1.5
Brazil	31.9	7.5	34.9	6.2	28.3	5.2
Chile	34.4	6.9	27.1	5.1	26.3	4.8
Colombia	21.1	7.7	19.2	6.9	20.9	6.7
Costa Rica[a]	30.3	5.8	33.1	6.8	30.1	4.3
Ecuador[b]	31.5	7.1	5.8	7.2	26.2	7.3
Nicaragua	47.0	6.2	35.9	6.2	36.1	5.9
Peru	—	—	—	3.0	—	2.0
Venezuela	32.2	12.0	31.0	11.2	35.1	13.7

— Not available.

Note: These are nonfinancial expenditures, so they exclude interest payments and international losses of the public financial sector (that is, the central bank).

a. Includes net lending.

b. Last available data are for 1990 and 1991.

Sources: IMF, *Government Financial Statistics*, various years; World Bank, *World Tables*, 1992; individual country reports.

In many countries, interest payments on public sector debt—both domestic and foreign—represent a large proportion of total public sector expenditures. In fact, by excluding these payments and concentrating on the so-called primary deficit, we find that most countries achieved substantial adjustments. Perhaps the most impressive case is that of Argentina, which in 1989 had a consolidated public sector deficit of almost 22 percent of GDP and a primary deficit of only 0.4 percent of GDP. In that year, and as a result of a remarkable surge in inflation, interest payments on the domestic, indexed debt in the non-financial sector surpassed 15 percent of GDP!

A large internal debt can seriously jeopardize macroeconomic stability when, as was traditionally the case in most of Latin America, it is concentrated on short-term maturity instruments. Changes in short-term interest rates stemming from changing world conditions, from macro-policy measures, or from purely perverse expectations have a huge impact on the public sector deficit. Many countries recognize this problem and are trying to reduce the stock of domestic debt as well as lengthen its maturity. Calvo (1988) argues that the presence of nonindexed domestic debt can produce self-fulfilling expectations that inflation will be high. This line of analysis is promising for understanding the Brazilian inflationary process, where during 1993 relatively low domestic debt and a primary surplus in the public sector existed alongside monthly inflation rates of 30 percent.

A peculiarity of Latin America's public finances is that in many countries the financial public sector is the source of sizable deficits through the so-called quasi-fiscal deficits. In most cases, these deficits stem from central bank operations that subsidize a particular group or particular operations. For example, two typical sources of quasi-fiscal deficits are dual exchange rates, where the central bank buys expensive foreign exchange at the ongoing rate and sells it cheaply to a particular user, and bailout operations of the financial sector, where the central bank acquires low-quality or nonperforming assets from a financial institution about to fail. Since this type of operation is usually financed by issuing interest-bearing obligations, the net effect is an operational loss for the central bank. This was the case in Chile, for example, where after the financial crisis of 1982–83, the central bank incurred very large losses (see table 4-10). In Argentina, in contrast, the main cause of the quasi-fiscal deficit was the payment of (high) interest rates on the legal reserves of commercial banks.

Credit Policy

An important component of the regional stabilization programs is the control of domestic credit to the public and private sectors (see figure 4-2 for data on selected countries). During the early years of the adjustment (1982–87), most of the burden of credit reduction fell on the private sector. This was, in part, a consequence of the sudden cut in the availability of foreign funds to finance public expenditures. Most governments reacted by borrowing heavily from the domestic banking system, crowding out the private sector. As a consequence, real interest rates increased sharply, and aggregate demand declined. However, as the adjustment proceeded and foreign financing was partially restored through debt restructuring, interest capitalization, and debt reduction, governments were able to ease credit restrictions to the private sector (see figure 4-3).

The financial deregulation undertaken by most countries during the late 1980s and early 1990s had important effects on how monetary policy was conducted in the region. In particular, central bankers had to learn how to manipulate monetary policy through indirect instruments as opposed to the traditional quantitative control of credit. For example, the reduction and harmonization of reserve requirements increased the ability of commercial banks to intermediate funds, reducing the authorities' direct control on liquidity. Likewise, gradual elimination of the direct allocation of credit forced monetary authorities to devise alternative methods of monetary control. Different countries opted for different solutions. The most advanced ones—Argentina, Chile, and Mexico, for example—developed an increasingly sophisticated

Table 4-10. Financial Public Sector Quasi-fiscal Deficit as a Percentage of GDP in Selected Countries of Latin America, 1986–91

Country	1986	1987	1988	1989	1990	1991
Argentina[a]	1.6	0.9	0.7	5.9	1.0	0.6
Chile[a]	—	3.9	3.2	1.8	2.2	1.9
Peru[b]	—	—	—	2.8	1.1	0.5
Uruguay[c]	3.9	2.8	3.1	4.0	4.1	—

— Not available.

a. Refers to the central bank.

b. Covers losses of the central bank and Banco Agrario.

c. Includes operational losses of the central bank and intervened banks.

Sources: IMF, *Government Financial Statistics*, various years; World Bank, *World Tables*, 1992; individual country reports.

system of open-market operations, while others used monetary stabilization securities issued by the central bank.

The opening of the Latin American economies to international transactions—both in goods and financial assets—also changed the way in which monetary policy is conducted. In particular, central bankers found that, in an open economy, policy inconsistencies can be very costly, and changes in the domestic economic conditions can clearly generate sizable capital movements that greatly affect monetary policy. For example, the 1991–93 surge in capital inflows into the region resulted in large increases in the supply of money that, in many cases, frustrated the monetary programs of central banks and generated pressures toward appreciation of the real exchange rate (the increase in capital inflows also affected real exchange rates throughout the region; see chapter 5). As the Colombian authorities discovered in 1991, in an open economy it even becomes difficult to sterilize the increases in international reserves. When this is attempted through the sale of domestic bonds, interest rate differentials are bound to appear, creating additional incentives for capital to flow into the country and further increasing the quantity of money (see Calvo 1991). Moreover, as Mexico found out during 1994, political developments can have devastating effects on an economy subject to unrestricted capital mobility (see chapter 9 for a detailed discussion).

Fiscal Adjustment and Tax Reforms: Three Case Studies

This subsection addresses in some detail the experiences of three countries—Chile, Mexico, and Argentina—with tax reforms and fiscal adjustment. Chile provides an exemplary case in which tax policy is managed so as to generate macroeconomic stability and facilitate the adjustment after the debt crisis. Mexico is an important case of a major tax reform, covering the revision of tax rates, the broadening of the tax base, and the improvement of tax administra-

Figure 4-2. Annual Growth Rates of Domestic Credit in Selected Countries of Latin America and the Caribbean, 1983–92

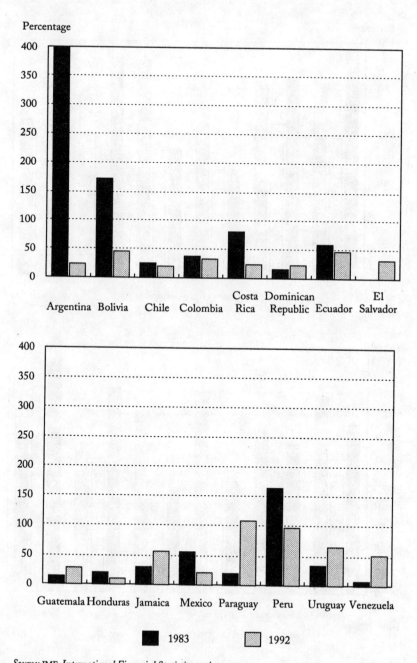

Percentage

Source: IMF, *International Financial Statistics*, various years.

Figure 4-3. Credit to the Private Sector as a Percentage of Total Domestic Credit in Selected Countries of Latin America and the Caribbean, 1980–92

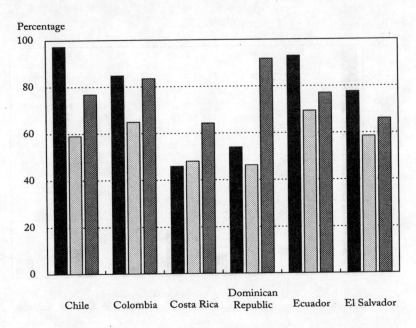

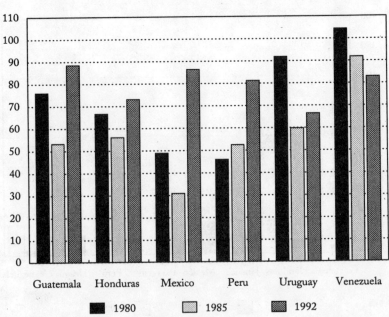

Source: IMF, *International Financial Statistics*, various years.

tion. Argentina shows that it is possible to reduce the fiscal deficit through a program that relies heavily on reductions in expenditures.

Chile. Between 1974, when the structural reforms were initiated, and the end of 1994, Chile went through three tax reforms. The first one, implemented in 1975, was the most profound and introduced sweeping changes in the country's public finances.[7] Its main purpose was to generate a substantial increase in tax revenues and to reduce the distortions generated by the old system. The principal features included the replacement of a cascade sales tax with a flat-rate value added tax at a 20 percent rate, full indexation of the tax system, elimination of all tax exemptions and subsidies, unification of corporate and other income taxes into a flat business tax, and integration of personal and business income taxes.

The combination of increased tax revenues and reduced government expenditures rapidly affected the fiscal deficit, which declined from more than 10 percent of GDP in 1974 to 2.6 percent in 1975 and to less than 1 percent in 1978. In the years that followed, and for the first time in more than two decades, Chile experienced a fiscal surplus. This situation changed only in 1983, when, in the midst of the recessive crisis, the reduction of tax collection generated a deficit.

In 1985, as a way to stimulate the economy after the debt crisis, Chile's public finance fundamentally changed direction. First, fiscal policy focused on redirecting public expenditures away from current expenditures and toward public investment. As a result, public investment increased more than 7 percentage points of GDP between 1985 and 1989. Additionally, a fiscal reform was enacted to encourage private savings via lower income tax rates. One of the most important components of this reform was the reduction of the tax rate on corporate earnings from 46 to 10 percent. At this point, with aggregate expenditures under control, this type of tax cut could be implemented without threatening the overall macroeconomic stability of the country. As a consequence of these policies, between 1985 and 1988 investment grew at a rate of 11 percent a year. In 1989, when fiscal finances were clearly under control—the nonfinancial public deficit had a small surplus—the rate of the value added tax was reduced from 20 to 16 percent as a way to encourage consumption.

The newly elected government of President Patricio Aylwin implemented a third fiscal reform in 1990 that sought to increase revenue to finance social programs and public investment. Economists associated with Aylwin's Concertación coalition calculated in 1989 that in order to implement significant social programs aimed at alleviating poverty, annual funds on the order of 4 percent of GDP were required (Tironi 1989). They argued that these resources could be obtained through a combination of the reallocation of expenditures, foreign aid, and increased tax revenues. To implement these programs rapidly, in April 1990 the executive submitted to the newly elected Congress a legislative project aimed at reforming the tax system. This package had three main features: (a) the corporate income tax was temporarily increased from 10 to 15 percent for 1991–93 and the base of the tax, which in 1985 had been defined as distributed profits, was broadened to total profits; (b) the progressivity of the personal income tax was increased by reducing the income level at which the maximum rate was applicable; and (c) the rate of the value added tax was increased to 18 percent from 16 percent (in the first half of 1993, the Chilean Congress maintained the 15 percent tax rate on corporate earnings).

To provide credibility to the fiscal adjustment and to reduce the public's speculation on whether these policies were only temporary, several institutional reforms were implemented. The most important was the creation, in December 1989, of an independent central bank whose board members were not directly subject to the vagaries of partisan politics. Initially the opposition to the military government strongly rejected this reform on the grounds that it was antidemocratic, arguing that taking monetary policy away from the control of a legitimately elected government greatly reduced the extent of democracy. By late 1989, however, the incoming administration realized that "tying its hands" could, after all, be convenient once it took over the government. This sentiment was strongly confirmed during the first two years of the Aylwin administration, as the performance of the central bank added significant stability and credibility to the government's economic program.

A second institutional reform that increased the credibility of fiscal policy announcements was enacted in late 1989, when legislation greatly restricted the public sector's involvement in production. This legislation severely limited the government's ability to engage in new joint ventures with the private sector and prohibited publicly owned firms from obtaining loans from the central bank. Finally, it may be argued that, in a way, the privatization of nearly 600 state-owned enterprises added credibility to the government's intentions of maintaining a balanced public sector (see chapter 6 for a detailed discussion of the Chilean privatization program).

Mexico. The Mexican tax reform was initiated in 1985, replacing an inefficient system fraught with corruption by a modern one based on a value added tax and an efficient income tax. Most domestic tax havens, subsidies, and exemptions were eliminated. In particular, the traditionally favorable treatment provided to, among others, truck owners, publishing houses, forestry, fishing, and livestock raising was abolished. Additionally, tax administration was greatly improved, reducing corruption and evasion.

Fiscal balance was achieved in 1986, and many tax rates were lowered as a way to provide additional incentives to the private sector. The corporate income tax was adjusted for inflation, and its rate was reduced from 42 percent in 1986 to 35 percent in 1991. Taxes on dividends were eliminated, and the maximum rate for the individual's income tax was lowered from 55 to 35 percent in 1991. All tax incentives for corporations were eliminated and replaced by an investment credit for firms that invest in areas other than Mexico City,

Monterrey, and Guadalajara. This credit is equal to the present value—computed using a 5 percent real discount rate—of depreciation expenditures.

As a way to curb tax evasion by corporations, Mexico devised an ingenious tax on assets at a 2 percent annual rate. This tax can be fully credited when the firm pays its corporate income tax. If in a particular year (or years) the firm incurs losses, it can carry forward the asset tax, fully indexed by inflation. This type of tax steadily gained in popularity throughout Latin America, and by late 1993 it had been adopted (in one form or another) by Argentina and Colombia.

To improve tax collection and reduce evasion, several significant administrative reforms were implemented. The administration of the value added tax was transferred from the states to the federal government, and a national data base of payers of the value added tax was constructed, greatly improving the audit and control process. For the first time, medium-size firms—those with annual sales of US$1.3 million or with more than 200 workers—were required to provide annual audits performed by a certified public accountant. The actual process of paying taxes was also simplified, since all commercial banks were allowed to receive tax payments from any firm or individual.

The Mexican fiscal reform was largely a success. In less than five years, a very large fiscal deficit was eliminated, and a modern tax system was put in place. Moreover, this success allowed authorities to devote a larger proportion of the budget to social programs through the Solidarity Program and other channels (see chapter 8). Also, the success of the fiscal adjustment allowed the government to reduce tax rates gradually, providing greater incentives for private sector investment. In June 1993, as a way to reinforce a degree of credibility and sustainability of its fiscal and macroeconomic reforms through time, Mexico announced that its central bank would be granted independence, as had been done in Chile and Argentina.

In spite of the tremendous fiscal effort, including the complete elimination of the public sector deficit, Mexico's inflation continued to be somewhat high: 12.9 percent in 1992. This persistent inflation was the result of two related factors. First, even though a preannounced rate of devaluation was used to anchor prices, some degree of inertia remained in the economy, reinforcing inflationary forces. Second, beginning in 1991 large capital flows into Mexico were monetized, putting pressure on domestic prices. These inflows increased the degree of real appreciation and created a policy dilemma in which the authorities had to decide whether to use the nominal exchange rate as an anchor to prices or whether to use periodic adjustments to avoid losses in competitiveness of the real exchange rate.

Argentina. When President Carlos Menem took over the government in mid-1989, Argentina was facing the worst economic crisis in its history. Inflation had reached 200 percent a month, output was plummeting, the foreign debt had not been served for more than a year, and the nation's morale was at an all-time low. Fiscal irresponsibility was at the center of all of this. Tax collection reached its lowest historical point in mid-1989, the prices of public services were ridiculously low, and expenditures were completely out of hand. The consolidated public sector deficit surpassed 21 percent of GDP.

From early on, the Menem administration understood that solving the country's problems required major action on the fiscal side (in spite of acknowledging the decisive role of fiscal imbalances, the two early Menem stabilization attempts—Roig/Rapanelli and González—only made limited progress in this area). Deep reforms aimed at increasing public sector revenues and reducing expenditures were needed. A succession of failed programs and unkept promises in the previous decade made the situation particularly difficult. Reducing the deficit clearly was not enough; credibility also had to be generated. This effort required fundamental institutional reforms that would allow the government to commit itself in a credible way.

Increasing tax revenues was clearly a priority in the new administration's program. During the second quarter of 1989, tax revenues were only 9.5 percent of GDP. Additionally, the tax structure was highly distorted. On the one hand, it relied heavily on export taxes and a number of inefficient tax surcharges; on the other, innumerable exemptions greatly reduced the effectiveness of the system. To make matters worse, tax administration had deteriorated steadily since the mid-1980s. The central tax office—Dirección General Impositiva—lacked resources and was plagued by corruption.

The Menem tax reform had several components. First, a broad and uniform value added tax was implemented that initially covered all goods and was extended to all services in November 1990. Second, a tax on fixed assets—similar to the Mexican tax discussed above—was put into place in 1990. Third, a tax on all bank checks was introduced in early 1991 (see Newfarmer 1992 for a detailed analysis of the Argentine public sector adjustment under the Cavallo plan). And fourth, taxes on exports were gradually eliminated. In addition to these measures for improving the efficiency of the system and increasing revenues, tax administration was strengthened. Computers were adopted, a list of all major taxpayers was compiled, the revenue directorate fired corrupt inspectors, wages paid to remaining inspectors were drastically raised, random inspections of the value added tax were greatly increased, and tax evaders were subject to stiff penalties, including the closure of their businesses.

To balance the public sector books, the Menem administration also took major action on expenditures. First, central government employment was reduced by approximately 100,000 people in 1991–92. This resulted in a simultaneous 10 percent reduction in the wage bill and an increase in the average wage of those still on the government's payroll (see Psacharopoulos 1992). Second, the federal government transferred almost 200,000 primary and secondary schoolteachers to provincial budgets. This was done on the basis of the Law of Coparticipation, which limited the federal government's contribution to the provinces to 58 percent of revenues. Third, in early 1991, the government passed a decree that strictly linked public expenditures to revenues, imposing a de facto balanced budget provision. Fourth, public sector prices were raised drastically to cover costs. And fifth, starting in 1990, the government engaged in an aggressive privatization program that not only generated direct revenue from sales but also eliminated the need to subsidize money-losing operations.

To make the stabilization program credible and accelerate the convergence of the domestic rate of inflation to world levels, the Argentine government introduced a set of important institutional reforms in March 1991. These were contained in the Convertibility Law, which fixed the exchange rate between the Argentine austral and the U.S. dollar and completely abolished all exchange and capital controls.[8] Additionally, this law established that the quantity of money could only be expanded if fully backed by international reserves.[9] This provision practically eliminated the possibility that the central bank would fund public enterprises, the federal government, or the provinces. Additionally, after international trade was opened in 1989–90, the fixed exchange rate was expected to discipline local prices. The current parity cannot be altered unless Congress passes a new law that would add credibility to the government's promises that the fixed exchange rate would be maintained and that inflation would subside.

Although the overall program rapidly reduced inflation, it also created a significant misalignment of relative prices (Dornbusch 1992). Prices of domestic (nontradable) goods became extremely high, putting a dent in the country's degree of competitiveness. However, the team led by Minister Domingo Cavallo showed great resolve in defending the parity and sticking to the original policy. A speculative attack against the peso in late 1992 was fended off successfully through restrictive credit policy and higher interest rates. Whether this policy will eventually be fully successful depends on whether the fiscal adjustment can be furthered in the short run and on whether significant gains in productivity can be attained in the domestic goods sector.

Exchange Rates, Inflation, and Disinflation

As many Latin American countries have painfully learned, in the long run, a fixed nominal exchange rate cannot be maintained under conditions of major fiscal imbalances financed by the creation of domestic credit. If domestic inflationary pressures exceed the international rate of inflation, international reserves decline, overvaluation takes over, and a speculative attack on the central bank's foreign exchange holdings eventually takes place (there is now an extensive literature on speculative attacks under fixed exchange rates; the pioneering piece is Krugman 1979; see also Edwards 1989d for case studies on the subject). Some countries that historically suffered from chronically high inflation dealt with this situation by adopting an adjustable, or crawling peg, system characterized by periodic adjustments of the nominal exchange rate according to inflation rate differentials. The motivation behind this type of system, first adopted by Brazil, Colombia, and Chile during the 1960s, is the recognition that, given an expansive fiscal stance, a competitive real exchange rate cannot be maintained with a system of fixed nominal exchange rates.

The historical experience of these countries contrasts sharply with that of another group of Latin American nations, mostly in Central America, which for many years had fixed exchange rates and low inflation rates. In the late 1970s, almost a decade after the collapse of the Bretton Woods system, many Latin American countries still had a system of fixed exchange rates (according to IMF, *International Financial Statistics*, in 1979 thirteen Latin American countries had a fixed exchange rate with respect to the U.S. dollar). This situation, however, changed after the debt crisis. Under heavy internal and external pressure, almost every country in the region had to adopt some kind of managed exchange rate regime during the mid-1980s (see table 4-11).

Initially, the adoption of more flexible exchange rate systems in Latin America was greeted with great enthusiasm by policymakers and experts alike (see Williamson 1981 for a forceful defense of the crawling peg exchange rate regime). It was argued that flexible systems, in particular crawling peg regimes, provided an adequate way to isolate the real sector from the effects of external shocks and domestic inflation. In the early 1990s, however, some observers, including the staff of the IMF, began to argue that flexible exchange rates allowed the Latin American countries to accommodate inflation and

Table 4-11. Countries in Latin America with Fixed Exchange Rates, 1979–91

1979	1982	1985	1990	1991
Bolivia	Dominican	Guatemala	Dominican	Argentina
Chile	Republic	Haiti	Republic	Nicaragua
Costa Rica	Ecuador	Honduras	Haiti	Panama
Dominican	El Salvador	Nicaragua	Panama	
Republic	Guatemala	Panama		
Ecuador	Haiti	Paraguay		
El Salvador	Honduras	Peru		
Guatemala	Mexico	Venezuela		
Haiti	Nicaragua			
Honduras	Panama			
Nicaragua	Paraguay			
Panama	Venezuela			
Paraguay				
Venezuela				

Source: IMF, *Annual Report on Exchange Rate Arrangements and Exchange Rate Restrictions,* several years.

institutionalize indexation, discouraging them from implementing serious anti-inflationary programs. According to this view, exchange rate policy in Latin America should return to greater rigidity—and even complete fixity—as a way to introduce financial discipline and credibility, eliminate inertia, and provide an anchor for prices.[10]

The proposition that fixed exchange rates should become an integral component of the region's efforts to achieve macroeconomic stability generated many questions among policymakers and their advisers. How is this system supposed to work? How has it performed in history? What are the tradeoffs between fixed rates and a more flexible system? Do preannounced declining pegs, of the *tablita* type, operate in a similar way? If a fixed exchange rate is adopted, how should the transition be engineered? How does this system affect the behavior and competitiveness of the real exchange rate? The crisis of the Mexican peso in December 1994 added considerable urgency to this debate. Some of these issues are addressed in the rest of this section.

Exchange Rates as Anchors: Analytical Aspects

Much of the recent enthusiasm for fixed nominal exchange rates is intellectually rooted in the modern literature on credibility and time consistency. According to this approach, which was pioneered by Calvo (1978) and Kydland and Prescott (1977), governments that have the discretion to alter the nominal exchange rate tend to abuse their power, introducing an inflationary bias into the economy. The reason for this is that under a set of plausible conditions, such as the existence of labor market rigidities that preclude the economy from reaching full employment, it is optimal for the government to surprise the private sector through unexpected devaluations. By engineering these unexpected devaluations, the government hopes to induce a reduction in real wages and, thus, an increase in employment and a boost in output. Naturally, in equilibrium the public is aware of this incentive and reacts by anticipating the devaluation surprises, rendering them ineffective. As a consequence of this strategic interaction between the government and the private sector, the economy reaches a plateau of high inflation.

A key policy implication of this literature is that, along the lines of the fiscal adjustment discussion presented in the preceding section, defining (and implementing) constraints that make government commitments credible improves society's welfare. This is where fixed exchange rates enter the picture. It is argued that the adoption of a fixed exchange rate constrains government's ability to surprise the private sector through unexpected devaluations. Promises of fiscal discipline become credible, and private sector actions do not elicit successive rounds of inflationary actions (see Edwards 1993a; Persson and Tabellini 1990). In particular, fixed exchange rates provide a reputational constraint on government behavior. The authorities know that if they undertake overly expansive credit policy, they will be forced to abandon the parity and devalue. As the 1993 experience with the exchange rate mechanism of the European Monetary System shows, exchange rate crises can indeed shatter the reputation of politicians.

In spite of its elegant appeal, this view has, in its simplest incarnation, some problems. First, in these simple settings, exchange rate policy has a very limited role. In fact, in most of these models, its only effect is to alter the domestic rate of inflation and, through it, to alter real wages. However, in most modern exchange rate models, nominal devaluations can also help to accommodate shocks to real exchange rate fundamentals—including shocks to the terms of trade—and to avoid misalignment of the real exchange rate (see Dornbusch 1991a; Edwards 1989d). Second, in economies with stochastic shocks, contingent exchange rate rules can, at least in principle, be superior to fixed rates (Flood and Isard 1989). Third, it is not clear why a country that can credibly commit itself to fixing the exchange rate unilaterally cannot commit itself to maintaining a fixed stock of domestic money or to maintain a predetermined rate of growth of domestic credit.

Devarajan and Rodrik (1992) and Kamin (1991), among others, examine the desirability of fixed exchange rates from a more general perspective. For example, in Devarajan and Rodrik (1992), policymakers face a tradeoff regarding exchange rate policy: while exchange rate flexibility has an inflationary bias, it also allows the country to reduce output variability. This is accomplished by smoothing, via exchange rate adjustments, the consequences of terms of trade shocks on output. In this model, it is not possible to rank a priori fixed and flexible (or active) exchange rate regimes. For large terms of trade shocks, flexible exchange rates are likely to be superior. Likewise, the more vulnerable the real economy is to these terms of trade shocks, the more desirable are flexible arrangements. In contrast, the greater the government's built-in inflationary bias, the greater is its temptation to abuse devaluations, and the less desirable is a flexible arrangement.

John Williamson (1991) deals with the issue of exchange rate regimes in developing nations. He argues that a fixed exchange rate is advisable as long as four conditions are met: (1) the country in question is small relative to the rest of the world, (2) the bulk of its international trade is undertaken with the country (or countries) with respect to which it plans to peg its currency, (3) the country wishes to have a rate of inflation similar to that of the country to which it is pegging its currency, and (4) institutional arrangements ensure that the commitment to a fixed rate is credible. Once these four conditions are met, the only remaining argument in favor of flexible exchange rates refers to terms of trade shocks. Although Williamson's list of requirements for a successful fixed exchange rate is eminently plausible, it leaves a number of unanswered questions. In particular, his analysis is silent on whether the adoption of a fixed exchange rate provides, in and of itself, an institutional constraint on fiscal policy. More specifically, it does not address the issue of whether the existence of a fixed exchange rate imposes reputational or other types of constraints on politicians (see Corden 1991a).

Nominal Exchange Rate Anchors and Latin America

The evaluation of fixed exchange rates as nominal anchors in real world situations should concentrate on two features of this system. First, to what extent do these regimes constrain the behavior of governments in the long run? And, second, how do these regimes work during the transition from high to low inflation? More specifically, does the adoption of a fixed exchange rate indeed accelerate the convergence of the domestic rate of inflation to world levels?

These issues have been addressed for the case of the Latin American nations (see, for example, Edwards 1993a, 1993b; Kiguel and Liviatan 1992). A recent study of the long-run experiences of four Latin American nations—the Dominican Republic, El Salvador, Guatemala, and Honduras—with fixed exchange rates suggests that the existence of a very long tradition of exchange rate stability provided some constraints on the behavior of the central bank.[11] Between 1950 and 1973, these central banks were careful not to violate the constraints imposed by the existence of a fixed parity. However, the historical evidence also indicates that these constraints are not fully operational under severe pressure stemming from (very) large terms of trade shocks. For example, in these four countries, the limits imposed by fixed rates on the creation of domestic credit became nonbinding during the late 1970s and 1980s and could not survive the combination of populist political pressures and severely negative terms of trade shocks. As a result of overly expansive policies, typical crisis situations evolved. However, the authorities artificially clung to the fixed rates for as long as they could. The empirical evidence clearly suggests that, by trying to avoid adjusting the exchange rate after the debt crisis and in light of the obvious imbalances, these nations were unable to engineer a rapid adjustment and incurred severe costs in the form of exchange rate overvaluation, controls, and trade distortions. Although not fully conclusive, these four historical episodes suggest that, in an international environment characterized by large shocks, exchange rate flexibility can greatly smooth the adjustment. Also, as is further argued in chapter 9 of this book, the Mexican experience of 1994 suggests strongly that fixed exchange rates are not particularly effective in situations in which the economy is subject to major political disturbances.

Regarding the performance of nominal exchange rate anchors in a stabilization package, recent evidence suggests that even if the fiscal deficit is under control, this type of policy is likely to generate some degree of real exchange rate appreciation during the transition; in some cases, this real appreciation can be substantial. (This was, for example, the case of Chile between 1978 and 1982; see Bruno 1991; Dornbusch 1992; Edwards 1993d; see also chapter 5 of this volume). Whether this will become a major policy problem and eventually force the abortion of the program depends on a number of factors, including the initial level of the real exchange rate, the existence of policies aimed at deindexing other contracts, the behavior of real exchange rate fundamentals, political developments, and the authorities' ability (and willingness) to undertake major fiscal and monetary adjustments when the economy faces negative sectoral shocks. As the world found out in late 1994, Mexico's inability to implement a substantial adjustment program after the assassination of presidential candidate Luis Colosio in March of that year generated significant tensions and a gigantic crisis.

To be effective, an exchange rate anchor should be adopted from a situation of undervaluation and be accompanied not only by consistent fiscal policies but also by strong and credible across-the-board deindexation policies. If, however, some contracts, and especially wages, continue to be indexed with respect to past inflation, the system will maintain a considerable degree of inertia, generating a sizable depreciation, as occurred in Chile during the late 1970s. If this type of situation is not managed carefully, the country can run into serious problems in which a speculative attack on the currency will provoke a major crisis and a return to macroeconomic instability. Appendix 4-2 addresses these issues in detail.

Although the merits of fixed exchange rates vary from country to country, it is possible to make some general statements. Both analytical work and historical evidence in Latin America and East Asia suggest that for economies facing a large external shock—either a terms of trade or financial shock—a more flexible exchange rate policy is preferred. This type of system allows them to accommodate foreign disturbances and to avoid situations of real exchange rate overvaluation. In fact, recent comparative studies persuasively show that maintaining competitive real exchange rates was at the heart of the splendid performance of East Asian economies during the last few decades. However, under flexible (or administered) exchange rates, there is always the danger that the authorities will exhibit a devaluationary and inflationary bias. This danger, however, can be greatly reduced by placing exchange rate policy within the purview of institutions removed from the contingent political cycle. This is the case in Chile, where exchange rate policy is undertaken by the independent central bank.[12] Moreover, to the extent that this type of institution is effectively developed, the adoption of more flexible exchange rate regimes appears to be more suitable for the vast majority of countries in the region in the years to come. Overall, the recent experiences of several countries—both industrial and developing—suggest that it is important to distinguish between the long run and transitional periods from high to lower inflation. Although during a stabilization program the adoption of a fixed rate as a way to guide expectations has merit, over the longer run a more flexible nominal exchange rate regime is likely to operate more effectively. Naturally, under either regime, fiscal policy has to provide the ultimate nominal anchor of the system.

Summary and Conclusions

In the mid-1980s, the sheer magnitude of debt payments represented a major obstacle for countries embarking on adjustment. Many countries were facing a debt-overhang situation in which policymakers did not perceive direct benefits from the market-oriented reforms. This situation was significantly altered in March 1989, when the Brady Plan, which called for voluntary debt-reduction agreements between banks and debtor countries, was implemented. The Brady Plan provided significant breathing room to a group of Latin American nations, allowing them to improve their performance substantially through lower fiscal imbalances, higher investment, and implementation of major reforms.

The data analysis presented in this chapter clearly shows that most countries in the region made substantial progress in attaining macroeconomic equilibrium. Public sector deficits were reduced, domestic credit expansion was curtailed, expenditures were cut significantly, and the tax system was reformed in many countries. Also, in an effort to reduce the public sector deficit—and simultaneously improve efficiency—several countries embarked on major privatization processes. In spite of this progress, several problems are yet to be resolved. First, in Brazil, the largest country in the region, fiscal disequilibrium continues to be somewhat elusive. Second, in many countries public finances were brought under control through major cuts in capital expenditures, which reduced public investment in infrastructure and somewhat jeopardized the prospects for future growth. Third, in some countries, the reduction in expenditures affected social programs, including health, nutrition, and education (see chapter 8).

The relationship among nominal exchange rate policy, inflation, and disinflation suggests that designing an appropriate exchange rate policy during the transition to disinflation is particularly difficult because, under most circumstances, a tradeoff exists between using the exchange rate as a nominal anchor to guide inflation downward and using it to maintain a competitive real exchange rate position in the country. However, under some circumstances—and if accompanied by adequate policies—a fixed (or predetermined) exchange rate may be useful for reducing inflation during the early phases of the stabilization program. Care should be taken, however, to avoid situations of real exchange rate overvaluation that could eventually lead to major disequilibria, speculation attacks, and balance of payments crises. The historical evidence of Latin American countries, as well as that of East Asian economies, suggests that, in environments where there are significant terms of trade shocks, a flexible exchange rate policy is superior to a completely rigid approach.

An important question is whether the progress recently attained by most countries on the macroeconomic front will be maintained and allow them to move toward long-run macroeconomic stability. From a long-run perspective, a key requirement for sustained macroeconomic balance is to isolate fiscal policy from the extremes of the political budget cycle, where governments in office generate inflation in the periods preceding elections in the hope that this will generate a boom and improve their political fortunes.

The history of Latin America is replete with incidents where fiscal balance was lost and inflation took over due to political pressures. Some countries recently tried to deal with these issues by implementing reforms that reduce the extent to which the central bank is influenced by short-term politics. Argentina, Chile, Colombia, Mexico, and Venezuela took steps in this direction by making central banks independent of the executive. Autonomous central banks, charged with achieving monetary stability, can certainly help to reduce macroeconomic imbalances (see de Gregorio 1994). It is important, however, to recognize that independent central banks are in no way substitutes for prudent and consistent fiscal policies. In fact, the history of central banking in Latin America during the 1930s suggests that, when faced with significant fiscal tension and major external shocks, even independent central banks may end up promoting inflation (Ortiz-Batalla 1993). In the final analysis, fiscal discipline is the only effective anchor.

Appendix 4-1: Debt and Debt Service Reduction Agreements

Since the inception of the Brady Plan in March 1989, six Latin American countries have obtained a debt-reduction agreement: Argentina, Brazil, Costa Rica, Mexico, Uruguay, and Venezuela. Debt restructuring packages within the Brady Plan were attractive to commercial lenders because they offered an ample menu of instruments from which creditors could choose according to the particular needs of their balance sheet.

The Enterprise for the Americas Initiative, launched by President George Bush in June 1990, included a concessional debt-reduction component from which Argentina, Bolivia, Chile, El Salvador, Jamaica, and Uruguay have benefited so far. Debt was reduced about 40 percent for severely indebted middle-income countries and up to 80 percent for low-income nations.

What follows is a brief description of the main debt-reduction arrangements currently under way in Latin America.

- *Face value of eligible debt.* This is the nominal value of the total debt covered by the agreement, including principal—both current and overdue—plus interest arrears (when they are included in the debt-reduction operation, such as in Argentina and Costa Rica).
- *Debt-equity swap.* Foreign currency debt is converted into local currency equity in a domestic firm. The investor may be the bank holding the loan or a company that buys the loan from a bank at a discount. The loan is then usually sold at near face value to the central bank of the host

country for local currency instruments, which are used to make the equity investment.

- *Debt–quasi-equity swap.* In this case, a multinational firm buys on-lendable loans in the borrower country and extends those loans to its subsidiary, thus funding the subsidiary at a preferential exchange rate.

- *Debt-for-development swap.* In a typical swap like this, an international agency buys debt in the secondary market at a substantial discount and exchanges that debt at a discount with the debtor country. In some cases, commercial banks donate debt. In return, the debtor issues a domestic bond and uses the domestic currency that is generated to finance development projects. In the case of debt-for-nature swaps, the financial instrument is called an environmental bond, and the proceeds from the conversion are used to finance parkland and tropical forest projects.

- *Buyback.* The original debt is canceled by a cash payment at a fraction of the original value (for example, 16 cents per dollar in Costa Rica).

- *Discounted bonds.* The creditor receives a long-term bond with a market interest rate but a lower face value. For instance, the new face value in the Mexican agreement was 65 percent. Discount Brady bonds typically have a thirty-year maturity. The value of their principal is guaranteed by a U.S. zero-coupon bond (that is, a bond that does not pay any interest before maturity). They have a rolling guarantee of one to two years of interest payments, implemented by setting up a special trust account as collateral with an amount equal to the value guaranteed. The face value and maturity of the collateral instruments are designed to match those of the debt being defeased.

- *Par bonds.* The creditor receives a bond with an identical face value but a lower interest rate. Collateral on the principal and interest—usually fixed—are equivalent to those of discounted bonds.

- *Additional loans.* In addition to exchanging the debt by using cash or bonds or both, the debt can be rescheduled to provide new funds under specified amounts and terms.

Appendix 4-2: Inflationary Inertia and Nominal Exchange Rate Anchors

This appendix examines the mechanics of exchange rate indexation and inflationary inertia and analyzes the circumstances under which the adoption of nominal exchange rate anchors are expected to be successful in a stabilization program. Issues related to credibility and a broad deindexation program that goes beyond the exchange rate are emphasized. The analytical discussion is supplemented with an empirical analysis of two recent historical experiences with nominal exchange rate policy and inflation in Chile and Mexico.

Indexation, Inertia, and Anchors

Consider the case of an economy that produces two types of goods: tradables and nontradables. Prices of tradables are assumed to be linked to international prices, while nontradables' prices are determined by the condition that this market clears at all times. To focus on inflationary issues, I abstract from problems related to changes in real exchange rate fundamentals, such as terms of trade, the degree of protection, and capital flows (the discussion that follows draws partially on Edwards 1989b, which further elaborates on these issues). I assume that initially the country follows a crawling peg exchange rate system in which the exchange rate rule consists of adjusting the nominal exchange rate by a proportion ϕ ($\phi \leq 1$) of lagged inflation differentials. I also assume that wages are adjusted according to a rule that includes lagged inflation as well as expected future inflation. Monetary policy is assumed to be passive and to accommodate inertial inflationary forces. This stylized economy, which captures some of the most salient aspects of many Latin American countries in the 1980s, can be depicted by the simple set of equations:

$$(4\text{-}1) \qquad \pi_t = \alpha\pi_{Tt} + (1-\alpha)\,\pi_{Nt}$$

$$(4\text{-}2) \qquad \pi_{Tt} = E_{t-1}(d_t + \pi_{Tt}^*)$$

$$(4\text{-}3) \qquad d_t = \phi\,(\pi_{t-1} - \pi_{T-1}^*)$$

$$(4\text{-}4) \qquad N^D\,(P_N/P_T Z_t) = N^S\,(W/P_N)$$

$$(4\text{-}5) \qquad w_t = \sum_{k=1}^{K} \gamma_k \pi_{t-k} + \sigma\pi_t^e$$

where the following notation is used:

π_t　= rate of change of the domestic price level

π_{Tt}　= rate of change of the price of tradables in domestic currency in period t

π_{Nt}　= rate of change of nontradables' prices in period t

d_t　= rate of devaluation in period t

π_{Tt}^*　= rate of world inflation in period t

E_{t-1}　= expectations operator, where expectations are assumed to be formed in period $t-1$

w_t　= rate of change in nominal wages in period t

Z_t = index of aggregate macroeconomic policies, which includes monetary expansion beyond passive accommodation of past inflation

N^D = demand for nontradables

N^S = supply for nontradables

π_t^e = expected inflation in period t

ϕ, γ_k = parameters that measure the degree of indexation in this economy

σ = parameter that determines the importance of expected inflation in the wage rule.

Equation 4-1 says that the domestic rate of inflation is a weighted average of inflation of tradables and nontradables. Equation 4-2 states that the law of one price holds ex ante and that the change in the domestic price of tradables is equal to the expected change in the exchange rate plus the expected rate of world inflation.[13]

Equation 4-3 is the devaluation rule and states that the exchange rate is adjusted in a proportion ϕ of inflation rate differentials. If $\phi = 1$, we have a typical purchasing-power-parity rule, where the rate of devaluation is equal to (lagged) inflation rate differentials. This type of policy is sometimes referred to as a real target approach.[14] Equation 4-4 is the market-clearing condition for nontradables. The demand for nontradables is assumed to depend on relative prices (P_N / P_T) and on aggregate demand (Z_t); the supply of nontradables is assumed to be a function of real product wages. Finally, equation 4-5, the wage adjustment rule, states that wage increases depend on two factors: lagged inflation up to K periods and expected future inflation. It is further assumed that $(\Sigma\gamma_k + \sigma) \leq 1$. The special case when $\sigma = 0$ and $\Sigma\gamma_k = 1$ corresponds to a situation where there is 100 percent backward-looking wage indexation. The value of K determines the degree of inflationary memory of this economy. Although w stands for the rate of change of nominal wages, it is perhaps more useful to think of this variable as capturing a broader category of other costs. In that sense, the coefficients γ_k can be interpreted as summarizing the degree of indexation of nonexchange rate contracts in the economy.[15]

This model can be solved in order to find an expression for the dynamics of inflation. To simplify the discussion, consider the case when wages are adjusted according to inflation in the last period only ($K = 1$). Further, assume that the wage adjustment rule is a strict weighted average of past inflation and expected inflation. That is, in equation 4-5, $\sigma = 1 - \gamma$. Before solving the model, it is necessary to make an assumption regarding inflationary expectations. I consider the case of rational expectations in which actual realizations of inflation in period t differ from the expectations formed at the beginning of that period by a random term μ: $\pi_t = \pi_t^e + \mu_t$.

After equations 4-1 through 4-5 have been manipulated, the dynamics of domestic inflation can be written as the following first-order difference equation:[16]

$$(4\text{-}6) \qquad \pi_t = a_1 \pi_{t-1} + a_2 \pi_{t-1}^* + a_3 \hat{z}_t + \mu'$$

where

$$(4\text{-}7) \qquad a_1 = \frac{(\eta + \alpha\varepsilon)\,\phi + \varepsilon\,(1-\alpha)\,\gamma}{(\eta + \varepsilon\alpha) + \varepsilon\,(1-\alpha)\,\gamma}$$

$$(4\text{-}8) \qquad a_2 = \frac{(\eta + \alpha\varepsilon)\,(1-\phi)}{(\eta + \varepsilon\alpha) + \varepsilon\,(1-\alpha)\,\gamma}$$

$$(4\text{-}9) \qquad a_3 = \frac{-\delta\,(1-\alpha)}{(\eta + \alpha\varepsilon) + \varepsilon\,(1-\alpha)\,\gamma}$$

and where η is the demand elasticity of nontradables with respect to relative prices ($\eta < 0$), ε is the supply elasticity of nontradables with respect to the real product wage ($\varepsilon < 0$), δ is the demand elasticity of nontradables with respect to aggregate demand pressures, and μ' is an error term related to μ.

In equation 4-6, coefficient a_1 provides a measure of the degree of inertia of domestic inflation. The closer a_1 is to unity, the more persistent inflation is and the higher the degree of inertia. The degree of inertia in the economy depends on the different elasticities involved *and* on the indexation parameters ϕ and γ.[17] Under full lagged indexation of the exchange rate—that is, ϕ is equal to one—the coefficient of π_{t-1} becomes unity $a_1 = 1$, and the system has no anchor. The time series of domestic inflation exhibits a unit root, and inflation could explode as a result of exogenous or aggregate demand shocks. Also, according to this equation, a reduction in the rate of exchange rate indexation ϕ results in a decline in the value of a_1 and, thus, in a reduction in the degree of inflationary inertia in the economy. This, of course, was the rationale for adopting nominal exchange rate anchors in a number of countries.

According to equation 4-6, if indexation is totally eliminated, and both ϕ *and* γ become simultaneously equal to zero, domestic inflation immediately converges to world inflation.[18] This situation corresponds to a Poincare-type stabilization program (see Sargent 1983). If, after the nominal exchange rate is fixed ($\phi = 0$), some degree of wage indexation remains ($\gamma > 0$), some inertia remains, and the real exchange rate is subject to consistent appreciation during the transition process. In a sense, then, the authorities face a tradeoff where the exchange rate anchor, on the one hand, reduces inertia and, on the other hand, generates a loss of international competitiveness.

An important assumption in the nominal exchange rate anchors approach to disinflation is that the adoption of a fixed nominal exchange rate is a credible policy and that the public believes that, from the date when the new policy is announced, the coefficient φ will remain lower (see Agenor and Taylor 1992 for a survey of alternative ways to test empirically for credibility effects). In fact, one of the most commonly used arguments for favoring nominal exchange rate anchors over monetary anchors has to do with credibility: since nominal exchange rates are more visible, they provide a more credible policy than the announcement of a constant level of monetary base (see Bruno 1991 for related discussions). It follows from equation 4-6 that if the policy of nominal exchange rate anchors is credible, a structural break would be observed empirically in the dynamic properties of inflation. This structural break would indeed take place at, or around, the moment the nominal anchor is implemented. From that point onward, the coefficient of lagged inflation in an equation of the type of equation 4-6 should decline, reflecting the reduction in the degree of persistence of the inflationary process. Of course, this assumes that economic authorities have controlled the structural roots of inflation: fiscal imbalance and monetary creation. If, however, the nominal anchor policy lacks credibility and the public doubts the extent to which the government will stick to the new policy, the estimated degree of inertia in equations similar to equation 4-6 will not be significantly affected by the adoption of the nominal exchange rate anchor (Edwards and Sturzenegger 1992 provide a model with endogenous credibility of the nominal exchange rate anchor). Empirically, there are several ways to investigate whether the adoption of exchange rate–based stabilization programs have changed inertia. Two approaches used above are (1) the use of interactive dummy variables to test for structural breaks in coefficient a_1 in equation 4-6 at the time (or around the time) of the policy change and (2) the use of varying coefficient techniques to estimate equation 4-6 (see Agenor and Taylor 1992).

Exchange Rates and Inflationary Inertia in Chile and Mexico

Data on Chile and Mexico are used here to investigate the relationship between exchange rate policy and inflationary inertia. These two countries provide interesting lessons because they both used the nominal exchange rate as an anchor in their disinflation programs of the 1970s and 1980s.

Chile. In the late 1970s, and after eliminating a stubborn fiscal deficit, Chile adopted a stabilization program based on the exchange rate. From February 1978 to June 1979, the program consisted of a preannounced declining rate of devaluation of the domestic currency. In June 1979, with inflation standing at an annual rate of 34 percent, the government fixed the nominal exchange rate at 39 pesos to the dollar. When the tablita was adopted in early 1978, and again when the peso was pegged to the dollar in June 1979, it was decided not to alter the wage indexation mechanism, which at that time was characterized by 100 percent adjustment to lagged price increases.

To investigate empirically the way in which the adoption of a nominal exchange rate anchor affected the degree of inflationary inertia in Chile, equations of the following type were estimated using quarterly data:

$$(4\text{-}10) \qquad \pi_t = b_0 + b_1 \pi_{t-1} + b_2 (D\pi_{t-1}) + b_3 \pi^*_{t-1} + b_4 \hat{z}_{t-1} + \mu_t$$

where the variable D is a dummy that takes the value of 1 for the period when the nominal exchange anchor is in place and 0 otherwise. If the anchors program is effective and credible, the estimated coefficient of b_2 should be significantly *negative*, indicating that this policy successfully reduced the degree of inertia in the system. Moreover, in the extreme case of a Poincare-style disinflation, inertia should disappear when the new policy is put in place, and $b_1 + b_2$ should not be significantly different from 0.

In the case of Chile, two dummies were used: the first one (DC1) has a value of 1 between the second quarter of 1978, when the declining rate of devaluation was first announced, and the first quarter of 1982, the last quarter when the nominal anchors approach was in effect. The second dummy (DC2) takes a value of 1 between the third quarter of 1979 and the first quarter of 1982; that is, DC2 covers the period when the nominal exchange rate was strictly fixed.

In the estimation of equation 4-10, π^* was defined as the quarterly rate of U.S. inflation and $\hat{z}_{t-1}$ as the rate of growth of domestic credit. The raw data were taken from the IMF's *International Financial Statistics* tape. Table 4-12 contains the results obtained using ordinary least squares. The results are quite interesting. In both cases, the interactive dummies are *not* significant and, in addition, have a positive sign. This indicates that the implementation of an exchange rate rule in 1978–79 did not alter the degree of inflationary inertia in Chile. These results could be the consequence of a combination of factors, including the fact that the nominal anchor was not credible and that wage rate indexation was left intact during this period.[19] These results suggest that the adoption of a predetermined exchange rate in Chile in 1978–79 was not associated with a change in the nature of the inflationary process that one expects from a credible policy of nominal exchange rate anchors. In particular, expectations, backward adjustment of the wage rate, and other contract practices (such as indexation) do not seem to have been affected in a significant way by the reform of the exchange rate system. As a consequence, the degree of inflationary inertia remained unchanged after the program was adopted in the late 1990s.

Mexico. In 1986–87, the Mexican government embarked on an ambitious stabilization and reform program aimed at regaining price stability, deregulating the economy, and opening foreign trade to international competition. During 1988, the exchange rate was fixed relative to the U.S. dollar, and from

Table 4-12. Exchange Rates, Indexation, and Inflationary Inertia in Chile: Results of Equation 4-10 Using Ordinary Least Squares

Variable	Nominal anchors approach	Fixed nominal exchange rate
Time period	Jan. 1974–Jan. 1982	Jan. 1974–Jan. 1982
Constant	−0.041	−0.049
	(−1.344)	(−1.397)
π_{t-1}	0.750	0.756
	(12.993)	(10.317)
$DC1^*\pi_{t-1}$	0.019	n.a.
	(0.688)	
$DC2^*\pi_{t-1}$	n.a.	0.025
		(0.430)
π^*_{t-1}	0.236	0.477
	(1.415)	(1.378)
$\hat{z}_{t-1}$	0.288	0.285
	(4.812)	(4.737)
$\bar{R}^2$	0.970	0.969
DW	2.042	2.036

n.a. Not applicable.

Note: The first dummy, DC1, has a value of 1 between the second quarter of 1978, when the declining rate of devaluation was first announced, and the first quarter of 1982, the last quarter when the nominal anchors approach was in effect. The second dummy, DC2, takes a value of 1 between the third quarter of 1979 and the first quarter of 1982, when the nominal exchange rate was strictly fixed. *t*-statistics are in parentheses.

1989 onward the rate of devaluation of the peso was preannounced. As in the case of Chile, and in an effort to guide expectations downward, the rate of devaluation was deliberately set below the rate of ongoing inflation. In successive revisions of the program, the preannounced rate of adjustment of the nominal exchange rate was reduced. These successive reductions are equivalent to reductions in the value of coefficient ϕ in equation 4-3. In Mexico, incomes policies became a central element of the anti-inflationary package, supplementing the exchange rate rule and the fiscal adjustment. Indeed, in late 1987, with the establishment of the Pacto de Solidaridad, unions, entrepreneurs, and the government worked out a political and economic plan for defeating inflation. Price and wage guidelines were important elements of this program.[20]

In the estimation for Mexico, the dummy variable *DM* was defined with a value of 1 between the second quarter of 1988, when the Pacto de Solidaridad was enacted, and the second quarter of 1990. The rate of growth of narrowly defined money was used as a measure of aggregate demand pressures. In every equation estimated for Mexico, the coefficient of $(DM\,\pi_{t-1})$ was significantly *negative*, indicating that the adoption of the preannounced exchange rate system and the other policies in the Pacto were credible, significantly changing the dynamics of inflation. The following result was obtained for the first quarter of 1979 through the second quarter of 1990:

$$(4\text{-}11) \qquad \pi_t = -0.060 + 0.896\pi_{t-1} - 0.194\,(DM\pi_{t-1}) + 0.698\pi^*_{t-1}$$
$$\quad (-3.546)(15.119) \qquad (-4.559) \qquad\qquad (1.726)$$

$$+\ 0.179\hat{z}_t + 0.220\hat{z}_{t-1} + 0.144\hat{z}_{t-2}$$
$$(2.789)\quad (2.476)\qquad (1.764)$$

$$\bar{R}^2 = 0.945$$
$$DW = 1.828$$

Period: first quarter 1979–second quarter 1990

Formal tests for the stability of the regression as a whole show that the dynamics of inflation in Mexico experienced a structural break in the first quarter of 1988, when the exchange-rate-based program and the Pacto de Solidaridad were enacted. The χ^2 (equation 4-4) statistic for structural stability turned out to be equal to 44.2, rejecting the null hypothesis that no structural break occurred in the first quarter of 1988.

The contrasting results between Chile and Mexico strongly suggest that adopting a nominal exchange rate anchor is not enough to counteract the inertia of the inflationary process. As the Chilean results show, it is possible to have such a system in place for a considerable period of time without making a serious dent in the dynamics of inflation. To the extent that the public does not perceive the new policy as credible, pricing behavior and contract clauses are not altered in any significant way, and the ingrained aspects of inertial inflation continue.[21] Although it is not possible to extract from these data the exact underlying macroeconomic reasons for the differences in effectiveness of these two programs, it is possible to speculate that the incomes policies implemented in Mexico alongside the pegged nominal exchange rate provided a broad sense of coherence to the stabilization program. In contrast, the continuation, and even reinforcement, of the lagged wage indexation rule gave contradictory signals to the private sector in Chile.

CHAPTER 5

The Opening of Latin America

AFTER DECADES OF PROTECTIONISM, MOST OF LATIN AMERICA BEGAN to open up to the rest of the world in the late 1980s. This process is perhaps the most impressive achievement of the reform programs, and it effectively ended more than four decades of import-substitution policies that encouraged what turned out to be a largely inefficient industrial sector.

The process leading to these trade reforms was not easy. In the mid-1980s, the protectionist view was still influential in many parts of Latin America. In fact, the debt crisis of 1982 provided a new impetus to the protectionist paradigm. Initially, many analysts interpreted the crisis as a failure of the world economic order and argued that the only way for Latin America to avoid a recurrence of this type of shock was to isolate itself further through selective protectionism and government intervention (Griffith-Jones and Sunkel 1986). This sentiment was compounded by the fact that a number of observers considered the liberalization reforms of the Southern Cone countries during the 1970s as a failure. This perspective is synthesized clearly by Lance Taylor (1991, pp. 119, 141), who argues that "trade liberalization strategy is intellectually moribund" and that there are "no great benefits (plus some costs) in following open trade and capital market strategies. . . . Development strategies oriented internally may be a wise choice towards the century's end."

Immediately following the eruption of the debt crisis, increased protectionism was indeed the path that Latin American countries chose. Even Chile, the strongest supporter of free trade, tripled its import tariffs. This sudden and drastic increase in the degree of protectionism was dictated largely by necessity. Faced with the need to generate an almost instantaneous reversal in the resource transfer of more than $30 billion, in the short run countries had very little alternative but to compress imports by some means or other. An increase in tariffs and quantitative restrictions was not surprising.

In the mid-1980s, Latin America's external sector was the most distorted in the world. Central America had the highest degree of import protection—in terms of both tariff and nontariff barriers—among developing countries, with

Table 5-1. Import Protection in the Developing World, 1985
(percentage)

Region	Total tariff protection[a]	Coverage of nontariff barriers[b]
Latin America and the Caribbean		
South America	51	60
Central America	66	100
Caribbean	17	23
Africa		
North	39	85
Other	36	86
Asia		
West	5	11
Other	25	21

a. Tariffs and paratariffs; weighted averages.
b. Measures as a percentage of import lines covered by nontariff barriers; weighted averages.
Source: Erzan and others 1989.

South America following closely behind (see table 5-1). However, by 1987–88, it became apparent that a fundamental change was needed in Latin America's development strategy.[1] In particular, policymakers realized that the long-standing protectionist trade policy was at the heart of the region's problems. With the help of the multilateral institutions, more and more countries reduced their levels of protection during the late 1980s and early 1990s. The process of trade reform proceeded at an accelerating pace. Tariffs were drastically slashed, many countries completely eliminated import licenses and prohibitions, and several countries began negotiating free trade agreements with the United States.

This chapter documents and evaluates the process of trade reform in Latin America and the Caribbean. It begins by providing a brief analytical discussion of the consequences of the traditional protectionist policies and of the expected results of liberalization reforms, including the role of supporting policies in assuring their success. This is followed by a discussion of the extent of trade reform in the region and an analysis of some of the results of the reforms. The analysis concentrates on productivity and exports and deals with the experiences of several countries. The next section explores the role of real exchange rates in the process of trade liberalization and analyzes the recent trend toward real appreciation. This is followed by a discussion of attempts to revive regional integration agreements and future prospects for free trade agreements with the United States. A statistical appendix investigates empirically the relationship between trade regimes and growth of productivity.

From Protectionism to Liberalization: Some Analytical Aspects

The recent trade liberalization programs in Latin America sought to reverse protectionist policies that for decades had been at the heart of the region's development strategy. To place these reforms in perspective, it is useful to analyze the way in which the protectionist policies affected the economic structure of Latin America and to discuss the expected effects of the liberalization policies.

Economic Consequences of Protectionism

Latin America's long tradition of protectionist policies molded the region's economic structure in fundamental ways. Perhaps the most important consequence of protectionism was that, from early on, high import tariffs and prohibitions in most countries generated a severe anti-export bias that discouraged both the growth and diversification of exports. In an early study using data from the 1960s, Bela Balassa (1971) found that Brazil, Chile, and Mexico had some of the most distorted foreign trade sectors in the world. These findings coincided with those obtained by Little, Scitovsky, and Scott (1970) in their pioneer study on trade policy and industrialization in the developing world. These works persuasively argue that the high degree of protection granted to manufacturing in Latin America resulted in serious discrimination against exports, misallocation of resources, inefficient investment, and deteriorating income distribution. Therefore, reversing the protectionist policies should be at the center of any attempt to reformulate Latin America's development strategy. However, at the time these proposals were made, Latin America was moving strongly in the opposite direction, pushing protectionist policies to a global level through the formation of customs unions with high common external tariffs.

The discouragement of export activities took place through two channels. First, import tariffs, quotas, and prohibitions increased the cost of imported intermediate materials and capital goods used to produce exportables that reduced their effective rate of protection. For years, a vast number of exportable goods, especially in the agriculture sector, had *negative* rates of protection to their value added. Second, the maze of protectionist policies resulted in overvaluation of the real exchange rate, which reduced the degree of competitiveness of exports. This anti-export bias explains the poor performance of the export sector in most countries, including the inability to develop nontraditional exports aggressively during the twenty years preceding the debt crisis. Paradoxically, policies that were supposed to reduce Latin America's dependence on the worldwide business cycle created instead a highly vulnerable economic structure in which the sources of foreign exchange were concentrated on a few products intensive in natural resources and imports were concentrated on a relatively small group of essential goods (CEPAL 1992a).

A second important consequence of traditional protectionist trade policies was the creation of a largely inefficient manufacturing sector. Instead of granting short-term protection to help launch new activities, high tariffs, quotas, and prohibitions became a fixture of the region's economic landscape. An important consequence of the pressures exercised by lobbyists and interest groups was that the protective structure became extremely uneven, with some sectors enjoying effective tariff rates in the thousands while others suffered from negative value added protection (Edwards 1992c).

The protectionist policies also had serious effects on labor markets. In particular, the protection of capital-intensive industries affected the region's ability to create employment. Various studies show that in developing countries more-open trade regimes result in higher employment and in a more even distribution of income than protectionist regimes. For example, after analyzing in detail the experiences of ten countries, Krueger (1983) concludes that exportable industries tend to be significantly more labor intensive than import-competing sectors. Moreover, employment tends to grow faster in outward-oriented economies, and the removal of external sector distortions tends to strengthen the process of employment creation in most developing nations. These results are broadly supported by other cross-country studies, including Balassa (1982) and Michaely, Choksi, and Papageorgiou (1991).

In the 1970s and early 1980s, some countries—most notably Brazil, Colombia, and Mexico—embarked on aggressive export-promotion schemes. These programs relied on heavy and selective subsidies and did not reduce the level of import protection. They failed to transform the export sector into an engine of growth (Rodrik 1993 argues that Brazil's export-promotion scheme was highly effective, but he does not discuss the net benefits; see also Nogués 1990). There are a number of possible reasons why, contrary to the case of East Asia, export promotion did not succeed in Latin America. First, as pointed out by Fishlow (1991b), decades of protectionism had generated relatively high wages that precluded the region from competing effectively in world markets. Second, in many countries the pro-export drive was not accompanied by a competitive real exchange rate (Nogués 1990). In most instances, the export-promotion effort took place in an environment of heightened macroeconomic uncertainty that resulted in volatile real exchange rates. This variability discouraged exports and, more important, private investment in the tradables sector (see, for example, Caballero and Corbo 1989; Edwards 1989d for empirical analyses of the relationship between real exchange rate uncertainty, exports, and investment). Indeed, real exchange rates exhibited significantly higher variability in Latin America than in East Asia. An important consequence of macro-instability is that it reduces the credibility of an export-promotion program. A third explanation for the limited success of export promotion in the Latin American countries is related to the role of rent-seeking activities. Selective interventions, such as those used in Latin America, tend to create substantial opportunities for appropriating large rents. In many cases, the attractiveness of these schemes is related directly to rent seeking and not to the export activity per se. According to Nogués (1990), this type of phenomenon explains the dismal performance of Argentina's export-promotion program. Between 1980 and 1984, Argentina provided $2.4 billion in incentives for industrial exports and exported a mere $6.7 billion. This suggests that a fundamental problem of Latin America's export-promotion schemes is that they were not closely linked either to results or to performance. In East Asia, programs that did not accomplish rapid results were promptly canceled; in Latin America, they were maintained for long periods of time (see Leipziger and Thomas 1993).

In terms of income distribution, the protective system generated large benefits to local industrialists—in particular, those able to obtain import licenses and concessions—and to urban workers. This, of course, was achieved at the cost of depressing the earnings and incomes of rural workers. During the 1970s, income distribution was significantly more unequal in Latin America than in Asia (see chapter 8).

Although several decades of protectionist policies accomplished the goal of creating an industrial sector in Latin America, they did so at a high cost. Exports were generally discouraged, the exchange rate became overvalued, employment creation lagged, and massive amounts of resources, including skilled human talent, were withdrawn from the productive sphere and devoted to lobbying for an ever-favorable treatment of unproductive sectors of the economy.[2] In the aftermath of the debt crisis, the long stagnation and even retrogression of the region's export sector—with an average rate of decline of 1 percent a year between 1965 and 1980—became particularly painful to the local public, analysts, and policymakers.

Trade Liberalization: Expected Results and Transitional Problems

The main objective of trade liberalization programs is to reverse the negative consequences of protectionism and, especially, its anti-export bias. According to basic theory, trade liberalization reallocates resources according to comparative advantage, reduces waste, and lowers the price of imported goods.[3] Moreover, to the extent that the new trade regime is more transparent—for example, through a relatively uniform import tariff—lobbying activities are greatly reduced, releasing highly skilled work from unproductive jobs. According to traditional international trade theory, once negative effective rates of protection and overvalued exchange rates are eliminated, exports not only grow rapidly but also become more diversified.

From a growth perspective, the fundamental objective of trade reforms is to transform international trade into the engine of growth. In fact, models of endogenous growth stress the role of openness.[4] For example, Romer (1989) has developed a model in which an open economy, by taking advantage of larger markets—*the* world market—can specialize in the production of a relatively larger number of intermediate goods and, thus, grow faster. Other authors concentrate on the relationship among openness, technological progress, and growth of productivity. Grossman and Helpman (1991) and Edwards (1992c), for example, argue that openness affects the speed and efficiency with which small countries can absorb technological innovations developed in the industrial world. This idea, based on an insight first proposed by John Stuart Mill, implies that countries with a lower level of trade distortions experience faster growth in total factor productivity and, with other things being equal, grow faster than countries that inhibit international competition.[5]

Several authors have tested the general implications of these theories using cross-country data sets (see Tybout 1992 for a general survey of empirical models on the relationship between trade orientation and growth of total factor productivity; see also de Gregorio 1992; Edwards 1992c). Although different empirical models yield different results, the general thrust of this line of research is that countries with less distorted external sectors do appear to grow faster. As Dornbusch (1991b) points out, openness possibly affects growth not only through one channel alone but also through a combination of channels, including the introduction of new goods, the adoption of new methods of production, the organization of new industries, the expansion in the number of intermediate goods available, and the conquest of new markets that permit the expansion of exports.

Because of the importance placed on reducing the anti-export bias, liberalization strategists also emphasize the role of exchange rate policy during a trade reform effort. Numerous authors contend that a large devaluation should constitute the first step in a trade reform process. In the presence of quotas and import licenses, a (real) exchange rate depreciation reduces the rents received by importers, shifting relative prices in favor of export-oriented activities and, thus, reducing the extent of the anti-export bias (see Bhagwati 1978; Krueger 1978, 1981; Michaely, Choksi, and Papageorgiou 1991).

Two fundamental problems have to be addressed in the transition toward freer trade. First, it is important to determine the adequate speed of reform. For a long time, analysts argued that gradual liberalization programs give firms time to restructure their productive processes and, thus, result in low dislocation costs in the form of unemployment and bankruptcies (Little, Scitovsky, and Scott 1970; Michaely 1985). These reduced adjustment costs, in turn, provide the political support needed for the liberalization program to succeed. Recently, however, the gradualist position has been under attack. There is increasing agreement that slower reforms tend to lack credibility, inhibiting firms from seriously restructuring. Moreover, the experience of Argentina in the 1970s shows that a gradual (and preannounced) reform allows those firms negatively affected by it to lobby (successfully) against the reduction in tariffs. According to this line of reasoning, faster reforms are more credible and thus tend to be sustained through time.

The thinking on the speed of reform has also been influenced by recent empirical work on the short-run unemployment consequences of trade liberalization. In a World Bank study on liberalization episodes in nineteen countries, Michaely, Choksi, and Papageorgiou (1991) argue that, even in the short run, the costs of reform can be small. Although contracting industries release workers, those expanding sectors that are positively affected by the reform process tend to create a large number of employment positions. In analyzing the employment consequences of trade reform, these authors distinguish between gross and net effects. The gross—or, in their words, disemployment—effect is defined as the unemployment associated with the contraction of some industries after the trade liberalization reform is undertaken. The net effect is defined as the total change in aggregate unemployment in the economy. Naturally, from an economic perspective, the net effect is the most interesting, because under most circumstances we would expect a reduction in the level of employment in those sectors that lose competitiveness and an increase in employment in those sectors that, as a consequence of a reform, expand (this and the paragraphs that follow are based on Edwards 1993c).

In most cases, Michaely, Choksi, and Papageorgiou compute variants of the before-and-after method of assessing the employment effects of trade reforms. However, three of the studies (Chile, Spain, and Yugoslavia) use a method that attempts to control for the evolution of other economic variables, such as the terms of trade, fluctuations in economic activity, and macroeconomic policies. The authors of the Chile and Yugoslavia studies found that, when controlling for other facts, the net effect of liberalization on employment was positive: as a consequence of the liberalization program, the aggregate rate of unemployment declined in these countries.[6] For Spain, the results differ depending on which liberalization episode is considered. While in the first two liberalization attempts (1960–66 and 1970–74), aggregate unemployment increased after the trade reforms, in the third episode (1977–80), net unemployment declined after liberalization.

Regarding the other countries in the study, unemployment increased after the following episodes: Argentina in 1967–70 and 1976–80; Israel in 1952–55 and 1962–68; Indonesia in 1966–72; Republic of Korea in 1978–79; the Philippines in 1960–65; and Turkey in 1980–84.[7] In most of these cases, however, the increase in unemployment was rather small and could be attributed to factors other than the reform itself. These results led the directors of the project to conclude that "by and large, liberalization attempts have *not* incurred significant transition costs by way of unemployment" (Michaely, Choksi, and Papageorgiou 1991, vol. 7, chap. 6, p. 80, emphasis added).

Undoubtedly, this project constitutes the most complete and ambitious attempt to understand the link between structural reforms and the labor market. However, as is usually the case with a collection of multiauthored country studies, the empirical and historical analyses are uneven and, at times, lack focus. For instance, some of the country studies fail to discuss in detail the role of labor market distortions, minimum wages, or indexation practices.

The link between trade liberalization reforms and labor market adjustment has also been studied for the liberalization experiences of the Southern Cone of Latin America during the 1970s. In the case of Chile, the existence of labor distortions, including minimum wages and indexation of wages to past inflation, generated a segmented labor market with a protected and an unprotected sector. The existence of a protected sector resulted in important wage rigidities that impaired the labor market's ability to adjust to the trade reform and other shocks. For example, Edwards and Edwards (1991) calculate that as a result of existing labor market rigidities, the trade liberalization reform generated short-run unemployment in Chile on the order of 3.5 percent (they use a segmented labor market model to quantify the effects of the Chilean trade reform on unemployment; see also Corbo, de Melo, and Tybout 1986; Ramos 1986).

The second problem that has to be addressed when designing a liberalization strategy refers to the sequencing of reform (Edwards 1984). This issue was first addressed in the 1980s in discussions dealing with the Southern Cone experience and emphasized the macroeconomic consequences of alternative sequences. It is now generally agreed that resolving the fiscal imbalance and attaining some degree of macroeconomic reform should be a priority in implementing a structural reform. Most analysts also agree that trade liberalization should precede liberalization of the capital account and that financial reform should only be implemented once a modern and efficient supervisory framework is in place (Lal 1985 presents a dissenting view; Hanson 1992 argues that under some circumstances the capital account should be liberalized early on).

Discussions of this issue focus more and more on the political economy of reform. In this setting, it is argued that policymakers should, in general, try to move rapidly and simultaneously on as many fronts as possible (Klaus 1990). McKinnon (1991), however, argues that in order to ensure an orderly and successful liberalization, the privatization of the banking sector should take place toward the end of the reform process.

The behavior of the real exchange rate is at the heart of the policy debates on the sequencing of liberalization. The central issue is that liberalizing the capital account, under some conditions, results in large inflows of capital and appreciation of the real exchange rate (Edwards 1984; Harberger 1985a; McKinnon 1982; this occurs if the capital account is opened in the context of an overall liberalization program and the country becomes attractive for foreign investors and speculators). The problem is that the appreciation of the real exchange rate sends a wrong signal to the real sector, frustrating the reallocation of resources called for by the trade reform. The effects of this appreciation are particularly serious if, as argued by McKinnon (1982) and Edwards (1984), the transitional period is characterized by abnormally high inflows of capital that result in temporary real appreciations, and generate very large (and unsustainable) current account deficits, as was the case in Mexico in 1993–94. According to this view, however, if the opening of the capital account is postponed, the real sector can adjust and the new allocation of resources is consolidated. According to this view, only at this time should the capital account be liberalized.

Recent discussions on the sequencing of reform expand the analysis to include other markets. More and more authors argue that the reform of the labor market—in particular the removal of distortions that discourage labor mobility—should, at least, proceed jointly with trade reform. The liberalization of trade in the presence of highly distorted labor markets may even be counterproductive, generating overall welfare losses in the country in question.

As the preceding discussion suggests, the behavior of the real exchange rate is a key element during a transition to trade liberalization. According to traditional manuals on how to liberalize, a large devaluation should constitute the first step in a trade reform process. Maintaining a depreciated and competitive real exchange rate is also important for avoiding an explosion in the growth of imports and a crisis in the balance of payments. Under most circumstances, reducing the extent of protection tends to generate a rapid and immediate surge in imports; however, the expansion of exports usually takes some time. Consequently, there is a danger that trade liberalization reform will generate a large trade balance disequilibrium in the short run. This will not happen if a depreciated real exchange rate encourages exports and helps to maintain imports in check.

Many countries historically failed to sustain a depreciated real exchange rate during the transition. This was mainly the result of expansionary macroeconomic policies that generated speculation, the loss of international reserves, and, in many cases, the reversal of the reform effort. In the conclusions to the massive World Bank project on trade reform, Michaely, Choksi, and Papageorgiou (1991, p. 119) succinctly summarize the key role of the real exchange rate in determining the success of liberalization programs: "The long-term performance of the real exchange rate clearly differentiates 'liberalizers' from 'nonliberalizers.'" Edwards (1989d) uses data on thirty-nine exchange rate crises and finds that, in almost every case, real exchange rate overvaluation generated drastic increases in the degree of protection.

Determinants of Successful Trade Liberalization Policies

Two economic aspects of trade liberalization are particularly important for analyzing the political economy of transition and the likelihood that reforms will be successful and sustained through time. First, it takes some time for the structural reforms to bear fruit. This means that, even though the reforms have a positive effect on the aggregate economy in the long run, they have costs in the short run. Moreover, a more-open economy may be more vulnerable to cyclical fluctuations. Transitional costs, however, are not even and affect some groups more than others. Second, even in the long run some groups lose and see their real incomes diminish. These groups benefited from the previous maze of regulations and, in most cases, tend to oppose the reforms from the beginning. Politically, then, trade reforms will only survive if they show some benefits early on and if those benefits expand gradually, affecting larger and larger segments of society. To the extent that this indeed happens, the reformist government will be able to force broader political coalitions to support the consolidation of the reform process.

Extensive comparative studies provide abundant evidence on the key determinants of a successful trade reform that persists through time and changes the trade structure of a country (Balassa 1971, 1982; Bhagwati 1978; Krueger 1978, 1980; Little, Scitovsky, and Scott 1970; Michaely, Choksi, and Papageorgiou 1991). These elements can serve as a guide for policymakers who want to implement trade liberalization policies that will be sustained through time. Existing historical evidence suggests that successful (in the sense of sustained) reforms are characterized, in the short and medium run, by at least some of the following elements:

- Exports, and in particular nontraditional exports, expand at a pace that exceeds the historical rate.
- Productivity growth increases at a fast pace, helping generate rapid growth for the economy as a whole.
- The trade balance does not exhibit "unreasonable" deficits; otherwise, the public would be skeptical about the viability of the reform and would speculate against the domestic currency.
- The overall level of unemployment stays at a relatively low level.
- Real wages increase, at least in the medium run. For this increase to affect a broad sector of society, trade liberalization should be supplemented by structural reforms aimed at deregulating other sectors of the economy.

It is interesting to note that, as is shown in the rest of this book, four of these five conditions were not met in Mexico in the 1993–94 period.

Recent Trade Liberalization Reforms in Latin America and the Caribbean

The pioneer in the trade liberalization process, Chile unilaterally eliminated quantitative restrictions and reduced import tariffs to a uniform level of 10 percent between 1975 and 1979. After a brief interlude with higher tariffs (at the uniform level of 35 percent), Chile imposed a uniform tariff of 11 percent and eliminated licenses and other forms of quantitative controls. Uruguay implemented a reform in 1978 and, after a brief reversal, pushed forward once again in 1986. Bolivia and Mexico embarked on their reforms in 1985–86, followed by a series of countries in the late 1980s. The members of the Caribbean Community (CARICOM) intensified trade liberalization reforms in the late 1980s and early 1990s. As of 1994, several nations, including Brazil, are proceeding steadily with scheduled rounds of tariff reductions and the dismantling of quantitative restrictions. However, it is still unclear whether all these reforms will be sustained and become permanent features of the Latin American economies.

The Latin American and Caribbean trade reforms were characterized by four basic elements: (1) reduction of the coverage of nontariff barriers, including quotas and prohibitions; (2) reduction of the average level of import tariffs; (3) reduction of the degree of dispersion of the tariff structure; and (4) reduction or elimination of export taxes. These measures generally were supported, during the early years of the reforms, by exchange rate policies aimed at maintaining a competitive real exchange rate. This section documents the extent of the recent liberalization programs; it is followed by analysis of the effects of the reforms, specifically on the growth of productivity and expansion of exports (portions of this section draw on Edwards 1992a).

Nontariff Barriers

A fundamental component of the trade reform programs was the elimination, or at least the severe reduction, of the coverage of nontariff barriers. During the early and mid-1980s in some countries, such as Colombia and Peru, more than 50 percent of import positions were subject to licenses or outright prohibitions. In Mexico, the coverage of nontariff barriers reached almost 100 percent of import categories in 1984, as was the case in most nations of Central America that year.

Table 5-2, which contains data on protectionism in the period before reform (1985 or 1987, depending on availability) and in the recent period (1991–92), shows that almost every country dramatically reduced the coverage of nontariff barriers.[8] In fact, some eliminated nontariff barriers altogether. The process through which nontariff barriers were eased varied from country to country. In some cases, such as Honduras, they were initially replaced by (quasi) equivalent import tariffs and then slowly phased out. In other countries, like Chile, they were eliminated rapidly without a compensating hike in tariffs.

In spite of the progress experienced in the last few years, significant coverage of nontariff barriers remains in a number of countries. In most cases, these nontariff barriers correspond to agricultural products. In Mexico, approximately 60 percent of the agriculture sector's tariff positions were still subject to

Table 5–2. *Opening in Selected Countries of Latin America, 1985–92*
(percentage)

| Country | Average protection of tariffs and paratariffs[a] | | Average coverage of nontariff barriers[a,b] | | Range of import tariffs | | | | | |
| | | | | | 1980s | | | Current | | |
	1985	1991–92	1985–87	1991–92	Year	Minimum	Maximum	Year	Minimum	Maximum
Early reformers										
Bolivia	20.0	8.0	25.0	0.0	1985	0.0	20.0	1991	5.0	10.0
Chile	36.0	11.0	10.1	0.0	1987	0.0	20.0	1992	11.0	11.0
Mexico	34.0	4.0	12.7	20.0	1985	0.0	100.0	1992	0.0	20.0
Second-phase reformers										
Costa Rica	92.0	16.0	0.8	0.0	1986	1.0	100.0	1992	5.0	20.0
Uruguay	32.0	12.0	14.1	0.0	1986	10.0	45.0	1992	10.0	30.0
Third-phase reformers										
Argentina	28.0	15.0	31.9	8.0	1987	0.0	55.0	1991	0.0	22.0
Brazil	80.0	21.1	35.3	10.0	1987	0.0	105.0	1992	0.0	65.0
Colombia	83.0	6.7	73.2	1.0	1986	0.0	200.0	1991	0.0	15.0
Guatemala	50.0	19.0	7.4	6.0	1986	1.0	100.0	1990	0.0	10.0
Nicaragua	54.0	—	27.8	—	1986	1.0	100.0	1990	0.0	10.0
Paraguay	71.7	16.0	9.9	0.0	1984	0.0	44.0	1991	5.0	86.0
Peru	64.0	15.0	53.4	0.0	1987	0.0	120.0	1992	5.0	15.0
Venezuela	30.0	17.0	44.1	5.0	1987	0.0	135.0	1991	0.0	50.0
Nonreformers										
Ecuador	50.0	18.0	59.3	—	1986	0.0	290.0	1991	2.0	40.0

— Not available.
a. Unweighted.
b. Data on nontariff barriers refer mostly to 1989 and, thus, are not necessarily compatible with those presented in table 5-1.
Sources: World Bank, several country-specific reports; UNCTAD 1987; Erzan and others 1989.

import licenses in late 1993. An important feature of the region's liberalization programs is that they proceeded much slower in agriculture than in industry, largely because the authorities desired to isolate agriculture from fluctuations in world prices and unfair trade practices by foreign countries.[9] However, an approach based on quantitative restrictions entails serious efficiency costs (Valdés 1992). Slowly, however, more and more countries are replacing quantitative restrictions with variable levies and are introducing a system for smoothing price fluctuations based on price bands.

Tariff Dispersion

The import-substitution development strategy pursued for decades in Latin America created highly dispersed protective structures. During the 1960s, Brazil, Colombia, and Uruguay had among the highest degrees of dispersion in effective protection in the world, while Chile had *the* highest rate of tariff dispersion in the world, with a standard deviation of 634 percent (Heitger 1987; World Bank, *World Development Report 1987*). Highly dispersed protective structures generate high welfare costs, because they increase uncertainty and negatively affect the investment process (Cardoso and Helwege 1991). These highly dispersed tariffs and nontariff barriers were the result of decades of lobbying by different sectors to obtain preferential treatment. As the relative power of the different lobbies changed, so did their tariff concessions and the protective landscape.

An important goal of the Latin American trade reforms was to reduce the degree of dispersion of import tariffs. Table 5-2 contains data on the range of tariffs for a group of countries for two points in time—mid-1980s (1985–87) and 1991–92—and clearly documents the fact that the reforms indeed diminished the range between minimum and maximum tariffs. In many cases, this meant *increasing* tariffs on goods that were originally exempt from import duties. In fact, in many countries, the minimum tariff was 0 percent in the mid-1980s. Generally, zero tariffs are applied to intermediate inputs used in the manufacturing process.[10] From a political economy perspective, the process of raising some tariffs, while maintaining a pro-liberalization rhetoric, was often difficult. Those sectors that traditionally benefited from the exemptions strongly opposed them as it became evident that their privileged situation was coming to an end.

An important question addressed by policymakers throughout the region is how much tariff dispersion should be reduced. Should the reforms implement a uniform tariff, or is some (small) degree of dispersion desirable? Although from a strict traditional welfare perspective, uniform tariffs are only advisable under very special cases, they have a strong administrative and political economy appeal. In particular, a system of uniform tariffs is very transparent, making it difficult for the authorities to grant special treatment to particular firms or sectors (Harberger 1990).

Average Tariffs

Reducing the average degree of protection is, perhaps, the fundamental policy goal of trade liberalization reforms. Traditional policy manuals on the subject suggest that once the exchange rate has been devalued and quantitative restrictions have been reduced or eliminated, tariffs should be slashed in such a way that both their range and average are reduced.[11] Table 5-2 contains data on average total tariffs (tariffs plus paratariffs) in 1985 and 1991–92. As can be seen, tariffs were significantly reduced in almost every country. Even those nations that acted somewhat cautiously on the reform front, such as Ecuador, made significant cuts in import tariffs, allowing a more competitive environment and reducing the degree of anti-export bias of the trade regime.

Countries that embarked on trade liberalization after 1990 moved at a much faster speed than those nations that opened up earlier. There has, in fact, been a clear change in what is perceived to be *abrupt* and *rapid* removal of impediments to imports. What fifteen years ago were seen as brutally fast reforms are now considered to be mild and gradual liberalizations. When Chile initiated trade reform in 1975, most analysts thought that the announced tariff reduction from an average of 52 to 10 percent in four and a half years was an extremely aggressive move that would cause major dislocations, including large increases in unemployment. In the early 1990s, more and more countries began opening up their external sectors very rapidly. For instance, Colombia slashed (total) import tariffs 65 percent *in one year*, from 34 percent in 1990 to 12 percent in 1991. This fast approach to liberalization was also followed by Argentina, Nicaragua, and Peru. Peru eliminated quantitative restrictions in one bold move, slashing import tariffs from an average of 110 percent in 1990 to 15 percent in March 1992.

Exchange Rate Policy

In the vast majority of countries, the first step in the recent process of trade reform was the implementation of large (nominal) devaluations. In many cases, this measure unified the exchange rate market. Most countries implemented large adjustments of the exchange rate as early as 1982 in order to face the urgencies of the adjustment process. The purpose of these policies was to generate real exchange rate devaluations and, thus, reduce the degree of anti-export bias of incentive systems.

As pointed out in chapters 2 and 4, many countries adopted crawling peg regimes, characterized by periodic small devaluations of the nominal exchange rate, as a way to protect the real exchange rate from the effects of inflation.[12] Table 5-3 contains data on real exchange rates for a group of Latin American countries. Once again, an increase in the index represents a *depreciation* of the real exchange rate and thus an improvement in the degree of competitiveness. Between 1980 and 1987, almost every country in the sample experienced very

Table 5-3. Bilateral Real Exchange Rate Relative to the U.S. Dollar in Selected Countries of Latin America and the Caribbean, 1980–93
(1985=100)

Country	1980	1983	1987	1992	1993[a]
Argentina	35.8	96.4	80.8	36.9	34.0
Bolivia	88.1	84.6	107.9	109.6	113.3
Brazil	70.7	88.7	78.0	51.7	45.7
Chile	55.3	75.3	94.8	75.1	75.2
Colombia	79.2	78.3	115.9	119.9	102.6
Costa Rica	65.8	103.0	94.9	88.2	82.9
Ecuador	105.6	104.5	153.3	165.7	153.9
El Salvador	172.6	133.9	121.0	103.7	—
Guatemala	124.9	120.5	162.0	149.5	—
Honduras	121.6	106.2	93.2	141.5	152.3
Jamaica	60.1	54.8	80.1	94.5	70.7
Mexico	83.3	119.8	123.9	68.7	63.8
Panama	102.0	100.7	98.8	107.8	106.5
Paraguay	74.4	60.7	111.4	113.0	—
Peru	77.3	80.6	46.2	21.7	23.6
Trinidad and Tobago	152.9	117.3	122.8	112.1	129.0
Uruguay	49.7	89.4	77.2	55.5	40.5
Venezuela	84.2	70.3	134.8	122.3	119.1

— Not available.

Note: Increases indicate currency depreciation against the dollar.

a. Preliminary.

Source: Calculated using data from the data base of the IMF's *International Financial Statistics,* various years.

large real depreciations. In many cases, however, these were partially reversed as a consequence of the inflow of large volumes of foreign capital after 1990 and the use of the exchange rate as the cornerstone of disinflation policies. Overall, however, in most countries the real exchange rate was depreciated significantly more by late 1991 than in 1981. This greatly encouraged exports, helping to revert decades of discriminatory policies.

Effects of Trade Liberalization

The trade liberalization reforms implemented in Latin America had three objectives: (a) to reduce the anti-export bias of the old regime and, thus, to encourage exports; (b) to help increase the growth of total factor productivity through greater competition and enhanced efficiency; and (c) to increase consumer welfare by reducing the real prices of importable goods. In this section, the evolution of productivity and exports in the period after the reforms is analyzed in some detail.

Trade Liberalization and Productivity Growth

The relaxation of trade impediments had a fundamental impact on the region's economies. Suddenly, Latin America's industry, which to a large extent had developed and grown behind protective walls, was forced to compete. Many firms did not survive this shock and went bankrupt. Others, however, faced the challenge of lower protection by embarking on major restructuring and increasing their level of productivity.

The ability (and willingness) of firms to implement significant adjustment depends on two main factors: the degree of credibility of the reform and the level of distortions in the labor market. If entrepreneurs believe that the reform will not persist through time, they have no incentives to incur the costs of adjusting the product mix and of increasing the degree of productive efficiency. In fact, if the reform is perceived as temporary, the optimal behavior is not to adjust but rather to speculate through the accumulation of imported durable goods. This was, as Rodríguez (1982) documents, the case in Argentina during the failed Martínez de Hoz reforms (see Corbo, Condon, and de Melo 1985 for a detailed microeconomic account of the process of adjustment in a large group of Chilean manufacturing firms).

In their studies on the interaction between labor markets and structural reforms, Krueger (1980) and Michaely, Choksi, and Papageorgiou (1991) find that most successful trade reforms indeed result in major increases in labor productivity. In most cases where this happens, labor markets are characterized by some degree of flexibility. Countries with rigid and highly distorted labor markets—including countries with high costs of dismissal, limitations on temporary contracts, and rigid minimum wage legislation—generally exhibit modest improvements in labor productivity after the trade reform process.

Some of the early Latin American reformers experienced important improvements in the productivity of labor. Labor productivity in the manufacturing sector increased at an annual rate of 13.4 percent in Chile between 1978 and 1981 and at a very significant annual rate of almost 4 percent in Mexico between 1986 and 1991, more than double the 1.6 percent annual rate of growth in that country between 1960 and 1982 (Edwards and Edwards 1991; Elías 1992; Sánchez 1992).

Recent models of growth suggest that countries that are more open to the rest of the world exhibit a faster rate of technological improvement and productivity growth than countries that are isolated. From an empirical point of view, this means that countries that open up their external sectors and engage in trade liberalization reforms experience an increase in growth of total factor productivity. The regression analysis presented in appendix 5-1 supports the notion that, when other variables (such as human capital formation, government size, political volatility, and the development gap) are held constant, the degree of openness of the economy is positively associated with the rate of growth of productivity. What is particularly important is that this result appears to be robust to the proxy used to measure the orientation of trade policy.

Table 5-4 contains data on the change in aggregate growth of total factor productivity in the period following the implementation of trade liberalization reform in six Latin American countries.[13] As can be seen, Chile and Costa Rica, two of the early reformers, experienced very large increases in growth of total factor productivity in the period following reform. The results for Chile coincide with those obtained by Edwards (1985), who finds that in the late 1970s, after the trade reforms had been completed, growth of total factor productivity was approximately three times higher than the historical average (it may be argued, however, that the major increase in growth of total factor productivity was the result of the complete structural reform package implemented in that country). Although the outcome is less spectacular, Argentina and Uruguay still exhibited substantial improvements in productivity growth in the period following reform. Bolivia, in contrast, presented a flat profile of total factor productivity growth. Sturzenegger (1992) argues that the very slow improvement in the growth of Bolivian productivity was, to a large extent, the result of negative terms of trade shocks and, in particular, the collapse of the tin market. In a series of recent studies, Ocampo (1991a, 1991b) calculates growth in total factor productivity in Colombia and finds that the increase in protectionism in 1982–85 was accompanied by a decline in productivity growth.

Perhaps the most puzzling result in table 5-4 is the slight decline in aggregate total factor productivity growth in Mexico after the reforms. Martin (1992) shows that this finding is robust to alternative methods of measuring growth of total factor productivity, including different procedures for correcting for capacity use. Also, Harberger (1992) finds that the growth in total factor productivity in Mexico was slower in 1986–90 than in 1975–82.[14] However, the aggregate nature of the data in table 5-4 tends to obscure the actual sectoral response to trade reform in Mexico. According to endogenous growth models, faster productivity will be observed in those sectors where

Table 5-4. Changes in Growth of Total Factor Productivity in Selected Countries of Latin America, 1978–82 to 1987–91

Country	Percentage change from 1978–82 to 1987–91
Argentina	1.91
Bolivia	0.11
Chile	4.96
Costa Rica	3.25
Mexico	−0.32
Uruguay	2.02

Note: For Chile, the pre-reform period is 1972–78.
Source: Martin 1992.

protectionism has been reduced and will not be observed in those still subject to trade barriers or other forms of regulation.

A distinctive characteristic of the Mexican reform is that, contrary to the Chilean case, it proceeded at an uneven pace. In particular, in 1993, most of the agriculture sector was still protected by relatively high tariffs and substantial nontariff barriers. Also, the existence of important distortions in the labor market probably dampened the effect of trade reform on productivity growth. Moreover, until 1992 the Mexican land tenure system was subject to a legal system—the *ejido* system—that, among other things, severely restricted the market for land and distorted economic incentives. Although most regulations on land ownership in the agricultural sector were legally eliminated in early 1992, these reforms have yet to have a practical impact because the titling process, where property rights are actually assigned, is still in its infancy. By late 1994, practically no *ejidos* had been converted into private landholdings (several observers argue that the titling process will, by itself, take between five and ten years). Also, during much of the period following the debt crisis, large fragments of the service sector in Mexico, including telecommunications and financial services, were under direct government control and subject to distortions.

Table 5-5 contains data on growth of total factor productivity in Mexico's manufacturing sector for 1940–89 (since these figures come from two different sources, they may not be fully comparable and, thus, should be interpreted with care). In the period following trade reform, the rate of productivity growth in the Mexican manufacturing sector exceeded that of every period after 1940 for which data are available. This suggests that, once the sectors actually subject to increased competition are considered, growth of Mexican productivity indeed improved after the trade reform. This proposition is supported by Weiss (1992), who uses regression analysis to investigate the impact of the trade reforms on productivity and cost margins. In a recent and detailed econometric study at a disaggregated level, Oks (1994) finds that trade reform has indeed had a positive impact on productivity growth in Mexico's manufacturing sector.

Table 5-5. Growth of Total Factor Productivity in Manufacturing in Mexico, Selected Years, 1940–89
(percentage)

Period	Growth in total factor productivity
1940–50	0.46
1950–60	0.53
1960–70	3.00
1970–80	—
1985–89	3.40

— Not available.
Sources: For 1940–80, Elías 1992; for 1985–89, Ibarra 1992.

An important question in evaluating the effects of trade reform refers to the speed with which productivity growth will react to the new incentives. Will the response be rapid, or will a long period of time pass before the fruits of the reforms are visible? Existing data for Chile provide some support for the idea that growth of total factor productivity will react quite fast. For example, Edwards (1985) finds that by 1979—the year the trade reform reached its goal of a uniform 10 percent import tariff—aggregate growth of total factor productivity had already reached 5.4 percent, significantly higher than the historical level. Agacino, Rivas, and Román (1992) find that growth of total factor productivity averaged 3.9 percent a year during 1976–81, greatly exceeding the historical average of approximately 1 percent, and varied significantly across industries. In some cases, average productivity growth exceeded the 10 percent annual mark—wood products and glass industries—while in others it was negative, such as in nonelectric machinery. Agacino, Rivas, and Román (1992) find that total factor productivity did not grow in Chile during the late 1980s. This result is consistent with the findings of Marfán and Bosworth (1994), who argue that after the reforms Chile experienced very moderate productivity growth. This result is puzzling and somewhat counterintuitive; according to the authors, it may be due to their treatment of cyclical changes in growth. Lefort and Solimano (1994) revisit the issue of productivity growth in Chile. After analyzing the evolution of six measures of growth of total factor productivity, they conclude that the reform process positively affected productivity in the 1976–81 period.

Trade Reforms and Exports

Important goals of the trade reforms were to reduce the traditional degree of anti-export bias of Latin American trade regimes and to generate a surge in exports. In fact, based on the East Asian model, more and more Latin American leaders have called for the transformation of the external sector into the region's engine of growth. The reduction of the traditional anti-export bias is expected to take place through three channels: a more competitive—that is, more devalued—real exchange rate, a reduction in the cost of imported capital goods and intermediate inputs used to produce exportables, and a direct shift in relative prices in favor of exports.[15]

The volume of international trade in Latin America, and, in particular, the volume of exports, increased significantly after the reforms were initiated.[16] For example, the volume of exports for the region as a whole grew at an annual rate of only 2.0 percent between 1970 and 1980, at a rate of 5.5 percent between 1980 and 1985, and at an annual average of 6.7 percent between 1986 and 1990. The real value of exports, however, evolved at a somewhat slower pace, because the terms of trade in every subgroup of countries deteriorated significantly during 1980–91 (see CEPAL 1992a). Although, strictly speaking, it is not possible to attribute this export surge fully to the reforms, ample country-specific evidence suggests that a more-open economy, and, in particular, a more depreciated real exchange rate, positively affected the growth of exports (Nogués and Gulati 1992). Some countries, especially Costa Rica, accompanied the reform process with the implementation of a battery of export-promotion schemes, including tax credits—through the Certificado de Abono Tributario—duty-free imports, and income tax exemptions. However, it has been argued that these systems are fiscally expensive and do not encourage exports effectively (see Nogués and Gulati 1992; Nogués 1990).

Table 5-6 presents detailed country-level data on the rate of growth of the total value of exports (in constant dollars) for four periods. Table 5-7 contains information on the evolution of the volume of exports throughout the period. Several facts emerge from these tables. First, while the growth in exports was rapid for the region as a whole, nontrivial variations occurred across countries; in some cases (such as Peru), the real value of exports declined. Second, the performance of exports (1982–87 and 1987–92) was not homogeneous. In the majority of the countries, exports performed significantly better during 1987–92 than in the previous five years, reflecting, among other things, the fact that it takes some time for exports to respond to greater incentives.

In Ecuador, the country whose trade reform has lagged the most, the volume of exports in recent years was below the 1970–80 historical average. In Bolivia and Chile, two of the early reformers, exports were very strong in 1987–91. The case of Chile is particularly interesting. Since most of its liberalization effort was undertaken prior to 1980, there are enough data points to allow a more detailed evaluation of export response to the new regime.

Table 5-6. Value of Exports of Goods and Nonfactor Services in Selected Countries of Latin America, 1970–93
(annual percentage rate of growth in constant prices)

Country	1970–80	1982–87	1987–92	1991–93[a]
Argentina	4.8	−0.1	6.6	1.8
Bolivia	0.6	0.6	8.1	−8.3
Brazil	9.9	9.7	5.5	7.5
Chile	10.2	6.5	10.9	3.9
Colombia	5.7	10.2	6.7	2.9
Costa Rica	5.9	5.7	10.9	12.2
Ecuador	14.0	3.3	9.1	2.6
Mexico	8.3	5.8	3.5	3.1
Paraguay	6.1	5.4	9.5	1.1
Peru	2.7	−4.5	0.8	1.6
Uruguay	7.2	4.2	7.1	−1.7
Venezuela	−7.3[b]	3.6	4.4	−7.0

a. Preliminary.
b. 1974–80.
Source: Data base of the International Economics Department, World Bank.

Table 5-7. Volume of Exports of Goods in Selected Countries of Latin America, Selected Years, 1970–93
(annual percentage rate of growth)

Country	1970–80	1982–87	1987–91	1991–93[a]
Argentina	2.1	0.8	12.8	−0.1
Bolivia	−1.7	−5.2	13.2	5.3
Brazil	8.2	8.0	1.5	11.2
Chile	7.4	7.6	7.4	10.5
Colombia	3.6	14.8	7.3	12.6
Costa Rica	3.8	6.2	7.5	15.4
Ecuador	14.6	6.8	8.2	6.7
Mexico	10.2	6.1	5.5	8.7
Paraguay	7.3	9.2	17.2	2.2
Peru	2.3	−4.0	1.3	5.2
Uruguay	5.4	−0.5	4.8	−0.6
Venezuela	−5.8	2.1	7.5	6.5

a. Preliminary.
Source: CEPAL, *Statistical Yearbook for Latin America and the Caribbean*, various years.

Between 1975 and 1980, when tariffs were reduced to a uniform 10 percent and nontariff barriers were completely eliminated, the behavior of Chilean exports was spectacular, growing (in volume) at an average of 12 percent a year—many times higher than the historical average in 1960–70 of only 2.6 percent a year. What is particularly impressive is that most of the surge in exports took place in the nontraditional sector (CEPAL 1992a).

Chile's success in the last few years was closely related to a boom in agriculture, forestry, and fishing exports. During the 1960–70 period, Chile was basically a net importer of agricultural goods. Today, agricultural, as well as forestry and fishing, exports are becoming increasingly important in the Chilean economy. In 1970, Chile exported $33 million in agricultural, forestry, and fishing products; by 1991, this figure had jumped to $1.2 billion! Notice that this excludes manufactured goods based on the elaboration of the agriculture sector. There is little doubt that economic policy lies behind the stellar behavior of the Chilean agriculture and export sectors in the last few years. First, the liberalization of international trade substantially lowered the costs of imported inputs and capital goods for agriculture, making the sector more competitive. In fact, the liberalization of international trade ended a long trend of discrimination against agriculture. This contrasts with Mexico, where agriculture has not yet benefited from the recent liberalization measures, including the reform of the old *ejido* system. Second, the exchange rate policy pursued aggressively in Chile after 1985 provided clear incentives for the expansion of exports. However, the current trend toward appreciation of the real exchange rate represents a cloud in the future of the sector. A third fundamental policy-based explanation of Chile's agricultural success has to do with the pursuit of a stable macroeconomic policy, which allowed entrepreneurs to have confidence in the system and to plan their activities over the longer run. Many export-oriented agricultural activities require sizable investments that are only undertaken in an environment of stability and policy continuity. And fourth, the strict respect for property rights, and the emergence of a stable and legal framework, also had significant, positive effects on the evolution of Chilean agricultural exports.

As tables 5-6 and 5-7 show, Mexico exhibited a slower rate of growth of total exports in the period after reform than during 1970–80. This, however, is largely an illusion, because during the 1970s Mexico's oil production increased very rapidly—at more than 18 percent a year. When nontraditional exports are considered, the performance after the reform is remarkable, with an annual average rate of growth for 1985–91 exceeding 25 percent (see table 5-8; a large percentage of this growth, however, was in the *maquiladora*, or in-bond sector).

After two successive years of decline, the volume of exports increased rapidly in Brazil during 1992 to 14.9 percent. Although it is too early to determine the exact forces behind this rapid growth, and whether it will be sustained, there is some indication that the highly depreciated real exchange rate and the reduction in the degree of protection increased the degree of international competitiveness of Brazil's exports (the reduction in internal demand could also have affected the recent rapid growth of exports). This interpretation is supported by Bonelli (1992), who finds that productivity growth in Brazil's manufacturing sector was positively affected by export orientation.

Table 5-8. Nontraditional Exports as a Percentage of All Exports in Selected Countries of Latin America, 1980–91

Country	1980	1982	1985	1987	1991
Argentina	0.27	0.31	0.28	0.31	0.35
Bolivia	0.15	0.09	0.05	0.19	0.30
Brazil[a]	0.57	0.59	0.66	0.69	0.71
Chile	0.38	0.22	0.35	0.39	0.36[b]
Colombia	0.41	0.42	0.41	0.55	0.64[c]
Costa Rica	0.36	0.38	0.37	0.42	0.50
Ecuador[d]	0.24	0.09	0.12	0.14	0.12
Mexico	0.13	0.20	0.18	0.38	0.50
Paraguay	0.58	0.71	0.82	0.68	0.69
Peru	0.21	0.23	0.24	0.27	0.28
Uruguay	0.61	0.58	0.66	0.67	0.71
Venezuela	0.04	0.07	0.09	0.13	0.17

a. Industrial products.
b. 1989 data; subsequent data are classified differently.
c. 1990 data.
d. Manufactured products.
Source: CEPAL, *Economic Survey of Latin America*, several years.

Table 5-9. Exports of Manufactured Goods as a Percentage of All Exports in Selected Countries of Latin America, 1970–91

Country	1970	1980	1982	1985	1987	1991
Argentina	0.14	0.23	0.24	0.21	0.31	0.28
Bolivia	0.03	0.02	0.03	0.01	0.03	0.05[a]
Brazil	0.15	0.37	0.38	0.44	0.50	0.55
Chile	0.04	0.09	0.07	0.11	0.09	0.11
Colombia	0.11	0.20	0.24	0.17	0.19	0.33
Costa Rica	0.19	0.28	0.25	0.22	0.24	0.25
Ecuador	0.02	0.03	0.03	0.01	0.02	0.02
Mexico	0.33	0.11	0.10	0.21	0.38	0.44[a]
Paraguay	0.08	0.04	0.09	0.06	0.10	0.11
Peru	0.01	0.17	0.16	0.13	0.17	0.19[a]
Uruguay	0.15	0.38	0.32	0.35	0.55	0.52
Venezuela	0.01	0.02	0.02	0.10	0.06	0.11[a]

a. 1990 data.

Source: CEPAL, *Statistical Yearbook for Latin America and the Caribbean*, several years.

A stated objective of trade reforms was to increase the degree of diversification of exports. In the period following the trade reforms, the importance of nontraditional exports, including manufacturing exports, increased steadily in the early reformers—Bolivia, Chile, and Mexico (see table 5-9). Also, in the majority of the countries, the share of the ten most important export goods in total exports declined significantly (CEPAL 1991).

Real Exchange Rate Behavior, Capital Inflows, and the Future of Trade Reforms in Latin America

After the mid-1980s, competitive real exchange rates played a key role in explaining the vigorous performance of most of Latin America's external sectors. In fact, it is not an exaggeration to say that the trade reforms were initially driven by highly competitive real exchange rates, making Latin American products very attractive in world markets. However, in most Latin American countries, real exchange rates experienced significant real appreciation and loss of competitiveness after 1992 (see figure 5-1; as in previous tables, an increase in the real exchange rate index captures a real exchange rate depreciation).

These real appreciations (and losses of international competitiveness) generated considerable concern among policymakers and political leaders. They were the result of two factors: first, many countries used exchange rate policy as an anti-inflationary tool, and, second, massive capital inflows into Latin America made foreign exchange too abundant (see Calvo, Leiderman, and Reinhart 1993).

Figure 5-1. Real Effective Exchange Rates in Selected Countries of Latin America, 1980–92
(1985=100)

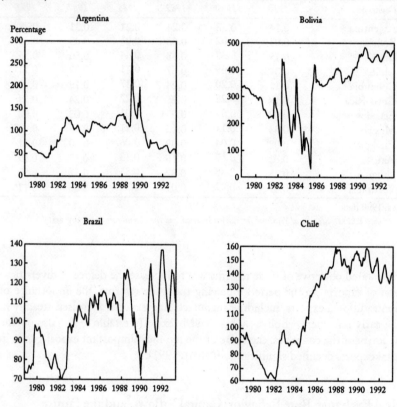

After eight years of negative resource transfers, there was a significant turn-around in capital inflows into Latin America in 1991–92 (see tables 5-10 and 5-11). The increased availability of foreign funds affected the real exchange rate through increased aggregate expenditures. A proportion of the newly available resources was spent on nontradables, including real estate, putting pressure on relative prices and on domestic inflation. An interesting feature of these capital movements is that a large proportion corresponded to portfolio investment and relatively little to direct foreign investment. As can be seen, Mexico was the most important recipient of foreign funds in the region in the last years. Indeed, the very large available foreign financing allowed Mexico to have a current account deficit on the order of 7 to 8 percent of GDP. As is argued in chapter 9, these very large (and unsustainable) current account deficits were at the heart of the Mexican peso crisis of December 1994. During

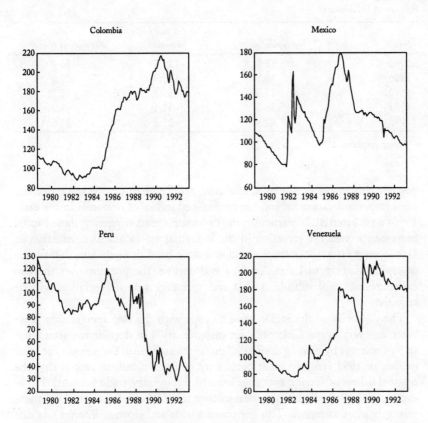

Source: IMF, *International Financial Statistics*, various years.

that year, a combination of factors—both political and exogenous—resulted in a sudden drying up of capital inflows to Mexico and in a large loss of international reserves. The abruptness of these developments did not allow the Mexican economy to adjust gradually to the new circumstances.

Real exchange rate appreciations generated by increased inflows of capital are not a completely new phenomenon in Latin America. In the late 1970s, most countries, but especially the Southern Cone nations, were flooded with foreign resources, which led to large real appreciations. Because this previous episode ended in the debt crisis, concern about the possible negative effects of these capital flows was high among some analysts from early on (see, for example, Edwards 1994b).

Whether capital movements are temporary—and thus subject to sudden reversals, as occurred in 1982—is particularly important in evaluating their

Table 5-10. Capital Inflows and Net Resource Transfers in Latin America,
1981–92
(billions of U.S. dollars)

Period	Net capital inflows	Interest and profit income	Net resource transfers
1982–85	55.3	−111.7	−56.4
1986–89	33.5	−138.7	−105.2
1990	17.0	−35.7	−18.7
1991	36.3	−31.1	5.2
1992	42.8	−21.2	21.6

Source: Jaspersen 1992.

possible consequences. Calvo, Leiderman, and Reinhart (1993) argue that the most important causes behind the generalized inflow of resources in the early 1990s were external. In particular, the two main events triggering these capital movements were the recession in the industrial world and the reduction in U.S. interest rates. Once these world economic conditions change, the volume of capital flowing to Latin America will decline, the pressure over the real exchange rate will subside, and a real exchange rate depreciation will be required.

The countries in the region tried to cope with the real appreciation pressures in several ways. Colombia, for instance, tried to sterilize the accumulation of reserves by placing domestic bonds—the so-called OMAs—on the local market in 1991 (an important peculiarity of the Colombian case is that the original inflow of foreign exchange entered through the trade account). However, to place these bonds, the local interest rate had to increase, making them relatively more attractive. This generated a wide and growing interest rate differential that favored Colombia, which attracted new capital flows that, in order to be sterilized, required new bond placements. This process generated a vicious cycle that contributed to a very large accumulation of domestic debt, without significantly affecting the real exchange rate. This experience shows vividly the difficulties facing authorities attempting to handle movements in the real exchange rate. In particular, real shocks, such as an increase in inflows of foreign capital, cannot be tackled successfully using monetary policy instruments.

Argentina tried to deal with the real appreciation by engineering a pseudo devaluation through a simultaneous increase in import tariffs and export subsidies. Although it is too early to know how this measure will affect the degree of competitiveness in the country, preliminary computations suggest that the magnitude of the adjustment obtained via a tariffs-cum-subsidies package may be rather small. Mexico followed a different route and decided to implement an exchange rate system based on a widening band. As part of this strategy, in October 1992, the pace of the daily adjustment in the nominal exchange rate was doubled to 40 cents. However, as the peso crisis of December 1994 showed, this measure was clearly not enough (see chapter 9 for a detailed discussion).

Chile tackled the real appreciation by implementing a broad set of measures, including conducting exchange rate policy relative to a three-currency basket, imposing reserve requirements on capital inflows, allowing the nominal exchange rate to appreciate somewhat, and undertaking significant sterilization operations. In spite of this multi-front approach, Chile did not avoid real exchange rate pressures. Between December 1991 and December 1992, the Chilean bilateral real exchange rate appreciated approximately 10 percent. This magnitude of appreciation was significantly smaller than that observed in other countries—Argentina and Mexico, for example. As a result, exporters and agricultural producers mounted increasing pressure on the government for special treatment, arguing that an implicit contract had been broken by allowing the real exchange rate to appreciate. This type of political reaction is, in fact, becoming more and more common throughout the region, adding a difficult social dimension to the issue of real exchange rates.

Although there is no easy way to handle the pressures of real appreciation, at least two avenues are possible. First, in countries where the dominant force behind movements of the real exchange rate is price inertia in the presence of nominal exchange rate anchor policies, the adoption of a more flexible nominal exchange rate system usually helps. This means that, to some extent, the inflationary targets have to be less ambitious because a periodic adjustment of the exchange rate results in some inflation (more specifically, with this option the one-digit inflationary goal has to be postponed). However, to the extent that this policy is supplemented by tight overall fiscal policy, there should be no concern regarding inflationary explosions.

Second, the discrimination between short-term (speculative) capital and longer-term capital should go a long way toward resolving the preoccupation

Table 5-11. *Net Capital Inflows as a Percentage of GDP in Selected Countries of Latin America, 1982–92*

Country	1982	1983	1984	1985	1986	1987	1988	1989	1990	1991	1992[a]
Argentina	2.5	0.4	2.3	2.8	1.6	2.2	2.8	0.3	0.5	3.0	5.7
Brazil	4.1	2.7	2.4	0.1	0.7	1.5	−0.5	0.3	1.1	0.2	—
Chile	4.2	2.6	10.5	8.6	4.3	5.4	5.0	5.5	11.7	3.0	7.8
Colombia	5.7	3.7	2.5	6.4	3.3	0.0	2.4	1.2	0.0	−1.9	—
Mexico	5.5	−1.6	−0.6	−1.1	0.9	−0.7	−0.8	0.7	3.5	7.1	8.7
Peru	7.8	3.8	5.3	2.4	3.6	3.7	5.4	2.9	3.6	2.2	3.4
Venezuela	−1.9	−4.7	−3.4	−1.7	−1.8	1.1	−1.7	−7.9	−7.4	3.7	5.8

— Not available.
a. Preliminary.
Sources: For GDP, data base of the World Bank, International Economics Department; for capital inflows, data base of the IMF on balance of payments.

with the effects of capital movements on real exchange rates. To the extent that short-term capital flows are more volatile, and thus capital inflows are genuinely long term, especially if they finance investment projects in the tradables sector, the change in the real exchange rate will generally be smaller and will be a true equilibrium phenomenon. In practice, however, discriminating between permanent and transitory capital inflows is difficult; in the end, policymakers are forced to make a judgment call.

Regional Trading Blocs in Latin America

There is little doubt that, as we approach the twenty-first century, the world economy is moving toward the formation of a small number of trading blocs. Although the European Economic Community and NAFTA are the best known cases, several other trading blocs, with different degrees of cohesion, are rapidly emerging. Among these, the Association of Southeast Asian Nations (ASEAN), with its dynamic and aggressive members, is especially promising. This is particularly so if the often-feared formation of a Yen Zone in the Pacific, including Japan and the ASEAN countries, takes shape in the next few years (see Schott 1991 for a general discussion of the recent formation and prospects of trading blocks in the world economy).

In the last few years, however, some new important trading blocs have emerged in the Western Hemisphere and are attracting the attention of policy analysts. Among these, the Mercado Común del Sur (MERCOSUR) and the Andean Pact, which jointly group nine Latin American countries, are two of the most important and have a volume of international trade that is expected to approach $250 billion a year by 2000 (MERCOSUR groups Argentina, Brazil, Paraguay, and Uruguay; the Andean Pact groups Bolivia, Colombia, Ecuador, Peru, and Venezuela). What makes the new integrationist effort in Latin America particularly interesting is that it takes place within a context that strongly favors export expansion and the growth of international trade throughout most of the developing world.

In addition to the somewhat large multimember trade agreements, there is a proliferation of recent bilateral integration agreements (see table 5-12 for a brief summary of trade agreements negotiated after 1990). The majority of the Latin American countries have expressed keen interest in joining NAFTA and see the bilateral—or small multilateral, for that matter—agreements as an intermediate step. Table 5-13 contains data on the evolution of intraregional trade and table 5-14 on bilateral trade for selected countries. Several important facts emerge from these tables. First, after reaching a low in 1985, intraregional trade expanded greatly in the late 1980s and early 1990s. Contrary to popular belief, intraregional trade as a proportion of total trade is still significantly below its 1975–80 level. Naturally, this means that there is significant room for expansion. In this context, intraregional trade in East Asia borders

(Text continues on page 149.)

Table 5–12. Regional Integration Agreements in the Americas after 1990

Agreement, date, and membership	Objective	Current status	Status/comment
Andean Trade Preference Act, 1991 Bolivia Colombia Ecuador Peru United States	Duty-free status for $324 million in imports from Andean countries to the United States	Operational	
Chile–Colombia Free Trade Agreement, 1993	Establishment of a free trade area	Operational as of January 1994	
Chile–Mexico Free Trade Agreement, 1991	Establishment of a free trade area by January 1996	Present maximum reciprocal tariff of 7.5 percent	Aggregate GDP, $241.2 billion; population, 94.9 million; intraregional trade, 0.1 percent of total foreign trade
Chile–Venezuela Free Trade Agreement, 1993	Establishment of a free trade area by 1999	Maximum tariff to imports from Chile to be 20 percent in 1994; Chile's tariff rate remains at 11 percent; tariffs scheduled to reach 0 percent in 1999	Aggregate GDP, $76.7 billion; population, 32.5 million; total foreign trade, $38.9 billion; intraregional trade, 1.4 percent of total foreign trade
Colombia–Venezuela Free Trade Agreement, 1992	Establishment of a free trade area by 1992	Common tariff agreed in 1992; conversations initiated with Mexico (Group of Three) to establish free trade area	Aggregate GDP, $91.3 billion; population, 52 million; total foreign trade, $34.7 billion; intraregional trade, 1.4 percent of total foreign trade

(Table continues on the following page.)

Table 5-12 (continued)

Agreement, date, and membership	Objective	Current status	Status/comment
El Salvador–Guatemala Free Trade Agreement, 1991	Establishment of a free trade area	Entered into operation in October 1991	
North American Free Trade Agreement, 1992 Canada Mexico United States	Establishment of a free trade area by 2009; elimination of tariffs in five, ten, or fifteen years, depending on the product; exceptions to Canadian agricultural and Mexican petroleum products; contains precedent-setting rights and obligations regarding intellectual property rights, services, trade, and investment; U.S.-Canada dispute settlement system extended to Mexico	Agreement signed and ratified; in phase as of January 1, 1994	Aggregate GDP, $6,204.6 billion; population, 362.7 million; total foreign trade, $1,223.8 billion; intraregional trade, 18.8 percent of total foreign trade
Group of Three: Colombia–Mexico–Venezuela Free Trade Agreement, 1993	Economic cooperation; in April 1993, the three countries agreed to establish a free trade area by 1994	Energy sector agreements signed; negotiations under way; draft accord of November 1993 provides for an immediate 0 tariff for some items and a ten-year transition for others, except in automobiles and agricultural goods; Mexico will cut tariffs faster than Colombia and Venezuela; signing date of January 1994 postponed because of Chiapas rebellion; agreement ratified by new Venezuelan authorities in February 1994	Aggregate GDP, $305.8 billion; population, 138.2 million; total foreign trade, $94.4 billion; intraregional trade, 0.8 percent of total foreign trade

Costa Rica–Mexico Free Trade Agreement, 1994	Establishment of a free trade area	Negotiations in progress; removal of all tariff and nontariff barriers between both countries; Mexican exports of goods that Costa Rica does not produce will enter duty-free beginning in 1995; tariffs on the remainder of Mexican exports to be reduced over five, ten, and fifteen years; most of Costa Rican exports will be allowed to enter Mexico duty-free in five years or less; rigid rule of origin requires goods to be made with inputs from the region	
Mexico–Central America Free Trade Agreement, 1992 Costa Rica El Salvador Guatemala Honduras Mexico Nicaragua	Establishment of a free trade area by December 1996	Safeguard regime, technical rules, and dispute-resolution agreements under negotiation; framework agreement for trade cooperation signed August 1992; Costa Rica engaged in bilateral negotiations with Mexico	Aggregate GDP, $240.3 billion; population, 112.4 million; total foreign trade, $72.4 billion; intraregional trade, 1.6 percent of total foreign trade
Venezuela–Central America Free Trade Agreement, 1992 Costa Rica El Salvador Guatemala Honduras Nicaragua Panama Venezuela	Provides for a nonreciprocal transition period in which unilateral tariff cuts will be made by Venezuela, with the eventual goal of a free trade agreement	Negotiations gained impetus after the Group of Three presidential summit in 1993 but have proceeded slowly since	

(Table continues on the following page.)

Table 5-12 (continued)

Agreement, date, and membership	Objective	Current status	Status/comment
Nueva Ocotepeque Agreement, 1992 El Salvador Guatemala Honduras	Establishment of a free trade area by 1993; long-run objective is to create a customs union; includes recent complementary agreements signed among these countries	Not clear	Aggregate GDP, $17.1 billion; population, 19.7 million; total foreign trade, $7.3 billion; intraregional trade, 11.8 percent of total foreign trade
MERCOSUR, 1991 Argentina Brazil Paraguay Uruguay	Establishment of a common market by January 1995; commercial liberalization program, macroeconomic policy coordination, common tariff, sectoral agreements	Present tariff preferences, 68 percent; dispute-resolution agreement signed; products gradually removed from national lists of exclusion; common external tariff negotiations hung up on differences over capital goods and electronics; process of liberalization well under way, but attaining a customs union by 1995 doubtful	Aggregate GDP, $492.3 billion; population, 190 million; total foreign trade, $76.3 billion; intraregional trade, 8.6 percent of total foreign trade
CARICOM–Colombia Free Trade Agreement, 1991 Antigua and Barbuda The Bahamas Barbados Belize Colombia Dominca Grenada Jamaica Montserrat St. Kitts and Nevis St. Lucia St. Vincent and the Grenadines Trinidad and Tobago	Provides for a nonreciprocal transition period in which unilateral tariff cuts will be made by Colombia, with the eventual goal of a free trade agreement	Negotiations are proceeding slowly due to CARICOM's demands for unilateral tariff reductions	

146

Agreement		
CARICOM–Venezuela Free Trade Agreement, 1993 Antigua and Barbuda The Bahamas Barbados Belize Dominica Grenada Jamaica Montserrat St. Kitts and Nevis St. Lucia St. Vincent and the Grenadines Trinidad and Tobago Venezuela	Provides for duty-free imports from CARICOM into Venezuela to be phased in over a five-year period; after five years, negotiations are to begin to eliminate tariffs on Venezuelan exports to signatory countries	Negotiations are proceeding slowly due to CARICOM's demands for unilateral tariff deductions
Colombia–Central America Free Trade Agreement, 1993 Colombia Costa Rica El Salvador Guatemala Honduras Nicaragua Panama Venezuela	Provides for a nonreciprocal transition period in which unilateral tariff cuts will be made by Colombia, with the eventual goal of a free trade agreement	Negotiations gained impetus after the Group of Three presidential summit of 1993 but have proceeded slowly since

Source: Lustig 1994; World Bank.

Table 5–13. *Intraregional Exports as a Percentage of Total Exports in Latin America and the Caribbean, 1970–93*

Country	1970	1975	1980	1981	1982	1983	1984	1985	1986	1987	1988	1989	1990	1991	1992	1993[a]
Argentina	21.1	25.9	23.8	19.7	20.4	14.1	18.5	18.7	23.9	21.6	20.5	25.9	26.3	30.3	34.1	37.3
Bolivia	9.7	35.9	36.7	42.6	51.6	55.0	52.8	60.2	64.5	57.8	47.7	44.0	45.6	51.2	40.7	44.6
Brazil	11.8	15.7	18.1	19.3	15.6	10.4	11.5	9.7	12.4	12.4	12.1	12.1	11.6	16.7	22.6	22.9
Chile	12.2	23.7	24.3	21.9	19.4	12.1	15.0	14.5	17.0	17.0	12.8	12.1	12.5	14.4	17.1	18.5
Colombia	10.5	21.7	17.6	23.7	21.7	14.0	13.5	14.0	11.4	17.3	16.0	16.0	16.9	24.1	23.0	24.8
Costa Rica	23.9	29.3	35.0	35.7	29.3	30.6	26.6	23.2	17.6	16.6	17.1	17.8	16.5	18.1	19.8	16.5
Mexico	9.8	14.3	6.9	9.8	8.8	7.5	6.4	5.4	6.7	7.8	7.5	7.1	6.6	4.3	4.8	4.9
Peru	6.5	16.7	21.2	12.8	15.4	10.4	11.9	14.1	14.5	16.1	14.5	15.3	15.4	16.1	18.1	21.7
Uruguay	12.8	29.3	37.3	26.6	30.8	23.7	26.2	27.8	39.2	30.3	27.4	36.8	39.0	40.4	41.9	45.7
Venezuela	33.5	33.2	37.4	36.6	21.4	20.9	19.2	18.3	20.0	23.9	21.6	21.5	22.8	20.1	27.2	30.3
All Latin America	17.6	21.0	22.2	21.1	17.5	14.0	13.7	12.6	14.1	14.9	14.3	15.4	16.0	16.1	18.6	19.0

a. Through October.
Source: IMF, *Direction of Trade Statistics.*

148

on 30 percent of total trade. In a recent study, Losada (1993) finds that, with reduced trade impediments, distance is the main determinant of bilateral trade, which suggests that in a context of generalized liberalization, investment projects, especially in infrastructure, aimed at facilitating intraregional trade will have a particularly high (social) rate of return.

An interesting development during the early 1990s is that intraregional direct foreign investment—that is, investment going from one country to another country within the region—greatly increased (see table 5-15). This suggests that privatization generated forces toward a market-driven integration going well beyond what planners envisaged during the 1960s.

MERCOSUR

MERCOSUR is a trade agreement signed by Argentina, Brazil, Paraguay, and Uruguay in 1991.[17] Its main goal is to eliminate all tariffs for intraregional trade by December 1994 and to establish a common external tariff that would guide international trade between the member countries and the rest of the world. What is particularly interesting about MERCOSUR is that it groups the two largest countries in South America—Argentina and Brazil—with two of the smallest (Chile, which was invited to join but declined, is moving briskly toward integration with Argentina through the signature of bilateral agreements). The data contained in table 5-16 clearly highlight some of the differences among these countries, including size, recent performance, and extent of international indebtedness. There is little doubt that the future of MERCOSUR will depend on the policies of Argentina and Brazil; Uruguay and Paraguay, as (much) smaller members, are likely to play a limited role in the political-diplomatic process that will determine the actual characteristics of the agreement. The big question is whether Brazil will be able to maintain its stabilization program on course and thereby reduce inflation to international levels in the near future. (Baldinelli 1991 discusses some of the most important macroeconomic policies in the MERCOSUR countries.)

The differences in strategy regarding the speed and depth of privatization and trade reform suggest that disagreements could easily erupt between Argentina and Brazil with regard to points closely related to MERCOSUR. In particular, many observers in Argentina are concerned that Brazil will insist on a relatively high common external tariff. The current structure of protection in the individual members of MERCOSUR shows that there may indeed be some room for disagreement. While Argentina recently embraced a significant free trade stance—slashing tariffs, considerably reducing nontariff barriers, and completely eliminating export taxes—Brazil is aiming at a higher and more variable tariff structure.

Table 5-17 contains data from 1992 on the level of intraregional trade for the MERCOSUR members. As can be seen, intraregional trade is more important for Argentina (with 17 percent) than for Brazil (11 percent; historically,

Table 5-14. *Intraregional Exports (Freight-on–Board Value) as a Percentage of Total Exports, 1980–93*

Exporting and importing area or country	1980	1981	1982	1983	1984	1985	1986	1987	1988	1989	1990	1991	1992	1993[a]
From Argentina to														
Brazil	9.5	6.5	7.4	4.6	5.9	5.9	10.2	8.5	6.7	11.8	11.5	12.4	13.7	30.4
Chile	2.7	2.1	2.2	2.4	1.8	1.3	2.0	2.3	2.8	3.7	3.7	4.1	4.7	6.7
Colombia	0.5	0.6	0.9	0.8	0.7	1.6	0.9	1.0	0.9	0.8	0.6	0.7	0.9	1.0
Peru	1.5	1.0	1.4	1.2	1.6	1.9	2.8	2.2	1.9	1.7	1.5	1.7	1.9	2.2
Venezuela	0.8	1.1	1.3	0.7	1.4	0.9	0.7	0.9	1.4	1.0	1.2	1.7	1.7	1.8
From Brazil to														
Argentina	5.4	3.8	3.2	3.0	3.2	2.1	3.0	3.2	2.9	2.2	2.1	4.7	8.5	9.2
Chile	2.2	2.7	1.4	1.0	1.0	0.9	1.1	1.4	1.6	2.1	1.5	2.1	2.6	2.8
Colombia	0.7	0.9	1.3	0.7	0.6	0.4	0.5	0.5	0.7	0.6	0.5	0.5	1.0	1.0
Peru	0.6	1.2	1.1	0.3	0.5	0.4	0.7	0.8	0.6	0.4	0.5	0.7	0.6	0.6
Venezuela	1.1	1.8	2.3	1.2	1.4	1.2	1.6	1.4	1.5	0.8	0.9	1.4	1.2	1.2
From Chile to														
Argentina	6.0	4.8	4.1	3.1	3.2	2.2	3.8	3.4	2.3	1.3	1.3	2.9	4.6	5.1
Brazil	9.6	7.3	8.3	4.3	6.2	5.4	6.9	6.8	4.7	6.4	5.7	5.0	4.5	5.2
Colombia	1.6	1.8	1.2	1.1	1.2	1.4	1.0	1.0	0.8	1.0	0.9	0.6	0.7	0.9
Peru	1.5	1.8	1.3	1.0	1.2	1.2	1.6	1.7	0.9	0.7	0.9	1.6	1.7	1.5
Venezuela	1.7	1.8	1.2	0.8	1.1	0.9	1.0	1.4	1.5	0.4	0.4	0.6	0.7	0.8
From Colombia to														
Argentina	1.7	1.7	1.2	1.4	1.7	1.0	1.3	0.8	1.0	0.6	0.4	0.5	1.0	1.3
Brazil	0.2	0.2	0.1	0.2	0.4	0.2	0.2	0.4	0.2	0.4	0.4	0.7	0.9	2.0

Chile	1.6	1.0	0.4	0.4	0.5	0.6	0.6	2.0	2.4	2.3	2.4	2.2	1.3	1.3
Peru	0.7	1.5	1.1	0.6	0.7	0.9	1.4	2.4	1.7	1.1	1.3	2.9	4.2	4.6
Venezuela	7.1	11.5	11.8	3.8	2.8	3.6	2.9	4.4	4.4	3.2	3.0	5.9	6.8	7.3
From Peru to														
Argentina	1.5	0.6	0.8	1.2	1.1	1.2	2.3	1.5	0.6	0.5	0.9	0.9	0.8	1.0
Brazil	3.2	1.5	2.2	2.0	1.5	1.8	2.9	4.2	3.0	4.5	3.9	3.1	4.7	0.0
Chile	1.2	1.8	1.2	1.5	1.6	1.7	2.0	1.2	1.5	1.9	1.7	1.3	1.2	1.2
Colombia	1.4	2.8	4.2	1.7	2.4	2.5	2.6	2.4	3.1	3.0	2.9	3.2	2.5	3.2
Venezuela	1.3	1.4	1.7	1.0	1.6	1.4	1.8	2.4	3.1	1.2	1.7	2.4	3.1	3.6
From Venezuela to														
Argentina	0.3	0.2	0.1	0.0	0.0	0.0	0.1	0.0	0.2	0.2	0.0	0.1	0.2	0.2
Brazil	3.5	4.7	5.3	3.7	3.2	1.8	0.8	1.4	1.5	2.0	1.9	1.8	2.8	2.9
Chile	1.3	1.7	1.4	1.4	1.4	1.7	1.4	1.3	1.4	1.2	1.0	0.8	0.8	0.3
Colombia	1.4	1.6	1.8	2.2	2.0	1.6	1.2	0.1	1.7	2.1	2.1	1.5	2.2	2.5
Peru	0.1	0.1	0.1	0.1	0.1	0.2	0.4	0.1	0.5	0.2	0.2	0.5	0.8	0.9
From the world to														
Argentina	0.6	0.5	0.3	0.3	0.3	0.2	0.3	0.3	0.2	0.2	0.1	0.3	0.4	0.4
Brazil	1.0	1.1	1.1	0.9	0.8	0.8	0.7	0.7	0.6	0.7	0.6	0.6	0.6	0.5
Chile	0.3	0.3	0.3	0.3	0.2	0.2	0.2	0.2	0.2	0.2	0.2	0.2	0.3	0.5
Colombia	0.3	0.3	0.3	0.3	0.2	0.1	0.2	0.2	0.2	0.2	0.2	0.1	0.2	0.2
Peru	0.2	0.2	0.2	0.1	0.1	0.1	0.1	0.1	0.1	0.1	0.1	0.1	0.1	0.1
Venezuela	0.6	0.6	0.7	0.3	0.4	0.4	0.4	0.4	0.4	0.2	0.2	0.3	0.3	0.2

a. Through October 1993 except for the case of exports from Argentina to Brazil, which corresponds to May 1993.
Source: IMF, *Direction of Trade Statistics.*

Table 5-15. Amount and Percentage of Direct Foreign Investment Coming from within Latin America, 1987 and 1992

Country	1987[a]		1992[b]	
	Amount (millions of dollars)	Percentage of total	Amount (millions of dollars)	Percentage of total
Argentina	21.07	28.0	99.00	32.6
Bolivia	0.01	1.1	31.89	31.6
Brazil	< 0.00	< 0.0	84.78	7.9
Chile	30.82	5.7	73.71	7.5
Colombia	< 0.00	< 0.0	58.65	27.2
Ecuador	17.70	30.1	4.70	38.2
Paraguay	0.05	5.1	50.30	43.0
Peru	17.85	65.3	46.91	29.0
Uruguay	15.51	56.4	3.24	59.3
Venezuela	22.49	4.7	94.39	40.8

a. Argentina, 1986; Paraguay, 1984.
b. Argentina, 1989; Bolivia, 1990; Brazil, Ecuador, and Venezuela, 1991.
Source: CEPAL 1993.

Brazil's intraregional trade was significantly lower, on the order of 4 percent of total exports). It is, in fact, Argentina that is bound to lose more if MERCOSUR is aborted. From a political economy perspective, this means that in negotiations regarding policies toward third parties, Brazil may have an important edge. If this is the case, and MERCOSUR is implemented around high import tariffs—with a range of 0 to 40 percent, which corresponds to the Brazilian liberalization target—it is very unlikely that its members will experience a net gain over the long run. More specifically, if Argentina were to join a trade agreement with a Brazilian-level common external tariff, the result would probably be a diversion of trade that would more than offset any benefits derived from the creation of trade.[18]

Table 5-18 presents the path that the elimination of tariffs is expected to take within MERCOSUR. Two main differences with respect to previous attempts at integration immediately stand out (on historical integrationist attempts in Latin America, see Edwards and Savastano 1988). First, there is a very high degree of automaticity in the integration process within MERCOSUR, and, second, the time frame allowed for integration is significantly shorter than those attempted previously. These features of the Asunción Treaty are a clear reflection that, even in an agreement dominated by a reluctant reformer such as Brazil, the rules governing opening up are aggressive and dynamic. An important, and as yet unresolved, question, however, is whether this ambitious, automatic intraregional liberalization program can be sustained in the presence of major macroeconomic imbalances in Brazil.

Table 5-16. *Economic Indicators for Members of MERCOSUR and the Andean Pact, 1992*

Indicator	MERCOSUR				Andean Pact				
	Argentina	*Brazil*	*Paraguay*	*Uruguay*	*Bolivia*	*Colombia*	*Ecuador*	*Peru*	*Venezuela*
GDP, 1992 (millions of U.S. dollars)	154,400	406,500	6,500	11,400	5,300	46,200	12,400	26,300	61,100
GNP per capita, 1992 (U.S. dollars)[a]	4,160	2,940[b]	1,410	2,840	680	1,300	1,060	1,080	2,920
GDP growth, 1980–92 (annual average, percent)	0.6	1.2	2.7	0.7	0.7	3.4	2.4	-0.7	2.1
Share of manufacturing in GDP, 1992 (percent)	22	22[b]	17	25	16[b]	20[b]	21[b]	—	16
Investment ratio, 1992 (percent)	17	19	24	13	16	18	20	16[b]	23
Merchandise exports, 1992 (millions of U.S. dollars)	12,000	36,200	920	1,700	600	7,300	3,000	3,500	14,000
Growth of exports, 1980–92[c] (annual average, percent)	3.5	7.1	7.2	4.2	3.4	5.7	5.0	-0.9[b]	2.0
Total external debt, 1992 (millions of U.S. dollars)	66,500	118,700	1,800	5,200	4,200	16,700	12,300	21,000	33,700
Inflation, 1980–92[d] (annual average, percent)	341	373	23	63	170	25	38	287	22

— Not available.

Note: All 1992 data are preliminary estimates.

a. Calculated according to the method of the *World Bank Atlas*.

b. 1991 data.

c. Exports of goods and nonfactor services, in constant prices.

d. Growth in GDP deflator, compound rate.

Sources: World Bank, *World Development Report 1993*, "World Development Indicators"; data base of the International Economics Department and country department staff estimates.

Table 5-17. Trade among Members of MERCOSUR, 1992

Country	Percentage of total exports	Amount (millions of U.S. dollars)
Argentina	17	2,100
Brazil	11	4,100
Paraguay	37	220
Uruguay	34	540

Source: Data base of the IMF, Direction of Trade Statistics.

Revival of the Andean Pact

In November 1990, more than two decades after its initial launching, the Andean Pact was renewed by the presidents of Bolivia, Colombia, Ecuador, Peru, and Venezuela (Chile, an original signatory of the pact, declined to participate). The new agreement, which came to be known as the Acta de la Paz, established a number of ambitious targets, including (1) the implementation of a regional free trade zone by 1992, (2) an agreement on the level and structure of the common external tariff by December 1991, (3) the implementation of the common external tariff by December 1995, (4) the liberalization of maritime and air transportation, and (5) the facilitation of foreign investment and capital mobility within the Andean group (Nogués and Quintanilla 1992 provide a detailed account of the Acta de la Paz).

Table 5-18. Percentage of Imports Subject to Free Trade in MERCOSUR, 1991–94

Date	Percentage
1991	
June	47
December	54
1992	
June	61
December	68
1993	
June	75
December	82
1994	
June	89
December	100

Source: Asunción Treaty.

There is great heterogeneity among the countries in the pact (table 5-16). These differences refer both to economic structure as well as to macroeconomic policy. For instance, while Bolivia is moving steadily toward low inflation and price stability, Venezuela is facing a new macroeconomic and political crisis. Despite large increases during 1992 and 1993, the volume of intraregional trade remains somewhat limited (see table 5-19). This reflects both the similarity of factor endowments across these countries and the existence of significant impediments related both to administrative and commercial regulations as well as to an extremely poor system of land transportation. The relatively low level of current intraregional trade suggests, in fact, the possibility of a significant diversion of trade once the customs union is launched. Whether this actually happens will depend largely on the level and structure of the common external tariff. This, in fact, is a highly controversial issue that is threatening the future of the pact.

As the discussion of the extent of the reforms showed, the Andean Pact nations have a significantly more homogeneous structure of protection than the MERCOSUR countries. In spite of this, there are still some important differences regarding the objectives of overall trade policy. While Bolivia and Peru pursued aggressive free trade reforms, Colombia and Venezuela maintained a more protectionist stance, arguing that higher tariffs are still necessary to encourage the formation of a strong industrial base. More recently, however, the Colombian government has been more inclined to accelerate its opening up and its integration with the rest of the world. The differences regarding commercial policies have already generated serious friction among the Acta de la Paz signatories, with Peru threatening to abandon the pact altogether if the common external tax is set at an "excessively protectionist" rate (the new political development in Peru, and especially the Fujimori "coup," added some uncertainty to the integrationist process).

In December 1991, and in accordance with the Acta de la Paz, a new agreement was signed by the Andean group's political authorities. The Act of Barahona established free trade zones among Bolivia, Colombia, and Venezuela starting on January 1, 1992. Ecuador and Peru were expected to join the free trade zone later. With respect to the common external tariff, the Act of Bara-

Table 5-19. Trade among Andean Pact Countries, 1992

Country	Percentage of all exports	Amount (millions of U.S. dollars)
Bolivia	13	90
Colombia	13	920
Ecuador	3	90
Peru	8	270
Venezuela	3	510

Source: Data base of the IMF, Direction of Trade Statistics.

hona established an extremely cumbersome mechanism, with exceptions across both countries and goods. More specifically, the common external tariff had four levels (0, 5, 10, and 15 percent), except for Bolivia, which only had levels of 5 and 10 percent. There were also exceptions for agricultural goods, automobiles, and noncompeting regional products; their tariff levels are still to be determined. From the beginning, this agreement on common external tariff had a serious problem, including the fact that rules of origin were not determined. For all practical purposes, the lowest tariffs (those of Bolivia) could become the effective common external tariff for the region as a whole.

In May 1992, only a few months after the common external tariff agreement, the future of the Andean Pact suffered a blow when Peru unilaterally suspended the preferential treatment granted to imports from within the pact. This action was part of a general Peruvian policy aimed at imposing a lower common external tariff. As a consequence, the governments of Colombia and Venezuela suspended negotiations with Peru. It is too early to say whether the Andean integrationist movement will continue to move forward or whether it will result in its (second) death. In fact, the border conflict between Peru and Ecuador has greatly increased the level of political-diplomatic tension in the region.

Revitalization of the Central American Common Market and Strengthening of the CARICOM

During the early and mid-1980s, and largely as a result of the international debt crisis, the Central American Common Market (CACM) began to break down. Most countries in the area responded to the debt crisis by imposing massive nontariff barriers, including multiple exchange rates. The most important consequence of this increase in protectionism was that the CACM's common external tariff ceased to be relevant as, de facto, members had different implicit tariffs for imports coming from outside the region. In 1986, the CACM received a fatal blow when the Central American payments clearing mechanism collapsed (partially as a result of Nicaragua's accumulation of very large debt; see Saborio and Michalopoulos 1992).

In July 1991, after several years of independently undertaking trade adjustment, the presidents of the Central American nations agreed to revitalize the CACM (the details of the agreement appear in the *Declaration of San Salvador,* July 17, 1991). Three important features of the renewed CACM are worth noting: first, the agreed common external tariff contemplated a range between 5 and 20 percent. This was significantly lower than the tariff structure of most Central American countries until recently and represented a clear move toward trade liberalization (see table 5-20). Second, the newly revitalized CACM included two new countries: Panama, which never joined the original agreement, and Honduras which withdrew from it in 1969. And, third, members of the CACM actively used export-promotion schemes to diversify and increase exports. Although it is still too early to know how successful these schemes are, Saborio and Michalopoulos (1992) suggest that they are costly from a fiscal perspective, without expanding exports significantly over and above what could be obtained through more competitive real exchange rates. The renewed CACM is a far cry from the agreement originally enacted in the 1960s. Instead of promoting an inefficient and forced process of industrialization behind protective walls, the countries in the region are uniting forces as a way to compete internationally and expand exports rapidly.

The attempts at commercial integration among the very small and extremely open Caribbean economies date back to the mid-1960s. In 1965, Antigua, Barbados, and Guyana subscribed to the articles of a Caribbean Free Trade Association (CARIFTA). Three years later, in May 1968, eight other Caribbean countries (Dominica, Grenada, Jamaica, Montserrat, St. Kitts-Nevis-Anguilla, St. Lucia, St. Vincent and the Grenadines, and Trinidad and Tobago) ratified this agreement; the remaining Caribbean nation, Belize, joined the association in 1971 (this paragraph and the two that follow draw on Edwards and Savastano 1988).

The CARIFTA agreement immediately freed most of the trade among its member countries from import and export duties and from nontariff barriers. A five-year schedule for eliminating intraregional tariffs was designed for the few import-substituting products exempted from the regulation. However, the agreement did not consider any measure related to the imposition of a common external tariff. Intraregional trade increased significantly after the establishment of CARIFTA; between 1967 and 1973, the share of intraregional trade rose from approximately 8 to 11 percent.

The gains from this integration, however, were strongly biased in favor of the more industrial countries of the agreement, which accounted for more than 90 percent of intraregional trade. Given this asymmetry in the distribution of benefits, the less industrial countries exerted pressure for broadening the scope of integration. In particular, they sought to establish mechanisms

Table 5-20. *Tariff Structures in the Central American Common Market*
(percentage)

Country	Pre-reform average tariffs[a]	Average legal tariff, 1987	1991 range	1993 range	1995 range
Costa Rica	52	26	10–50	5–30	5–20
El Salvador	48	23	5–35	5–25	5–20
Guatemala	50	25	5–37	5–20	5–20
Honduras	41	20	4–35	5–20	5–20
Nicaragua	54	21	5–20	5–20	5–20

a. Ad valorem equivalent of average external tariff.
Source: Saborio and Michalopoulos 1992.

that would imply a more favorable treatment for them within the agreement. As a result, CARICOM was established in August 1973. Its objectives went further than commercial integration; they included harmonizing monetary and fiscal policies and creating planning agencies for agricultural and industrial development. Also, a common external tariff for imports from nonmember countries was established. Despite the almost immediate adoption of the common external tariff, the adverse external terms of trade caused by the oil shock of the 1970s prompted protectionist responses—in the form of restrictive import licensing—from Guyana and Jamaica. This action not only negatively affected the level of intraregional trade—the share in total trade dropped to 8 percent in 1975 and 7 percent in 1976—but also provoked antagonism and retaliatory responses from the other members of CARICOM. Although conciliatory measures were subsequently attempted, the share of intraregional trade remained around 7 percent, and the trade flows continued to be heavily concentrated among the four more industrial countries of the region.

In February 1991, the CARICOM heads of state decided to revive the association and to rationalize the trade regime. The most important step was to reduce the common external tariff band from 0–70 percent to 0–45 percent. In October 1992, a further step was taken when the common external tariff was reduced to a 5–20 percent range within a period of four to five years. Although the pace of reform was somewhat slower than that followed by some other recent reformers, this measure clearly put the CARICOM nations on the path of liberalization and outward orientation.

The North American Free Trade Agreement

As in most of Latin America, Mexico's trade policy was characterized for decades by a significant degree of protectionism and inward orientation. Starting in late 1985 and as a component of a major structural adjustment plan, Mexico embarked on an ambitious unilateral program of trade liberalization. Import tariffs were halved, and import licenses were reduced from 92 to 20 percent.

After almost a decade of intensive, and often confrontational, trade negotiations, the United States and Mexico agreed in November 1990 to move toward a free trade agreement. In February 1991, Canada, Mexico, and the United States began negotiating the North American Free Trade Agreement, and later that year the U.S. Congress approved the fast-track treatment of the agreement. On August 12, 1992, the three parties announced that a consensus had been reached on the exact nature of the proposed agreement.

Both the United States and Mexican negotiators had originally expected that the U.S. government would submit the agreement to Congress in the summer of 1992. However, U.S. presidential politics, plus deep disagreements regarding details of the agreement, delayed its submission until late 1993. The most important areas of contention between U.S. and Mexican negotiators referred to (1) defining the rules of origin for specific products, (2) establishing the rules for agricultural trade, (3) determining the treatment that would be given to automobiles, (4) workers' protection in Mexico, and (5) environmental rules in Mexico, especially on the border. Of these, perhaps the most important problem was defining rules of origin. After a grueling debate, and the hasty implementation of a number of side agreements, the U.S. Congress finally passed NAFTA in November 1993. The agreement established very different speeds of liberalization for different sectors. For example, according to the final text, in order for motor vehicles to be subject to free trade within NAFTA, their regional value added should initially be at least 50 percent. This figure, however, will increase slowly for a period of eight years, until it reaches 62.5 percent. Regarding the agriculture sector, the agreement proposes, for most items, the slow elimination of tariffs over a period of fifteen years.

Various authors predict that NAFTA will have a severely negative effect on Mexico's agricultural sector (ITAM 1994). In fact, the January 1994 uprising in Chiapas by the Zapatista Mayan Indians was, at least in part, the result of the perception that NAFTA would destroy traditional agriculture in that state. A recent study by Velez and Rubio (1994) indicates that production of most grains in Mexico—sorghum, wheat, barley, soy beans, beans, and maize—will suffer considerably by implementation of the free trade agreement. Grain production in Mexico is extremely inefficient and subject to a high degree of protection. To avoid the devastating impact that free trade could have on Mexican agriculture, NAFTA considered the implementation of high initial tariffs at a level that would replicate the protection granted by traditional licenses. These duties will be phased out gradually through time. For instance, NAFTA established an initial import tariff on barley of 128 percent, which will be eliminated gradually in ten years. Maize is, perhaps, the most dramatic case of inefficient production. Mexico's average yields are approximately 1.7 tons per hectare, barely one-fourth of average yields in the United States. NAFTA established a tariff quota for maize imports into Mexico. Initially, Mexico will be able to import 2.5 million tons of maize duty-free. During the first year of NAFTA, imports above that level will be subject to a 215 percent tariff, but it will be completely liberalized in fifteen years.

As Nogués and Quintanilla (1992) argue, the heavy media coverage received by NAFTA negotiations tended to overshadow the broader commitment made by the Mexican government toward freer trade. In fact, after becoming a member of the General Agreement on Tariffs and Trade (GATT) in 1986, Mexico consistently and systematically pursued freer trade policies. This was reflected in the reduction in trade impediments, in the signing of bilateral trade agreements with Chile (1991), and in the discussions to sign free trade agreements with Venezuela (1993), Colombia, and Central America. The recent negotiations to become a member of the Organization for Economic Cooperation and Development also underlie the importance of freer trade as a fundamental component of the national development strategy for the next decade. However, for this policy position to be translated into additional gains in productivity and welfare, it will be necessary to reduce tariffs and license coverage even further and to extend the reforms to all areas of the economy, especially agriculture.

The GATT and the Prospects for Global Trade Liberalization

There is little doubt that Latin America has embarked on one of the most substantial unilateral trade liberalization reforms in modern economic history. However, a serious concern among the region's political leaders is the lack of reciprocity from the industrial countries. While the Latin American nations greatly opened up their trade sector to foreign competition, most industrial nations continued to follow protectionist practices. In fact, as captured in table 5-21, the industrial countries traditionally imposed significant restrictions on Latin American exports. These trade impediments mostly took the form of nontariff barriers, including quotas, prohibitions, and licenses. The approval of the GATT's Uruguay Round package in December 1993 provides some hope that in the years to come multilateralism will produce a more-open system of world trade (see table 5-22 for a summary of the Uruguay Round's most important implications for Latin America).

Before 1947, when the first round of multilateral trade negotiations was held in Geneva, average tariff protection in industrial countries was above 100 percent (this discussion is based on Losada 1994). Fueled by the Smoot-Hawley Tariff Act of 1930, protectionist ideas grew during the 1930s, 1940s, and 1950s. After seven rounds of GATT-sponsored negotiations, average tariff protection had been reduced to 5 percent by 1993; however, most industrial countries continued to use an extensive array of nontariff barriers that effectively raised the degree of protection. By 1993, imports from developing countries into some industrial countries were, for all practical purposes, prohibited.

The liberalization of world trade contemplated in the Uruguay Round will be implemented gradually throughout a period of ten years. From an institutional point of view, one of the most important elements of the agreement is the creation of the World Trade Organization, which replaced the GATT in 1995. Negotiations about market access, which will largely determine the extent of the liberalization effort, were completed in mid-1995.

Some authors (Corden 1984, for example) predict that regional integration schemes will act as intermediate steps toward a more perfect multilateral system based on the GATT and the World Trade Organization. There are, however, some problems with this idea. The current structure of trading blocs is not cooperative across groups, so that the gains from more trade within a bloc have to be compared with the losses from less trade between blocs. Moreover, the United States is currently pushing a policy of reciprocity rather than free trade.

Table 5-21. Protection in OECD Countries against Latin American Exports,
Mid-1980s
(percentage)

Country	Import–weighted level of nontariff barriers
Argentina	63.0
Brazil	38.3
Chile	23.8
Mexico	8.4
Peru	12.8
Uruguay	23.2
Venezuela	3.2
Central America	17.1
Average for Latin America and the Caribbean	28.6

Source: Leamer 1990.

The Uruguay Round covers trade in agriculture and textiles and the regulation of services and investment. Overall, according to the agreement, industrial countries will have to reduce the average trade-weighted tariffs on exports from developing countries 34 percent in ten years (from 6 to 4 percent). Developing countries, in turn, will have to increase the coverage of duties bound and to remove export subsidies. In some cases, the reduction will be impressive; for instance, Brazil is committed to lowering import tariffs from a maximum of 105 percent to a ceiling of 35 percent. Trade-distorting investment measures, such as local content requirements, will be eliminated in five to seven years.

The streamlining of the protection of intellectual property is expected to help some developing countries that have started exporting knowledge-intensive goods, such as software and agricultural technology. However, the liberalization measures agreed to in December 1993 are rather timid in some areas, especially agriculture, and the timetable for implementation is too lengthy. Safeguard rules are expected to be softened and could be introduced in a discriminatory way and without compensation. Unfortunately, these antidumping measures could give rise to a new form of disguised protectionism.

The successful completion of the Uruguay Round is expected to provide both static and dynamic gains to the world economy. The developing countries will receive about one-third of these gains. Trade is expected to grow 12 percent in the next ten years, due exclusively to the Uruguay Round. Developing countries will not receive a significant share of the dynamic gains, however, since economies of scale and technological spillovers through greater innovation are likely to accrue to exporters of industrial goods.

Table 5-22. Main Results of the Uruguay Round for Latin America and the Caribbean

Area	Results
Market access	Overall cut of 33 percent in import tariffs on industrial products, reductions in peaks and escalation; tariffs reduced in five equal annual steps, starting when the World Trade Organization comes into effect; weighted average tariff down from 6.4 to 4.0 percent in industrial countries; share of duty-free imports from 20 to 43 percent in industrial countries; developing-country tariff bindings increased from 12 to 56 percent of imports
	Lower than average tariff cuts made in sensitive sectors, such as textiles, clothing, footwear, and transport equipment
	42 percent reduction in tariffs on tropical agricultural products and 57 percent on tropical industrial products in industrial countries; erosion of preference margins experienced by some developing countries
	34 percent cut in tariffs on natural resource–based products; larger than average gains for some metals and minerals, smaller gains for fish
	Developing countries with high per capita income required to phase out subsidies within eight years
Agriculture	Gradual liberalization process in the sector: over six years for industrial countries and ten years for developing countries; bindings on agricultural tariffs increased from 81 to 95 percent of imports (industrial countries) and from 23 to 90 percent (developing countries); virtual elimination of all nontariff barriers; minimum tariff cut of 15 percent on all tariff lines by industrial countries, with an average tariff reduction of 36 percent over six years from a 1986–88 base; restrictions against imports subject to a tariff commitment
	Export subsidies reduced 36 percent in value and 21 percent in volume over the implementation period; domestic support programs reduced 20 percent
	Special safeguard provisions enacted that permit the imposition of additional duties up to certain limits, triggered by both price and volume clauses

162

Textiles and clothing	Four-step phaseout of the Multi-Fibre Agreement over ten years; gradual integration of the sector into the World Trade Organization; expansion of outstanding quota restrictions; provisions to redistribute quotas in favor of quota-constrained and efficient exporters; developing-country exporters accounting for less than 3 percent of a country's imports of a product exempted from safeguard action if all developing-country members with less than a 3 percent share account for less than 9 percent overall
Intellectual property rights	National treatment and most-favored-nation clauses applied to all intellectual property rights; subsidies for research activities are declared nonactionable; minimum standards provided for copyrights, trademarks, industrial design, patents, and so forth
	Patent protection for twenty years in all areas of technology, including pharmaceuticals
	One year's delay in the implementation of trade-related intellectual property rights after the establishment of the World Trade Organization; the delay for developing and transitional economies extended to five years, except for the most-favored-nation and national treatment clauses
Services	Multilateral rules extended to a large segment of world trade (20 percent); general agreement on trade in services that establishes the nondiscrimination principle, including most of the GATT-type provisions
	Framework for establishing and maintaining liberalization commitments; continuing negotiations related to safeguards, subsidies, and government procurement; special appendixes that address specificity of sectors

Source: Author's elaboration from several GATT documents.

Appendix 5-1: Productivity Growth and Openness: An Econometric Analysis

Factor accumulation explains between half and two-thirds of long-run growth (Fischer 1988). The large unexplained residual in growth accounting exercises has been attributed to technological progress or productivity gains. From a policy perspective, a key question is, What determines these productivity improvements? In particular, it is important to understand whether national domestic policies, including financial and trade policies, can affect the pace of productivity growth. If this is the case, policymakers will have more freedom to pursue avenues that enhance long-run performance.

The recent interest in endogenous growth models has revived applied research on the determinants of growth. Some authors emphasize the role of openness in determining the pace at which countries can absorb technological progress originating in the rest of the world (Grossman and Helpman 1991). Edwards (1992c), for example, assumes that there are two sources of growth of total factor productivity: (1) a purely domestic source stemming from local technological improvements (innovation) and (2) a foreign source related to the absorption of inventions generated in other nations (imitation). More specifically, the country's ability to appropriate world technical innovations (or to imitate) is assumed to depend on two factors: positively, on the degree of openness of the economy and on the gap between the country's level and the world's stock of total factor productivity. The first channel is the openness effect discussed by Lewis (1955): more-open countries have an advantage in absorbing new ideas generated in the rest of the world. In this context, more open refers to a less distorted foreign trade sector. The second channel is a catch-up effect common to growth models based on convergence notions.

If the aggregate production function is defined as $y_t = Af(K_t, L_t)$, then total factor productivity is $A_t = y_t / f(\bullet)$, and total productivity growth is $(\dot{A}/A)$. The role of the two sources of technical progress—innovation and imitation—can be captured by the following simple expression:

$$(5\text{-}1) \qquad \frac{\dot{A}}{A} = \alpha + \left[\beta\omega + \gamma\left(\frac{A^* - A}{A}\right) \right]$$

where α and γ are parameters, A^* is the level of the world's (appropriable) total factor productivity, and ω is the rate of growth of the world's total factor productivity (that is, $A^*_t = A^*_0 e^{\omega t}$). β is a parameter between 0 and 1 that measures the country's ability to absorb productivity improvements originating from the rest of the world and is assumed to be a negative function of the level of trade distortions in the economy (δ).

$$(5\text{-}2) \qquad \beta = \beta(\delta) \; ; \; \beta' < 0$$

where δ is an index of trade distortions that takes a higher value when international trade, both in imports and exports, becomes more distorted.

Parameter α is the basic rate of domestic productivity growth or innovation, which for simplicity is assumed to be exogenous. $[\gamma(A^* - A) / A]$ is the catch-up term that says that domestic productivity growth is faster in nations where the stock of knowledge lags behind the world's accumulated stock of appropriable knowledge.[19]

In this setting, the path through time of domestic total factor productivity is given by

$$(5\text{-}3) \qquad A_t = \left[A_0 - \left(\frac{\gamma}{\gamma + \omega(1 - \beta) - \alpha} \right) A_0^* \right] e^{-(\gamma - \alpha - \beta\omega)t} + \left(\frac{\gamma}{\gamma + \omega(1 - \beta) - \alpha} \right) A_0^* e^{\omega t}$$

This, of course, is the solution to differential equation 5-1. It follows from equation 5-3 that the long-run rate of growth of domestic total factor productivity depends on whether $(\gamma - \alpha - \beta\omega) \gtreqless 0$. If $(\gamma - \alpha - \beta\omega) > 0$, in the steady state, total factor productivity grows at the rate of the world's productivity ω. This means that the level of domestic total factor productivity (and of GDP) is a function of the degree of trade intervention, with higher trade distortions resulting in a lower level of real income. A key implication of this result is that countries that engage in trade liberalization programs are characterized, during the transition between two steady states, by higher rates of productivity growth and, thus, by faster rates of GDP growth.

A second case appears when $(\gamma - \alpha - \beta\omega) < 0$. Long-run growth of total factor productivity $(\dot{A}/A)$ depends on how large the world's rate of growth of total factor productivity (ω) is relative to the domestic rate of productivity improvement. If $\omega > (\alpha - \beta) / (1 - \beta)$, domestic total factor productivity grows in the steady state at the world rate ω. If, however, $\omega < (\alpha - \gamma) / (1 - \beta)$, and $(\gamma - \alpha - \beta\omega) < 0$, the long-run equilibrium rate of growth of total factor productivity is equal to $(\alpha + \beta\omega - \delta)$ and depends negatively on δ, the country's level of trade distortions (of course, in this case, $[\alpha + \beta\omega - \delta] > \omega$). That is, in this case, more-open countries (those with low δ) grow faster during steady-state equilibrium, because the domestic source of technological inventions is strong enough to drive, even in the steady state, the aggregate rate of technological innovations.

This model suggests that growth of total factor productivity depends on the degree of trade distortions in the economy and on a catch-up term that measures the gap between the country's and the world's level of productivity. A cross-country data set is used to test these implications of this model. More specifically, equations of the following type can be estimated:

$$(5\text{-}4) \qquad \rho_n = b_0 + b_1 \delta_n + b_2 g_n + \Sigma a_i x_{in} + \mu_n$$

where ρ_n is the average rate of growth of total factor productivity in country n; δ_n is, as before, an index of trade distortions; g_n is the catch-up term; the x_{in}s are other possible determinants of growth of total factor productivity; and μ is an error term.

Barro (1991), Edwards (1992c), and Roubini and Sala-i-Martin (1992), among others, suggest that, in addition to the degree of openness, productivity growth is also affected by the following factors: (a) human capital, usually measured by educational attainment; (b) the importance of government in the economy, measured by the ratio of government expenditure to GDP; (c) the degree of political instability; and (d) the inflation rate. In the estimations of equation 5-4, these variables are incorporated as possible determinants of productivity growth. Variables are defined in the following way:

- *Growth of total factor productivity.* A problem faced in the estimation of equations of the type of equation 5-4 refers to the measurement of growth of total factor productivity. In particular, it is difficult to obtain longtime series of capital stocks for a large number of countries. In this appendix, three measures of growth of total factor productivity constructed by Edwards (1992c) are used.

- *Trade distortions.* Traditionally, studies that investigate the relationship between trade policy and economic performance have difficulties measuring the extent of trade distortions. This problem is tackled by using two variables. First, most of the basic estimates use the ratio of total taxes on foreign trade—import tariffs plus export taxes—over total trade as a proxy for trade distortions. This variable is measured as an average for 1971–82. Since this variable, denoted TRADETAX, measures the true extent of trade distortions with error, in the estimation of the total factor productivity growth equation, an instrumental variable technique that tries to correct for measurement error is also used. The second proxy is the 1971–82 average trade dependency ratio—imports plus exports as a percentage of GDP. These two indexes of trade distortions were constructed with raw data obtained from the IMF.

- *Catch-up term.* Following the recent literature on endogenous growth (Barro 1991; Edwards 1992c), initial GDP per capita—for 1971 in this case—is used as a measure of the gap between a particular country's level of productivity and that of the world. This variable is denoted as GDP71; the data were obtained from Summers and Heston (1988). The coefficient of this variable is expected to be negative.

- *Human capital.* Two indexes are used. The first is the attainment of secondary education in 1981; the second is the increase in secondary education coverage between 1961 and 1981. When alternative indexes, such as secondary and higher education were used, the results obtained were not altered. The data were obtained from the World Bank's *World Development Report*. The coefficient of this variable is expected to be positive.

- *Role of government*. This index is defined as the share of government over GDP and is taken from Summers and Heston (1988). Barro (1991) argues that this coefficient should be negative, capturing the effect that greater government activities tend, in general, to crowd out the private sector.
- *Political instability*. This variable is defined as the average perceived probability of a change in government and was obtained from Cukierman, Edwards, and Tabellini (1992; this index was computed from a probit analysis of government change using pooled data for 1948–81). Its coefficient in the total factor productivity growth equations is expected to be negative, reflecting the fact that in politically unstable situations economic agents do not devote their full energies to pursuing economic objectives.
- *Inflation tax*. This variable is defined as the average collection of inflation taxes for 1971–82 and was computed as πm, where π is the rate of inflation and m is the ratio of narrowly defined money to GDP. The coefficient of this variable is expected to be negative, reflecting the effects of higher inflation on uncertainty and economic activity.

Tables 5-23 and 5-24 summarize the results obtained from the estimation of several versions of equation 5-4. Table 5-23 contains weighted least squares estimates—with population in 1971 as weight—for all three measures of growth of total factor productivity; table 5-24 presents instrumental variables' regressions for the TFP1 definition of productivity growth (in simple ordinary least squares estimates, heteroskedasticity was detected; Barro 1991 and Edwards 1992c, among others, also use weighted least squares in equations of this type; when the other two indexes were used, the results were not altered significantly).

As can be seen from these tables, the results are highly satisfactory. Almost every coefficient has the expected sign and is significant at conventional levels. Particularly important for the discussion pursued in this chapter is that in every regression the proxies for trade distortions and openness are highly significant. Moreover, the computation of standardized beta coefficients indicates that trade impediments are the second most important explanatory variable of growth of total factor productivity, after the catch-up term (in equation 5-5, the standardized beta coefficient of TRADETAX is –0.75; that of GDP71 is –0.78).

Both the TRADETAX coefficient and the trade dependency ratio are imperfect proxies of trade distortions. In particular, they do not directly capture the role of quantitative restrictions on trade. In order to deal with this measurement error, using problem instrumental variables, versions of some of these

Table 5-23. Regressions for Growth of Total Factor Productivity, Cross-Country Results of Several Versions of Equation 5-4

Definition of TFP growth	TFP1		TFP2		TFP3	
	Equation 5-5	Equation 5-6	Equation 5-7	Equation 5-8	Equation 5-9	Equation 5-10
Constant	−0.013	−0.012	−0.018	−0.005	0.074	0.030
	(−1.041)	(−1.326)	(−1.418)	(−0.439)	(6.163)	(1.772)
GDP71	−1.85E-06	−7.28E-07	−1.8E-06	−1.08-06	−3.69E-06	−1.48E-06
	(−3.433)	(−1.929)	(−2.960)	(−2.451)	(−3.673)	(−2.187)
TRADETAX	−0.076	—	−0.074	—	−0.199	—
	(−3.033)		(−2.620)		(−4.902)	
Trade dependency	—	0.017	—	0.025	—	0.025
		(3.147)		(3.910)		(2.480)
Government	−6.14E-04	−4.20E-04	−6.50E-04	−4.10E-04	−2.00E-03	−2.00E-03
	(−2.429)	(−1.708)	(−2.292)	(−1.433)	(−5.157)	(−4.827)
Education	1.19E-04	1.56E-07	5.9E-06	1.30E-04	—	1.20E-04
	(1.536)	(2.130)	(0.675)	(1.560)		(0.895)
ΔEducation	—	—	—	—	1.60E-04	—
					(1.453)	
Political instability	−0.017	−0.017	−0.026	−0.043	−0.014	−0.023
	(−2.117)	(−2.480)	(−2.846)	(−5.253)	(−1.670)	(−1.802)
Inflation tax	—	8.3E-05	—	8.8E-05	—	2.7E-05
		(0.540)		(0.487)		(0.921)
R^2	0.400	0.351	0.492	0.487	0.598	0.416
Number of observations	54	52	54	52	52	52

— Not applicable.

Note: For exact explanations of how TFP1, TFP2, and TFP3 were constructed, see Edwards 1992c. *t*-statistics are in parentheses. R^2 is the coefficient of determination. See Edwards 1992c for a list of the countries considered in this regression.

Table 5-24. Regressions on Growth of Total Factor Productivity
(instrumental variables and dependent variable TFP1)

Variable	Equation 5-11	Equation 5-12
Constant	0.036	0.050
	(1.689)	(2.037)
GDP71	–3.4E-06	–3.7E-06
	(–2.766)	(–2.677)
TRADETAX	–0.171	–0.185
	(–2.432)	(–2.314)
Government	–4.9E-04	–5.5E-04
	(–1.708)	(–2.292)
Education	3.00E-05	4.80E-05
	(2.130)	(0.675)
Political instability	–0.029	–0.040
	(–2.333)	(–2.823)
Inflation tax	–8.1E-05	–2.5E-05
	(0.766)	(–0.939)
R^2	0.248	0.392
Number of observations	52	52

Note: t-statistics are in parentheses; R^2 is the coefficient of determination. The following instruments were used: a constant, GDP71, government, education, trade dependency, ratio of imports to GDP, political instability, and inflation tax. These equations were weighted by population in 1971.

equations are also estimated. In estimating equations 5-5 and 5-6 again, the trade penetration ratio of imports to GDP is used as an instrument for TRADE-TAX.[20] The results, presented in table 5-24, confirm those discussed previously and provide additional support for the view that, after controlling for other factors, countries with more-open and less distorted foreign trade sectors tend to exhibit a faster rate of growth of total factor productivity, over the long run, than nations with a more distorted external sector.

CHAPTER 6

Privatization and Deregulation

PRIOR TO THE 1980S, A NUMBER OF LATIN AMERICAN COUNTRIES embarked on isolated attempts to increase the role of market forces. The Alessandri reforms in Chile in the late 1950s and the modernization effort led by Krieger-Vassena in Argentina during the 1960s are two examples of these historic interludes with reduced regulations. However, what distinguishes these episodes from the structural reforms initiated in the late 1980s is that no efforts were made to privatize government-owned firms (the privatization of bus services in Buenos Aires in 1962 constitutes an early exception). Moreover, during some episodes—the Alessandri reforms in Chile in 1958–64, for example—the promotion of market forces took place side by side with initiatives aimed at increasing the role of the state as a producer (this role was pursued by the Corporación de Fomento de la Producción, CORFO; see Ffrench-Davis 1973).

The emphasis on privatization is part of a new vision of economic development in the region that, as discussed in chapter 3, gained force during the late 1980s. It is this emphasis on privatization that clearly sets the recent structural reforms apart from previous efforts to deregulate the Latin American economies. Privatization, more than any other policy, changed the economic landscape in Latin America. Between 1985 and 1992, more than 2,000 publicly owned firms, including public utilities, banks, insurance companies, highways, ports, airlines, and retail shops, were privatized throughout the region.[1]

As with other reforms, however, the pace of privatization varied from country to country. While in some countries, such as Chile and Mexico, approximately 90 percent of state-owned enterprises had been divested by mid-1993, in others—Bolivia and Ecuador, for example—the process was much slower. In still others, including Uruguay, the privatization effort ran into political difficulties in 1993 and basically came to a halt. In both Chile and Mexico, the government maintained control of the largest state-owned enterprises—CODELCO in Chile and PEMEX in Mexico—partially for historical and political reasons. The nationalization of Mexico's oil sector happened at such a pivotal moment in the history of that country that even Presidents Carlos Salinas

Table 6-1. *Privatization of State-owned Enterprises in Selected Countries of Latin America, 1980–92*

Country	Number of firms privatized	Percentage of total state-owned enterprises
Argentina	45	15
Brazil	42	6
Chile[a]	501	96
Mexico	1,001	87
Venezuela	77	62

a. For 1974–91.
Source: World Bank, several country-specific reports.

and Ernesto Zedillo have found overturning it very difficult. The case of CODELCO in Chile is similar. The large Chilean copper mines were national-ized in 1971 by a historic vote of both chambers of the Chilean Congress (however, a major financial scandal unraveled in 1994 involving huge losses from futures trading, and this created significant public pressure for privatiz-ing CODELCO). Table 6-1 provides general data on the magnitude of the privatization effort in selected countries; table 6-2 lists some of the recent large (over $100 million) privatizations in Latin America during 1988–91.

This chapter analyzes the privatization and deregulation efforts in Latin America in the 1980s and early 1990s. It begins with an analytical discussion of the policy options and tradeoffs facing governments engaged in massive divestiture programs. Next, case studies are provided for Chile, Mexico, and Argentina. This is followed by analysis of the actual procedures used during privatization; the impact of these programs on fiscal revenues, efficiency, and aggregate welfare; and issues related to the implementation of a modern regu-latory framework.

Privatization and Deregulation: Analytical Issues and Policy Options

Throughout most of Latin America, the importance of state-owned enter-prises grew steadily between the 1950s and early 1980s. The creation of a sub-stantial state-owned enterprise sector was an important component of the structuralist development strategy and responded to a number of objectives. First, it was considered an efficient way of dealing with externalities and, in particular, with natural monopolies and oligopolies. Second, state ownership was generally seen as a way to serve the public interest and advance social objectives, such as the provision of (some) services at low prices to the popula-tion at large. And third, a large public sector was thought to reduce the vul-nerability of the economy to external shocks (on the use of public ownership as a way to deal with externalities, see, for example, Willig 1993). In many

Table 6-2. Privatization Transactions of More Than $100 Million in Selected Countries of Latin America, 1988–91
(millions of U.S. dollars)

Country and enterprise	Transaction date	Gross transaction date	Sale technique[a]	Sector
Argentina				
Aerolíneas Argentinas	April 1990	260	Private offer	Airline
ENTEL	November 1990	1,244	Private offer	Telecommunications
Brazil				
Aracruz	May 1988	130	Public offer	Pulp and paper
Usiminas	December 1991	1,430	Private offer	Steel
Chile				
Compañía de Teléfonos	January 1988	170	Private offer	Telecommunications
Colombia				
Papelcol	August 1990	100	Private offer	Pulp and paper
Mexico				
Aerovías de México	November 1988	339	Private offer	Airline
Banamex	September 1991	2,300	Private offer	Banking
Bancomer	October 1991	2,550	Private offer	Banking
Banpaís	June 1991	182	Private offer	Banking
Cananeas	September 1990	475	Private offer	Mining
Banca Cremi	June 1991	248	Private offer	Banking
Mexicana de Aviación	June 1989	140	Private offer	Airline
Mexicana de Cobre	October 1988	1,360	Private offer	Mining
Multibanco Mercantil	June 1991	204	Private offer	Banking
Nikko Hotel	October 1988	110	Private offer	Hotel
Sicartsa 1	November 1991	170	Private offer	Steel
Sidermex North	November 1991	145	Private offer	Steel
TELMEX	December 1990	1,760	Private offer	Telecommunications
Tereftalos Mexicanos	November 1988	106	Private offer	Chemical
Venezuela				
CANTV	November 1991	1,885	Private offer	Telecommunications
VIASA	September 1991	145	Private offer	Airline

a. Does not include sales subsequent to the first transaction (such as employee offers, international public offers) or debt-equity-swap components.

Source: Kikeri, Nellis, and Shirley 1992.

cases, the enthusiasm for a large state-owned enterprise sector was related to the national security doctrine and was strongly supported by the local armed forces (Fishlow 1989). Moreover, in some cases—Salvador Allende's Chile and Alán García's Peru—the creation of a dominant public sector became the central tool in efforts to build a socialist-oriented society. Toward the middle to late 1970s, the coverage of the state-owned enterprise sector had grown beyond the so-called strategic sectors and, in most countries, included firms in industries that were competitive and had traditionally functioned efficiently. In Brazil, for example, the state grew in economic importance after the first oil shock (the *estatização* period; Fishlow 1989). In spite of a rhetoric favoring private sector development, the state expanded its economic role both indirectly through major financing provided by the National Development Bank and directly through the acquisition of productive firms.

In almost every country, the growth of the state-owned enterprise sector was accompanied by the development of massive regulatory legislation that restricted the freedom of the private sector. Entry into and exit from certain industries were tightly controlled, the price and quantity of goods produced were regulated, and the creation of new firms was subject to endless bureaucracy (for a fascinating account of regulatory overkill, see De Soto 1986). The financial sector was submitted to particularly serious restrictions that affected the allocation of credit and the level of interest rates paid to depositors and charged to borrowers. Additionally, labor relations became more rigid, reducing the degree of international competitiveness of the labor force and depressing the creation of employment. The effort to regulate and control a very broad range of private activities stemmed from a distrust of competition and markets. Also, it was thought that regulating labor markets would shield the poor from the vagaries of cyclical fluctuations.

A major shortcoming of this thinking—and one that became particularly apparent in the 1980s—was that it did not confront the costs of massive regulation, including government failures and outright corruption. Additionally, the traditional approach failed to realize that excessive regulation generated large gains for small groups that were able to obtain industrial licenses and import permits and that, in general, could circumvent the regulatory maze. As it turned out, instead of increasing the degree of efficiency and equity of the economic system, the combination of a very large state-owned enterprise sector and massive regulations generally resulted in a lethargic public sector, an antiquated private sector motivated by rent seeking and corruption, income inequality, and a growing underground economy (of course, there were some exceptions to this picture; for a broad analysis of the evolution of state-owned enterprises and the privatization effort of the 1980s and 1990s, see Glade 1988).

By the mid-1980s, in most countries, state-owned enterprises were incurring major losses that imposed a heavy burden on public finances, fueled the inflationary process, and resulted in very poor provision of services. The eruption of the debt crisis made evident that the path followed until then was costly and ineffective; despite good intentions, the presence of a mammoth public sector and sweeping distortions did not shield the Latin American economies from major external shocks.

When faced with the imperious need to tackle massive fiscal imbalances during the late 1980s, many policymakers saw the sale of publicly owned assets as a natural way to obtain liquid resources in the short run. Additionally, many supporters of reform argued that rapid privatization would provide some basic political foundations to the economic transformation; in particular, it was thought that distributing shares broadly to the population would create thousands of supporters of the new economic system (see Hachette and Luders 1992). However, in many countries the privatization process initially ran into serious political opposition. Not surprisingly, those groups that for decades had benefited from excessive regulation and the growing public sector—state-owned enterprise unions, bureaucrats, and private agents that had been able to "capture" regulators—were unwilling to give up their advantages (regulators are captured when an interest group can, directly or indirectly, dictate what they should do; see Becker 1983; Stigler 1971). The privatization process slowly acquired political support. In many countries, this was attained through the implementation of schemes that distributed to workers (usually at a low price) a percentage of shares in the privatized firms. Also, in many countries, as the quality of services improved, many consumers actively supported new rounds of privatization.

The decision to embark on massive privatization posed gigantic challenges for the region's governments, including the need to decide which state-owned enterprises to sell and how to sell them. Perhaps the most difficult task—and one that was not always tackled fully—was to create a new regulatory framework consistent with a private sector becoming rapidly involved in areas that, traditionally, had been reserved for the government. A critical issue was to distinguish between those sectors that could be self-regulated—industries characterized by open competition or, at least, contestability—and those that required active government regulation. In general, the majority of privatized firms fell in the first category; however, a small but important group, including utilities and the financial sector, were characterized by externalities and generally functioned more efficiently when subject to well-defined regulations (a particularly difficult issue was setting the bases required to develop regulatory rules that credibly committed the government not to expropriate the private sector's newly acquired assets; as argued by Spiller 1992, this issue was particularly relevant for the case of utilities).

Privatization

When the early Latin American reformers embarked on their privatization efforts, very little was known, both at the academic and managerial levels, about how to undertake a massive divestiture of public property. This forced the authorities to improvise and to learn on the job. Mistakes were made, and, especially in Chile, the process ran into difficulties and partial reversals. Slowly through time, however, new information was acquired, and general principles were established. Although no general agreement on all aspects of privatization was attained, the knowledge on the subject is significantly better today than it was a few years ago (several Latin American professionals have even become consultants to Eastern European governments on privatization issues). Many of these lessons are not strictly related to economics or finance but rather have to do with the political economy of privatization. Avoiding, or at least reducing, political opposition from interest groups is clearly as important as setting up a technically correct program.

Some of the most important lessons from the Latin American experience refer to the need to distinguish between different sectors and sizes of firms when designing a privatization program. Failing to follow this simple principle caused serious problems in Chile's privatization effort in the middle and late 1970s (see Edwards and Edwards 1991). In general, accumulated experience suggests that while small firms in the manufacturing sector can be sold early on and rapidly, the divestiture of large monopolies, banks, insurance companies, and public utilities that wield monopoly power is substantially more complicated. In particular, in most cases, it is desirable to define a clear regulatory framework before firms are put on the block. In many countries, this is difficult to do, because there is very limited, if any, experience with the implementation of modern regulatory legislation. The international financial institutions, and especially the World Bank, have taken an active stance on this issue, providing financial and technical support to countries engaged in the design of new regulations.

Governments usually have multiple objectives when they engage in privatization: increasing (net) revenues to the government, reducing the size of the public sector, increasing efficiency, and spreading ownership more broadly. Typically there are tradeoffs among these objectives. On the one hand, maximizing government revenue may require selling large blocks of shares to single bidders, such as local conglomerates or foreign multinationals. On the other hand, broadening ownership may require selling shares at a very low price—or even at a zero price—to a wide segment of the population. The Latin American experience suggests that when government objectives are not clarified and prioritized early in the process, serious conflicts are bound to arise, and the privatization effort may run into political difficulties (for a discussion of the Chilean privatization program, see Hachette and Luders 1992).

Experience also shows that, independent of the main objectives of the privatization program, it is fundamentally important that sales be carried out with absolute transparency and without any suspicion of impropriety. Lack of transparency usually results in political opposition to public sector divestiture. In the majority of countries, the public feels that it "owns" public firms and becomes frustrated if the fruits of privatization seem to be accruing fully to private parties. In Argentina and Chile, for example, the lack of transparency of some early privatization introduced deep suspicion into the system.

Modes of Privatization. It is useful to distinguish at least four modes of privatization: (a) sale of a controlling percentage of shares to a private company or consortium; (b) initial public offering of shares on a stock exchange, either domestic or international; (c) employee buyout; and (d) liquidation of the firm and sale of its assets (see Seabright 1993 for a similar classification). Each of these modalities can help to attain particular goals. For example, the sale of controlling interest is usually consistent with a speedy privatization that raises significant revenues in the short run. Public offerings of shares, in contrast, help to broaden ownership. Some countries, such as Chile and Mexico, offered shares at preferential prices to small investors. This created a broad constituency of shareholders that supports the privatization process and is concerned with the way in which the private sector is regulated. Public offers in foreign stock exchanges, such as Argentina's offer of the petroleum company YPF's stock in New York in June 1993, can increase the international appeal of certain firms and signal the government's seriousness regarding privatization. Employee buyouts generally reduce the extent of opposition to privatization in certain sectors. Most Latin American countries resorted to a combination of these four modes of privatization. In some cases, two or more of these modalities were used during the sale of a particular firm—the telephone company, ENTEL, in Argentina and the electric utility, ENDESA, in Chile, for example. By combining these methods, the authorities hoped to achieve several objectives as well as minimize the extent of political opposition to the privatization process.

As a way to avoid excessive concentration and potential monopolistic behavior, some countries broke up public monopolies before offering them to the private sector (however, an important technical issue is whether it is more efficient to break up large monopolies vertically or horizontally). This was the case, for example, in Argentina, where the Buenos Aires telephone company and the natural gas distribution company were divided into several independent firms before being sold. This breakdown of public utilities was complemented by a new regulatory framework aimed at curbing potential abuses by the newly privatized firms. Also, Argentina, Chile, and Mexico made efforts to agree with the buyers of public utilities on future expansion programs and price-setting mechanisms. Argentina, however, only devised the regulatory framework after the telephone company had been sold. This increased the uncertainty facing potential buyers, reducing the price offered.

Sequencing. An important question in designing a wholesale divestiture program is the sequence in which firms in different sectors should be privatized. In particular, should banks and other financial institutions be sold early on, or should they be maintained under public property for a longer time? McKinnon (1991) argues that because of moral hazard considerations, the privatization of banks should come near the end of the reform process. McKinnon's position is partially based on the Chilean experience of the 1970s in which banks were sold early to emerging, and not fully solvent, conglomerates (the *grupos*), which used them to finance the acquisition of firms subsequently privatized. During this process, the newly privatized banks engaged in extremely risky and financially questionable operations and accumulated large volumes of bad loans—many to related companies owned by the same conglomerate. Due to the existence of a (implicit) government guarantee on deposits, the public did not distinguish between solid and financially troubled banks. This process—which, in the first place, was able to develop because of the lack of an appropriate supervisory framework— produced a major financial crisis in 1982–83, when some of the largest Chilean banks became insolvent and had to be taken over by the government.

This episode starkly illustrates the importance of implementing a modern supervisory framework *before* privatizing banks. However, it is unclear whether, as McKinnon (1991) argues, this justifies delaying the divestiture of financial institutions beyond what is required to put the new regulations in place. In fact, there are compelling reasons for privatizing banks during the early stages of the reform process but only *after* the new regulatory framework is firmly in place. First, to move from a protectionist to a competitive environment, manufacturing and other firms have to engage in major restructuring activities that allow them to increase productivity. This requires financing, which, under most circumstances, is difficult to obtain from a largely inefficient and old-fashioned state-owned banking system. Second, a banking system dominated by large government-owned banks usually stands in the way of macroeconomic stabilization efforts. In these cases, the culture of the public bank often prevails, and credit is granted at a pace that is inconsistent with overall macroeconomic equilibrium. This was the case in Nicaragua, where the inability to control the state-owned Banco Nacional de Desarrollo jeopardized the macroeconomic stabilization program in the early 1990s (personnel of the bank continued to operate within the populist mode that characterized the Sandinista administration, crowding out private investment and limiting the country's ability to meet the International Monetary Fund's targets). Also, delaying the privatization of the banking system may delay the creation of a dynamic and modern capital market, negatively affecting resource allocation and intermediation.

Privatization and Public Finances. Massive divestiture programs of the type implemented in Latin America have important effects on public finances. First, the proceeds of the sales themselves constitute public sector revenue, improving the fiscal accounts in the short run. Most experts contend that these revenues should not be considered permanent income and, thus, should not be used to finance increases in current expenditures. Although, in theory, political leaders agree with this prescription, in reality governments in a number of countries (Argentina, Brazil) relied on privatization revenues to delay the implementation of other deficit-reducing measures. Privatization also affects public revenues through a second channel: many state-owned enterprises in Latin America have faced longtime financial problems requiring large and continuous injections of government funds. Naturally, once these firms are sold to the private sector, the government ceases to be responsible for their finances. This can save large volumes of public funds, as was the case in Chile during the first round of privatization. To the extent that privatized firms become profitable and pay taxes, divestiture also affects public finances in the longer run. When a profitable firm is privatized, however, the public sector ceases to receive those funds, having a negative effect on public finances. In the aggregate, however, privatization had an overall positive fiscal impact in most Latin American countries (see Galal, Saez, and Torres 1992; Psacharopoulos 1992).

The restructuring of firms in distress has become an increasingly important issue in the design of privatization plans. Should the government restructure state-owned enterprises—both financially and technologically—before they are sold, or should this task be left to the new owners? The way in which this problem is handled has economic as well as political consequences. From a financial perspective, if the government undertakes the restructuring, including laying off redundant workers, it will be able to sell the firm at a higher price. Restructuring tends to be expensive, however, with costs associated with both the acquisition of new equipment and the dismissal of workers. Moreover, governments do not have a comparative advantage when restructuring inefficient state-owned firms (Seabright 1993). As discussed in greater detail in chapter 8, labor legislation in most Latin American countries does not consider economic distress as a valid cause for "just" layoffs. This means that substantial resources are required to finance severance payments. In some countries, such as Mexico and Chile, this problem was partially solved by working out agreements with unions in the firms to be privatized, whereby workers consented to layoffs in exchange for a portion of the firm's stock.

Many Latin American countries are moving to privatize their social security systems. This development, pioneered by Chile in the early 1980s, is particularly advanced in Argentina, Peru, and, to a lesser extent, Mexico. These reforms have two main objectives: first, to replace financially troubled pay-as-you-go pension schemes with fully funded capitalization systems based on individual retirement accounts and, second, to develop a large presence for institutional investors in the (emerging) capital markets (see chapters 7 and 8 for further details). Also, the creation of privately administered pension funds opens an opportunity for developing new channels for privatization. For, instance, in the second round of Chilean divestitures in the mid-1980s, pension funds were given the opportunity to buy shares at subsidized prices, helping, in this way, to further the goal of spreading ownership (see Luders 1991).

Political Economy Issues. From a political economy point of view, the way in which privatization is undertaken—in particular, who is allowed to bid and how the shares are paid for—has important consequences. In this regard, there are three pressing questions: Should workers in firms being privatized receive a proportion of the shares, either free or at reduced prices? What role should foreigners have in the privatization effort? When foreigners are allowed to bid, should they pay for the firms in cash or through a debt-equity swap?

The preferential treatment of workers in privatized firms was broadly used in Argentina, Chile, Mexico, and Nicaragua as a tool to reduce political opposition to the divestiture process. This practice, however, has important distributional consequences, tending to benefit segments of the labor force that, through political pressures, were able to extract sizable rents from society in the past (in most countries, workers in state-owned enterprises are part of the protected sector and tend to receive higher salaries than workers in the unprotected or informal sector; see Harberger 1971). Moreover, these programs discriminate against public employees who work in sectors usually not subject to privatization, including defense, education, and health. From a fairness and distributive perspective, schemes aimed at distributing some shares to broad segments of the population—through the newly privatized social security system or some other mechanism—are preferable to schemes that concentrate on workers in the privatized firms themselves.

Historically, most Latin American countries restricted the participation of foreign-owned firms in certain sectors of the economy (for example, the original charter of the Andean Pact explicitly limited the maximum ownership percentage for foreign firms). In recent years, however, and as a result of a combination of factors, including the surge in privatization and the reduction of foreign financing, many restrictions on foreign ownership were relaxed. One of the most interesting features of the new economic landscape in Latin America is that foreign companies now own (or control) companies in sectors that, until very recently, were considered to be out-of-bounds and strategic, including telecommunications and air transport.[2] More interesting, perhaps, is the fact that Latin American firms have begun to bid for companies being privatized in other countries within the region. For instance, Chilean firms recently acquired Argentine companies in the electric distribution sector, and Argentine and Brazilian companies presented bids in Mexican privatization.

Most governments restrict, either explicitly or implicitly, the percentage of a privatization that can be financed through debt-equity swaps. In Brazil, this has been the subject of considerable debate. The administration of President Itamar Franco strongly argued for reducing the proportion of debt allowed in these operations. Recent experience shows that political problems tend to develop when foreign firms are perceived as reaping substantial benefits, while local groups, including consumers, experience some losses. This, for example, was the case in the privatization of ENTEL in Argentina and TELMEX in Mexico (Galal, Saez, and Torres 1992). In spite of significant changes in attitudes regarding foreign participation in investment projects, the issue of foreign ownership of certain firms is still politically sensitive in many countries. In Mexico and Venezuela, for example, the privatization—to foreigners or, for that matter, to nationals—of the oil giants PEMEX and PDVSA is an out-of-bounds topic. In Chile, recent discussions of the possible privatization of the national copper corporation CODELCO generated a serious political fallout (a high official of the coalition leading party—the Christian Democrats—had to resign after suggesting that CODELCO be privatized; however, in early 1994 pressures to privatize CODELCO reemerged).

Efficiency and Welfare Consequences of Privatization. Recent studies support the view that privatization increases efficiency, as measured by productivity growth, in the newly privatized companies as well as in those companies remaining in the public sector (see Glade 1988; Hachette and Luders 1992; Psacharapoulos 1992). For example, Galal, Saez, and Torres (1992) report that labor productivity increased significantly after a number of large Chilean and Mexican privatizations. In the case of the Mexican telephone company, total factor productivity increased more than 15 percent in 1991 alone. In the case of Colombia, at least three of four recent privatizations—an automobile assembly plant, a large refuse collection company, and a bank—brought important increases in productivity and efficiency (see Zuleta and others 1992). In what is probably the most ambitious, detailed study of privatization in the region, Hachette and Luders (1992) perform a number of econometric tests based on the financial statements of individual firms to determine whether privatization increased efficiency in Chile. They find a statistically significant, although quantitatively small, efficiency advantage for privatized firms.

Privatization is also expected to have an effect on consumer welfare. However, determining the magnitude of the effect is difficult because it involves quantifying elements related to the prices of services provided by monopolies, alternative rationing schemes, and profits accruing to foreigners. In spite of these difficulties, several authors attempt to provide approximate orders of magnitude for the welfare consequences of privatization (see, for example, Galal, Saez, and Torres 1992).

In a number of cases, consumer welfare increased through a reduction in prices, an improvement in the quality of service, and an expansion in the services provided by the privatized firms. In Argentina, water prices declined and service quality increased after privatization of the water distribution company. In Colombia, consumer welfare increased through the reduction of prices in the automobile and banking sectors (however, because of the massive change in other economic conditions, it is not clear whether the reduction in consumer prices and increase in service efficiency can be attributed to the divestiture process; see Zuleta and others 1992). Galal, Saez, and Torres (1992) argue that, although aggregate welfare increases in most privatizations, in some cases consumer welfare is negatively affected because of expected increases in real prices (as occurred with TELMEX in Mexico). This, however, is not completely clear since the new and old regimes use different mechanisms to ration services. Public telephone companies throughout Latin America were infamous for their use of rationing through queuing: having to wait ten years to obtain a phone line was all too common. The expectations are that, under the privatized regime, the ability of consumers to obtain services, although at a higher price, will increase significantly.

Regulation

The purpose of economic regulations is to establish legal rules that restrict, or alter, the free functioning of markets. In the presence of market failures—natural monopolies, information asymmetries, and externalities, for example—well-designed regulatory frameworks have the potential to increase social welfare by inducing firms to act in a manner that (somewhat) resembles competitive behavior. Regulations can take many forms, including the provision of minimal services and the administrative determination of price caps, rates, and barriers to entry or exit (Spulber 1989). There is a tendency in many parts of the world, including Latin America, to overregulate and thus encourage rent seeking, corruption, and inefficiency. One of the most challenging tasks facing Latin American countries—or any country engaged in a privatization process, for that matter—is to design modern and efficient regulatory frameworks that protect consumers and enhance efficiency without choking private initiative.

From an analytical perspective, regulatory rules are equivalent to incomplete contracts between private firms and regulators. This means that both parties constantly face the temptation to behave strategically by taking advantage of contingencies not fully specified in the regulatory contract or simply by walking away from it. Consider, for example, the interaction between a privately owned utility and the regulatory authority. The regulators have an incentive to promise a high price to the utility, as a way of inducing it to expand capacity. However, once the firm actually incurs the cost of the investment required to increase production, the regulator is tempted to renege on its promise and set a low price for the utility's output. This, of course, is a typical case of time inconsistency, where the interaction between strategically motivated agents has the potential to harm society.[3] This type of strategic behavior usually yields socially suboptimal outcomes because firms anticipate the behavior of the government and invest less than they would otherwise (on the general economics of time inconsistency, see Blanchard and Fischer 1989; for a classic treatment of the subject, see Calvo 1978). This undesirable (third-best) result can be avoided if the appropriate type of safeguarding institutions are in place and if regulators can credibly commit themselves to certain courses of action in the future.

Various authors argue that the development of efficient regulatory frameworks and safeguarding institutions is, in fact, an important prior requirement for the successful privatization of utilities, including telecommunications, electricity, and water provision (Spiller 1992). Because of the specificity of their assets, public utilities are particularly vulnerable to expropriation (either administrative or outright) by the government. Thus, in the absence of appropriate institutions, efforts to privatize utilities generate only limited interest. Moreover, bidders tend to offer what are perceived to be low prices for these companies. The recent privatization of the telephone companies in Argentina and Venezuela provide two highly contrasting cases that underscore this point. In Argentina, a controlling share of the telephone company was sold before a credible regulatory framework had been put in place; as a result, only three bidders offered prices deemed to be very low. In Venezuela, in contrast, the design of modern regulations prior to the sale attracted a large number of bidders (seven) that offered what experts considered to be (very) attractive prices. Interestingly enough, Argentina did enact a modern and efficient regulatory system after the telephone company was sold, generating significant capital gains to the two foreign consortia selected in the initial bidding process.

The ability to create a regulatory framework that allows the government to commit itself credibly to fulfill its promises and, in particular, not to expropriate the assets of the privatized firms, depends on three institutional factors (this approach toward regulations is influenced by Douglas North's analysis of the role of institutions in economic development; see North 1985, 1990; Spiller 1992 for details). The first relates to customs and traditions regarding property rights. In many Latin American countries, this tradition is weak—many private agents have vivid memories of past abuses and expropriations—which makes the implementation of credible regulatory rules somewhat difficult. The second factor is the degree of independence and efficiency of the judiciary, including the transaction costs involved in resolving conflicts between parties. And the third refers to the form of political organization and degree of political polarization.

Many countries, especially the poorer ones, have weak judiciary systems that operate under antiquated conditions and are plagued by financial problems. Moreover, the judiciary is often dependent on contingent political forces, introducing serious elements of suspicion into the conflict-resolution mechanism. In that regard, institutional reforms aimed at strengthening the judicial system, helping it to modernize and gain some degree of independence, have a positive impact on the creation of a modern state and, eventually, on the consolidation of market-based reforms.

The political system affects the form and credibility of regulation in several ways. In highly arbitrary political regimes, where the executive can change rules and laws with the stroke of a pen, it is difficult to enact legislation-based regulatory frameworks that are credible. In countries with a well-functioning presidential democracy, however, regulation based on specific laws can be quite credible. In this case, the actual level of credibility depends on the extent of political competition. If there is a high (and healthy) degree of competition among political parties, it is unlikely that an agreement to change the rules of the game will be attained easily; the degree of credibility thus tends to be high. Spiller (1992) uses this institutionally based framework to explain the differences in utilities' regulatory frameworks across some Latin American and Caribbean countries. For example, Chile's institutional setting—a fairly independent judiciary and a competitive presidential political system—explains why regulation in that country is based on very specific laws that establish criteria for entry and the determination and adjustment of rates (for the specifics of Chile's regulatory system of electric utilities, see Philippe 1991). In contrast, Jamaica's institutions—an independent judiciary, a strong tradition of respect for court decisions, and a two-party parliamentary regime—determine the use of license- or contract-based regulation.[4]

In industries where there are informational asymmetries—the financial sector being a particularly important one—the costs of monitoring a firm's actions affect the degree of optimal intervention and regulation. In Latin America, governments traditionally were unable to oversee banks' actions. This led to serious financial crises in Chile, Colombia, and Uruguay that ended in the virtual nationalization of large portions of the financial sector.

For regulatory agencies to maintain a certain degree of independence, and thus not become mere agents of the government or be captured by the regulated firms, it is important for their staff to be selected on technical bases and for agencies to have financial autonomy. In some countries—Argentina and Chile, for example—legislation that created the regulatory commissions specifically provided them with funds, adding transparency to the regulatory process. In many countries, however, the main constraint on implementing a credible and modern regulatory system that protects consumers and ensures stability is not the availability of funds, but the absence of skilled technical personnel. A definitive move toward a modern state clearly requires the creation of new institutions, including a strong, technically sophisticated, and independent civil service. In a study on the East Asian "miracle," the World Bank (1993a) argues that an independent and technocratic civil service largely isolated from political pressures was at the heart of the extremely rapid growth observed in that part of the world during the last few decades.

Privatization Programs in Chile, Mexico, and Argentina

As in other areas, Chile is a pioneer in the privatization process in Latin America, having engaged in a first round of massive divestiture during the middle and late 1970s. Mexico followed in the mid-1980s and Argentina in 1989. More recently, other countries, including Peru and Venezuela, moved aggressively toward privatization. This section discusses some of the most salient features of the privatization experiences in Chile, Mexico, and Argentina (see table 6-3 for a synoptic view of the main features of divestiture programs in these three countries and, for comparison, in Peru).

Table 6–3. *Privatization in Selected Countries of Latin America: A Schematic View*

Item	Argentina	Chile		Mexico	Peru
		First round	Second round		
Approximate starting date	1989	1974	1984	1984	1991
Main objectives	Reduce size of government; increase efficiency and government revenues	Maximize government revenues; reduce size of government	Spread ownership; reduce importance of government	Reduce size of government; modernize Mexican economy	Reduce state-owned enterprises–induced fiscal deficit; modernize Peruvian economy
Number of firms privatized[a]	45	470	80[b]	908	12
Percentage of state-owned enterprises privatized	15	82	96[c]	79	20
Role of foreigners	Significant; firms from both industrial nations and Latin American countries	Very limited; mostly in the form of joint ventures	Significant; through debt-equity swaps	Major role in some areas (such as steel, telecommunications)	Foreigners encouraged to participate
Debt-equity swaps	Yes; percentage allowed decided on case-by-case basis	No	Yes; on case-by-case basis; limited percentage	No	Not to date

Political opposition	Significant initially, now very minor	Yes; not voiced because of political situation	Yes	Very minor	Yes
Efficiency gains	Some to date	Major restructuring to improve productivity	Significant productivity improvements	Yes; very large in some cases	Too early to know
Workers offered shares at preferential prices	No	No	Yes; on case-by-case basis	Yes; workers have right of first refusal by law	Yes
Government credit	No	Yes	No	No; cash only	Cash only to date; some loans from Banco de la Nación to finance layoffs
Sequencing	Airlines and phone company first; electricity; steel; gas; water	Banks first; manufacturing firms next; regulatory framework last	Rule of the game; reprivatization; regulatory framework; large firms and public utilities	Small firms first; public utilities; banks	Small enterprises first; regulatory framework; banks; large state-owned enterprises
Scope of divestiture	Partial	Full	Partial; controlling packages sold	Partial; in some cases government retained nonvoting shares	Full in most cases

a. Until 1991.
b. Excludes reprivatization.
c. Accumulated.
Source: World Bank, several internal country reports.

Table 6-4. Privatizations in Chile, 1974–90

Round and year	Number of companies	Mode
First round		
First phase, 1974	More than 325	Free-of-charge return
Second phase, 1975–78	228	Debt-led divestiture
Second round		
First phase, 1984–86	About 50	Onerous divestiture of odd sector
Second phase, 1985–90	About 30	Widespread sale of state-owned enterprises

Source: Luders 1991.

Chile. Between 1974 and 1992, the Chilean government privatized more than 500 firms. This process was carried out in two rounds—the first during the middle and late 1970s and the second during the middle and late 1980s. These two efforts were separated by a brief interlude, between 1982 and 1984, when, as a result of the financial crisis discussed in chapter 3, there was a partial reversal in the process, and the government took over more than fifty banks and firms (see table 6-4 for a summary of the Chilean privatization program).

The first round of privatization (1974–82) had two distinct components. The first was the return of firms seized by the Unidad Popular during 1970–73 to their original stockholders.[5] The second was the sale of a large number of banks and firms to the private sector. Some of these companies were nationalized during the Allende administration, while others traditionally were under government control. The process was centralized by a special unit within the government holding company (CORFO), and sales were conducted through bids and direct sales. In many cases, CORFO rejected all bids and negotiated with the two highest bidders. This process introduced an element of arbitrariness into the process, making it politically unpopular. The typical sale conditions included a small down payment with the balance due in yearly installments.

Commercial banks were privatized first. In spite of explicit legislation aimed at avoiding excessive concentration of ownership, controlling interests in most banks were bought by emerging local conglomerates. Immediately after banks were sold, a large number of manufacturing firms were offered to the private sector. Between 1974 and 1978, 114 firms were privatized, and 259 firms seized during the Allende government were returned to their stockholders (Edwards and Edwards 1991).

Luders (1991) describes this early round as a debt-led privatization process in which buyers—mostly the *grupos*—borrowed heavily in order to pay for newly acquired firms. This increased borrowing took place through three basic channels. First, the conglomerates used the recently privatized banks to obtain loans to finance part of their purchases. Second, and perhaps more important, the government encouraged higher indebtedness by providing substantial volumes of credit directly to prospective buyers. And, third, foreign banks were eager to extend loans to the Chilean conglomerates either to acquire new firms or to finance the operations of ongoing concerns.

There has been a long debate in Chile on whether these early firms were sold at a fair price or whether buyers were subsidized. Although the early procedure sometimes lacked transparency, there is no evidence of a deliberate underpricing of assets. Many of the early firms were sold at relatively low prices because they were in extremely poor financial condition, had a large number of redundant personnel, and incurred significant losses. Additionally, political instability and the lack of a credible regulatory framework that committed the government to supporting the private sector reduced the market value of these assets.

In an effort to sell a large number of companies fast, the government did not attempt to restructure them before offering them to the public. Many of these firms were in serious financial difficulties, and all of them had major productivity problems. Buyers were expected to implement the steps necessary to improve efficiency. To that effect, the government placed few restrictions on the buyers' ability to lay off redundant workers. This contrasts sharply with the Mexican case, where authorities made serious efforts to avoid layoffs in the privatized firms. In retrospect, the cost of restructuring the privatized firms was clearly much higher than the *grupos* officials had anticipated. For years, many companies—including those in the export sector, which was supposed to be favored by the new policies—incurred large losses. The *grupos* increasingly tapped the credit market in order to cover them, generating what Harberger (1985b) calls a false demand for credit. This put severe pressure on real interest rates in the late 1970s and early 1980s, adversely affecting Chile's macroeconomic balance.

By 1982, when the Chilean economy entered a deep crisis, various *grupos* became insolvent, and the government took over fifty firms and banks. This unexpected reversal in the privatization process constituted a serious setback for the government's program. The authorities rapidly decided to privatize these firms and banks once again. However, the sour experience of the early privatization indicated that this time a different scheme was needed. In the second round of privatization, the government expressly avoided creating a situation where a few (technically insolvent) conglomerates would buy a large number of firms.

The outcome of the first phase of Chilean privatization, including the partial reversal, the failure of some of the largest banks, and the bankruptcy of large conglomerates, was a direct consequence of how the firms and banks were sold. First, in spite of existing (and antiquated) legislation, no real effort was made to supervise the newly privatized financial sector. In particular, as

Table 6-5. Privatization in Chile, Method of Payment and Buyers, 1985–89

Enterprise	Method of divestiture	First buyers
CAP	Stock market	Varied investors
	Direct sale to workers	Own workers
	Redemption of equity[a]	
CHILEFILMS	Auction	Domestic investors
CHILGENER	Stock market	Varied investors
		Foreign investors
		Pension funds
	Direct sale to workers	Own workers
CHILMETRO	Stock market	Varied investors
		Pension funds
	Direct sale to workers	Own workers
CHILQUINTA	Stock market	Varied investors
		Pension funds
	Direct sale to workers	Own workers
CTC	Stock market	Varied investors
		Pension funds
	Direct sale to workers	Own workers[b]
		Public sector employees
	Auction	Foreign investors
	Increase in equity	Foreign investors
ECOM	Direct sale to workers	Own workers
EDELMAG	Direct sale to public	Small regional investors[c]
ELECDA	Direct sale to public	Regional investors[c]
	Stock market	Varied investors
	Expropriation settlement[d]	Small investors
ELIQSA	Direct sale to public	Regional investors[c]
	Direct sale to workers	Own workers
	Stock market	Varied investors
	Expropriation settlement[d]	Small investors
EMEC[e]	Auction	Domestic investors
EMEL[e]	Direct sale to workers	ENDESA employees
EMELARI	Direct sale to public	Regional investors[c]
	Direct sale to workers	Public sector employees
	Expropriation settlement[d]	Small investors
EMELAT[e]	Auction	EMEL
		ENDESA employees
ENAEX	Auction	Foreign investors
	Direct sale	FAMAE[f]
ENDESA	Stock market	Varied investors
		Pension funds
	Direct sale to workers	Own workers
		Public sector employees
	Direct sale to public	
	Expropriation settlement[d]	Small investors

Enterprise	Method of divestiture	First buyers
ENTEL	Stock market	Varied investors
		Pension funds
	Direct sale to workers	Own workers
	Direct sale	Chilean army
	Expropriation settlement[d]	Small investors
IANSA	Direct sale	Sugar beet producers[g]
	Direct sale to workers	Own workers
	Stock market	Varied investors
		Foreign investors
ISE GENERALES	Stock market	Varied investors
	Direct sale to workers	Own workers
ISE VIDA	Stock market	Not available
LABORATORIO	Stock market	Varied investors
CHILE		Pension funds
	Direct sale to workers	Own workers
LAN CHILE	Stock market	Varied investors
	Direct sale to workers	Own workers
	Auction	Domestic and foreign investors
PEHUENCHE	Direct sale to workers	Own workers
	Subscription of new shares ENDESA	
PILMAIQUEN[e]	Auction	Foreign investors
PULLINQUE[e]	Auction	One investor[h]
SACRET	Direct sale to workers	Own workers
SCHWAGER	Stock market	Varied investors
		Pension funds
	Direct sale to workers	Own workers
	Expropriation settlement[d]	Small investors
SOQUIMICH	Stock market	Varied investors
		Pension funds
	Direct sale to workers	Own workers
TELEX-CHILE	Auction	Foreign investors

a. The total number of shares in CAP's equity was 438,089,188, of which 83.3 percent belonged to CORFO in April 1986. In June 1986, CORFO withdrew 288,641,076 shares, for which CAP paid $0.25 per unit. As a result of the annulment of the shares, private ownership increased from 17 to 49 percent, with a corresponding decline in CORFO's ownership.

b. Only newly issued shares.

c. These companies were partially sold to the general public only from that region. This was called regional popular capitalism.

d. The Allende government intensified the process of agrarian reform from 1971 to 1973, expropriating a large number of farms. Some former owners sued the government. In 1987, a law was passed authorizing the government to settle the claims in shares of public enterprises at book value.

e. Originally a subsidiary of ENDESA.

f. FAMAE is an enterprise of the Chilean army.

g. IANSA is a monopsony in the market for sugar beets in Chile.

h. It was not possible to find out whether it is foreign or domestic.

Source: Galal, Saez, and Torres 1992.

early as 1976 when a mid-size commercial bank, the Banco Osorno, collapsed, government officials were aware that the *grupos* were using banks to acquire new firms, inflating share prices to provide collateral for new loans, and using these, in turn, to buy still other companies. Second, the government sought to maximize revenue from privatization, with little concern for the resulting concentration of property and political power.

During the second round of privatization, the authorities' main objectives were to reduce dramatically the size of the government and to broaden ownership. The first step consisted of reprivatizing those firms that had failed during the financial crisis of 1982. This time, however, the government did not provide credit and carefully checked the financial credentials of prospective buyers. Financial institutions, including two of the largest banks, were privatized through a scheme known as "popular capitalism," in which private individuals were allowed to buy a limited amount of shares—up to US$7,000—at a below-market value (see Luders 1991 for details).

During the late 1980s, the Chilean government broadened the scope of privatization by selling large public utilities and firms that had long been in government hands, including the largest steel mill, the national airline, and most utilities—telephones, electricity, and water. During this phase, the government exercised great pragmatism, combining different modes of privatization even for a given firm. Shares were sold—usually at discount—to workers, to foreigners, to pension funds, and to local private companies. To avoid the distributive impact of selling shares exclusively to workers of the privatized firm, the government sometimes offered shares to anyone employed in the public sector. Foreigners participated actively in this second round of privatization, taking advantage of the attractive debt-conversion program described in chapter 4—the Chapter 19 scheme. Table 6-5 contains a list of privatized companies, buyers, and mode of payment for 1985–89.

During the second phase of privatization, the Chilean government introduced sweeping regulatory reforms. Particularly important were the laws establishing operating and servicing rules for utilities. The main principle behind this new set of regulations was that entry and price setting were left to the market in those areas with a high degree of competition or contestability. The government would regulate technical aspects, including those related to safety, and set prices in areas where markets were imperfect. These ambitious reforms, however, ran into problems during the early 1980s. For example, the General Law of Telecommunications of 1982 was ambiguous regarding the regulatory rights to approve concessional requests and did not establish an efficient and transparent procedure for setting rates (Galal 1993). These shortcomings were partially remedied in 1985 and 1987, when the authority of the regulatory body was clarified and a clear procedure, based on a rate-of-return framework, was established for determining telecommunications tariffs.[6] In early 1994, however, regulators set what were considered to be low rates for the telephone company. This generated a serious crisis in which share prices tumbled, and the trading of its American Depositary Receipts in New York had to be suspended.

Many observers predicted that the new Chilean democratic government that took over in 1990 would put an end to the divestiture process and even repeal some of the privatizations of the military regime. However, nothing of this kind happened. In fact, after heated debate on the subject, the government of President Aylwin continued the privatization process, and in 1993, share packages of six firms, including railway lines and transportation companies, were sold to the private sector (see *El Mercurio,* international edition, January 7–14, 1993). There is little doubt that, as the public associates the rapid growth of the last few years with the new economic mode, there will be no turning back in the Chilean divestiture program.

Mexico. Between 1983 and 1993, the Mexican government privatized approximately 1,000 state-owned firms. At the end of the Salinas administration in 1994, the number of state-owned enterprises in Mexico had been reduced from 1,155 in 1982 to less than 80 (however, the Mexican government still owns some important firms, including the oil giant PEMEX; the government showed its clear commitment to privatization and restructuring when, in 1987, it allowed Aeroméxico, a state-owned airline, to go bankrupt). In many ways, the Mexican divestiture program is exemplary. It proceeded smoothly, with minimal political opposition (see Sánchez 1992).

The Mexican privatization program began slowly in 1983. During its first phase (1983–87), sixty-four small and medium firms were sold to private interests. Most of the early privatization corresponded to manufacturing companies operating in fairly competitive sectors that did not require significant changes in the regulatory framework. During this initial phase, the impact of sales on fiscal revenues was rather modest; gross proceeds were approximately US$2.6 billion.

Starting in 1988, the privatization process accelerated, as very large public firms, including service sector monopolies, were put on the block. These sales included the telephone company TELMEX—which on its own generated a revenue of US$1.8 billion—the two major airlines, eighteen banks that had been nationalized immediately after the debt crisis, a gigantic steel complex, and other large corporations. This second round of privatization raised more than US$12.0 billion.

The procedure used was both simple and effective. The complete process was handled by a decentralized unit in the Finance Ministry and usually followed three steps. The first was valuation of the firm to be privatized by an investment bank; this value was then used for reference but did not constitute a minimum "reserve" price during the sale process. The second step was to offer the firm for public sale. The conditions of sale were remarkably straightforward: cash only. In some cases, if the firm was considered to be too large, only a controlling percentage was sold. The third step corresponded to the actual sale of the company in question. A commission at the ministerial level—the Income and Expenditures Commission—made the final adjudication, which in most cases corresponded to the highest bidder (for detailed discussions of the process, see Gil Díaz 1992).

The privatization program enjoyed substantial political support in Mexico, more than in any other country (notice that the Zapatista rebels did not make privatization a main issue in their negotiations with the Salinas and Zedillo administrations). This was the result of a series of factors. First, the whole Mexican reform program was designed in consultation with labor unions and the private sector through the tripartite agreement known as "Pacto." In an informal way, the Pacto de Solidaridad operated beyond macroeconomic stabilization, covering some of the most important structural reforms. Second, according to existing regulations, unions had the right of first refusal in any privatization. They could buy any percentage of the firm being offered, with the condition not to resell that stake for a given period of time. Between 1984 and 1991, unions bought controlling packages in sixteen companies. Also, unions from a number of very large companies, including TELMEX and Aeroméxico, bought substantial packages of shares at a discount. And third, the government entered into informal agreements with buyers that there would be no layoffs (there were a few exceptions to this, including the two airlines, Aeroméxico and Mexicana de Aviación). This was the case even with firms such as TELMEX that had clear labor redundancy.

In 1991, the Mexican government began to privatize the nineteen banks that had been nationalized at the outset of the debt crisis. The process was completed in 1992 and hailed as a big success, because every bank was sold at several times its book value. In the years immediately preceding the privatization, Mexican banks were relatively inefficient by international standards, with operating costs almost twice as high as those of U.S. banks. However, as a result of increased competition—both among themselves and from new institutions—productivity growth is expected to increase in the years to come (Gavito Mohar, Sánchez García, and Trigueros Legarreta 1992).

Most of the banks were bought by Mexican industrial conglomerates whose goal was to expand their activities to the financial sphere. What makes this situation particularly interesting (and potentially delicate) is that in Mexico, in contrast with most of the region, banks are allowed to invest in equities. This means that, contrary to the Chilean case of the 1970s, the ownership structure of the banks and their conglomerates is out in the open. However, to avoid financial crises of the type that engulfed most of Latin America during the 1980s, it is fundamentally important to continue strengthening the recent regulatory legislation. Given the close links among banks, brokerage houses, and manufacturing firms, it is crucial to consolidate accounting at the conglomerate level. Only in this way will the authorities be able to monitor the soundness of individual banks and avoid collusion and unexpected surprises. The

Mexican peso crisis of 1994 showed that, in spite of efforts to strengthen the overall regulatory framework, the Mexican banking system continues to be weak.

By beginning the privatization process with small firms and moving slowly to larger and more sophisticated companies, the Mexican government avoided committing large and costly mistakes during the early phases. From a political economy point of view, an important feature of the Mexican program is that the interministerial Income and Expenditures Commission, which had the final word on all matters related to privatization, operates on the basis of complete unanimity. This meant that agreements had to be worked out among the different ministries, avoiding political conflicts and sensitive public disagreements (Gil Díaz 1992 emphasizes this point).

The Mexican privatization program had positive effects on efficiency and productivity (see ITAM 1992). In the case of Aeroméxico, for example, labor productivity more than doubled between 1981 and 1990, and total factor productivity increased more than 20 percent. The second airline, Mexicana, also experienced substantial gains in productivity: labor productivity increased 47 percent, while total factor productivity grew 12 percent after privatization. Moreover, in a number of services, including the telephone company and the airlines, aggregate welfare increased as well. For instance, the aggregate welfare gains from the privatization of TELMEX are expected to exceed 10 percent of its market value and those from the privatization of Aeroméxico to improve 6 billion pesos (Tandon 1992).

The deregulation of transportation and the operation of ports was one of the most important achievements of Mexico's modernization program. According to a study by Fernández (1992), the traditional control by four unions of all operations in the Mexican port of Veracruz resulted in huge inefficiencies. A common practice—and one observed in many other countries in the region—was for members of the union to charge exorbitant prices and then subcontract the job to nonunion workers at a small fraction of the original fee. Out of each $1,000 charged for moving containers, the nonunion worker performing the job obtained only $50! The difference, of course, represents the rents obtained by the union for having the right to restrict entry. In Brazil, where a 1934 law grants monopoly to the stevedores' union, the situation is not very different. Nor was it different in Chile where, until 1981, the stevedores' union had an absolute monopoly and charged more than double the cost for performing some operations (union members obtained contracts and then subcontracted to so-called *medio pollos,* who in turn subcontracted to *cuartos de pollo,* who performed the task).

Mexico began to deregulate and modernize ports in mid-1991. The new regulation established free entry of service firms, eliminated service segmentation, allowed freedom to subcontract across firms and free determination of service rates, and restricted the number of unions to one per company. The results of the new legislation were spectacular: the cost of services declined more than 30 percent, and the volume of containers handled in Veracruz increased 47 percent in one year.[7]

A second important piece of legislation is the Law of Navigation and Maritime Trade, which allowed private parties to build and operate ports. This resulted in the creation of a number of specialized ports—for cement products, mining, and petrochemicals—that greatly reduced the costs of transportation (Fernández 1992; Sánchez 1992). Argentina also restructured private ports, and the volume of exports of grain increased significantly.

The effects of transportation regulations are not restricted to ports; they also affect the trucking industry. Mexico provides a particularly telling example of both the costs of this type of regulation and the benefits of reform. Until 1988, trucking activities were tightly restricted and subject to severe barriers to entry. The government had the right to grant concessions to private parties for one or more of the nine established routes. In most cases, only those companies with a concession could provide trucking services. The one exception was truckers who obtained special permits allowing them to transport one (and only one) type of good on a particular route. Companies with concessions or with permits were subject to loading and unloading restrictions. Trucks were often allowed to unload in a given city but were prohibited from loading and, thus, had to make the return trip empty (see Fernández 1992).

As a result of this maze of regulations, the Mexican trucking industry was not reliable. Moreover, costs were extremely high, exceeding by almost 50 percent what they would have been in a competitive environment. In June 1989, the trucking industry was reformed, and, subject to safety requirements, free entry was established. According to the new law, any truck could move freely and load and unload in any city, port, or railway station. Additionally, fees were deregulated and completely freed in 1990. As a result, the number of licensed trucks increased 62 percent in two years, fees declined as much as 50 percent on some routes, and the quality of service improved dramatically (Fernández 1992).

The deregulation of transportation services vastly improved the ability of Chile and Mexico to compete internationally. By reducing the costs of shipping almost 50 percent, small and medium firms that would otherwise be marginal were able to expand their export activities (Fernández 1992; Gil Díaz 1992). Recent efforts to deregulate maritime and land transport in Colombia and Venezuela are also showing promising results. The recent decision by the Brazilian Senate to begin deregulating ports may very well provide additional impetus to the expansion of Brazilian exports as well.

Argentina. State-owned enterprises have long been a financial drag on Argentina's treasury. During the 1980s, financing requirements for state-owned enterprises surpassed 50 percent of the total nonfinancial public sector

Table 6-6. Revenue from Privatization in Argentina, through 1992
(millions of U.S. dollars)

Enterprise	Cash	Bonds	Transferred liabilities
Aerolíneas Argentinas	260.0	1,610.0	n.a.
Altos Hornos Zapla	3.3	29.7	n.a.
Central Alto Valle	22.1	n.a.	n.a.
Central Dock Sud	25.0	n.a.	n.a.
Central Guemes	10.0	76.2[a]	n.a.
Central oil extraction areas	1,387.4	n.a.	n.a.
Central Pedro de Mendoza	8.5	n.a.	n.a.
EDELAP	5.0	134.0[a]	n.a.
Electricity			
SEGBA Central Costanera	90.1	n.a.	n.a.
SEGBA Central Puerto	92.2	n.a.	n.a.
SEGBA Edenor	30.0	397.9[a]	n.a.
SEGBA Edesur	30.0	481.0[a]	n.a.
ENTEL (phone company)	2,270.9	5,000.0	n.a.
Grain elevators	6.0	n.a.	n.a.
Highways	Canon	n.a.	n.a.
Induclor	17.8	50.6	n.a.
Liniers cattle market	Canon	n.a.	n.a.
Llao Llao Hotel	3.7	12.0	n.a.
Monomeros Vinilicos	9.3	26.5	n.a.
Natural gas (seven firms)	218.0	1,095.0[a]	823.0
Palermo Hippodrome	61.5	n.a.	n.a.
Petropol	4.5	12.1	n.a.
Petroquímica Río Tercero	7.3	n.a.	n.a.
Polisur	14.1	41.0	n.a.
Railways	Canon	n.a.	n.a.
Real estate	107.0	n.a.	n.a.
Secondary oil extraction areas	458.3	n.a.	n.a.
Silos Buenos Aires	Canon	n.a.	n.a.
Silos Quequen	Canon	n.a.	n.a.
SOMISA	140.0	12.1	250.0
Tandanor	59.8	n.a.	n.a.
Television and radio stations	13.9	n.a.	n.a.
Total	5,455.7	6,794.9	1,073.0
		2,184.1[a]	

n.a. Not applicable.
a. Bonds at cash value.
Source: Unpublished data from Argentina's Subsecretaría de Privatizaciones, 1993.

deficit, directly contributing to the eruption of hyperinflation in 1989. Toward the end of that decade, it became increasingly clear to analysts and policymakers that a permanent solution to the country's macroeconomic instability would require a massive restructuring and divestiture of public enterprises. The Reform Act of 1989 established that publicly owned enterprises were eligible for privatization. Originally, the plan ran into political opposition, especially from the militant Peronist unions. Slowly, however, as the quality of services provided by most of the newly privatized firms improved and the structural adjustment program began to bear fruit in other spheres, the program began to enjoy support among the population at large.

Between 1989 and 1992, fifty-one firms were privatized for a total of approximately US$18 billion in cash and debt reduction. Drawing from the experiences of other countries, the Argentine government strengthened the regulatory framework for public utilities and other sectors where it formerly had an important presence (see table 6-6 for data on the most important Argentine privatizations, including the amount of the sales and method of payment).

The Argentine privatization program responded to a number of objectives. First, to reduce inflation and stabilize the macroeconomy, the Menem administration urgently needed to reduce the fiscal burden imposed by state enterprises. The most effective and rapid way to accomplish this was to divest most public enterprises. Second, integral components of the Menem administration's vision of a modern Argentina were a reduction in the size of the state and a major decentralization. And third, the modernization process required a major improvement in the quality of public services, including telecommunications, electricity, transportation, and ports. A long history of failed attempts to increase the efficiency of state-owned enterprises convinced the new administration that this could only be achieved through a major participation of the private sector in these areas (Menem's main economic strategist, Domingo Cavallo, articulated his vision of a "new" Argentina in his 1985 book *Volver a crecer*).

Beginning in 1989, the privatization process was coordinated by a special unit created in the Ministry of Economics and headed by the undersecretary of privatization. Actual sales of state-owned enterprises were undertaken by ad hoc commissions that included representatives from the central unit, sectoral policy areas, auditing bodies, and, in some cases, provincial governments (Alexander and Corti 1993). Most privatizations were carried out with legislative approval and oversight, providing political legitimacy to the process. The initial round of privatization was approved by the Emergency Law of 1989; during the second round, a bicameral commission had the right to approve specific sales of state-owned assets (if the commission failed to reach consensus on a specific privatization, the executive could act on its own). As a way to reduce the monopoly power of the privatized firms, state-owned utilities were divided into two or more companies before the privatization. This was the case of telecommunications, electricity, and natural gas.

The Argentine government used several privatization procedures. The most popular method was to create new corporations that owned or operated public assets; as a way to increase the attractiveness of the firms to be privatized, the old state enterprises retained most liabilities. Shares of the newly formed companies were then offered to the public and sold through a two-envelope competitive bidding process. The first envelope included the technical characteristics of the offer, while the second dealt with its financial features. In some cases, instead of selling the actual asset, the government offered operating concessions for up to ninety-nine years. This was the case for some highways, ports, and railways. In the case of railways, concessions were granted to bidders that required the lowest amount of subsidy for a period of ten years. In the case of the urban-rural railway system, the winning bidder requested a subsidy of approximately US$100 million a year, significantly lower than the almost US$500 million that the government had been placing into the system every year. An interesting aspect of the privatization of railways is that the total labor force was reduced from more than 95,000 to a mere 5,000, increasing productivity by several orders of magnitude!

Other procedures were also used to sell certain assets. For example, government holdings in chemical and industrial firms were sold to majority stockholders, and some assets, especially real estate, were auctioned to the highest bidder. A controlling percentage of the petroleum company YPF was sold as an ongoing concern through a combination of mechanisms including a public offering of American Depositary Receipts in New York.

The Argentine government recognized early on that a successful privatization process required a new, modern regulatory framework. However, in practice, the implementation of new regulatory laws was slow and often lacked transparency. For example, the telecommunications company, ENTEL, was put on the market before the new regulations had been fully implemented, dissuading several potential bidders from participating in the process (Hill and Abdala 1993). In particular, participants were concerned that their assets might be expropriated in the future. The most important element of uncertainty referred to the possibility that tariffs would be fixed at levels below those required to obtain a minimum rate of return. Eventually, three consortia bid for 60 percent of the shares of the two newly created telephone companies. The government retained 40 percent of the shares, of which 10 percent were sold to the telephone company workers, 20 percent to the general public, and 10 percent to telecommunications cooperatives. The two consortia paid US$214 million in cash plus US$5 billion in Argentine foreign debt for a 60 percent stake in the telephone company.

In an effort to dispel the buyers' concerns regarding future changes in the rules of the game, the Argentine government created a new regulatory agency—the Comisión Nacional de Telecomunicaciones—and gave it power to determine prices and to regulate concessions and entry requirements. The commission was funded by a tax on telecommunications revenues and was comprised of five members appointed by the president of the republic. The first commissioners, however, lacked technical expertise and were not fully committed to the privatization process or the notion of privately operated utilities. As a result, the commission remained inactive and failed to resolve some of the most serious problems facing the sector. A particularly serious issue emerged when the Convertibility Law of 1991 banned all indexation formulas, leaving the newly determined telephone tariffs vulnerable to inflationary erosion (Herrera 1993). According to Hill and Abdala (1993), the commission's unwillingness to replace the indexation formula reduced the credibility of the Argentine government's commitment to providing clear rules for the newly privatized firms. In early 1992, and partially due to World Bank suggestions, the telecommunications commissioners were replaced by a new team that was highly committed to Argentina's new development path. The new commission acted rapidly, making quick decisions on pending petitions for rates and entry into new areas such as mobile and cellular phones.

An important feature of the Argentine privatization process, one that sets it apart from those of Chile and Mexico, is that Argentina started with very large and controversial companies—the national airlines and the telephone company. This was largely a political decision. The Menem administration realized that, after the hyperinflation and frustrated modernization efforts of the Alfonsín government, the only way to signal a decisive commitment to privatization was to move swiftly and to put major state-owned enterprises on the block. Initially, many observers were skeptical about the government's ability to diffuse the opposition of activist unions. However, as the process proceeded, more and more analysts realized that this process could indeed be one of massive and rapid modern privatization.

Another important feature of the Argentine privatization—and according to some observers, a worrisome one—is that, as in the case of Chile during the first round of privatizations in the 1970s, a small number of local conglomerates acquired controlling packages in many of the privatized firms (these conglomerates were the Techint group, Pérez-Companc, Comercial La Plata–Soldati, and the Astra group). This increased the degree of industrial concentration, especially in public utilities. Although the government responded by trying to speed up the modernization of the regulatory framework, including price-setting mechanisms, it is too early to know whether monopolistic practices will be fully avoided. In the years to come, it will be important to monitor closely whether the new regulatory framework indeed provided an adequate environment for the development of natural monopolies in private sector hands.

The Argentine privatization program had an important impact on the country's public finances. Psacharopoulos (1992) correctly anticipated that the deficit of public enterprises would decline from 3.4 percent of GDP in 1989 to –0.06 percent of GDP in 1994. The reason behind this drastic change is that inefficiencies and politically controlled prices led to systematic losses in state-owned enterprises. For the system as a whole, the reduction in government outlays (primarily in the form of subsidies and transfers) will more than offset the reduction in income stemming from the limited number of profitable operations.

The privatization process allowed the Argentine government to reduce drastically its public (foreign and domestic) debt. As of the first quarter of 1993, the face value of public debt had been reduced approximately US$14 billion. Additionally, the government had received approximately US$6 billion in cash. Naturally, this provided welcome breathing room at a time when the need to consolidate public finances was at the heart of the adjustment program.

As a result of privatization, the payroll in public enterprises declined drastically: from 250,000 in 1989 to approximately 60,000 employees by the end of 1993. This major reduction in public sector employment was accomplished through three channels: transfers to newly privatized firms, early retirement, and voluntary quits with severance payments. The average cost in severance payments was around US$7,200 per employee, or US$690 million in total. This cost was partially covered with World Bank adjustment loans, which required clear audit conditions for disbursement. The reduction in redundant personnel prior to the privatization allowed the government to obtain higher prices and allowed buyers to start operating with fairly lean crews. Additionally, the existence of generous severance payments rendered existing collective bargaining agreements void, allowing buyers to negotiate from scratch with the remaining labor force (the bargaining process was still subject to the fairly distorted Argentine labor legislation; see chapter 8 of this book; Alexander and Corti 1993).

An important lesson of the Argentine privatization process is that humility and humbleness are essential ingredients. Even when authorities are convinced of the need to modernize the regulatory framework, the new regulation is likely to become operational only slowly. In some cases, mistakes will be made along the way. More generally, it takes time to build institutions that are credible and able to fulfill their economic role. This means that it is especially important to set the bases for new institutions early on and to make corrections when there are indications of problem areas.

CHAPTER 7

Capital Market Deregulation, Savings, and Investment

FOR MANY DECADES, A MAJORITY OF LATIN AMERICAN COUNTRIES imposed tight controls on the financial sector. Ceilings on interest rates were common, and credit was allocated to sectors that social planners deemed exciting and promising. The creation of new financial institutions was often blocked as a way to reduce the extent of speculative and unproductive activities. These policies responded to two related factors. First, based on simplistic interpretations of Keynesian theories, it was thought that, by controlling interest rates at reasonably low levels and by expanding the scope of government direct intervention, investment would greatly increase. Second, starting in the 1940s, a great distrust of market mechanisms prompted politicians to impose controls on almost every aspect of economic life. Raúl Prebisch, the intellectual father of CEPAL and structuralism, was one of the original popularizers of Keynesian economics in Latin America. In his 1947 book, *Introducción a Keynes*, he devotes several chapters to the behavior of interest rates and argues that government intervention aimed at controlling interest rates accelerates growth (pp. 104–6). He contends that lower interest rates *encourage* savings and that the government should "lower interest rates to a level where full employment is achieved" (p. 138). And later, "[it is] required that the State assumes control over certain variables, . . . [including] interest rates. Regarding investment, it is likely that it should be socialized as the only means to achieve full employment, since the manipulation of the interest rate will not be sufficient" (pp. 139–40, translated from Spanish).

Financial control was expected to increase aggregate savings, accelerate capital accumulation, boost the efficiency of investment, and stimulate overall growth. Things, however, did not work as expected. These policies resulted in a low degree of monetization, generated significant lobbying activities (including corruption) aimed at obtaining credit quotas, reduced the quality of private investment, depressed the growth of productivity, and discouraged financial intermediation and savings. During 1960–85, the ratio of loanable funds to GDP in a group of Latin American countries was only 75 percent of that of a comparable group of Asian nations (the Latin American countries were Argentina, Brazil, Chile, and Colombia; the Asian countries were India, the Philippines, Sri Lanka, and Turkey; McKinnon 1991).

The dominant development paradigm in Latin America during the 1960s and 1970s was challenged in the 1970s by the view that financial liberalization was essential to encourage growth. According to this approach, pioneered by McKinnon (1973) and Shaw (1973), a growth-conducive financial policy requires free interest rates, low reserve requirements on bank deposits, and sophisticated financial intermediaries, including stock exchanges (see, for example, Luders 1968). It was not, however, until the 1980s that this view was accepted by a large number of policymakers and political leaders. This change in perception of the role of the financial market in the development process is part of the new economic synthesis that emerged in the region in the past few years. As a consequence of this new perspective, and influenced by the experience of other regions, the reform of the financial sector became an important component of most recent programs for structural adjustment throughout Latin America. By allowing the sector to develop, it was expected that financial intermediation would increase and that firms would be able to finance expansion programs more easily. Also, by creating a transparent market-based system of credit allocation, lobbying activities were expected to decline and the productivity of investment to increase.

According to the traditional literature on financial liberalization and reform, the deregulation of capital markets affects economic growth through two channels: higher savings rates and improved allocation of investment. While higher savings allow an increase in capital accumulation, improved allocation of investment results in higher marginal productivity of capital (Fry 1988 summarizes these theories and some tests related to them).

Recently, however, several authors have suggested that the link between the financial sector and economic performance takes place through a different avenue. King and Levine (1993a), for example, argue that financial institutions have an advantage in processing information regarding the potential degree of creativity and inventiveness of entrepreneurs. Thus, a well-developed financial sector is able to identify promising projects—projects that result in rapid growth of productivity—and to monitor the extent to which entrepreneurs indeed make progress. These authors have developed a formal theoretical model that suggests that countries with more developed financial sectors have an advantage in sorting out highly productive innovations and, thus, tend to grow faster than countries with repressed financial sectors. This approach, then, differs from the traditional McKinnon and Shaw views in two important respects: first, it recognizes that the processing of information is at the center of the capital market functions, and, second, it emphasizes growth of productivity (rather than accumulation of physical capital) as the fundamental source of economic development. King and Levine (1993b) present preliminary empirical evidence that supports their model: using an eighty-country data set, they find that, after controlling for other factors, higher degrees of financial intermediation are positively associated with growth of productivity over the long run.

Recognition that the acquisition and processing of information regarding investment projects is one of the fundamental roles of the capital market has important policy implications. Since information is a public good—that is, consumption by one individual does not preclude others from consuming it—the tendency in competitive markets is to produce less information than is socially desirable (on the theory of public goods, see Samuelson's 1954 classic treatment). Stiglitz (1994) contends that this has two important consequences. First, since financial institutions know that it is difficult to monitor them when information is limited, they are tempted to act recklessly, either undertaking (excessively) risky actions or committing fraud. And, second, since the public is aware of the incentive problem facing financial institutions, it entrusts to them fewer resources than it would under the (hypothetical) case of full information (Stiglitz and Weiss 1981 show that if firms are highly leveraged—as financial institutions usually are—they tend to act as risk lovers and gamble other people's money). This, of course, constitutes a market failure that, in theory, can be minimized through government intervention. In fact, the nature of information as a public good and the existence of information asymmetries constitute the fundamental theoretical rationale for designing a regulatory framework in financial markets. In the absence of such a framework, financial institutions are bound to get overextended, make bad loans, and, eventually, collapse at a huge cost to society (the collapse of a large number of banks in Argentina, Chile, Colombia, and Uruguay during the late 1970s and early 1980s was closely related to the lack of adequate regulation). From a policy perspective, it is difficult to design regulations that, while avoiding moral hazard, do not introduce significant distortions that reduce the financial market's ability to identify entrepreneurs who have the greatest potential to innovate and foster growth of productivity. The implementation of this type of regulatory framework constitutes, indeed, one of the most serious challenges to the financial sector reforms in Latin America.

In designing regulatory legislation for the financial sector, it is important to recognize that, to a large extent, the inadequate availability of information can be reduced significantly through actions mandated by the government but undertaken by the private sector itself. The use of credit-rating agencies and outside auditors to monitor the accounts of financial institutions are only two examples of quasi self-regulation. The long history in Latin America strongly suggests that overregulating the financial sector, especially intervening through direct government actions, can be disastrous. It can negatively affect the efficiency of the capital market, while at the same time creating rent seeking and heightening corruption.

As with other reforms, the degree of progress in financial deregulation has varied across the region. While some countries are farther along, others only recently began to create modern and dynamic capital markets. This chapter analyzes the recent experience in Latin America with financial reform and investigates the behavior of investment and savings.

Financial Repression in Latin America: Historical Background

In the late 1970s and early 1980s, the degree of sophistication of the financial sector varied significantly across Latin American countries. In some, such as Argentina, Brazil, Chile, and Uruguay, the banking system was somewhat developed, although still subject to important distortions. In others, including Bolivia, the Dominican Republic, Ecuador, Nicaragua, Peru, and Venezuela, the financial sector fitted almost perfectly the textbook description of financial repression: interest rates were subject to controls, the government allocated credit arbitrarily, securities markets were discouraged, and new financial institutions faced significant barriers to entry. In virtually every country, financial regulations and controls were translated into a low level of financial intermediation. As table 7-1 shows, with the exception of Venezuela and Honduras, the ratio of broad money to GDP was below 30 percent in the early 1980s (this ratio is within the range of 90 to 100 percent in more industrial nations; see McKinnon 1991). This section provides a historical analysis and reviews the state of the financial sector in Latin America as of the mid-1980s. This discussion serves as a background for the analysis of recent financial sector reforms provided in the rest of the chapter.

Many of the historical inefficiencies of the Latin American financial sector can be traced to the region's macroeconomic imbalances. High and variable rates of inflation discouraged the public from holding deposits in the domestic financial sector, generating the very low degrees of financial depth reported in table 7-1. In most countries, overvalued exchange rates encouraged speculation against the local currency and reduced the volume of resources intermediated by local financial institutions. Also, the need to collect a sizable inflation tax led central banks to impose very high reserve requirements on commercial banks, reducing their ability to intermediate funds. This is illustrated in table 7-2, which shows that effective reserve ratios in Latin America greatly exceeded those of the industrial countries in the late 1970s and 1980s.

In most Latin American countries, the banking system was traditionally at the heart of the financial sector, and other institutions were highly underdeveloped. Until the late 1980s, securities markets were relatively primitive, and market capitalization declined during the first half of that decade. With the exception of Chile, institutional investors played no significant role in the development of financial markets in Latin America until the early 1990s. Macroeconomic instability also precluded the issue of long-term securities, forcing firms to rely on inefficient sources of funds to finance new projects.

As a consequence of an array of regulations, emerging stock markets stagnated during the early 1980s. In most countries, they were extremely thin and highly concentrated on a few stocks. Government red tape discouraged firms

Table 7-1. Ratio of Broadly Defined Money to GDP in Selected Countries of Latin America, 1980–86
(percentage)

Country	1980	1983	1986
Argentina	22.6	16.1	16.3
Bolivia	15.5	12.1	5.3
Brazil	13.1	11.0	13.2
Chile	15.0	19.9	17.9
Colombia	22.9	28.0	27.5
Ecuador	19.3	17.1	20.9
Guatemala	20.5	24.0	22.3
Honduras	26.1	30.6	31.7
Mexico	23.6	23.9	24.3
Peru	12.7	11.6	12.0
Uruguay	20.3	20.3	15.8
Venezuela	31.5	41.9	42.3
Average	20.3	21.4	20.8
Standard deviation	5.4	8.7	9.4

Note: Calculated using stocks at the end of the period for broadly defined money.
Source: Morris and others 1990.

from issuing new shares, and speculators easily manipulated stock prices. In Brazil, for example, six stocks accounted for 70 percent of daily trading during the late 1980s. Additionally, most stock exchanges lacked trained staff, and adequate equipment was scarce. Small investors were deterred by the lack of transparency in most operations.

Historically, most Latin American countries imposed significant barriers to entry into the financial sector. Permits for the creation of new institutions were either not granted or subject to substantial red tape. In Uruguay, for example, the banking law effectively froze the number of banks and bank branches at their 1965 level (strictly speaking, new banks could be formed, but they were forbidden to take deposits; see Pérez-Campanero and Leone 1991). In Costa Rica and Nicaragua, the government had the exclusive right to own and operate commercial banks. In other countries, government-owned banks operated without a hard budget constraint, making the survival of small private banks almost impossible. As a result of this maze of regulations, the region developed an inefficient financial sector that exhibited high unit costs and substantial spreads between deposit and lending interest rates (McKinnon 1991; Morris and others 1990).

For many years, the government controlled the movement of interest rates. Ceilings were often set below ongoing rates of inflation, generating negative real interest rates. For a group of twelve countries, the average real rate of interest on bank deposits was negative during most years between 1980 and

1985 (Morris and others 1990; see tables 7-3 and 7-4). Naturally, these negative real rates of interest had serious consequences for resource allocation, including the funding of new productive projects, and greatly encouraged capital flight.

Most countries had strict (and arbitrary) guidelines regarding the sectoral allocation of credit. This was done through four main channels. First, government-owned development banks lent to certain sectors at below-market interest rates. In some cases, the central bank itself performed the role of a development agency, providing subsidized loans to favored sectors, usually agriculture, housing, and small enterprises. Second, commercial banks were required to lend a certain proportion of their portfolio to specific sectors. Third, the central bank provided preferential rediscount rates for loans granted by commercial banks to specific industries. And fourth, commercial banks were subject to differential reserve requirements, depending on the characteristics of their loan portfolios.

During the early and mid-1980s, a substantial share of total credit in many countries was directly allocated through these nonmarket mechanisms. For example, an estimated 30 percent of total loans in Colombia were directly allocated in 1986; the share was more than 40 percent in Argentina, more than 25 percent in Mexico, and 80 percent in Brazil. In Brazil, according to the World Bank, the subsidies implicit in the different officially controlled credit programs amounted to almost 8 percent of GDP a year (Morris and others 1990).

The practice of directly allocating credit was rationalized on the basis of efficiency and equity. It was argued that unless resources were administratively directed, specific sectors would receive a volume of loans below what was socially optimal. Existing empirical evidence, however, suggests that under most circumstances, administratively allocated credit does not reach the intended uses; it usually ends up being directed to a few large borrowers, who

Table 7-2. *Effective Reserve Requirements on Bank Deposits in Selected Countries, 1971–80*

Country	1971	1975	1980
Germany[a]	10.3	10.2	8.7
United Kingdom	5.3	6.9	2.8
United States	7.8	6.7	4.6
Brazil	34.4	28.4	33.4
Chile	52.0	35.9	28.2
Colombia	33.1	29.3	45.2
Mexico	20.7	79.2	51.4
Uruguay	32.5	35.9	11.9

a. Federal Republic of Germany before reunification.
Source: McKinnon 1991.

enjoy large rents (McKinnon 1991). The successful East Asian economies tackled this problem by organizing contests among exporting firms. Those that managed to increase their exports rapidly—independently of the sector—had access to the official financial market at relatively low interest rates (World Bank 1993a).

Traditionally, one of the most serious problems facing the Latin American financial sector was the lack of an adequate supervisory framework. Often, financial institutions were subject to very lax prudential rules and engaged in highly risky ventures. The disclosure of information was minimal or nonexistent, the quality of the loan portfolio was not analyzed, external auditors were seldom required to inspect the books in detail, and the rollover of questionable loans was allowed. Additionally, the accrual of interest on nonperforming loans was common, and unsecured loans (often to firms related to the banks) were permitted. Virtually everywhere the government provided (implicit) free deposit insurance regardless of the soundness of bank portfolios, creating situations of serious moral hazard. Moreover, provisions for bad loans were rarely made. In Argentina, Mexico, and Uruguay, provisions stood at less than 25 percent of nonperforming loans in 1985 (Morris and others 1990).[1]

In many cases, the combination of inadequate regulation, lax supervision, and free deposit insurance encouraged all parties involved—financial institutions and the public—to engage in excessively risky behavior. This situation

Table 7-3. Annualized Real Deposit Interest Rates in Selected Countries of Latin America, 1980–86
(percentage)

Country	1980	1983	1986
Argentina	3.6	18.9	16.3
Bolivia	−19.9	−66.2	−19.6
Brazil	3.8	8.7	4.3
Chile	8.9	0.9	3.2
Colombia	7.7	11.6	10.4
Ecuador	−1.9	−24.6	−0.2
Guatemala	−1.6	4.3	−19.0
Honduras	−7.4	1.7	5.1
Mexico	−0.1	−22.4	−2.9
Peru	−16.2	−20.2	−20.5
Uruguay	5.2	10.8	−6.7
Venezuela	−5.4	6.8	−1.7
Average	−2.3	−5.8	−2.6
Average without Bolivia	−0.7	−0.3	−1.1
Standard deviation	8.6	22.8	11.4
Standard deviation without Bolivia	7.0	14.4	10.7

Source: Morris and others 1990.

Table 7–4. Real Interest Rate Spreads in Selected Countries of Latin America,
1980–86
(percentage)

Country	1980	1983	1986
Argentina[a]	11.4	20.8	3.5
Bolivia	6.7	5.6	19.5
Chile	4.6	9.7	5.2
Colombia[a]	0.9	3.3	8.0
Ecuador	4.5	4.3	3.9
Guatemala[a]	1.8	2.9	2.2
Honduras[a]	5.7	8.2	8.9
Mexico[a]	5.6	17.7	26.4
Peru	5.4	7.4	6.4
Uruguay	10.4	11.4	20.3
Venezuela[a]	1.0	3.8	3.6
Average	5.3	8.6	9.8

a. Average annual interest rates.
Source: Morris and others 1990.

became particularly serious in the Southern Cone countries during the late 1970s, when Argentina, Chile, and Uruguay freed interest rates and allowed commercial banks to expand their activities greatly. The lack of information disclosure requirements generated situations of adverse selection in which good and bad risks were not distinguished. As interest rates increased, riskier borrowers were willing to pay even higher rates, hampering the soundness of bank portfolios. Macroeconomic instability exacerbated this situation; an increasingly high variance in project yields made it particularly difficult for banks to distinguish different risks (McKinnon 1991). Moreover, because of the existence of (implicit) insurance, moral hazard developed; banks and depositors perceiving that under bad states of nature, their losses would be covered by the monetary authority, as indeed occurred in the three countries (Ramos 1986).

The debt crisis of 1982 had a severe impact on an already inefficient and weak Latin American financial sector. The sudden drying up of foreign financing and the historical lending practices of many institutions conspired to create a situation in which a large number of firms could not pay their loans—or the interest, for that matter—to local banks. The proportion of nonperforming loans skyrocketed, exceeding in some cases more than 20 percent of total portfolios (Morris and others 1990). The debt crisis hit the financial sectors of Argentina, Chile, Colombia, Mexico, and Uruguay particularly hard. For instance, the largest private commercial bank and forty-two small and medium-size financial institutions had to be liquidated in Argentina during 1980–82 (Baliño 1991). In Chile, eleven financial institutions, whose portfolios represented almost 15 percent of total loans, were liquidated in 1981–82. A year later, the crisis had widened, and seven insolvent banks were taken over by the government. Two of them were liquidated; the other five were rehabilitated and privatized through the sale of share packages to small investors and privately managed pension funds (Larraín 1988; Velasco 1992). In Uruguay, the central bank tried to protect depositors by selling troubled banks to foreigners, who required that the banks be restructured and purged of bad loans before taking them over. The crisis, however, dragged on until 1986, when new failures forced the government to intervene in four commercial banks (Pérez-Campanero and Leone 1991). At the macroeconomic level, the debt crisis put an end to an era of ample foreign savings. In the mid- and late 1980s, it became clear that increasing domestic savings would be a fundamental task for the years to come. More and more experts agreed that this would require a new and dynamic approach toward capital markets.

Financial Deregulation in Latin America: Regional Trends and Selected Experiences

Starting in the late 1980s and early 1990s, many Latin American countries implemented major financial reforms aimed at increasing the degree of financial intermediation and raising the efficiency of investment. Although the experiences of specific countries varied significantly, most reforms tried to tackle the most serious problems, particularly (a) the deregulation of interest rates, (b) the elimination of direct credit allocation rules, (c) the reduction and harmonization of reserve requirements for commercial banks, (d) the relaxation of barriers to entry, (e) the encouragement of security markets and of institutional investors, and (f) the creation of modern and efficient supervisory legislation. This section evaluates the progress achieved by these reforms until 1993, beginning with a brief regional overview and moving to a detailed discussion of the experiences of Chile, Argentina, Bolivia, and Colombia.

Regional Overview

Table 7-5 presents a synoptic view of financial deregulation in eight countries. The information is organized according to the policy objectives discussed above and shows that until 1993 progress was somewhat uneven across both countries and policies. Most countries completely eliminated interest rate ceilings, and market forces determined interest rates. Those countries that maintained preferential interest rates for selected activities—Colombia, Mexico, and Venezuela, for example—opted to link the subsidized rate to market interest rates. Typically, the cost of funds for the favored sectors was set at a certain percentage of the rate prevailing in the market. This allowed the preferential rate to move through time according to market forces and represented

Table 7-5. Financial Reforms in Selected Countries of Latin America until Mid-1993

Country	Interest rate determination	Directed credit	Reserve requirements	Barriers to entry	Securities markets	Institutional investors	Supervisory framework
Argentina	Market-determined	Eliminated, except for multilateral institutions' credit lines	Lowered	Free entry; foreign-owned banks allowed	Deregulated	Expected to increase in importance with pension fund reform	Strengthened in 1992 when Comisión Nacional de Valores given more responsibility
Bolivia	Freely determined since 1985; large spreads	Severely reduced after the four largest public financial institutions closed	Rationalized in 1988	Greatly reduced after 1991	No important developments yet	Expected to increase	Improved after the reform of the superintendency of banks
Brazil	Mostly market-determined, but some sectors still borrow at subsidized rates	Several niches still remain; state-owned enterprises can borrow at below-market rates	Not completely rationalized yet	Reduced after 1991 with the elimination of "carta patentes" (licenses)	Still subject to substantial distortions	Very minor role	Not very efficient to date; it needs reform
Chile	Freely determined since mid-1970s; spreads declined in past few years	Eliminated, except for sectoral credit lines from multilateral institutions, which are auctioned	Rationalized across deposits and institutions	New institutions encouraged; number of banks increased to thirteen domestic and twenty-two foreign	Rapidly expanding; low degree of market capitalization	Increasingly important role of private pension funds after 1981	Modified in mid-1980s; modern and efficient; risk classification of portfolios required

(Table continues on the following page.)

Table 7-5 (continued)

Country	Interest rate determination	Directed credit	Reserve requirements	Barriers to entry	Securities markets	Institutional investors	Supervisory framework
Colombia	Freely determined, although some sectors still subject to subsidized rates	Percentage of directed credit to agriculture reduced to 6 percent of deposits	Reserves used as monetary control instrument; increasing variability	Barriers reduced; government-owned banks still important	Some attempts made; little results yet	Not important yet	Reformed in principle; banks subject to Basel Accord standards
Mexico	Freely determined after 1988–89; development banks lend at below-market rates	Eliminated in commercial banks; some directed loans corresponding to multilateral lines	Reserve requirements eliminated for peso-denominated deposits	In principle, new law of 1991 allows free entry; some restrictions for foreign-owned banks (30 percent maximum)	Increasingly dynamic; affected by foreign investors; widely fluctuating in 1991–92; additional reforms required	Pension fund reform expected to have impact in short run; foreign institutional investors playing growing role	Reformed; banks subject to Basel Accord in theory; portfolio risk analysis required; overall supervision still weak, however
Nicaragua	Freely determined after 1990; very high in real terms; very large spreads	Yes, through three large government-owned banks	High, not fully rationalized	Private banks face no formal barriers; significant competition from government banks	No developments yet	None	Being developed; current framework deficient
Venezuela	Freely determined; agriculture and housing rates are below market	Some credit directed to agriculture; percentage declined	Reduced to 15 percent for all deposits	In principle, free entry for locally owned banks; restrictions for foreign banks	New draft law proposed; approval not expected	Not important	New law of superintendency in draft form

Source: World Bank and IMF data.

a marked improvement over the historical practice of having completely fixed rates for certain sectoral operations. In particular, the new practice was more transparent, separating the magnitude of the subsidy from the inflationary conditions of the country.

As can be seen from table 7-5, the direct allocation of credit was greatly reduced in the region. In fact, with the exception of development lines of credit provided by the multilateral institutions, most countries eliminated forced sectoral loans. Argentina, Bolivia, Chile, and Jamaica adopted auction systems to distribute development credit among eligible users. This practice, set up with the assistance of the World Bank, forced credit users to reveal their willingness to pay for funds, considerably reducing the inefficiency costs associated with arbitrarily allocated subsidized credit schemes.

In many countries, the deregulation of interest rates and the elimination of direct credit allocation were supplemented by the reduction and rationalization of reserve requirements. This combination of policies allowed the financial system to expand the degree of intermediation, pressured firms to increase the quality of their investment projects, and forced banks and other lenders to make a greater effort to identify promising investors. In spite of this progress, and mostly due to macroeconomic imbalances and lack of credibility of the reforms, in most countries financial instruments continued to be concentrated on very short maturities; Chile was the major exception.

In most countries, barriers to entry were reduced as a result of the financial reforms. Despite the tendency to encourage competition and the creation of new institutions—both domestic and foreign—many countries made limited progress in this area because the private sector concentrated on acquiring financial institutions being privatized rather than on developing new ones. However, in a few countries, such as Nicaragua, new private banks rapidly entered the market, expanding the scope of the financial sector.

Almost every country in table 7-5 made some efforts to adopt a modern regulatory system aimed at minimizing destabilizing practices rooted in moral hazard and adverse selection. The reforms adopted fall in three main categories: requirements for capital adequacy of different financial intermediaries, regulations governing the disclosure of information and the activities of supervisory agencies, and norms that clearly define the steps to be taken in case some financial institutions face distress. This new legislation was expected to create a modern financial sector that is not vulnerable to isolated risky practices or to aggregate fluctuations in the economy as a whole. Most countries also developed rules requiring banks to abide by the Basel Accord regulations.

Despite serious efforts, the process of putting together a modern regulatory framework proved to be more difficult than expected. The lack of trained personnel, including inspectors and accountants, in many cases slowed down the process, as did rivalry between government institutions with overlapping responsibilities.

The goal of financial deregulation in most Latin American countries was to withdraw the government from directly participating in the allocation of credit and the setting of interest rates. According to the currently dominant view in the region, the role of the government should be restricted to monitoring and setting prudential regulation and supervision. This approach differs from that followed in most East Asian economies, where traditionally the government played a more active role in financial markets. For example, in Japan, Republic of Korea, and Taiwan (China), the government authorities allocated credit, channeling large amounts of resources at preferential rates to successful exporters (from a theoretical point of view, this system may solve the public good and externality problems typical of capital markets; see Stiglitz 1993; World Bank 1993a). This system resulted in a fragmented financial sector in which the official market coexisted with an informal or curb market (however, segmentation of the financial market may have negatively affected investment in some economies; see Edwards 1987 on Korea). Despite this segmentation in the East Asian economies, deposit interest rates in the official segment remained mostly positive. This contrasts sharply with Latin America, where negative real rates of interest were the main feature of the era of financial repression. It is too early to know how the Latin American approach to financial reform will ultimately compare with the East Asian model. Two comments are in order, however. First, most of the Latin American reforms were undertaken in the midst of a major crisis, which suggests that a more gradual approach, with selective direct interventions, would have been very difficult, if not utterly impossible, to implement. At the time the reforms were initiated, the overwhelming feeling was that direct government involvement had failed badly and that the Latin American countries had to move toward a radically different model. In fact, by the late 1980s, most Latin American leaders felt that tinkering at the margins was no longer an option. Second, the mostly hands-off approach followed in virtually every country in Latin America resulted in very high real interest rates.[2] This, in turn, encouraged moral hazard, placing the health of the financial sector at risk. Consequently, the need for an efficient supervisory and monitoring system was particularly urgent.

An important consequence of the financial reforms, and one that has been widely discussed by the financial media, is the tremendous expansion of the Latin American stock market between 1989 and the first half of 1994. Table 7-6 presents the evolution of the U.S. dollar value of total trade from 1989 through the third quarter of 1993 for a selected group of countries. Certain countries—Argentina, Mexico, and Venezuela—had a tenfold increase in the value of transactions during this period, although that growth was not smooth. Quite the contrary, Argentina and Venezuela experienced large fluctuations. In most countries, stock market volatility was largely the result of highly variable prices (see table 7-7 for the evolution of real stock prices in local currency and a comparison with Asian and Middle Eastern economies).

Table 7-6. Total Value Traded in Emerging Stock Markets of Latin America in the First and Third Quarters, 1989–93
(millions of dollars)

Country	1989 First	1989 Third	1990 First	1990 Third	1991 First	1991 Third	1992 First	1992 Third	1993 First	1993 Third
Argentina	94	485	151	293	314	1,671	2,644	4,049	2,835	2,393
Brazil	6,591	2,914	2,669	2,033	1,524	4,494	9,651	5,115	6,669	13,345
Chile	140	216	241	147	331	628	544	455	600	713
Colombia	23	15	16	17	20	53	151	156	80	217
Mexico	1,097	2,094	3,314	2,614	2,795	10,534	13,577	7,694	9,539	15,699
Peru	—	—	—	—	—	—	—	42	252	493
Venezuela	36	21	35	379	803	472	1,275	731	271	441

— Not available.

Source: IFC, *Quarterly Review of Emerging Stock Markets,* various years.

In spite of their tremendous takeoff and the enthusiasm they generated among worldwide investors, Latin American stock markets continued to be underdeveloped. For example, the number of stocks listed declined between 1989 and 1993 in Argentina, Brazil, Colombia, and Mexico. Also, as table 7-8 shows, price-earning ratios were volatile—indeed, significantly more than in the comparison group. The implementation of appropriate regulatory and

Table 7-7. Local Stock Market Price Indexes in Emerging Markets for the First and Third Quarters, 1990–93
(in local currency and constant prices)

Economy	1990, third	1991 First	1991 Third	1992 First	1992 Third	1993 First	1993 Third
Argentina	100	60	97	129	77	75	85
Brazil	100	111	219	160	349	372	555
Chile	100	175	255	260	220	222	225
Colombia	100	107	94	245	279	213	256
Mexico	100	135	199	269	182	230	230
Peru	—	—	—	—	100	264	399
Venezuela	100	174	158	165	121	81	78
Korea, Rep. of	100	105	107	90	74	94	99
Malaysia	100	124	109	120	119	125	163
Pakistan	100	105	148	204	44	41	42
Philippines	100	188	155	176	212	213	283
Taiwan (China)	100	191	176	171	123	166	130
Turkey	100	66	34	34	28	30	62

— Not available.

Source: IFC, *Quarterly Review of Emerging Stock Markets,* various years.

Table 7-8. Ratio of the Number and the Price of Listed Stocks to Earnings[a] in Emerging Stock Markets in the Third Quarter, Selected Economies, 1989–93

	1989		1990		1991		1992		1993	
Economy	Number	Price	Number	Price	Number	Price	Number	Price	Number	Price
Argentina	184	36.4	174	−4.4	174	21.9	175	16.1	176	39.3
Brazil	594	8.4	584	7.2	568	8.4	567	10.0	555	14.1
Chile	213	4.9	216	6.2	219	18.9	231	14.6	263	16.9
Colombia	82	7.8	80	11.1	80	11.2	80	39.2	80	18.1
Mexico	255	7.2	205	10.3	200	13.0	197	11.0	192	14.1
Peru	—	—	—	—	—	—	—	—	231	35.0
Venezuela	60	5.1	66	19.3	66	25.2	66	20.6	92	13.9
Korea, Rep. of	535	37.2	669	19.1	687	23.5	687	15.5	694	20.6
Malaysia	242	30.7	266	19.9	303	24.2	357	22.5	402	30.0
Pakistan	416	9.1	473	10.4	519	12.8	620	16.7	644	18.3
Philippines	144	14.6	151	24.3	159	21.0	168	19.0	174	21.5
Taiwan (China)	165	46.1	193	22.0	212	23.3	245	16.9	275	21.0
Turkey	50	6.6	100	40.1	131	14.1	140	10.0	147	26.2

— Not available.

a. Total market capitalization divided by total earnings of firms on a yearly basis.

Source: IFC, *Quarterly Review of Emerging Stock Markets,* various years.

supervisory legislation along the lines discussed in the country studies presented below is an important precaution for further deepening these emerging markets. The Mexican peso crisis of 1994 generated a generalized (and, in some cases, major) decline in the region's stock markets (see chapter 9 for details).

Selected Country Experiences

The experiences of four countries—Chile, Argentina, Bolivia, and Colombia—with financial deregulation during the past few years provide an interesting cross section of countries that have developed their capital markets to different degrees. While Chile began its financial deregulation process in 1974, Argentina and Colombia only starting in the late 1980s made efforts to provide a framework that would allow the development of a vigorous financial sector. The analysis concentrates on the issues identified as being the most important for the Latin American financial reforms.

Chile. The deregulation of the Chilean financial sector began in early 1974, immediately after the military overthrew the Unidad Popular coalition. At that time, Chile's capital market was highly repressed: interest rates were controlled and were negative in real terms, barriers to entry were severe, directed credit was the norm, and reserve requirements were high and uneven. In 1974, the degree of financial deepening reached a historical low, with a ratio of broad money to GDP barely above 5 percent. The first step in the deregulation process was to lower reserve requirements for commercial banks, which during the last days of the Unidad Popular government had been raised to 100 percent for marginal deposits. Next, barriers to entry were relaxed, and finance houses—the *financieras*—were allowed to operate in May 1974. These institutions could freely determine interest rates paid on deposits and concentrate their operations on consumption loans. The freeing of interest rates was broadened in October 1975, when ceilings on bank deposit rates were lifted. The next step was the privatization of banks, which were mostly bought by the newly formed conglomerates, the so-called *grupos*. The one area in which Chile did not make early progress was the enactment of a modern supervisory framework. Banks and other institutions had great leeway to engage in all sorts of transactions, including providing large loans to related firms. Monitoring was lax, requirements on the disclosure of information were minimal, the examination of bank books was pro forma, and the quality of bank portfolios was not assessed. This situation was aggravated by the presence of an implicit deposit insurance scheme that encouraged moral hazard, greatly weakening the financial sector (the implicit insurance scheme was established in late 1976 and early 1977, when the government bailed out the depositors of two failing financial institutions: Banco Osorno and Financiera La Familia; see Edwards and Edwards 1991).

The sweeping deregulation of the domestic financial sector contrasted sharply with the authorities' guarded attitude toward international capital movements. Between 1974 and 1979, capital controls were very tight. Initially this policy was aimed at avoiding capital flight. Slowly, however, and as Chile became an attractive international risk, these controls also prevented capital from flowing into the country. It was only in mid-1979 that a very limited degree of capital mobility was allowed. Inflows increased dramatically after that date, reaching the staggering level of 12 percent of GDP in 1981. The relaxation of capital controls in 1979 was premature, however, because it encouraged overborrowing and generated forces that greatly overvalued the real exchange rate (Edwards 1985; Harberger 1985b).

The Chilean financial reform of the 1970s had spectacular effects on financial intermediation and the stock market. The ratio of broadly defined money to GDP increased from 5.3 percent in 1974 to more than 20 percent in 1981; the ratio of effective bank reserves dropped from 72 percent in 1972 to 28 percent in 1982. The number of banks increased from nineteen in 1973 to thirty-five in 1981, and real credit to the private sector increased more than 1,000 percent during that period. In spite of these achievements, the early Chilean financial reforms had three weak spots. First, lax supervision allowed banks and other financial intermediaries to accumulate an unsustainable proportion of nonperforming loans (this regulatory framework contrasted sharply with the tight control of the pension funds discussed below; see Gallagher 1992). Second, throughout the period, (real) interest rates remained extremely high—real deposit rates averaged more than 25 percent in 1981—putting severe pressure on the financial health of the manufacturing sector. These high real interest rates were the result of a combination of factors, including rising expectations of devaluation in 1980–81, growing demand for credit to finance large losses incurred by *grupos*-owned firms—the false demand for credit discussed in chapter 6—and a high country risk premium during 1981–82. And third, although financial intermediation expanded rapidly, domestic savings did not grow as many supporters of the program had expected.

In 1981–82, Chile entered a deep crisis that affected economic activity and employment and threatened to destroy the financial sector. The authorities reacted to the crisis by taking three broad measures. First, several financial institutions were rehabilitated and their loans restructured. Private sector debts to the banking system were rescheduled in 1983 and 1984 into long-term loans with an interest rate of 5 to 7 percent in real terms. The central bank bore the costs of this operation and purchased the nonperforming portfolio of the commercial banks, which, in turn, committed themselves to repurchasing these bad loans with their profits (Larraín 1988; Ramírez and Rosende 1992). Second, failed banks were reprivatized through the popular capitalism procedure described in chapter 6, and, third, a detailed regulatory framework for the financial system, including a new banking law, was enacted in 1986.

In designing the new banking law, the Chilean authorities sought to accomplish two goals. The first was to set an incentives system that would avoid the monitoring, moral hazard, and adverse selection problems that plagued the system during the early years of the reforms. Very strict requirements for the disclosure of information were imposed, the extent of banking secrecy was limited, and banks were required to have the quality of their portfolio evaluated twice a year by independent risk-rating agencies. Additionally, the coverage of deposit insurance was reduced, and depositors were informed, through a wide public information campaign, that no additional bailouts would take place. The second objective was to establish an explicit mechanism for dealing with (potential) bank difficulties in the future. The idea was to develop a semiautomatic system that would avoid, as long as possible, government bailouts. The law established in great detail the steps to be taken in case a bank fails to meet reserves or debt-equity ratio requirements. If a bank faces difficulties, it can rapidly enter into an agreement with its creditors to transform the debt into equity in the bank (Ramírez and Rosende 1992). According to this provision, once the bank is out of trouble and starts generating profits, it has to repurchase the shares from its debtors.

The reform of the social security system initiated in May 1981 represented a key step in the development of Chile's financial markets. This reform replaced a basically insolvent pay-as-you-go regime with a capitalization system based on individual retirement accounts managed by private companies known as Administradoras de Fondos de Pensiones, AFP.[3] A key feature of the system is that workers have the freedom to choose their AFP and can shift their funds freely among them. A detailed and modern regulatory framework—enforced by an institution especially created for this purpose, the Superintendency of AFPs—ensures free determination of fees and commissions and free entry into the industry. These two elements created the conditions for markets to function competitively and efficiently. In contrast with the case of banks, the Superintendency of AFPs established from the first day very precise norms to secure the diversification and transparency of the AFPs' investments (Iglesias and Emmerij 1991).

Currently, pension funds are the largest institutional investors in the Chilean capital market, with assets representing 26.5 percent of GDP in 1990 (compared with 0.9 percent in 1981). The average real return to investment of Chilean pension funds between 1981 and 1990 was 13 percent. The real return of individual accounts (after subtracting fees) varied between 10.4 percent and 9.2 percent. These impressive results reflect, in part, the fast expansion of a previously underdeveloped financial market.[4] The dynamism exhibited by the Chilean capital market during the past ten years forced constant revisions to the norms governing the eligible securities for AFP investments. Initially, these institutions were not allowed to hold common stock or foreign securities. These regulations, however, were recently relaxed by the Aylwin administration, which broadened the scope of instruments that can be maintained in the AFP portfolios. This provided additional impetus to the local stock market, allowing firms to finance expansion plans in an increasingly efficient fashion. Perhaps the most important effect of Chile's liberalization of the financial sector was that it encouraged (private) savings. The increase in the savings rate was steady but slow. By 1993, the ratio of gross domestic savings to GDP bordered 30 percent, significantly higher than the historical ratio of 20 percent.

In 1990, Chile took important steps toward improving the allocation of development credit. In that year, and with the assistance of the World Bank, a system was implemented for auctioning long-term credit provided by the multilateral agencies. The local financial institutions that successfully bid for these funds are free to charge a market-clearing interest rate to the final user. To avoid collusion, only those institutions that meet certain requirements can bid for these funds. This system, which was also adopted by Bolivia and is under consideration in a number of countries, including Argentina, reduces the traditional inefficiency associated with developing credit earmarked for specific uses.

The recent success of the Chilean economy was rapidly reflected internationally. Secondary market prices for Chilean foreign debt surpassed 90 percent in 1992, and international institutions are eager to participate in the new

Chilean miracle. As pressures to lift controls on capital inflows mount, Chilean observers cannot avoid recalling the experience of the late 1970s and early 1980s, when excessive borrowing overvalued the real exchange rate and generated the great financial crisis of 1982. The authorities are now acting with prudence, taking gradual steps to relax capital controls.

Argentina. The Argentine capital market suffered from structural problems for decades (this discussion draws partially on unpublished work by Fernando Losada). The government recurrently turned to the financial system to deal with its own budgetary difficulties. This became particularly common after the debt crisis, when subsequent administrations were forced to incur debts with the banking system in the form of compulsory reserve requirements. These reached more than 65 percent of deposits in December 1988, reducing the loanable capacity of banks and thus their profitability. The intermediation process became extremely inefficient, diverting funds from productive projects toward often loss-making and corruption-ridden publicly administered housing and investment programs. The central bank paid interest on mandatory reserves as a way to compensate private financial institutions and keep the system at work. Its capacity to carry out monetary policy was severely constricted, because virtually no assets were left for monetary absorption.

The Alfonsín government implemented steps to deregulate the financial sector in October 1987, when interest rates were freed, and a more resolute attitude toward troubled banks was taken. Also, at that time an effort was made to improve portfolio management in both the National Mortgage Bank and the National Development Bank. The public sector borrowing requirements remained substantial, however, and continued to crowd out the private sector.

In early 1988, the government owned thirty-six banks, which accounted for 45 percent of banking deposits and provided 71 percent of bank credit. Employment in the financial sector totaled more than 140,000 people, 60 percent of whom worked for official banks. After the failure of the Primavera Plan in 1988, more and more funds abandoned the domestic financial system, dangerously reducing central bank reserves. In a desperate attempt to avoid a final run on scarce foreign exchange, the authorities freed the exchange rate, and the economy followed a path of increasing instability that ended in the hyperinflation of July 1989.

The adoption of the Convertibility Plan in March 20, 1991, marked the beginning of an era of financial deregulation in Argentina. The convertibility law established a fixed exchange rate with respect to the U.S. dollar and severely limited the government's ability to finance the public deficit. Moreover, to acquire credibility, the monetary base had to be fully backed by liquid international reserves.

President Menem signed an omnibus decree on October 31, 1991, ordering the reform of the state, including deregulation of the financial market. This decree was followed by resolutions that established the following measures: (a) exemption of securities' issuance from the stamp tax, (b) abolition of the tax on transfers of securities, (c) exemption of stock, bond, and securities transactions from income tax, (d) allowance of freely determined fees and commissions by brokerage houses, (e) granting of power to the Securities and Exchange Commission for authorizing markets for future contracts and options, (f) full elimination of capital and exchange controls, and (g) rationalization of reserve requirements, eliminating discrimination according to the type of loan.

The convertibility law reformed the norms related to the noncapitalization of interest, allowing parties to reach agreements based on market interest rates. In August 1991, a law protecting dollar-denominated deposits was enacted, followed a few weeks later by a bill modifying the law of common investment funds. Additionally, legislation was approved that introduced tax exemptions to make investments in securities more attractive and that reformed the corporate bonds law.

As part of the effort to make the financial sector more dynamic, the foreign investments law was amended to grant foreign and domestic capital equal treatment. The Foreign Capital Investment Register was converted from an approval mechanism to a simple statistical list. Also, Argentina became a member of the Multilateral Investment Guarantee Agency, sponsored by the World Bank, in October 1990. Thus, foreign investments were provided insurance coverage against political risks. The government also signed investment guarantee agreements with Belgium, France, Germany, Great Britain, Spain, Switzerland, and the United States. Since late 1992, the government has been studying a program for auctioning long-term development credit provided by multilateral institutions similar to the one implemented in Chile and Bolivia since 1990.

The Argentine privatization program proceeded at a fast pace. However, relatively little progress was made on the sale of government-owned financial institutions. The federal government, in fact, intends to retain ownership of the largest bank—Banco de la Nación Argentina—and provincial government banks continue to have a dominant role in the financial market. What is somewhat troublesome is that a number of provincial banks are in a very weak financial position, which makes the consolidation of the public finances more difficult. Some local observers point out that the government is interested in keeping control over some discretionary allocation of credit; since the central bank is now a fully independent institution, the Banco de la Nación is the only channel for directly (and decisively) affecting the financial market.

Stock markets did not evolve smoothly during the first stage of the reform program. The Buenos Aires Stock Exchange boomed in 1990, when volumes traded increased ten times. After that, it experienced several spasms. This instability conspired against the confidence of domestic investors in the capital market. The stock price index crashed 48 percent in the second half of 1992 and then recovered strongly until mid-January 1993. Some forecasts indicated a price to earning ratio of 13.1 for 1993 compared with 16.9 for 1992 ("Buenos Aires Eases Back after Roller Coaster Ride," *Financial Times*, February 4, 1993). Eventually, that ratio reached 40.0 in 1993, indicating a remarkable and unexpected increase in market capitalization.

In 1993, the Argentine government committed itself to reforming social security, replacing the inefficient and insolvent pay-as-you-go regime with a capitalization system similar to the one operating in Chile since 1981. This should add impetus to the financial market. However, before implementing this program the government has to deal with the large overhang of the current system by recognizing payment arrears or confiscating unpaid benefits. Clearly, both options are financially and politically difficult. Moreover, until mid-1993, trade unions successfully blocked the approval of the social security reform in Congress. Whether the government will be able to change the political tide with respect to this issue is still to be seen and will depend on President Menem's and Minister Cavallo's powers of persuasion.

Bolivia. Hyperinflation sharply reduced financial intermediation in Bolivia during the mid-1980s, after which the financial system recovered quite rapidly. The base of deposits almost doubled from $465 million in 1985 to $820 million at the end of 1990 and more than $1.7 billion at the end of 1992. The ratio of broadly defined money to GDP almost quadrupled during that period, reflecting a general increase in the degree of credibility in the system. In spite of this progress, the economy is still highly dollarized—around 90 percent of deposits and loans are denominated in U.S. dollars—and most of the time deposits are held for 120 days or less. Nominal boliviano interest rates have continued to be high in real terms, and interest rates on dollar-denominated certificates of deposit have been much higher than in the United States, indicating a significant degree of country risk.

In 1985, the Bolivian government began reforming the financial sector. The main reforms included the liberalization of interest rates and the exchange rate system (the rate of exchange with respect to the U.S. dollar is freely determined in daily auctions; see Cariaga 1990). Reserve requirements on commercial banks were lowered and rationalized, and strict leverage limits were established. The supervision of the financial system was removed from the central bank, and a new autonomous Superintendency of Banks was created. Since late 1988, all financial information has to be reported to the regulatory agencies, and accounting practices are harmonized across institutions, allowing the superintendency to scrutinize banks' portfolios and limit their credit exposure.

Publicly owned financial institutions historically financed unproductive ventures, impairing the productivity of investment and imposing heavy losses on the economy. This changed as the financial reforms reduced the volume of credit directly allocated by the government. In spite of this, the quality of the loan portfolio of public banks continue to be significantly weaker than that of private institutions. In mid-1991, the government committed itself to close the Banco Agrícola, the Banco Minero, and the Fondo de Exploración Minera and to cease lending operations of the Banco del Estado. The number of workers in the sector was reduced. In addition, an effort was made to limit the concentration of lending by strengthening the documentation requirements for large bank borrowers.

As a result of these reforms, a primary market for securities developed and continues to grow. This market is particularly active for central bank instruments, which are auctioned weekly without prior announcement of the volume intended for sale. Interest rates on these securities generally exceed deposit rates by more than 2 percentage points. More recently, however, rates for certificates of deposit declined and maturities increased, indicating growth in public confidence in the system.

In spite of the broad scope of the reforms, the Bolivian capital market continues to be thin and relatively concentrated. Currently the system is dominated by the thirteen private local banks, which hold 70 percent of the assets, loans, and deposits. There are also three state-owned banks, four foreign banks, one mining fund, twelve savings and loan associations, and various cooperatives. As is the case in most of the poorer nations in the region, a significant proportion of total banking credit is financed by the central bank through development credits provided by donors or the multilateral agencies. As of 1991, agriculture and industry accounted for almost half of the total loans outstanding. As a way to improve the allocation of development credit, the central bank adopted a system for auctioning these credit lines to private banks very similar to the one in Chile. In addition to these formal institutions, Bolivia's informal financial sector is very active and may be as large as the formal system. Much of Bolivia's underground economy, including drug-related activities, is channeled through this informal market (see Sturzenegger 1992 for a discussion of the role of the drug sector in the Bolivian economy).

Although Bolivia has made a serious effort to improve the performance of the capital market, many problems have yet to be resolved. Real interest rates remain high, discouraging investment. Spreads are also high, reflecting the underdeveloped nature of the Bolivian structure of financial intermediation, and seem to be induced by structural rather than policy causes (that is, unduly high operating costs and large volumes of nonperforming loans). The system of contractual savings (insurance, pensions, and social security) is especially problematic, because it discourages the demand for securities. Additionally, and perhaps more important, the Superintendency of Banks has limited personnel for implementing some of the more important tasks. In that regard, Bolivia illustrates the fact that in the smaller and poorer nations it is necessary—even critical—not only to reform the existing legislation but also to provide supervisory personnel with the right skills to perform their jobs. If this effort is lacking, the newly enacted body of supervisory rules will be largely irrelevant.

An additional weakness of the Bolivian financial sector is that the four public financial institutions are in a very weak financial condition and the capital base of the financial system is very low (the debt to equity ratio was 11.8 in 1990). The new banking law foresees a minimum capital of SDR3 million (special drawing rights) for a financial institution. In fact, several World Bank missions have advised the government to liquidate both public and private institutions that are insolvent. Continued efforts and political will are required to continue the reforms and solve some of the problems discussed here.

Colombia. As in most of Latin America, the Colombian financial sector was highly distorted and regulated during the 1960s and 1970s. Almost every financial distortion discussed above was prominently present: the number of banks was controlled, and ownership was highly concentrated; interest rates were subject to ceilings; forced credit allocation was very important; securities markets were discouraged; and supervision was lax. In the early 1980s, Colombia experienced a serious financial crisis when two private conglomerates that were at the center of a web of related and questionable financial transactions failed. As a result of this, two medium-size banks—the Banco Nacional and Banco del Estado, which held 5 percent of deposits—had to be taken over by the government. This led to a tightening of government regulations and to the flight of deposits from the banking system. These two developments negatively affected an already weakened financial sector, sharply reducing the degree of profitability of some of the most important intermediaries.

In 1982, the two largest banks (Banco de Colombia and Banco de Bogotá) and the largest finance company (Corporación Financiera Grancolombiana) developed serious financial problems and had to be taken over by the authorities. All in all, between 1982 and 1986, the Colombian government intervened in more than twenty financial institutions, including banks, brokerage houses, and insurance companies (Montes-Negret 1988).

Colombia's experience illustrates how private securities markets can deteriorate even with fairly stable rates of inflation and stable fiscal policies. By the end of the 1980s, fewer than 100 companies were listed on the stock exchanges compared with 400 in the 1960s, and privately issued securities (stocks and bonds) amounted to 2 percent of total financial system liabilities compared with 20 percent in 1965 (the increase in political and drug-related violence also affected the securities market; entrepreneurs were afraid that listing their companies publicly would make them the target of terrorist attacks). The transaction costs of either offering securities to the market or trading securities were very high—almost 600 basis points in excess of the basic cost of funds in the case of primary offerings. Wealth also became more concentrated during most of the 1980s, because float (the percentage of free voting share relative to total share in circulation) was often no greater than 10 percent for most companies (the material in this and the next paragraph draws on Glaessner 1992).

The deterioration in Colombia's securities markets during the 1970s and 1980s can be traced partly to three factors: increased government intervention in the intermediation of savings, both through government ownership of intermediaries and through an extensive network of directed credit and forced investment programs; real trade restrictions coupled with a significant government presence through ownership of certain nonfinancial companies, which lessened the incentive to undertake investments and raise capital to remain competitive; and capital controls and entry barriers to the provision of financial services, either by offshore institutions or by domestic institutions (on the stock exchanges). These policies created disincentives for companies to raise capital through public offerings and permitted easier retention of control.

The financial crisis of the 1980s highlighted the serious shortcomings of the Colombian financial sector. In the early 1990s, and as a part of a grand program to modernize the economy, the government decided to reform the financial market. In December 1990, Congress passed a law allowing the executive to implement sweeping reforms, and a few months later—in April 1991—the Gaviria administration presented its reform program, which was completed by the end of 1994 (see Psacharopoulos 1992). The most important measures in the package include the relaxation of barriers to entry, the reduction and rationalization of reserve requirements, and the freeing of most (but not all) interest rates.

To increase the degree of competition of the banking sector, the government privatized some of the banks that failed during the first half of the 1980s; it also devised ways to strengthen the Banco de Colombia in order to eventually sell it to private interests. From a supervisory perspective, an effort was made for all banks to comply with the capitalization standards set forward by the Basel Accord.

Forced bank investments on government securities were sharply reduced. Also, direct lending requirements to the agriculture sector were limited to 6 percent of total loans for large and medium-size farmers and to 1 percent for small farmers. The proportion of loans directed to large and medium-size farmers was expected to decline gradually, until such loans became fully market determined in 1994. Additionally, to reduce the degree of distortions associated with direct credit, the government introduced substantial flexibility in the interest rates charged for these resources. Fixed nominal interest rates and rate ceilings were replaced by a system of flexible charges in which preferential rates are linked to market interest rates.

In 1991, the Colombian Congress approved a general law (Ley Marco 9/91) that liberalized international capital transactions and reduced the extent of exchange controls. Partially as a result of this legislation, capital inflows increased significantly during 1991, 1992, and 1993, putting pressure on the supply of money and generating a large appreciation of the real exchange rate. The government responded by increasing (marginal) reserve requirements and attempting to sterilize the inflows of foreign capital. However, these policies resulted in higher interest rate differentials that attracted additional inflows of capital, provoking another round of real appreciation.

In spite of the implementation of a policy package aimed at modernizing the financial sector, there are still many lagging areas, including the development of securities markets. Specific legal and regulatory reforms at the microeconomic level, coupled with institutional reforms, are needed to generate an incentive-neutral environment for companies to issue securities and for investors to demand them (Glaessner 1992). Regarding the offering of securities, legal and regulatory changes are needed to define clearly the rights of parties in bond or preferred equity offerings and increase the diversity of instruments that can be originated (such as permitting commodity-indexed debt or asset-backed securities).

There is a need to change regulations that discourage controlling shareholders from issuing free voting shares. Additionally, institutional reforms involving tougher enforcement of tax provisions for companies of all sizes would reduce incentives for small and medium enterprises not to undertake public offerings as part of an effort to evade taxes. Finally, streamlining regulatory procedures for public offerings by permitting processes such as self-registration and reducing regulatory overlap would decrease the very high transaction costs now associated with public offerings.

Another important shortcoming of the Colombian financial reforms is that, as in many other countries in the region, they failed to generate the expected increase in domestic private savings. Increasingly, analysts and policymakers are realizing that although microeconomic financial reforms are a necessary condition for increasing savings, they are not a sufficient one. A major jump in aggregate domestic savings requires additional macroeconomic measures, including ensuring long-term stability, and further fiscal adjustments.

Savings and Investment

Development economists have long understood that savings are at the heart of the development process. Increased savings allow capital to accumulate at a faster pace and the economy to grow faster. Recent models of endogenous growth provide an equilibrium—steady state–based—analytical framework that supports this proposition; see, for example, the family of Ak models pioneered by Rebelo 1991; see Gersovitz 1989 for a detailed survey on the links between savings and development. One of the important stylized facts of world history is that massive increases in savings precede significant takeoffs in economic growth. Arthur Lewis (1955) recognizes this in his classic work on development in dual economies; he argues that one of the central problems in the theory of economic development is to understand the process by which a community that was previously saving a low percentage of GDP increases savings dramatically.

Latin America, however, traditionally had a low rate of domestic savings. In 1980, for example, gross domestic savings were on average 20 percent of GDP, slightly higher than in 1965, when they stood at 19 percent. This stagnation contrasts sharply with East Asia, where the average gross savings ratio increased from 23 percent of GDP in 1965 to almost 30 percent in 1980 (World Bank, *World Development Report,* various years). In spite of the availability of foreign resources to supplement domestic savings, the average investment rate was rather low in Latin America during 1960–80, when gross investment averaged 23 percent of GDP. What made things worse was that for decades savings—both domestic and foreign—were used to finance projects with doubtful rates of return. The maze of distortions and regulations that traditionally affected Latin America's financial sector had a negative impact on resource allocation, the efficiency of (private) investment, and, perhaps more important, the growth of productivity (see, for example, the discussion in World Bank, *World Development Report 1991*).

The debt crisis had important consequences for the behavior of investment throughout the region. During the years of muddling through, investment was drastically reduced as a way to accommodate the sudden drying up of capital flows. In the case of public investment, the cuts were so deep that in some countries existing infrastructure was not even maintained. Although in recent years there has been a marked recovery, in the majority of the countries investment rates have not yet reached their levels before the debt crisis (see figure 7-1).

There is little doubt that a sustained acceleration in growth will require significant increases in both the volume and quality of investment. Even if, as existing evidence suggests, the different structural reforms generate important improvements in growth of productivity, the rate of capital accumulation clearly has to be increased beyond its current levels. A key question, however, is how this higher investment will be financed. Since the availability of foreign funds on a stable basis is likely to be tight, most countries will have to rely heavily on higher domestic savings to fund the increase in investment.[5] Improving the volume of savings and the quality of investment is, in fact, an overriding goal of the structural reform policies long advocated by many economists for the region. Higher domestic savings will not only contribute to growth, but will also help attain sustainable current account balances. Indeed, as is argued in chapter 9, the drastic reduction in private savings contributed significantly to the Mexican crisis of 1994.

Recent Behavior of Savings in Latin America

The early literature on financial liberalization argues that one of the most important objectives of these reforms was to generate, among other things, a significant increase in domestic savings. In the original models of financial repression of McKinnon (1973) and Shaw (1973), allowing (real) interest rates

Figure 7-1. Ratio of Gross Domestic Investment to GDP in Selected Countries of Latin America and the Caribbean, 1980–91

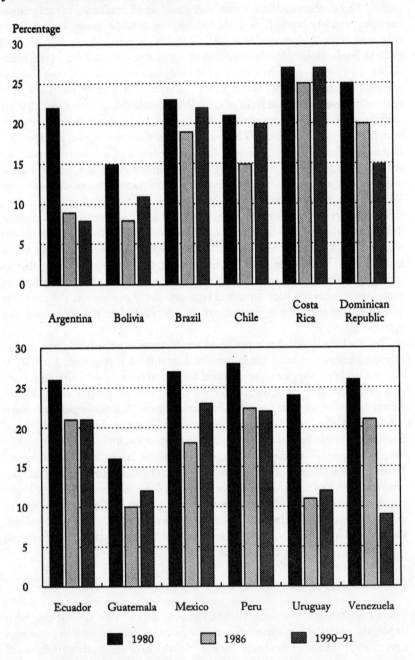

Source: World Bank, *World Tables*, various years.

to rise to market levels alters the intertemporal rate of substitution, encouraging aggregate savings (see Fry 1988 for surveys of this type of model). However, empirical studies for a large number of countries—both industrial and developing—find only a weak interest rate elasticity of aggregate domestic savings. Boskin (1978) finds a very low elasticity for the United States. Several studies of the developing countries, including Giovannini (1983), fail to find any effect of changes in interest rates on private savings. McKinnon (1991, p. 22) acknowledges that "aggregate savings, as measured in the GNP accounts, does not respond strongly to higher real interest rates."

Various hypotheses have been offered to explain this phenomenon. First, in financial models, higher (real) interest rates result in portfolio readjustments, including a higher degree of financial intermediation, but not necessarily in higher aggregate savings as defined in national accounts. Moreover, in general equilibrium macroeconomic settings, an increase in interest rates tends to have two offsetting effects on savings: on the one hand, there is an intertemporal substitution effect away from current consumption, which tends to increase domestic savings. On the other hand, higher interest rates generate a negative wealth effect, which tends to reduce savings (if the objective of savers is to receive a certain fixed income, higher interest rates lower the amount required to attain the flow of income desired). Depending on which of these two forces dominates, higher interest rates are associated with either an increase or a decline in aggregate savings.

In spite of the relative unresponsiveness of savings to higher interest rates, financial reforms still have important effects on growth through improvement in the quality of aggregate investment, especially private investment. For example, in a series of studies Gelb (1989), Fry (1988), and McKinnon (1991) find robust evidence supporting the proposition that a reduction in the degree of repression of the capital market tends to increase the productivity of investment. This body of work suggests that reducing financial instability, especially inflation, also has an important positive effect on the return to investment. Recent work by King and Levine (1993a) provides additional support to the idea that more developed financial sectors are associated with faster growth of total factor productivity.

Broad comparative analyses of savings behavior are often plagued by data problems (Gersovitz 1989). Savings are usually estimated in a questionable way (mostly as residuals). Until very recently, no comparable data on private savings were available for a large number of countries, and data on net savings are still very scarce. Figure 7-2 contains data on the evolution of (gross) domestic savings rates for selected Latin American countries between 1980 and 1992. As can be seen, in the majority of the cases savings were higher in 1992 than in the mid-1980s but were still below their 1980 level. Chile and Mexico, two of the earliest reformers, provide contrasting cases. In Chile, gross domestic savings increased steadily after 1980, reaching almost 27 percent of GDP in 1993, partially as a result of the social security reform; in

Figure 7-2. Ratio of Gross Domestic Savings to GDP in Selected Countries of Latin America and the Caribbean, 1980–92

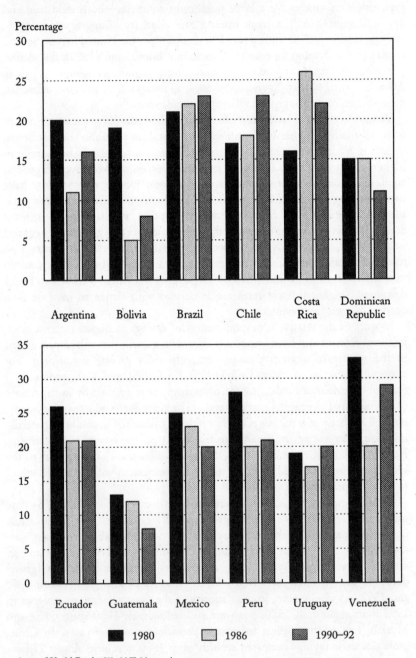

Source: World Bank, *World Tables,* various years.

Mexico, aggregate domestic savings declined gradually during this period. Although it is too early to determine the final impact of the recent financial reforms on aggregate savings, historical and comparative evidence indicates that financial reforms will not generate the massive increase, in the short to medium run, expected by the early supporters of financial liberalization policies.

Figures 7-3 through 7-13 display the evolution of private, government, and aggregate gross national savings for eleven countries. The data cover all years for which information exists. Several interesting facts emerge from these figures. First, the recent behavior of national savings rates was very similar to that of domestic savings rates. Second, in most countries government savings improved in the last few years. This is largely the result of the adjustment programs implemented after the debt crisis throughout the region. Finally, private savings in many countries declined substantially. What makes this situation particularly interesting—and in some sense puzzling—is that this decline in private savings took place at the same time that significant reforms aimed at liberalizing domestic capital markets were implemented in most countries. As is argued in chapter 9, this decline in private savings certificates constitutes one of the weakest spots in Latin America's economic landscape.

An important question is how Latin American savings rates compare with those of other regions. Table 7-9 contains the average and distribution of private, government, and aggregate national savings for a group of Latin American, Asian, African, and industrial countries for the 1970–82 and 1983–92 periods. During the more recent period, Latin America's private savings rates were the lowest in the world. Also, these more aggregated data confirm that, after the debt crisis, private savings rates tended to decline in Latin America. The story regarding government savings is very different: during the most recent period, the Latin American countries in this sample exhibited comparatively high rates. In fact, the region had the highest median and the second highest average government savings rates. This is particularly important because the generation of relatively high government savings is a recent phenomenon in Latin America and one that is based on somewhat fragile bases. In fact, it would not be surprising if, in some countries, fiscal discipline were to slip in the near future, reducing the government's contribution to aggregate savings. When private and government savings are consolidated, the picture continues to look bleak, with Latin America being once again at the bottom of the scale.

Average regional data, such as those presented in table 7-9, tend to obscure the behavior of individual countries. To add flavor to the comparisons, figures 7-14 through 7-18 display the evolution of savings rates for five high-performing Asian countries. The contrast with the Latin American figures is quite stunning. The East Asian economies had aggregate savings rates that were not only very high—on the order of 30 to 40 percent—but also very stable. Moreover, the contribution of government savings to total national

(Text continues on page 238.)

Figure 7-3. Savings as a Percentage of GDP in Argentina, 1985–92

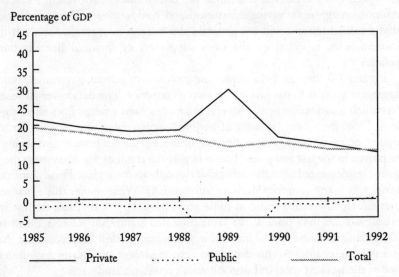

Source: IMF, *World Economic Outlook 1994.*

Figure 7-4. Savings as a Percentage of GDP in Bolivia, 1988–92

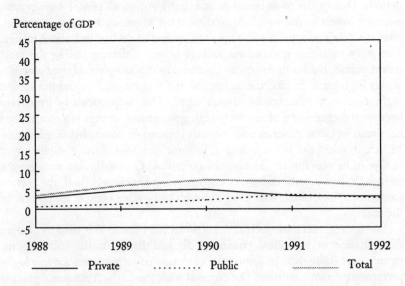

Source: IMF, *World Economic Outlook 1994.*

Figure 7-5. Savings as a Percentage of GDP in Brazil, 1977–92

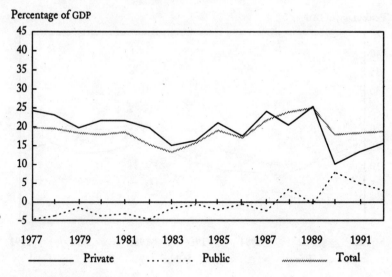

Source: IMF, *World Economic Outlook 1994.*

Figure 7-6. Savings as a Percentage of GDP in Chile, 1983–92

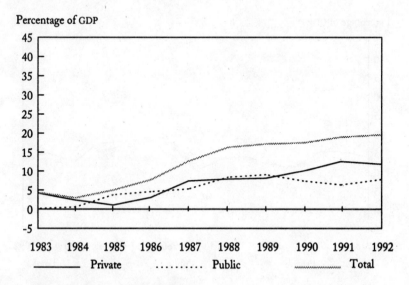

Source: IMF, *World Economic Outlook 1994.*

Figure 7-7. Savings as a Percentage of GDP in Colombia, 1980–92

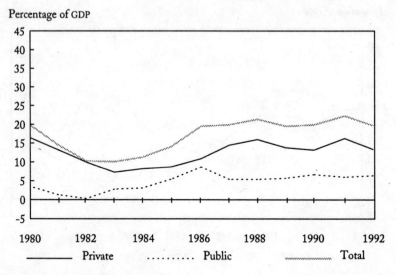

Source: IMF, *World Economic Outlook 1994.*

Figure 7-8. Savings as a Percentage of GDP in El Salvador, 1978–92

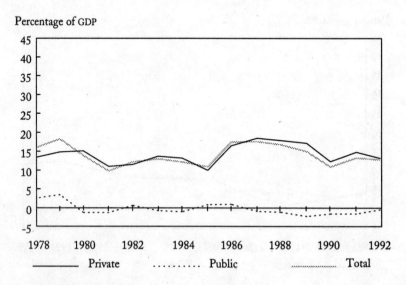

Source: IMF, *World Economic Outlook 1994.*

Figure 7-9. Savings as a Percentage of GDP in Mexico, 1980–92

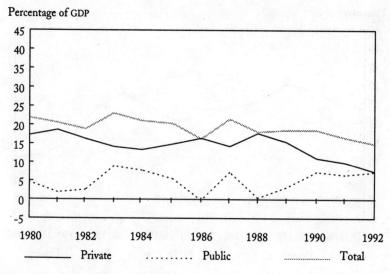

Source: IMF, *World Economic Outlook 1994.*

Figure 7-10. Savings as a Percentage of GDP in Paraguay, 1985–92

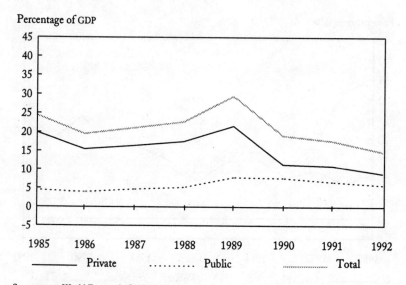

Source: IMF, *World Economic Outlook 1994.*

Figure 7-11. Savings as a Percentage of GDP in Peru, 1979–92

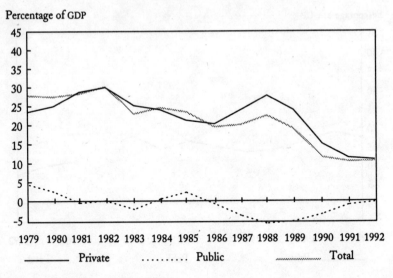

Percentage of GDP

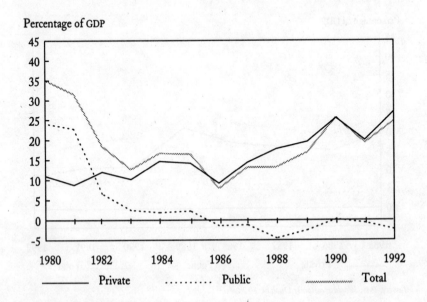

Source: IMF, *World Economic Outlook 1994.*

Figure 7-12. Savings as a Percentage of GDP in Trinidad and Tobago, 1980–92

Percentage of GDP

Source: IMF, *World Economic Outlook 1994.*

Figure 7-13. Savings as a Percentage of GDP in Venezuela, 1980–92

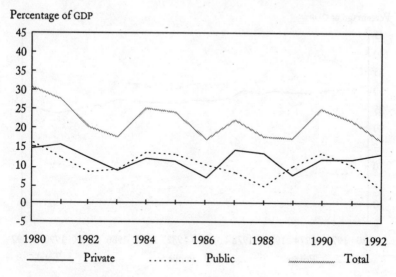

Percentage of GDP

——— Private   · · · · · · · · Public   ⌇⌇⌇⌇⌇ Total

Source: IMF, *World Economic Outlook 1994.*

Table 7-9. Regional Comparison of Private and Government Savings Rates, by Quartile and Region, 1970–92

Type of savings and region	1970–82				1983–92			
	First	Median	Third	Average	First	Median	Third	Average
Private savings								
Latin America	13.1	13.2	21.7	16.1	10.9	14.7	17.9	13.8
Asia	—	—	—	—	17.4	19.1	22.9	20.2
Africa	11.4	14.4	18.9	15.2	10.7	16.7	19.5	15.6
Industrial countries	18.0	21.6	23.4	21.3	18.3	21.3	23.4	21.3
Government savings								
Latin America	–0.7	1.7	6.6	3.3	–1.3	2.4	5.5	2.2
Asia	0.0	2.7	8.8	4.4	0.0	1.6	9.0	3.9
Africa	–1.6	0.9	2.1	0.6	–1.3	1.0	4.5	0.9
Industrial countries	–0.5	2.0	3.8	1.8	–3.6	–0.1	1.3	–0.8
National savings								
Latin America	14.5	19.4	27.7	19.8	14.0	17.8	19.1	15.3
Asia	4.9	24.8	26.7	18.8	18.8	23.8	28.5	24.5
Africa	10.8	15.5	18.7	16.4	10.6	17.5	22.1	16.8
Industrial countries	19.6	22.8	25.8	23.1	17.5	19.1	23.4	20.4

— Not available.

Source: Unpublished data from the IMF.

Figure 7-14. Savings as a Percentage of GDP in Japan, 1970–92

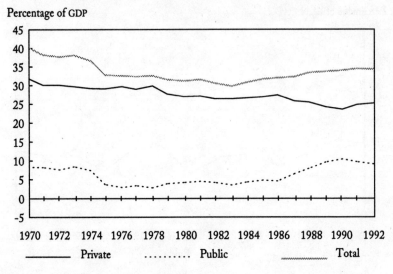

Source: IMF, *World Economic Outlook 1994.*

Figure 7-15. Savings as a Percentage of GDP in Malaysia, 1985–92

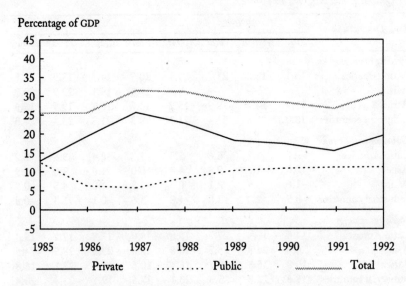

Source: IMF, *World Economic Outlook 1994.*

Figure 7-16. Savings as a Percentage of GDP in Singapore, 1985–92

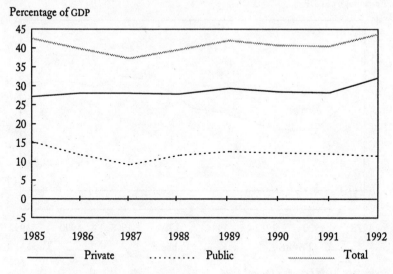

Source: IMF, *World Economic Outlook 1994.*

Figure 7-17. Savings as a Percentage of GDP in Thailand, 1985–92

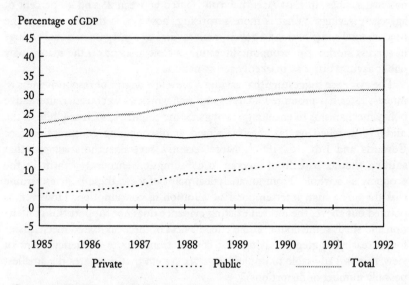

Source: IMF, *World Economic Outlook 1994.*

Figure 7-18. Savings as a Percentage of GDP in Republic of Korea, 1978–92

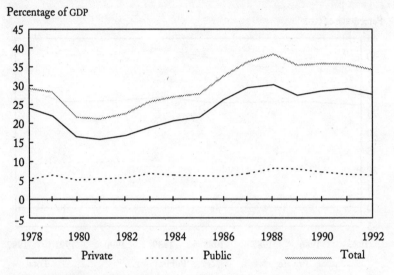

Percentage of GDP

————— Private   ·········· Public   ⌇⌇⌇⌇⌇ Total

Source: IMF, *World Economic Outlook 1994.*

savings was significantly higher in East Asia than in Latin America. While, historically, government savings in Latin America barely contributed to national savings, in East Asia they contributed between 25 and 40 percent of aggregate savings. What is more surprising, however, is that in spite of the fundamental contribution of government savings to aggregate national savings in success stories, the economic literature is almost silent on the reason why public savings differ so markedly across nations.

The evidence suggesting that savings have a low degree of responsiveness to interest rates has prompted analysts and policymakers to consider alternative policy mechanisms to encourage savings. Some countries, such as Chile in the mid-1980s, relied on tax reforms aimed at discouraging consumption (see Edwards and Edwards 1991). More recently, several authors suggest that shifting the tax base from income to consumption encourages thrift in the economy as a whole. From an analytical point of view, these policies assume that there is a high intertemporal substitution in consumption. However, as pointed out above, the limited existing evidence does not support this contention and sheds some doubt on the effectiveness of these tax-based mechanisms for increasing aggregate savings (of course, from a pure efficiency point of view, it is still advisable to implement a tax system that generates the smallest possible number of distortions).

Evidence from a score of countries, including the East Asian miracle economies, suggests that the increase in private domestic savings rates is a rather slow process (World Bank 1993a). This evidence also indicates that a drastic increase in private savings is usually the result of two factors: macroeconomic stability and the creation of an institutional environment that instills confidence in small savers (the case of postal savings in East Asia is a good example of this type of institution). To the extent that macroeconomic stabilization becomes consolidated, private savings tend to increase. More important, however, the development of new institutions, such as new social security systems, could play an important role in increasing private savings from their historical levels.

In spite of recent developments, the literature on private savings is still somewhat fragmented, with different authors emphasizing specific issues, including the effects of social security contributions (Feldstein 1980), interest rates (Gylfason 1993), and liquidity constraints (Jappelli and Pagano 1994). This fragmentation is also present in the empirical literature on the subject; authors typically concentrate on a few possible determinants of private savings (see Gersovitz 1989; Aghevli and others 1990; Hayashi 1986 provides a fascinating analysis of Japanese savings and deals with the opposite question to the one we are addressing: he asks why Japan's savings rate is so high).

Edwards (1994) uses a fifty-country data set to analyze why Latin America's savings rates are so low.[6] The coefficients of determination are rather high, surpassing in every case 0.5. As suggested by the life cycle hypothesis, the coefficient of the age dependency ratio is significantly negative, indicating that demographics play an important role in explaining differences in private savings across countries. This coincides with the results obtained by a number of authors, including Leff (1968) and Modigliani (1980) in their pioneer work. The rate of growth of per capita GDP is significantly positive. This result is also obtained by Bosworth (1993) and Carroll and Weil (1993). This suggests that there is a two-way causality relationship between growth and savings: higher growth generates higher private savings, and higher savings allow for higher capital accumulation and thus faster growth (to address the endogeneity problem, Edwards estimates his equations using instrumental variables techniques). Within this context, the key policy question is how to enter this virtuous circle.

In his regression analysis on private savings, Edwards also includes indexes of the extent of development of the financial market (ratio of money to GDP), the degree of financial repression (real interest rates), and the severity of borrowing constraints (ratio of private sector credit to total credit). The coefficient of the money to GDP ratio is always significantly positive, suggesting that countries with a deeper financial system tend to have higher private savings rates. The coefficient of private credit is negative, as suggested by the borrowing constraint perspective. This is the case both when private credit is included jointly with the ratio of money to GDP and when it is excluded. The coefficient of real interest rates is insignificant in every regression where it is included. This is consistent with results obtained by a number of previous researchers (see McKinnon 1991, for example) but contradicts the theoretical implications of a number of models (Carroll and Summers 1991; Gylfason 1993). When measures of the efficiency of the financial system, such as the spread between lending and interest rates on deposits, are included, their coefficients are not significant (from theoretical and empirical points of view, the possible effects of interest rates—and other incentives—on private savings continues to constitute a major controversy).

The coefficient of government savings is significantly negative in every regression. More important from a policy perspective, however, is that this coefficient is always significantly different from –1.0. This indicates that, although higher government savings crowd out private savings, they do not do so one-to-one and that Ricardian equivalence does not hold strictly. In most regressions, this coefficient is approximately –0.5, suggesting that an increase in government savings of 1 percent of GDP generates a reduction in private savings of 0.5 percent of GDP. National savings, then, increase in the aggregate by 0.5 percent of GDP. The coefficient of the share of social security expenditures by the government over total public expenditure is negative and significant at conventional levels. This is consistent with previous findings by Feldstein (1980) and gives some support to the notion that reforms that replace government-run (and partially funded) social security systems with privately run capitalization systems result in higher rates of private savings.[7] The current account balance is insignificant in every regression. Also, the coefficients of income distribution and political instability are not significant in any of the regressions where they are included. The majority of the Latin American countries exhibit negative residuals in every regression: their actual private sector rates are below estimated rates. Overall, these results suggest that, in the case of Latin America, private savings are low because of a combination of factors, including demographics (Latin America has a much higher age dependency ratio than the countries in the rest of the sample), growth, and policy variables such as social security and government savings.

From a policy point of view, these results, as well as others, suggest that the most direct way to increase private aggregate national savings in the short and medium runs is to raise government savings through changes in the public deficit. In a comprehensive study, Corbo and Schmidt-Hebbel (1991) use a thirteen-country data set to analyze the macroeconomic consequences of higher public savings. In particular, they investigate the extent to which an increase in government savings is reflected in a decline in private savings. They find that, although government savings crowd out private savings, the magnitude of this effect is far below the one-to-one relationship suggested by the simple Ricardian equivalence doctrine; overall, their empirical analysis strongly indicates that an increase in public savings will be translated into higher aggregate savings (on Ricardian-Barro equivalence, see Barro 1974).

Moreover, on average, increasing public savings by reducing expenditures is more effective than increasing taxation. The most appropriate mix of higher tax revenues and reduced expenditures to increase public savings depends on the specific characteristics of the country in question. If the level of tax compliance is low, and the tax effort is clearly below par, an increase in tax revenues is needed. However, under most circumstances, some reduction in expenditure is likely to be optimal. For instance, in most countries in the region, it seems feasible to reduce the military budget as a way to finance both the expansion of social programs and the generation of higher public savings.

The preceding discussion raises two important questions: Why do government savings differ so markedly across countries? What are the most effective mechanisms for increasing government savings? Several authors rely on insights from public choice and game theory to study government behavior (see Persson and Tabellini 1990 for a comprehensive discussion). Many of these models assume that political parties alternate in power and that the group in office acts strategically, in an intertemporal sense, when making decisions whose economic consequences span more than one period (Cukierman, Edwards, and Tabellini 1992). In this setting, the political party in office is reluctant to implement policies whose fruits will be reaped by its opponents. This type of approach has been used to address cross-country differentials in government savings rates (Edwards 1994). According to this approach, the authorities' incentive to increase government savings—and thus the ability to produce public goods—depends on two fundamental political economy variables. First, it depends on the probability that the party in power will still be in office in the subsequent period. If this probability is low, the opposition party is likely to be in office once the projects mature and will get the credit from the increased production of the public goods. Naturally, under these circumstances, the incentives to increase savings are low. The recent political economy literature on inflation and stabilization associates the probability that the incumbent will remain in office with the degree of political instability in the country in question. This analysis predicts, then, that the higher the degree of political instability, the lower the government's savings. The second determinant of the government's incentives to save is the extent to which the political parties have different preferences. In the extreme case when their preferences are exactly the same, government has a high incentive to save, even if the probability of remaining in office is low. The difference in parties' preferences is known as the degree of political polarization. This analysis predicts that, with other things being equal, a greater degree of polarization results in lower government savings. In regression analyses, however, it is difficult to find empirical counterparts for political polarization. Some authors, such as Cukierman, Edwards, and Tabellini (1992), for example, argue that the frequency of politically motivated attacks and assassinations are appropriate proxies.

Figure 7-19. Ratio of Private Gross Domestic Investment to GDP in Selected Countries of Latin America, 1980–91

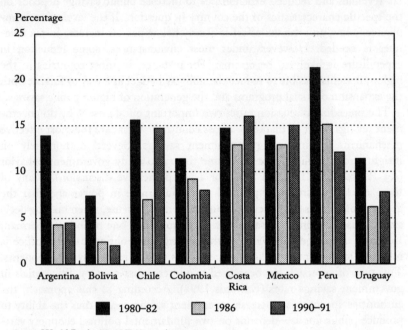

Percentage

Source: World Bank, *World Tables*, various years.

Edwards's (1994) econometric estimates of cross-country government savings equations provide some support for the political economy approach. In every equation, the coefficient of the political instability index is significantly negative, as suggested by this approach. Moreover, when alternative measures of political instability are used, such as the estimated probability of changes in government, the results are maintained.

The development of new institutions, such as new social security systems tailored after the Chilean experience, plays a fundamental role in increasing private savings from their historical levels. Government savings, in turn, are positively affected by the creation of social and political institutions that reduce the degree of political instability. This suggests, then, that the strengthening of democracy has important, and fairly direct, positive effects on growth and economic progress.

It is important to note that the decision to increase government savings does not necessarily imply that public investment should be increased at an equal pace. In fact, both decisions should be kept separate. Whether specific public investments should be undertaken has to be decided on a project by project basis. This requires implementing highly professional procedures for appraising public investment projects. In those countries where an expansion in public investment is not justified, the government should still increase its savings and channel those resources to the capital market.

Recent research undertaken at the World Bank (1993a) suggests that East Asia experienced a virtuous circle of growth and private savings. Using time-series econometric techniques, Bank researchers find that, in the miracle economies, higher growth increases disposable income and encourages private savings. Higher savings, in turn, permit a higher level of capital accumulation and, thus, reinforce higher growth. Of course, a key question in this context is how to get this virtuous circle going? In most East Asian economies, this was achieved through increases in public savings during the earlier phases of the process. These experiences provide, then, some support for the importance of public savings, and further fiscal adjustments, in Latin America during the years to come.

Investment and Infrastructure

Figure 7-19 contains data on the ratio of gross private investment to GDP for selected countries. As can be seen, in many of the cases it is possible to detect a familiar U-shaped behavior: private investment experienced a drastic dip in the mid-1980s, only to recover in the early 1990s. While in some countries the recovery is complete, in Bolivia, Colombia, and Peru, the private investment ratio is still significantly below its 1980 level.

However, the volume of private investment is only part of the story. In most countries, the composition of private investment changed significantly. For instance, after decades of stagnation, investment in agriculture and related activities soared in Chile, resulting in a surge in productivity growth and an increase in agriculture-related exports from less than $40 million in the early 1970s to almost $1.3 billion in 1991. Moreover, the real return to investment in Chile was extremely high in the early 1990s, generating significant growth in privately administered pension funds. A growing proportion of private investment was also directed to the manufacturing sector, whose export-related activities expanded rapidly (Edwards and Edwards 1992).

In Mexico and Argentina, the composition of private investment also changed in the past few years. In both countries, investment in nontraditional activities increased significantly. In Mexico, the structural reforms resulted in a restructuring of the petrochemical sector, and new investments in modern technologies will allow the sector to withstand new competition and, in some product lines, move into exports (Kessel 1992). In both Argentina and Mexico, the private sector began channeling an important percentage of its investment toward infrastructure, including privately run ports and roads.

Public investment was affected in a particularly severe way in the aftermath of the debt crisis. As figure 7-20 shows, in most countries with available information, public gross domestic investment was significantly lower in 1990–91

Figure 7-20. Ratio of Public Gross Domestic Investment to GDP in Selected Countries of Latin America, 1980–91

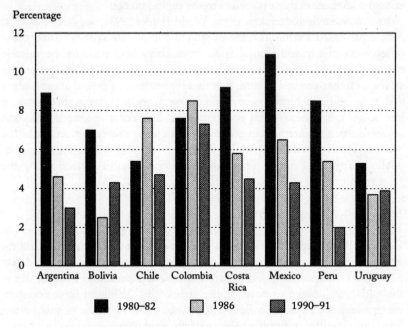

Source: World Bank, *World Tables*, various years.

than in 1980. Moreover, in a number of countries, net public investment was negative during the past decade. This was the result of three factors. First, the need to reverse the international transfer of resources in the early and mid-1980s forced almost every country in the region to reduce expenditures. In most cases, public investment shouldered a disproportionate share of this adjustment. Second, the fiscal adjustments of the late 1980s were largely accomplished through major reductions in public expenditures, including public investment. And third, the reduced role of the state in the development process affected public investment; many activities that in the past were considered to be exclusively within the realm of government activities, including utilities, are now performed by the private sector.

An important consequence of the decline in public investment during the 1980s was the deterioration in the region's infrastructure, including roads, bridges, ports, and power generation (for a discussion of the state of infrastructure in Latin America, see Fleisig 1992). Recent empirical studies for a number of countries, including the United States, point out that investment in infrastructure has a particularly large effect on growth. For example, Aschauer (1989) argues that due to the existence of significant externalities, infrastructure investment has almost twice the effect on growth that private investment has. These findings have prompted policymakers, including the Clinton administration in the United States, to emphasize the need to step up capital accumulation in basic infrastructure.

Although the externalities argument is eminently plausible for some types of infrastructure, it is very important not to push this idea too far. In fact, the economic history of Latin America is replete with cases of gigantic public sector projects—many of them in infrastructure—with very low, and even negative, social returns. In general, public sector investment projects should be assessed from a microeconomic perspective and should only be undertaken to the extent that their (social) rate of return exceeds a predetermined level. Not following this rule is a clear invitation to return to the practices of the past, when exceedingly frivolous projects were implemented in the name of some allegedly worthy cause.

A systematic economic appraisal of projects requires developing an appropriate institutional setting, with qualified personnel to undertake this task at a large scale. This was done in Chile, where almost every large public sector project is subject to a stern battery of tests before being undertaken. Unfortunately, most other countries have been slow to design and implement project evaluation units. For example, during the execution of the 1991 budget, the Argentine government exercised little, if any, project analysis (Psacharopoulos 1992).

One of the most startling aspects of public sector investment in Latin America is that most countries have extremely small budgets for maintenance and operation. The result is the extremely rapid deterioration of the stock of capital. What makes this situation particularly serious is that maintenance outlays are typically small relative to investment costs and have extremely high (social) rates of return. Preliminary analyses suggest that one of the most effective ways to improve the quality of infrastructure in the region is to expand maintenance and operating budgets (see Fleisig 1992). Paradoxically, however, constraints placed on lending in many of the multilateral institutions discourage a more efficient and extensive use of maintenance. Changes in these regulations that would allow multilateral institutions to cofinance maintenance would go a long way toward improving the quality of the region's infrastructure in the years to come.

An important challenge is to ensure that the newly privatized infrastructure and utilities can raise the funds required for their expansion. This problem presents a particular challenge for the World Bank, which for many decades helped to finance public infrastructure projects but is not allowed (by charter) to finance the private sector directly. The recent experience of Chile clearly suggests that, contrary to popular belief, the private sector can raise a substantial volume of funds at fairly long maturities to finance major infrastructure expansions. This, for example, is the case of the electric utility ENDESA. Two main factors are behind this ability to fund large projects: consolidated macroeconomic stability and an institutional and regulatory environment that enables the government to commit itself credibly to not expropriating the utilities' assets in the future. In other countries in the region, however, the ability to fund these substantial projects will develop more slowly. In these cases, the international financial institutions are actively involved in efforts to implement creative techniques for lengthening bond maturities and improving the access of utilities to long-term financial markets.

Direct Foreign Investment

For many years, the Latin American countries severely restricted direct foreign investment. In the early 1970s, the countries of the Andean Pact implemented a regulation—Resolution 24 of the Cartagena Accord—that restricted the right of foreigners to control manufacturing firms and placed broad controls on their ability to remit profits to their home countries. In other cases, foreigners could not participate in sectors deemed to be strategic. As a result of these regulations and of the inward-looking policies pursued in most countries, direct foreign investment played a minor role in the process of capital accumulation during the 1970s; in most countries, it amounted, on average, to less than 1 percent of GDP a year (Edwards 1991).

Many analysts argue that in the aftermath of the debt crisis, direct foreign investment should play a larger role as a source of foreign funds for developing countries. However, the total volume of resources is likely to be limited and shared by more and more potential host countries, including the nations of Eastern Europe and Central Asia. After pointing out that bank loans and bonds issues are unlikely to be a major source of foreign funds during the years to come, Cardoso and Dornbusch (1989, p. 1434) propose that "the immediate obvious candidate [for providing foreign resources] is direct foreign investment. Unfortunately, the role of direct foreign investment has never been very large."

Increasingly, however, analysts agree that a fundamental role of direct foreign investment is to allow the host country to come in contact with new techniques and new management styles. Even if its volume is modest, direct foreign investment helps to diffuse innovations, encourages the imitation of best practices in more industrial countries, and accelerates the pace of productivity growth.

Under these circumstances, a key question is what makes particular countries attractive for foreign investors. A first, and obvious, factor is the body of regulations directly affecting direct foreign investment activities, including restrictions on the remittance of profits. In recent years, most Latin American countries introduced reforms to their direct foreign investment legislation: instead of being chased out of these countries as they were in the 1960s and 1970s, foreign companies are now being lured in through a variety of schemes. For example, in 1990 Bolivia approved a new law ensuring equal treatment for foreigners and locals in all sectors, with the exception of mining and hydrocar-

Table 7-10. Regulations on Direct Foreign Investment in Selected Countries of Latin America, through 1994

Country	Sectors restricted to state	Sectors restricted to nationals	Controlling interest by foreigners allowed	Restrictions on profit remittances	Privatization financed by debt-equity swaps
Argentina	None	None	All sectors	None	Yes
Brazil	Oil, gas, tele-communica-tions	Banking, transporta-tion, media, health	Yes, except in computers	None	Yes
Chile	None	None	All sectors	None	No, program canceled early 1993
Colombia	Alcoholic beverages	Defense, toxic materi-als disposal	All sectors	None, up to registered investment	No
Mexico	Petroleum, hydrocarbons, nuclear energy	Transport, media	Most sectors	None	No
Peru	None	None	All sectors	None	Yes
Venezuela	None	None	All sectors	None	

Sources: Ferretti 1991; IMF, *Annual Report (of the Board of Directors),* various years; IMF, several country-specific reports.

bons; Venezuela went through successive rounds of liberalization of direct foreign investment restrictions between 1989 and 1990; and Brazil greatly relaxed the restrictions on the repatriation of profits in mid-1990. Table 7-10 summarizes the current regulations affecting direct foreign investment in selected countries. As can be seen, these are quite liberal and contrast sharply with those of the 1960s and 1970s.

One of the most important determinants of the distribution of direct foreign investment across countries is the soundness of economic policies. Foreign investors tend to avoid countries with major distortions and controls and are attracted to nations with consistent and predictable macroeconomic policies. Policies that move the economy toward greater openness and international competitiveness, as well as reduce the size of the government, tend to encourage direct foreign investment (see Edwards 1991). In that regard, the reforms undertaken in most Latin American countries during the past few years positioned them very well to receive direct foreign investment funds. This was indeed the case in some of the early reformers—Chile and Mexico—which saw drastic increases in direct foreign investment in the past few years (see figure 7-21). Even in these cases, however, direct foreign investment is still a relatively small proportion of GDP, indicating that the Latin American nations should seriously persevere in their efforts to increase domestic savings.

Figure 7-21. Ratio of Net Foreign Direct Investment to GDP in Selected Countries of Latin America, 1980–92

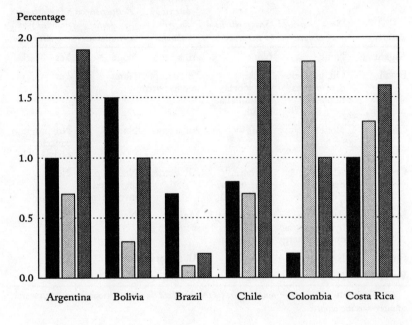

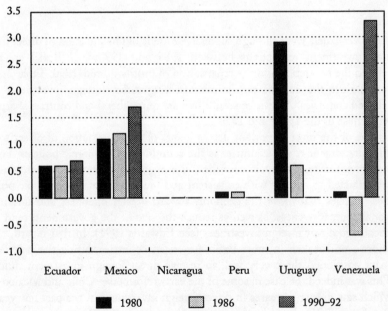

Sources: For 1980–90, IMF data; for 1991–92, World Bank data.

Appendix 7-1: Financial Development and Productivity Growth

New theories of the role of the financial sector in the development process emphasize the connection between the degree of financial deepening and the growth of productivity. For example, King and Levine (1993a) have developed a model in which the financial sector plays a key role in processing information regarding investment opportunities and profitable projects. Within this framework, the financial sector has a clear comparative advantage for monitoring the allocation of investment funds (on modern theories of the link between financial intermediation and growth, see McKinnon 1991).

From an empirical perspective, this approach suggests that, after controlling for other factors, countries with a more developed financial sector exhibit a faster rate of growth of total factor productivity than those with a less developed one. In this appendix, this proposition is tested using the data set from appendix 5-1. Cross-country regressions of the following type are estimated using weighted least squares:

$$(7-1) \qquad TFP_i = \alpha_0 + \Sigma_j \beta_j X_{ji} + \gamma FIN_i + u_i$$

where TFP_i is the rate of growth of total factor productivity in country i; the Xjs are other variables affecting growth of total factor productivity, including the degree of openness and the size of government; and FIN_i is an index of the degree of financial development in country i. According to the theories discussed above, the regression coefficient γ is expected to be positive, reflecting the fact that countries with a higher degree of financial development exhibit higher growth of productivity than those with a lower degree.

In the estimation of equation 7-1, the data set described in appendix 5-1 on trade policy is used (the results presented in table 7-11 correspond to the definition of growth of total factor productivity, TFP2; when the other two definitions are used, similar results are obtained). The data on the growth of total factor productivity correspond to an average for 1971–82. A particularly difficult issue in the estimation of equation 7-1 refers to the definition of the indicator of financial repression, FIN. In the analysis reported here, three alternative indicators are used: (a) the ratio of narrowly defined money to GDP during the initial year (M1GDP), (b) the ratio of broadly defined money to GDP in 1971 (M2GDP), and (c) the ratio of domestic credit to the private sector relative to GDP, also in 1971 (DCGDP). In addition to the indexes on financial development, the following regressors are incorporated into the analysis. The first is initial real GDP per capita (GDP71). As in the analysis on openness, this variable measures the gap between the country in question and the industrial nations and captures the catch-up effect on growth of productivity. It is expected that the higher the initial level of GDP per capita, the lower the growth of total factor productivity. The second regressor is growth in coverage in secondary education (GSEC). It is expected that faster increases in human capital accumulation will result in more rapid growth of total factor

Table 7-11. Productivity Growth and Financial Development, Cross-Country Results
(weighted least squares, *t*-statistics in parentheses)

Variable	Equation 7-2	Equation 7-3	Equation 7-4
Constant	0.016	0.016	0.015
	(2.255)	(2.273)	(2.114)
GDP71	−1.85e-06	−1.96e-06	−1.97e-06
	(−3.677)	(−3.784)	(−3.639)
Secondary education	2.67e-04	2.63e-04	2.54e-04
	(3.101)	(3.041)	(2.885)
Trade distortions	−0.075	−0.077	−0.076
	(−3.303)	(−3.366)	(−3.240)
Government	−3.69e-04	−3.71e-04	−3.78e-04
	(−1.387)	(−1.434)	(−1.424)
Political instability	−0.036	−0.034	−0.030
	(−3.439)	(−3.136)	(−2.790)
M1GDP	0.007	n.a.	n.a.
	(2.189)		
M2GDP	n.a.	0.004	n.a.
		(1.741)	
DCGDP	n.a.	n.a.	0.005
			(1.227)
R^2	0.571	0.551	0.534
Number of observations	45	46	46

n.a. Not applicable.
Note: Population was used as weight.

productivity. The third is the share of government consumption in GDP. As argued in chapter 5, its coefficient is expected to be negative. The fourth is political instability, which is defined as the expected probability of a change in government (Cukierman, Edwards, and Tabellini 1992). Its sign is expected to be negative, reflecting the fact that innovation is negatively affected by political instability. And fifth is an index of the extent of trade restrictions, whose coefficient is expected to be positive. Countries with more-open foreign trade are able to absorb technological innovation more rapidly and thus have a faster rate of growth of total factor productivity than countries with less-open foreign trade.

Table 7-11 contains the results obtained using a group of forty-five countries for which data are available. The regressions are estimated using weighted least squares, where population is used as the weight (standard tests suggest the presence of heteroskedasticity). As can be seen, the results are quite interesting. As in the case of the regressions reported in appendix 5-1, trade restrictions and government and political instability are significantly negative, as is real GDP in 1971. The most interesting result from the point of view of this chapter is that the indexes of initial financial deepening are positive, as expected, and that M1GDP and M2GDP are significant at conventional levels. These regressions, then, provide some preliminary support for the view that financial depth and development are associated with growth of productivity, as is argued by the proponents of financial reform.

CHAPTER 8

Poverty, Income Distribution, and Human Resources

POVERTY AND INEQUALITY HAVE LONG BEEN SALIENT FEATURES OF THE Latin American economies. The inability to deal effectively with these issues is, perhaps, the clearest and saddest illustration of traditional policies. Decades of government intervention and regulations did little to reduce income inequality. As Sheahan (1987) points out, Latin America is the only region in the world where the share of income going to the poorest 20 percent of the population consistently declined between 1950 and the late 1970s. Moreover, income inequality preceded the debt crisis and the modernization programs of the 1980s and 1990s (see table 8-1). In the late 1970s, the percentage of income received by the poorest 20 percent was lower in Latin America than in any other part of the developing world. The degree of income inequality is particularly striking when compared with that of resource-poor East Asia (see table 8-2).

After a decade of adjustment, one of the main—if not *the* main—challenges facing Latin America is finding ways to reduce poverty and reverse decades of inequalities. Addressing the needs of the poorest strata of society is not just a social issue but also a political one. Only to the extent that poverty is reduced and living conditions of the poor are improved will the structural reforms implemented during the last decade be sustained. Moreover, satisfying the needs of the poor for education, nutrition, and health will directly affect economic growth: as a larger proportion of the population acquires basic human capital, the economy will grow more rapidly (Barro 1991).

Although between 1960 and 1980 economic growth improved living standards, as measured by educational attainment, health conditions, nutrition, and other social indicators, by the early 1980s a large percentage of the region's population—approximately 91 million people—still lived in poverty. Even though many of the policies aimed at reducing poverty in the 1960–80 period, including agrarian reforms, minimum wage legislation, and labor market regulations, were well intentioned, they made limited progress in this area. In

Table 8-1. *Percentage of Income Received by Lowest 20 Percent of Population, for Selected Regions, 1960–78*
(percentage)

Region	1960	1970	Around 1978[a]
Sub-Saharan Africa	5.2	4.1	6.2
Middle East and North Africa	4.9	5.0	5.3
East Asia and Pacific	5.3	6.0	6.2
South Asia	4.5	7.0	—
Southern Europe	5.5	4.3	5.0
Latin America and the Caribbean	3.7	3.4	2.9

— Not available.

a. The 1980 edition of *World Tables* refers to these figures as "most recent estimate."

Source: World Bank, *World Tables*, 1980.

Table 8-2. *Income Distribution in Selected Economies of Latin America and Asia, Various Years, 1970–80*
(percentage of all income)

Economy and year	For lowest 40 percent	For highest 10 percent
Argentina, 1970	11.0	35.2
Brazil, 1972	7.0	50.6
Costa Rica, 1971	12.0	39.5
El Salvador, 1976–77	15.0	29.5
Mexico, 1977	9.9	40.6
Panama, 1973	7.2	44.2
Peru, 1972	7.0	42.9
Venezuela, 1970	10.3	35.7
Median	10.1	40.1
Hong Kong, 1980	16.2	31.3
Indonesia, 1976	14.4	34.0
Korea, Rep. of, 1976	16.9	27.5
Malaysia, 1973	11.2	39.8
Philippines, 1970–71	14.2	38.5
Thailand, 1975–76	15.2	34.1
Median	14.8	34.1

Note: The sample is restricted to the group that the World Bank classifies as middle-income economies.

Sources: World Bank, *World Development Report 1982, World Development Report 1986.*

Table 8-3. Percentage of the Population Living below the Poverty Line in Selected Countries of Latin America, 1970 and 1981

Country	1970	1981
Argentina	8.0	8.0
Brazil	49.0	43.0
Chile	17.0	16.0
Colombia	45.0	43.0
Costa Rica	24.0	22.0
Honduras	65.0	64.0
Mexico	34.0	29.0
Panama	39.0	37.0
Peru	50.0	49.0
Venezuela	25.0	24.0
Average	39.0	35.0

Sources: Reported in Cardoso and Helwege 1992; the data for 1970 are from Altimir 1982; those for 1981 are from Molina 1982.

1981, more than one-third of Latin America's population had income below the poverty line (see table 8-3).

The debt crisis that erupted in 1982 worsened an already battered social picture. The sudden halt in foreign financing, the deterioration in the terms of trade, and the resulting need to implement significant macroeconomic adjustment programs severely affected real income throughout the region. In 1991, only ten out of thirty economies with available data had a GDP per capita above that of 1980: Antigua and Barbuda, the Bahamas, Barbados, Belize, Chile, Colombia, Dominica, Jamaica, St. Kitts and Nevis, and St. Vincent and the Grenadines. Naturally, this decline in real GDP per capita affected overall well-being and, in most countries, deepened poverty in the 1980s. In 1993 more than 10 million children under the age of five were malnourished in Latin America, and a large proportion of the population did not receive appropriate health or educational services. Although many countries reacted to the crisis by implementing emergency social programs, the overall level of poverty and inequality increased. Additionally, the restructuring of the economy generated, in many countries, highly segmented labor markets and a burgeoning informal urban sector.

An important direct consequence of the adjustment programs of the 1980s was the reduction, in most countries, of government spending devoted to social programs (an exception to this was social security spending, which is treated in greater detail below; for an analysis of the evolution of government spending in the early 1980s, see Hicks 1992b). Somewhat surprisingly, many social indicators—infant mortality, school enrollment, and life expectancy, for example—improved despite these problems (see table 8-4). Psacharopoulos (1992) presents a series of possible explanations for this puzzle. First, there may be a significant lag between changes in inputs that go into social programs (that is, public social spending) and changes in outcomes, summarized by social indicators. Recent data showing that the rate of improvement in these indexes is leveling off provide some support for this view. Second, aggregate data may be misleading, hiding what is occurring within each country. In fact, the World Bank argues persuasively that countrywide data tend to hide serious inequalities within a given country. When these more detailed data are analyzed, it becomes clear that social indicators are not improving in all segments of society. Third, in many countries, the reduction in the level of social spending is coupled with an increase in the efficiency with which funds are used and in the support that private nongovernmental organizations extend to social programs. Although publicly provided inputs declined substantially, the availability of total effective inputs was not reduced by that much—and, maybe, not reduced at all (Grosh 1992).

For many years, acceleration in the rate of economic growth was considered to be the main (if not the only) vehicle for reducing inequalities and poverty. In particular, it was argued that the right type of growth, based on comparative advantages, employment creation, and productivity growth, would generate higher wages and better economic conditions for the poor. Increasingly, however, empirical evidence indicates that, although crucially important, higher growth is not enough. Because it takes a long time for the fruits of

Table 8-4. Social Indicators in Latin America and the Caribbean, 1970–90

Indicator	1970	1980	1990
Illiterate population as percentage of population, ages fifteen and older	29.0	23.0	15.3
Enrollment rates, ages six to eleven	71.0	82.3	87.3
Gross enrollment rates, secondary level	31.6	47.4	54.9
Population per physician	2,053	1,315	1,083
Percentage of the population with access to safe water	53.7	70.1	79.8[a]
Infant mortality rate	84.9	63.0	48.2
Life expectancy at birth	60.1	64.3	67.5

Note: Figures are weighted averages of economies in Latin America and the Caribbean with populations of more than 1 million persons.

a. 1988 data.

Sources: Raw data are from the data base of the World Bank, International Economics Department; CEPAL, *Statistical Yearbook for Latin America and the Caribbean,* 1991.

faster growth to reach the most vulnerable and poorest segments of society, many institutions, including the World Bank, argue strongly that there is a need to implement a two-pronged approach toward poverty reduction in which faster growth is supplemented with social programs targeted at providing social services to the neediest (Psacharopoulos 1992).

As pointed out in chapter 3, the expansion of social programs was absent in most early structural adjustment programs. Slowly, however, politicians recognized that the need to reduce poverty and expand possibilities was urgent, both politically and economically. In fact, in the new democratic environment, consolidation of the reform process and achievement of economic and social stability required that the fruits of reforms be spread across society. The urgency of dealing effectively with the social sectors has increased significantly in the aftermath of the Mexican peso crisis of 1994. Because foreign resources have diminished, growth opportunities have also declined in the short run. This means that programs aiming directly at reducing poverty should be improved. This chapter explores the state of the social sectors, the evolution of social policies, and the evolution of labor market regulations and their relation to social programs.

Poverty and Income Distribution

The lack of adequate data makes the analysis of poverty and income distribution in Latin America a difficult and frustrating task. Little is known about living conditions in rural areas, the informal sector, or migration patterns. Moreover, much of the existing data are at the aggregate level and tend to hide major differences across regions, racial groups, and gender. Despite these problems, several institutions, including CEPAL and the World Bank, have made serious efforts to depict human conditions in the region (see CEPAL 1985; Psacharopoulos 1992).

Poverty not only is widespread in Latin America—the bottom 20 percent of the population receive less than 4 percent of total income—but increased during the last decade. Psacharopoulos (1992, p. 16) argues that "much of the poverty in the region relates to the exceptionally high degree of income inequality affecting Latin America."

Table 8-5 summarizes income distribution in Latin America during the 1980s. For as many countries as possible, data are provided for more than one year. In six of the twelve countries with more than one observation, income distribution, as measured by the Gini coefficient, deteriorated in the 1980s. In the other six countries—Colombia, Costa Rica, Guatemala, Paraguay, Uruguay, and Venezuela—it improved. However, these data are of poor quality and should be interpreted with caution. For example, for many of the countries, the available information is concentrated on the urban sector. Also, in some cases, data for the early 1980s actually refer to 1985 or 1986, when the

Table 8-5. Income Distribution in Selected Countries of Latin America, 1980s
(Gini coefficient)

Country	Early 1980s	Late 1980s
Argentina (Buenos Aires)	0.389	0.461
Bolivia (urban)	0.479	0.515
Brazil	0.574	0.625
Colombia (urban)	0.578	0.515
Costa Rica	0.451	0.410
Guatemala	0.532	0.528
Honduras[a]	0.528	0.533
Panama	0.376	0.446
Paraguay	0.450	0.400
Peru	0.427	0.438
Uruguay (urban)	0.452	0.420
Venezuela	0.512	0.498

a. Early and late values are not strictly comparable due to differential survey coverage.
Sources: Psacharopoulos 1992, 1993.

region was already feeling the effects of the debt crisis and was facing dramatic adjustments.

Some time ago, the public policy literature moved away from relative measures of well-being, such as income distribution, and emphasized absolute social indicators, including the percentage of the population living under poverty conditions. As a result of this, serious efforts have been made to construct poverty lines in Latin America. These are generally defined as the income required by a household of a predefined size to meet a minimal standard of living. This standard of living is, in turn, constructed around food consumption; it is estimated that an adult should consume no less than 2,500 calories a day. A typical consumption basket that covers this required intake is computed and priced for each country. The food basket is then increased by a certain factor to allow for the consumption of other items and thus to calculate the poverty threshold. In Latin America, it has become a tradition to multiply the food basket by a factor of 2.0 to construct urban poverty baskets and by a factor of 1.5 to compute rural baskets. Households with a (monetary) income below this hypothetical basket are defined as being below the poverty line (households with a level of income below the cost of the food basket are defined as being below the destitution line; this condition is also called extreme poverty).

Constructing poverty lines requires a detailed profile of income distribution and consumption surveys. Obtaining this information is not only expensive but also time-consuming. This becomes particularly evident when analysts try to obtain poverty lines for more than a moment in time, implying that comparators of poverty lines through time should be interpreted with great care. Table 8-6 contains data on poverty lines for a group of Latin American countries for the early and late 1980s. This table uses a uniform poverty basket for

Table 8-6. Percentage of Individuals in Poverty and Extreme Poverty in Selected Countries of Latin America and the Caribbean, 1980 and 1989

	Poverty[a]		Extreme poverty[b]	
Country	1980	1989	1980	1989
Argentina (Buenos Aires)	3.0	6.4	0.2	1.6
Bolivia (urban)	51.1	54.0	22.5	23.2
Brazil	34.1	40.9	12.2	18.7
Chile	—	10.0	—	1.5
Colombia (urban)	13.0	8.0	6.0	2.9
Costa Rica	13.4	3.4	5.4	1.1
Dominican Republic	—	24.1	—	4.9
Ecuador (urban)	—	24.2	—	4.0
El Salvador (urban)	—	41.5	—	14.9
Guatemala	66.4	67.0	36.6	39.5
Honduras (urban)	48.7	54.4	21.6	22.7
Jamaica	—	12.1	—	1.1
Mexico	16.6	22.6[c]	2.5	7.3[c]
Panama	27.9	31.8	8.4	13.2
Paraguay (Asunción)	13.1	7.6	3.2	0.6
Peru (Lima)	31.1	40.5[d]	3.3	10.1
Uruguay (urban)	6.2	5.3	1.1	0.7
Venezuela	4.0	12.9	0.7	3.1

— Not available.

Note: The computations are based on common poverty lines.

a. Defined as having an income of $60 per person per month or less.

b. Defined as having an income of $30 per person per month or less.

c. Based on an unweighted sample that may not accurately reflect the composition of the population.

d. Based on extrapolation from 1985–86 poverty figure.

Source: Psacharopoulos 1993.

all countries in the region, defined at US$60 in 1985 purchasing-power-parity dollars a month.[1] In four out of the twelve countries with comparable figures—Colombia, Costa Rica, Paraguay, and Uruguay—the percentage of the population below the poverty line declined.

The unequal distribution of income is generally recognized to be at the heart of poverty in Latin America. Various authors have attempted to explain the determinants of income inequality in different countries at a given moment in time. Altimir and Piñera (1979) provide some preliminary work that emphasizes the crucial role of education. Fiszbein and Psacharopoulos (1992) use data on ten countries—Argentina, Bolivia, Brazil, Colombia, Costa Rica, Guatemala, Honduras, Panama, Uruguay, and Venezuela—to analyze the fundamental determinants of income inequality during the 1980s. They decompose Theil's inequality indexes in an attempt to isolate those structural variables that are better able to explain inequality. In performing the decomposition, variables in four categories are used—education, age, sector of employment (agriculture, mining, manufacturing, and so on), and type of employment (employed, self-employed, employer). These four variables explain approximately 50 percent of the variability of the Theil index in the countries under consideration.

The level of education appears to be the single most important determinant of inequality at a given moment in time. To investigate the determinants of income distribution, Fiszbein and Psacharopoulos estimate a statistical model to compute the probability of being at the bottom of the distribution.[2] In addition to the four structural variables discussed above, they add gender. Along the lines of previous results, education is overwhelmingly the main determinant of the probability of being in the bottom 20 percent of income distribution. In Panama, for example, people with zero to five years of education have an 83 percent estimated probability of being in the lowest 20 percent of the distribution. The corresponding figure is 69 percent for Argentina and 42 percent for Brazil. These figures contrast sharply with those for people with thirteen or more years of education; in most countries, the likelihood that they will be in the bottom 20 percent of the distribution is less than 5 percent.

The importance of education in determining inequality was recently confirmed in a series of detailed studies for Brazil during the 1960s and 1970s. Using disaggregated data for six metropolitan areas, Barros (1992) and Cardoso, Barros, and Urani (1993) find that two-thirds of the increase in inequality between 1960 and 1970 was rooted in education. However, the importance of education as an explanation of inequality in Brazil declined during the 1970s. For this period, their analysis strongly suggests that unemployment and macroeconomic instability provide most of the explanation for cyclical changes in inequality.

With all else remaining equal, the probability of being at the bottom of the distributional scale is higher for females than for males. For example, in Venezuela, households headed by single mothers are significantly more likely to be below the poverty line. Moreover, poor women tend to be older and to have less ability to improve their skills through training and education (Márquez 1992). According to Psacharopoulos (1992, p. 15), "Working women continue to be concentrated in low-paying, low-productivity jobs . . . where there is little chance of advancement."

Countrywide aggregate data tend to hide significant variations in poverty and income distribution within countries. Brazil provides the starkest example of intracountry differences in human development. For example, while Rio Grande do Sul has social indicators comparable to those of Portugal and the Republic of Korea, the region of Paraíba has indicators similar to those of Kenya (Calvacati de Albuquerque 1992). These regional differences are reflected in almost every social indicator: illiteracy ranges from 11 percent in the urban south to more than 55 percent in the rural northeast, and mean years of schooling are 5.2 in the southeast and 1.7 in the rural northeast. Large regional differentials in human development and poverty are also present in other countries. For example, in Honduras maternal mortality is five times higher in rural areas (624 per 100,000) than the national average. In El Salvador, 80 percent of infant mortality takes place in rural areas. In Mexico, infant mortality is twice as high in the poorer states as in the wealthier ones.

In many countries, ethnicity is directly related to poverty and inequality. In 1989, almost 60 percent of Guatemala's indigenous population had zero to five years of education compared with only 24 percent of the nonindigenous population. In Bolivia, 12 percent of the indigenous population had no education, while only 2 percent of the nonindigenous population fell in that category.

Macroeconomic Instability and Cyclical Variations in Poverty and Inequality

For many years, it was thought that income distribution only changed slowly through time. This belief was based largely on data from the industrial nations, which suggest that there is significant persistence in distributional data. Most analysts argued that in the absence of major shocks, such as a revolution or war, the distribution of income would change only gradually as the result of policies aimed at improving education and other social services. New research based on time-series data for some Latin American countries suggests, however, that in some countries income distribution can change significantly in relatively short periods of time. For example, the Gini coefficient in Brazil exhibited large cyclical variations between 1980 and 1991, and education played only a minor role in explaining cyclical changes in inequality (Cardoso, Barros, and Urani 1993). Based on a disaggregated data base for six Brazilian metropolitan areas, macroeconomic instability—measured by the inflation rate and by changes in the real exchange rate—had significantly negative effects on Brazil's distribution of income. More specifically, overvaluation of the real exchange rate negatively affected the poor, as did increases in the level and variability of inflation.

The broad results by Cardoso, Barros, and Urani (1993) were confirmed by a multicountry study by Cárdenas and Urrutia (1992). These authors use a large cross-section data set for 110 countries to investigate changes in the United Nations Development Programme's human development index (which is a weighted average of three social indicators: life expectancy, adult literacy, and income per capita; its usefulness for analyzing the evolution of human conditions is subject to considerable controversy). They find that higher inflation, as well as more variable inflation, negatively affect the evolution of the human development index. Their regression results also suggest that, as pointed out above, faster growth improves social indicators, as does greater social government expenditure.

There are two fundamental reasons why macro-instability deepens poverty. First, in many countries, overvaluation of the real exchange rate hurts labor-intensive exports and thus employment and wages. Second, the poor are significantly more vulnerable to macroeconomic imbalances, because they cannot protect themselves from the direct and indirect consequences of the inflation tax. These findings support the view that programs aimed at reducing macro-economic disequilibria—and, in particular, programs that reduce inflation—tend to improve income distribution. In fact, poverty improved in Bolivia in the 1980s largely because of the end of hyperinflation in 1986.

Repeated experiences in Latin America with populist policies underscore the links between macroeconomic disequilibrium and income distribution. Dornbusch and Edwards (1991) contend that, although populist episodes have specific and unique characteristics in different nations, they have common threads as well. In particular, populist regimes historically tried to deal with income inequality by using overly expansive macroeconomic policies. These policies, which relied on deficit financing, generalized controls, and a disregard for basic economic equilibria, almost unavoidably provoked major macroeconomic crises that hurt the poorer segments of society. As the case studies collected in Dornbusch and Edwards (1991) show, at the end of every populist experiment, inflation is out of hand, macroeconomic disequilibria are rampant, and real wages are lower than they were at the beginning of these experiences. The overriding historical lesson is that macroeconomic policy should not be used to pursue social or redistributive goals. Every time this principle is violated, the most vulnerable and poor segments of society are severely hurt.

Income Distribution, Poverty, and Growth

There is ample evidence that over the medium and long run, faster growth is the main determinant of poverty reduction, improved social conditions, and reduced inequality. For example, in their cross-country analysis, Cárdenas and Urrutia (1992) find that GNP growth is the main determinant of improvements in social conditions. Morley (1992, p. 4) also makes this point when he argues that "economic growth is a potent force for poverty reduction." This is clearly illustrated by the cases of Brazil, Colombia, Costa Rica, and Mexico in the decade preceding the debt crisis, when accelerated growth substantially reduced poverty. In Costa Rica, GNP per capita grew 41 percent between 1961 and 1971 and poverty was cut in half. Naturally, a slowdown in growth—or worse yet, a period of decline in GDP, as occurred in the 1980s throughout most of the region—is generally associated with an increase in the proportion of the population living below the poverty line.

Faster economic growth reduces poverty through two channels. First, it tends to increase employment, improving the opportunities for productive

Table 8-7. *Urban Unemployment in Selected Countries of Latin America,*
1984–92
(average annual percentage rate)

Country	1984	1985	1986	1987	1988	1989	1990	1991	1992ᵃ
Argentina	4.6	6.1	5.6	5.9	6.3	7.6	7.5	6.5	6.9
Bolivia	6.9	5.8	7.0	7.2	11.6	10.2	9.5	7.0	6.8
Brazil	7.1	5.3	3.6	3.7	3.8	3.3	4.3	4.8	5.9
Colombia	13.4	14.1	13.8	11.8	11.2	9.9	10.3	10.0	10.5
Costa Rica	6.6	6.7	6.7	5.9	6.3	3.7	5.4	6.0	4.3
Chile	18.5	17.0	13.1	11.9	10.2	7.2	6.5	7.3	5.0
Ecuador	10.5	10.4	10.7	7.2	7.4	7.9	6.1	8.5	—
Guatemala	9.1	12.0	14.0	11.4	8.8	6.2	6.4	6.5	—
Honduras	10.7	11.7	12.1	11.4	8.7	7.2	6.9	7.6	—
Mexico	5.7	4.4	4.3	3.9	3.5	2.9	2.9	2.7	3.2
Panama	12.4	15.7	12.7	14.1	21.1	20.4	20.0	19.8	18.0
Paraguay	7.3	5.1	6.1	5.5	4.7	6.1	6.6	5.1	6.0
Peru	8.9	10.1	5.4	4.8	7.9	7.9	8.3	5.9	—
Uruguay	14.0	13.1	10.7	9.3	9.1	8.6	9.3	8.9	9.3
Venezuela	14.3	14.3	12.1	9.9	7.9	9.7	10.5	10.1	8.0

— Not available.
a. Preliminary.
Source: CEPAL, *Economic Survey of Latin America,* several years.

activities among the poor. This suggests that the type of growth is important
in determining how fast poverty is reduced. Growth that emphasizes labor-
intensive sectors is generally more effective in reducing poverty than growth
that is biased against exports and employment-generating activities. Second,
to the extent that growth is associated with increased productivity, wages also
improve, and under most circumstances, the poorest segments of society see
an improvement in their life conditions. Again, the model of growth is important in determining the extent to which this channel operates. Growth based
on comparative advantages and reduced trade distortions is conducive to faster
wage increases among the poor, especially in the rural sector. Also, investment
in human capital significantly increases productivity, encourages the growth of
real wages, and reduces inequality.

The debt crisis, and the adjustment period that followed, negatively
affected both employment and real wages in Latin America. As table 8-7
shows, (urban) unemployment was extremely high in the years following the
crisis.[3] Although in many countries unemployment is beginning to decline, in
late 1992 and 1993 the level of unemployment was still alarmingly high in
most countries. Moreover, given the demographics of the region, the next few
years will be characterized by significant increases in labor supply, putting
additional pressure on employment. Table 8-8, in contrast, shows the evolution of average real wages in selected countries. As can be seen, with four

exceptions—São Paulo in Brazil, Chile, Mexico, and Uruguay—real wages in 1992 were below their 1984 level. These tables show, in a shocking way, the impact of the debt crisis and the subsequent adjustment on social conditions in the region.

As growth is beginning to recover, so are wages and employment. In many countries, however, the pace is somewhat modest, suggesting that in the years to come growth alone will not be sufficient to reduce poverty at a fast enough pace. The Mexican crisis, however, has introduced serious challenges for the continuous recovery of wages in many countries. The Psacharopoulos (1992, p. 14) estimates that if GDP grows at 4.2 percent a year and if income distribution improves with growth—as it has historically—by the year 2000 the incidence of poverty in Latin America could be reduced to 11 percent. A growth rate of 4.2 percent a year is significantly higher than the region's average during the last decade (1.7 percent a year), but in the aftermath of the Mexican crisis it will be difficult to obtain.

The poverty and especially the distributive impacts of structural reform policies have an important effect on the political support for—and thus the durability of—the reform process. In the midst of a major crisis, it is possible for political leaders to initiate major reforms with limited political support from the public (initially, the reforms were supported by a rather small constituency, mostly comprised of exporters). The deeper the crisis, the greater the incentives that politicians face to attempt new policies and the greater the tolerance of the public toward novel economic approaches (Haggard and Kaufman 1992; Haggard and Webb 1993). In that sense, the debt crisis provided a unique opportunity for leaders from traditional Latin American political parties—Peronistas in Argentina, PRI in Mexico, Acción Democrática in Venezuela—to implement policies that favor competition.

Table 8-8. Average Real Wages in Selected Countries of Latin America, 1984–92
(1980 = 100)

Country	1984	1985	1986	1987	1988	1989	1990	1991	1992[a]
Argentina	116.9	106.1	102.0	93.5	92.7	84.6	80.3	76.2	75.6
Brazil	105.1	111.8	121.5	105.4	103.2	102.3	87.6	87.8	105.5
Chile	97.2	93.5	95.1	94.7	101.0	102.9	104.8	109.9	114.9
Colombia	118.1	114.6	120.1	119.2	117.7	119.4	113.4	115.3	116.7
Costa Rica	84.7	92.2	97.8	89.2	85.2	85.7	87.2	83.1	—
Mexico	74.8	75.9	71.5	71.3	71.7	75.2	77.9	83.0	85.0
Peru	87.2	77.6	97.5	101.3	76.1	41.5	36.2	41.8	42.5
Uruguay	72.2	67.3	71.9	75.2	76.3	76.1	70.6	73.2	75.1

— Not available.

a. Preliminary.

Source: CEPAL, *Economic Survey of Latin America,* several years.

The fact that reforms are initiated, however, does not ensure that the reforms will be durable. As time goes by, memories of the crisis will fade, and, unless a broad political constituency emerges, the sustainability of the reforms will be in jeopardy. Two conditions must be present for this wide political endorsement to take place: first, growth has to accelerate, and second, and perhaps more important, the benefits of this faster growth should accrue to a large proportion of the population. On the contrary, if the reforms tend to maintain (or increase) the degree of income inequality, political polarization will result, and the probability of policy reversal will increase. Alesina and Tabellini (1988) and Aizenman (1990), among others, argue that unequal income distribution tends to paralyze governments and to prevent them from moving forward in the structural reform process. Along similar lines, Dornbusch and Edwards (1991) point out that poor (and worsening) income distribution is often at the heart of populist experiments. An important question is whether the current emphasis on poverty reduction by international development agencies is sufficient to increase the likelihood of consolidation. A potential problem with this strategy is that even if poverty—defined as the percentage of the population below the poverty line—is reduced, income distribution may become more unequal. This would be the case, for example, if income were redistributed toward the extremes, shrinking the percentage received by the middle class. Social unrest in Argentina (Santiago del Estero, Jujuy), Mexico (Chiapas), and Venezuela (Caracas) suggests that the tolerance for increasing inequality is reaching a limit. Political leaders throughout the region have reacted to these problems by designing plans that significantly increase social expenditures. Whether these programs will be effective—and, more important, whether they will be carried out without hampering the progress achieved in macroeconomic stability—remains to be seen. Moreover, the Mexican crisis has posed a formidable challenge to the reformers. The key question is whether, in the midst of new rounds of austerity, sufficient support for modernization will be obtained. The answer to this question is likely to be affected by the degree of political reform undertaken in Mexico.

Human Development in Latin America after Initiation of the Structural Reforms

A broad evaluation of life conditions requires understanding how a series of social variables, including nutrition, health, and education, behave through time. In this section, the evolution of some of the most important indexes of human development during the last decade is discussed, with special emphasis on the years following reform (the discussion draws extensively on Psacharopoulos 1992). The analysis concentrates on health and population, nutrition, education and human capital formation, social security, and water and sanitation.

Table 8-9. Health Indicators in Latin America and the Caribbean, 1980–90

Economy	Life expectancy at birth (years)		Under-five mortality rate (per 1,000 live births)		Babies with low birth-weight[a], most recent estimate
	1980	1990	1980	1990	
Antigua and Barbuda	71	74	—	24	8.2 (1982)
Argentina	69	71	46	35	6 (1985)
Bahamas	67	69	—	—	4.8 (1984)
Barbados	72	75	—	12	19.0 (1975)
Belize	64	68	—	29	—
Bolivia	54	60	207	160	15 (1985)
Brazil	63	66	103	83	8 (1985)
Chile	69	72	43	27	7 (1985)
Colombia	66	69	78	50	15 (1985)
Costa Rica	72	75	31	22	9 (1985)
Dominica	—	75	—	20	10.5 (1983)
Dominican Republic	63	67	102	78	16 (1985)
Ecuador	63	66	107	83	10 (1985)
El Salvador	57	64	110	87	15 (1985)
Grenada	67	70	—	38	12.2 (1975)
Guatemala	58	63	130	94	10 (1985)
Guyana	61	73	—	71	11 (1985)
Haiti	52	70	197	130	17 (1985)
Honduras	60	65	140	84	20 (1985)
Jamaica	71	73	29	20	8 (1985)
Mexico	67	70	83	49	15 (1985)
Nicaragua	58	65	132	78	15 (1985)
Panama	70	73	43	31	8 (1985)
Paraguay	66	67	70	60	6 (1985)
Peru	58	63	144	116	9 (1985)
St. Kitts and Nevis	—	70	—	—	13.4 (1975)
St. Lucia	68	72	—	23	9.7 (1985)
St. Vincent and Grenadines	67	70	—	27	10.0 (1982)
Suriname	65	68	—	38	13.0 (1985)
Trinidad and Tobago	68	71	29	17	3.9 (1984)
Uruguay	70	73	43	25	8 (1985)
Venezuela	68	70	50	43	9 (1985)

— Not available.

a. Percentage born weighing less than 2.5 kilograms.

Sources: World Bank, *Social Indicators of Development,* various years; World Bank, *World Development Report,* various years; UNICEF, *The State of the World's Children,* various years; WHO, *Global Nutritional Status: Anthropometric Indicators,* various years.

Health and Population. In most countries in the region, health indicators improved during the 1980s but at a slower pace than in the 1970s (see table 8-9). This, for instance, was the case for infant mortality rates in the Dominican Republic and Venezuela and for life expectancy in Ecuador, Guatemala, and Honduras (Grosh 1990).

As with poverty and inequality, health indicators vary significantly within each country, for example, according to the level of schooling of the mother. In Peru, in the early 1990s the infant mortality rate was 5.6 times higher for mothers with almost no education than for mothers with thirteen or more years of schooling. This ratio was 5.3 times in Colombia and 4.8 times in Bolivia. In Bolivia, infant mortality also varies according to ethnicity, with the indigenous non-Spanish-speaking population having a 35 percent higher rate than the Spanish-speaking population. The main determinant of infant mortality in Latin America is low weight at birth, and the most effective way to reduce infant mortality is to target food supplements to undernourished pregnant and lactating mothers. In most of Latin America, this is done through maternal and child health care programs. Although these programs help to lower mortality rates, many should be redesigned to improve efficiency (Psacharopoulos 1993).

A traditional problem with health provision in Latin America is that in many countries the emphasis is on funding and subsidizing curative medicine rather than on basic preventive care. This approach is not only inefficient but also highly regressive, because its benefits tend to accrue to the middle and upper classes. Recent efforts to tackle this problem are hampered by the lack of adequate medical support staff, including nurses, technicians, and nurses aides. Also, the lack of proper distribution of drugs stands in the way of an effective expansion of curative care (Psacharopoulos 1992).[4]

The lack of adequate sanitary conditions is at the heart of Latin America's health problems. Diarrhea and other water-related diseases cause a high percentage of the region's infant mortality. During the 1980s, more than 80 million urban dwellers and 18 million rural dwellers obtained drinkable water services. Despite these improvements, sanitary conditions are still far from adequate. This was clearly reflected in the outbreak of cholera in the late 1980s. A particularly serious problem is the inadequate treatment and disposal of sewage. In many countries, this problem is related to the neglect of infrastructure maintenance during the 1980s. Most Latin American countries lack the required institutional support for adequately maintaining infrastructure investment.[5] To upgrade existing water and sewage facilities, the region as a whole will need to invest $10 billion to $15 billion in the next few years. Additionally, approximately $10 billion will be required during the next decade to provide water and sewage to areas that currently lack these services (Yepes, Gutierrez, and Gyamfi 1992).

For more than two decades, serious efforts have been made to control the rate of growth of population. An expansion in family planning, including an

Table 8-10. Rates of Population Growth in Selected Countries of Latin America and the Caribbean, 1960–92
(percentage)

Country	1960–70	1970–80	1980–90	1990–92
Argentina	1.5	1.7	1.4	1.2
Bolivia	2.4	2.6	2.5	2.4
Brazil	2.8	2.4	2.1	1.7
Colombia	3.0	2.2	2.0	1.7
Costa Rica	3.4	2.8	2.9	5.6
Chile	2.2	1.6	1.7	1.6
Dominican Republic	3.2	2.6	2.2	—
Ecuador	3.2	3.0	2.7	2.4
El Salvador	3.4	2.4	1.4	2.1
Guatemala	2.8	2.8	2.9	2.9
Guyana	2.2	0.7	0.5	0.8
Haiti	1.7	1.7	1.9	2.1
Honduras	3.1	3.4	3.4	3.1
Jamaica	1.4	1.3	1.3	1.0
Mexico	3.3	2.9	2.3	2.1
Nicaragua	3.2	3.1	2.8	3.8
Panama	3.0	2.8	2.1	2.0
Paraguay	2.9	3.0	3.1	2.8
Peru	2.9	2.7	2.2	2.1
Trinidad and Tobago	1.4	1.1	1.3	1.2
Uruguay	1.0	0.4	0.6	0.6
Venezuela	3.5	3.6	2.6	2.2
Average for region	2.8	2.4	2.1	1.0

— Not available.
Source: OAS 1992.

increase in the use of contraceptives, has resulted in a significant decline in total fertility rates in the region. However, in the poorer countries, the total rate of fertility remains high, exceeding five children per mother in Bolivia, Guatemala, Honduras, and Nicaragua.

Excess fertility in Latin America has serious social consequences (this and the paragraphs that follow draw on an unpublished memorandum from Sandra Newhouse; see table 8-10 for comparative data on population growth throughout the region). There is a strong negative correlation between fertility and educational attainment: poor and uneducated women tend to give birth at a very early age and tend to have many children. As a result of the very high rate of unwanted pregnancies among poor women, the number of street children increased significantly in the recent past. Addressing the fertility problem in Latin America constitutes an efficient way of dealing with problems of poverty and health among women (illegal abortions are prevalent in the region: in Brazil, approximately 4 million illegal abortions are performed each year, exceeding the number of births by 33 percent!). In particular, reproductive health services allow for early intervention in family planning and prevention of other serious diseases, including AIDS.

Although during the 1970s and 1980s, most Latin American countries had active family planning programs, a number of problems developed. Many women did not fully understand how contraceptives should be used and often received treatment under unsanitary conditions. The rate of discontinuity was very high: many poor women abandoned systematic family planning methods shortly after joining a program. As a consequence, efforts are being made to develop the institutional capacity needed to ensure the sustainability and continuity of family planning programs.

Nutrition. Latin America experienced improvements on the nutritional front during the 1980s, to the extent that in the early 1990s malnutrition in the region was below that of the developing world as a whole (14.2 and 21.5 percent, respectively; see Psacharopoulos 1992). Despite this progress, in 1993 more than 10 million children below the age of five were malnourished, mostly in Brazil and Mexico.

This progress in nutritional attainment occurred despite the very small volume of resources devoted to tackling this problem. On average, less than one-quarter of 1 percent of GDP is spent on nutritional programs in Latin America (see Selowsky 1992 for a discussion of how budgetary reallocations could affect nutritional programs; see also table 8-11). Depending on the country, effective nutritional programs cost between $30 and $50 per beneficiary a year (Psacharopoulos 1993). Quadrupling, or even doubling, the amount of resources devoted to nutritional programs would go a long way toward eliminating the problem. From a budgetary point of view, this would mean modest changes in resource allocation. The funding to targeted nutritional programs could be increased through a combination of measures, including greater public sector efficiency and reduced expenditures in other areas, such as the military.

Nutritional programs clearly improve the efficiency of the educational system. Well-fed children are more attentive in school and learn at a faster rate. More specifically, programs aimed at increasing the nutritional intake of children from birth to three years of age are likely to have a significant effect on learning abilities and generate very large social returns, increasing productivity and, eventually, the ability to obtain high-paying jobs (Psacharopoulos 1992).

General food subsidies for staples, such as rice and beans, are an inefficient and regressive way of tackling nutritional problems. These programs, which are very popular among politicians, usually benefit the richer segments of the population at a very high budgetary and efficiency cost. More and more countries are moving away from such schemes and are adopting targeted programs aimed at reaching the poor sectors of society that need support. This is the case, for example, in Chile, Mexico, and Venezuela.

Table 8-11. Malnutrition in Selected Countries of Latin America and the Caribbean, 1985

Country	Number of malnourished children	Number of children covered by feeding programs	Cost per beneficiary (U.S. dollars)	Percentage of GNP spent
Argentina	—	968,228	35.0	0.02
Bolivia	760,200	482,227	21.1	0.49
Brazil	5,024,200	13,957,298	16.9	0.28
Chile	35,000	1,342,208	47.8	0.34
Colombia	487,900	1,197,966	13.9	0.11
Costa Rica	10,800	64,554	43.9	0.35
Dominican Republic	58,000	107,095	28.8	0.07
Ecuador	264,000	172,955	32.9	0.31
El Salvador	123,200	110,820	31.3	0.20
Guatemala	502,500	254,292	7.5	0.14
Honduras	164,800	140,000	30.7	0.53
Mexico	1,584,600	5,037,724	10.3	0.05
Paraguay	25,200	21,565	20.5	0.06
Peru	428,800	2,704,801	57.5	0.96
Uruguay	20,500	139,564	28.7	0.31
Venezuela	275,400	448,185	12.2	0.09

— Not available.

Source: Musgrove 1991.

For some years, one of the most popular ways of targeting nutritional subsidies has been based on school feeding programs (Grosh 1993). New evidence, however, suggests that these programs may not be as efficient as once thought. First, if children are partially fed at school, they tend to receive less food at home. Second, significant leakages occur in the distribution channel, and, in most cases, only a fraction of the food reaches the targeted population. Finally, such programs offer very little variety in the food, greatly reducing their appeal to the beneficiaries. Linking nutritional programs to the primary health system may be a more effective way of providing support. In this case, the most efficient modality is one where food subsidies are distributed in the form of coupons or food stamps, and the beneficiary uses the existing market network to obtain the food (Castañeda 1992; Grosh 1993; Psacharopoulos 1993).

Social Security. Social security has for many years been a fundamental element in the provision of health and pension services throughout Latin America (Mesa-Lago 1991). Many families, especially from the middle classes, obtain basic income support and health services through the social security system. Moreover, social security represents one of the few social services where expenditures increased systematically during the 1980s.

However, most social security institutions in the region are inefficient and underfunded and siphon significant funds from general revenues. Unless major reforms are implemented, there will be a series of major financial crises (see, for example, Cox-Edwards 1992). In fact, the insolvency of the social security system is a serious, unresolved fiscal problem in many countries, including Argentina, Brazil, Guatemala, and Venezuela.

In most mature social security systems, including those of Argentina, Brazil, and Mexico, the ratio of pensioners to contributors is very high, imposing a heavy burden on the working population. In Argentina, for example, there is one retiree for every three contributors. This figure is almost two in the case of Chile. An important question is the extent to which participants in social security systems see their contributions (or a fraction of them) as payroll taxes (in the ideal system, participants would consider their contributions as part deferred payments and part insurance premiums). If they consider them to be payroll taxes, the social security system is introducing an additional burden to the labor market, reducing the creation of employment (table 8-12 summarizes social security contributions and benefits in ten Latin American countries). Cox-Edwards (1992) argues that in all countries, with the exception of Chile and Peru, there is only a very weak actuarial connection between contributions and benefits.

Clearly there is room for increasing the degree of managerial efficiency of social security institutes. In the early 1990s, administrative costs exceeded 15 percent of expenditures, as opposed to 3 percent in the industrial nations (Psacharopoulos 1993). Also, in many countries, two or more institutes frequently serve the same region or population, creating a clear duplication of effort.

In terms of economic efficiency and equity, social security systems have serious problems in most countries in the region. First, in most cases existing pension funds encourage early retirement, placing a serious burden on the country at a time when the retiree is in the prime of his or her productive years. Second, pensions are rarely related to the individual's contributions to the system. This is particularly true for higher income individuals, who often obtain lavish pensions after making only small and limited contributions to the general pension funds. Third, as health providers, social security systems tend to encourage expensive and highly technological curative care. And fourth, the poor are often excluded from social security. In Brazil, only 18 percent of the lowest income group, which account for more than 40 percent of the population, are covered by social security. They receive only 3 percent of total social security benefits (McGreevey 1990).

In most countries, the contributions to the health component of the social security system are independent of marital status, family size, and age. Benefits, however, automatically extend to dependents. As the age structure of the population changes, the active population is less willing to support these systems (Cox-Edwards 1992).

Table 8-12. Social Security Contributions and Other Payroll Taxes in Selected Countries of Latin America
(percentage unless otherwise noted)

| Country | Contributions | | | | | Benefits | |
	Health care	Additional family coverage	Retirement	Workers' compensation	Other programs	Pensions	Health care and other benefits
Argentina	31	None in public system	9	Insurance premium	15	Benefit-defined pension, inherited by spouse and minor children	Medical care extended to dependents; disability; maternity leave; unemployment insurance; low-cost mortgages
Bolivia	10	None in public system	8.5	1.5	None	Benefit-defined pension, inherited by spouse and minor children	Medical care extended to dependents; disability; maternity leave
Brazil		28–30[a]	6.5	1–3	15.4	Benefit-defined pension, inherited by spouse and minor children	Medical care extended to dependents; disability; maternity leave; unemployment insurance
Colombia	7	5	6.5	Included	2.0	Benefit-defined pension, inherited by spouse and minor children	Medical care extended to dependents; disability; maternity leave; public sector
Chile	7	Varies with plan	10	0.9–3.4	None	Contribution-defined above a minimum level	Choice of plan; maternity leave

(Table continues on the following page.)

Table 8-12 (continued)

Country	Contributions					Benefits	
	Health care	Additional family coverage	Retirement	Workers' compensation	Other programs	Pensions	Health care and other benefits
Ecuador		20.2[a]		Included	None	Benefit-defined pension, inherited by spouse and minor children	Medical care extended to dependents; disability; maternity leave
Mexico		18.05[a]		0.26–6.56	5.0	Benefit-defined pension, inherited by spouse and minor children	Medical care extended to dependents; disability; maternity leave; low-cost mortgages
			2			Contribution-defined	
Nicaragua	9	None in public system	8	Included	None	Benefit-defined pension, inherited by spouse and minor children	Medical care extended to dependents; disability; maternity leave
Peru	9	May vary with plan	9	Insurance premium	7.5	Contribution-defined above a minimum level	Choice of health plan; public sector training; low-cost mortgages
Venezuela		Public sector 6.75 / Private sector 23–25		Included	5.0	Benefit-defined pension, inherited by spouse and minor children	Medical care extended to dependents; disability; maternity leave; unemployment insurance; public sector training

a. Covers health care, additional family coverage, and retirement.

Source: Cox-Edwards 1992.

In the early 1980s, Chile embarked on a major reform of its social security system, replacing a traditional (and financially troubled) pay-as-you-go pension system with one based on individual retirement accounts. In the new system, health provision is also based on choice. Workers contribute 7 percent of their taxable income to an insurance program. They can choose between a public system managed by the national health fund (FONASA) or private health providers (ISAPRES). Approximately 80 percent of the population is affiliated with the public system and 20 percent with the private system. The Chilean social security reform had important results. First, the traditional drag on public finances was eliminated. Second, the system became much more efficient (although there is still room for improvement, and the minimal pension may be too low to cover requirements; on details of the Chilean system, see Cheyre 1991). And third, the capitalization system encouraged the Chilean capital market by creating a number of large institutional investors, giving decisive impetus to increases in savings.

Education, Human Capital Formation, and Social Conditions

For a long time, economists have argued that the accumulation of human capital, through improvements in the coverage and quality of education, constitutes one of the fundamental pillars of successful development strategies (T. W. Schultz 1961, 1980 is the undisputable modern pioneer of this view in economics; see also Harberger 1972; Psacharopoulos 1993). In the last few years, this idea has gained renewed popularity thanks to the development of a new family of growth models that incorporate the possibility of increasing returns to scale and positive externalities (Lucas 1988; Romer 1986; see the discussions of new endogenous growth models in chapter 5). For example, Azariadis and Drazen (1990) contend that once a certain threshold in education is achieved, economy-wide externalities increase the degree of productivity growth and thus overall economic performance.

Lucas (1993) suggests that Korea's ability to double living standards every eleven years since the mid-1960s is propelled by increases in productivity fueled by the accumulation of human capital. Recent empirical studies strongly support this view, indicating that the existence of a highly educated labor force, whose skills improve rapidly year after year, is partially behind the tremendous economic success of Korea and other East Asian economies. For example, in an econometric study on the growth experiences in that part of the world, Fukuda (1993) finds that secondary school enrollments play a significant role in explaining cross-economy growth differentials. These results support those reported by Barro (1991) for a group of developing economies. Pyo (1993) carefully constructs time series for the stock of human capital in Korea for the period 1955–90 and finds that the increase in educational coverage contributed to that economy's fast rates of growth. In another study that examines why the "Gang of Four"—Hong Kong, Korea, Singapore, and Taiwan (China)—outperformed virtually every comparison group during the last twenty-five years, Easterly (1993) finds that education showed a remarkably robust effect in explaining cross-country growth: independent of the econometric technique applied and of the data used to define growth, primary and secondary education attainments have large and significantly positive coefficients in growth regressions.

Table 8-13 presents data on educational attainment for a group of Latin American countries in 1989, as well as information on three of the East Asian miracle economies: Hong Kong, Korea, and Singapore. There are significant differences in educational coverage across Latin America, and in every category with available data, educational coverage in the East Asian tigers is significantly above the average for Latin America and the Caribbean.

Education contributes not only to aggregate (macroeconomic) growth but also to an individual's ability to generate high earnings. Many studies show that education (jointly with experience) is one of the most important statistical determinants of workers' rewards in the labor market. For example, using panel data for the Greater Santiago area in Chile for 1974–80, Cox-Edwards (1984) finds a significantly positive coefficient of education in Mincer-type equations on earnings (Mincer 1965). Moreover, the higher the degree of education, the lower the vulnerability of earnings with respect to cyclical fluctuations in the economy (a series of studies directed by George Psacharopoulos at the World Bank reaches similar conclusions; see the essay in Psacharopoulos 1993). Additionally, Psacharopoulos and Fiszbein (1992) find that the degree of education is a major determinant of the probability that a given individual will have earnings below the poverty line.

Education, then, plays a multiple role in the development process. It has important effects both at the macro-aggregate level, where it is a key source of growth, and at the microeconomic level, where it is a fundamental vehicle for moving out of poverty. A series of studies on Latin America, as well as other parts of the world, suggests strongly that the rate of return (both private and social) is particularly high for investments in primary education (Psacharopoulos 1993; Selowsky 1969). Psacharopoulos and Ng (1992) use household survey data to estimate private and social rates of return for primary, secondary (both general and vocational), and university education for fourteen Latin American countries. They find that the primary social rate of return exceeded that of secondary education in eleven of the fourteen cases—the exceptions being Chile, Costa Rica, and Honduras. Private rates of return were estimated for eighteen countries. In thirteen, the rate of return was higher in primary than in secondary education. In spite of this evidence, throughout Latin America net primary school enrollment rates are below 85 percent—this is the case, for example, in Bolivia, Brazil, Colombia, El Salvador, Guatemala, Haiti, and Nicaragua. By comparison, the net primary education enrollment rate in East Asia is 100 percent of primary school-age children (World Bank, *World Development Report 1992*, table 29).

*Table 8-13. School Enrollment in Selected Economies of Latin America,
the Caribbean, and East Asia, 1989*

Economy	Net primary enrollment	Secondary enrollment[a]	Tertiary enrollment[a]	Primary pupil to teacher ratio
Latin America and the Caribbean				
Argentina	—	74	41	19
Brazil	84	39	11	23
Chile	89	75	19	29
Colombia	69	52	14	30
Costa Rica	86	41	27	32
El Salvador	70	26	17	40
Guatemala	—	21	—	35
Jamaica	99	61	5	34
Mexico	100	53	15	31
Peru	95	67	32	29
Trinidad and Tobago	91	83	6	28
Average	87	50	18	27
Asia				
Hong Kong	100	73	—	27
Korea, Rep. of	100	86	38	36
Singapore	100	69	—	26

— Not available.
a. As a percentage of the eligible population.
Source: World Bank, *World Development Report 1992.*

In 1989, Latin America spent on average $118 annually per primary education student, down from $164 in 1980 and significantly less than the East Asian economies (Wolff, Schiefelbein, and Valenzuela 1993). This budgetary reduction affected some of the most important inputs into the educational process: teachers' salaries declined drastically, lowering teachers' morale; textbooks were less available than before; and preschool financing was cut. This, not surprisingly, had an important effect on the quality of education, including the children's ability to learn and retain basic concepts as they moved up the educational ladder.

In most countries, there is insufficient access to early and preschool education. Additionally, women lag in almost every educational category, including programs similar to Head Start, even though the social return on early training of women is exceedingly high. It not only increases productive employment opportunities but indirectly affects fertility and nutritional attainment (Psacharopoulos 1993).

One of the most serious problems in Latin America's educational system is the extremely high repetition rates, which rank among the highest in the developing world. In Bolivia, for example, the repetition rate ranges from 16 percent in Beni to more than 35 percent in Chuquisaca, although the rate of repetition in the English-speaking Caribbean economies is significantly lower than in the rest of the region (Psacharopoulos 1993).[6] In 1990, the cost of repetition exceeded $4 billion for the region as a whole.

The average quality of Latin America's primary education is extremely poor (Wolff, Schiefelbein, and Valenzuela 1993). For example, an international comparative study on reading abilities of nine year olds found that Venezuelan students ranked last out of students in twenty-seven countries; Trinidad and Tobago students did better but still significantly below the average. A 1992 study on mathematics and science achievement for thirteen year olds found that Brazilian students from São Paulo and Fortaleza were outscored by students from China, Israel, Jordan, Korea, and Taiwan (China), as well as by students from every industrial economy in the sample. The only economy Brazil outscored was Mozambique. Finally, a 1992 study on mathematics and science for thirteen year olds in five Latin American countries—Argentina, Colombia, Costa Rica, the Dominican Republic, and Venezuela—found that, with the exception of elite schools, test performance was significantly below that of average countries, such as Thailand and the United States (Costa Rica was the exception, where second-tier schools had very strong test scores).

Latin America's traditional neglect of primary education contrasts sharply with its treatment of higher education, which is highly subsidized. This has serious regressive distributive effects, reducing the volume of resources available to the poorest sectors of society, where, in some countries, illiteracy is rampant (Psacharopoulos 1993). Although the quality of higher education (especially in the sciences) has to improve significantly if the region is to compete successfully in the world economy, this has to be done in an effective and fair way. In most cases, university students acquire a very high earning capacity and are able to pay (at least retroactively) for their education. The establishment of efficient scholarship and loan systems can broaden the access to university training and, at the same time, permit a recovery of costs.

The newly emerging economic structure in Latin America, based on markets, competition, and outward orientation, requires a dynamic and highly productive work force. Only in this way will it be able to face the international market, increase wages and living standards, reduce poverty and inequality, and move to a second phase of export growth. However, creating such a work force is a time-consuming process that will not bear fruit in a year or two. There is thus an urgent need to reinforce the provision of education. Quality can be upgraded through improved management and allocation of educational resources and increased funding. In particular, rapid increases in the resources devoted to preschool and primary education are likely to produce very high social rates of return. Teachers should be trained using modern techniques, their skills should be periodically renewed, and their salaries should be increased to levels similar to those of relevant comparison groups. Parents should get more directly involved in the educational system by having a larger role in the decisionmaking process. If Latin America maintains its traditional neglect of education and fails to improve the quality and coverage of the system, the likelihood that the structural reforms will be sustained in the long run will be greatly reduced. As the experience of the East Asian miracle economies shows, a solid educational base is required to increase productivity and compete successfully internationally. Moreover, a broad and high-quality educational system usually provides a ticket for social peace, harmony, and general prosperity.

Labor Market Regulations in Latin America

For decades, the Latin American nations used labor legislation as a tool to achieve social goals. Employment protection, minimum wages, and bargaining rules were aimed at protecting workers from capitalists' voracity. Although in most countries this type of legislation played an important role in setting labor standards during the 1930s and 1940s, it eventually created a highly distorted labor market. Excessive protectionism encouraged the creation of an informal sector, created dual economies, and generated significant rents.

In most countries, the deregulation of the labor market did not form part of the reform program. In many ways, labor was the forgotten sector. However, the existence of a dynamic and flexible labor market is a fundamental component of the successful adoption of market-oriented policies. It helps to reallocate resources and allows the economy to respond rapidly to new challenges stemming from increased foreign competition. Moreover, freeing the labor market of distortions tends to have positive distributive consequences because it encourages the expansion of employment and increases wages in the poorest segments of society. In most Latin American countries, labor market distortions generate segmentation where protected and unprotected sectors coexist side-by-side. Moreover, after the eruption of the debt crisis, the combination of labor market distortions and macroeconomic austerity conspired to create a large and growing informal sector in many countries. Removing the most serious distortions tends to increase the unprotected sector wage rate, to reduce the protected sector wage rate, to increase overall employment, and to reduce the duality between the formal and informal sector. The extent of labor market regulation in Latin America contrasts sharply with the extreme flexibility of the highly successful East Asian economies—Hong Kong, Indonesia, Korea, Malaysia, Singapore, Taiwan (China), and Thailand. In fact, recent studies by the World Bank (1993a), Krueger (1993), and Nam (1993) persuasively argue that flexibility in labor markets is one of the most important determinants of these countries' economic miracle. Labor market flexibility allows small and medium firms to adapt rapidly to new market conditions, to remain competitive internationally, and to take advantage of technological advances. Discussions of European economic problems and sluggishness focus more and more on the costs associated with rigid and protected labor markets. Unless labor distortions are reduced in Europe, recovery will be slow and painful (*Financial Times*, June 22, 1993). This section analyzes the most important distortions in labor markets in the region and discusses alternative ways of reforming this key sector.

Textbooks usually mention minimum wages as the predominant labor market distortion to be removed in market-oriented reforms. At the present time, however, this is not the most pressing issue in Latin America. In fact, with a few exceptions, minimum wages declined throughout the region in the last few years and are now largely a nonbinding restriction (see table 8-14). This, of course, does not mean that (potential) hikes in minimum wages will not have negative effects on employment in the future.

The most serious labor market distortions in Latin America can be classified in three categories: (a) high costs of dismissal, which reduce flexibility and make a firm's restructuring difficult and slow; (b) high payroll taxes, which reduce the incentives to expand employment and negatively affect the degree of international competitiveness of local firms; and (c) the nature of labor–management relations, which encourage confrontation and costly settlement procedures (much of the discussion in this section is based on Cox-Edwards 1992).

Costs of Dismissal

Latin American labor legislation has a long tradition of trying to protect employment stability. This is done through a series of measures, including placing severe limitations on temporary hiring and imposing substantial costs—in the form of severance payments—on unjust dismissals. These policies have two consequences for labor markets. First, they increase the cost of labor, discouraging the creation of employment. Second, because of the specific way in which the legislation is often put into effect, they strongly discourage training activities that result in the acquisition of new skills.

The impact of employment protection laws largely depends on how firms perceive them. If specific rules, such as severance payments, are seen as a delayed payment scheme, their effects on hiring and other decisions are minimal. If they are perceived as a tax on the use of labor, they have serious effects on the way firms deal with labor. Given the way in which severance payments are legislated, firms do not view them as delayed payments but as a tax (Cox-Edwards 1992).

Table 8-15 summarizes the main characteristics of employment protection legislation in ten countries. Several important features emerge from this table. First, in almost every case severe restrictions are placed on temporary contracts. This contrasts sharply with labor legislation in the United States, where the employment-at-will doctrine prevails (in contrast with the United States, most Latin American countries lack unemployment insurance). In principle, restricting temporary hires increases labor costs, discouraging employment, and introduces rigidities that tend to slow down responses to changes in the

Table 8-14. Minimum Urban Real Wages in Selected Countries of Latin America, 1984–92
(1980 = 100)

Country	1984	1985	1986	1987	1988	1989	1990	1991	1992[a]
Argentina	167.5	113.1	110.0	120.8	93.5	42.1	40.2	56.0	44.5
Brazil	87.4	88.9	89.0	72.6	68.7	72.1	53.4	59.9	55.4
Colombia	113.5	109.4	114.2	113.0	109.9	110.8	107.9	104.3	103.2
Costa Rica	104.4	112.2	118.7	117.9	114.6	119.4	120.5	111.8	—
Chile	80.7	76.4	73.6	69.1	73.9	79.8	87.5	95.6	100.0
Mexico	72.3	71.1	64.9	61.5	54.2	50.8	45.5	43.6	42.0
Paraguay	93.8	99.6	108.3	122.6	135.2	137.5	131.6	125.8	115.0
Peru	62.3	54.4	56.4	59.7	52.0	25.1	23.4	15.9	16.3
Uruguay	88.8	93.2	88.5	90.3	84.5	78.0	69.1	62.0	61.5
Venezuela	66.5	96.8	90.4	108.7	89.5	72.9	59.3	55.1	—

— Not available.
a. Preliminary.
Source: CEPAL, *Economic Survey of Latin America,* several years.

international competitive scene. Second, there is a steep difference in severance payments for justified and unjustified dismissal. What is particularly
important is that in most countries just dismissal excludes economic reasons,
such as financial distress and increased foreign competition. This means that,
in most cases, firms that are restructuring by reducing the size of their labor
force incur high costs to compensate those workers who are unjustly laid off.

The amount of severance pay in the case of just dismissal varies significantly
across countries. Colombia, Uruguay, and Venezuela require one month's pay
per year of service, but in Uruguay the ceiling can be as high as six months'
pay. Mexican law establishes a payment of three months' wages in cases of just
dismissal. Bolivia does not require compensation for just dismissal, but workers are entitled to one month's pay per year of service in case of voluntary
retirement. Dismissed workers in Ecuador receive 25 percent of the final
month's pay per year of service, plus up to three months' wages. Paraguayan
law mandates that individuals be paid fifteen days of pay for each three years
of service. By and large, severance payments in Latin America are higher than
in a number of other countries, including Germany, Spain, and the United
Kingdom (Cox-Edwards 1992; the *Financial Times,* June 22, 1993, recently
argued that in Belgium "severance pay is relatively high—usually about two-
thirds of salary for four months"; this, of course, is very low compared with the
Latin American data in table 6-8).

A third characteristic of labor protection legislation is that severance payments for unjust cause are directly related to the worker's tenure in the firm
and typically take the form of x month's salary per year of service. This introduces some serious, and arbitrary, distortions. For example, firms tend to
retain older workers, even if they are less productive than younger ones. Relat-

Table 8-15. *Job Protection Legislation in Selected Countries of Latin America*

Country	Restrictions on temporary contracts	Probability period	Advance notice before dismissal	Severance with just cause	Severance without just cause	Economic cause of severance
Argentina	2 years, nonrenewable	3 months	1–2 months	No severance pay	$W \times T$[a]	$5 \times (W \times T)$[a]
Bolivia	Renewable once	3 months	3 months	No severance pay	$W \times T$	$W \times T$
Brazil	2 years, nonrenewable	12 months	1 month	FUND[b]	$1.4 \times$ (FUND)	$1.4 \times$ (FUND)
Colombia	3 years, nonrenewable	2 months	45 days[c]	FUND[b]	FUND + (15–40 days' wages) $\times T$	FUND + (15–40 days' wages) $\times T$
Chile	1 year, nonrenewable	12 months	1 month	No severance pay	$1.2 \times (W \times T)$[d,e]	$(W \times T)$[d]
Ecuador	2 years, nonrenewable	3 months	1 month	$0.25 \times (W \times T)$ + FUND	$0.25 \times (W \times T)$ + FUND + $(3 \times W)$, if $T < 3$ $(T \times W)$, if $0.25 < T < 3$ Pension, if $T > 25$	$0.25 \times (W \times T)$ + FUND + $(3 \times W)$, if $T < 3$ $(T \times W)$, if $0.25 < T < 3$ Pension, if $T > 25$
Mexico	No restrictions	None	1 month	$W \times 3$	(20 days' wages) $\times T$	(20 days' wages) $\times T$
Nicaragua	2 years, nonrenewable	12 months	1–2 months	$W \times T$	$2 \times (W \times T)$	$2 \times (W \times T)$
Peru	2 years, nonrenewable	3 months	None	FUND[b]	FUND + $(W \times T)$	FUND + $(W \times T)$
Venezuela	Renewable once	3 months	1–3 months	(10–30 days' wages) $\times T$	$1.5 \times$ (10–30 days' wages) $\times T$	$1.5 \times$ (10–30 days' wages) $\times T$

Note: W represents a monthly wage; T represents years of tenure on the job.

a. In this case, the law establishes a maximum monthly wage. Thus, there is a cap on severance.

b. In this case, the employer establishes a fund from which it draws resources to cover severance payments.

c. A minimum severance payment equivalent to forty-five days' wages is payable in case of dismissal.

d. In this case, the law establishes a maximum number of years on the job. Thus, there is also a cap on severance.

e. The burden of proof is on the employer. Failure to prove allegations of just cause may invoke a penalty of up to 50 percent over the normal severance $(W \times T)$.

Source: Cox-Edwards 1992.

ing severance payments to years of service also reduces the employer's incentive to invest in human capital formation, especially if these investments are not specific to the firm, because the value of increased skills is higher in firms not affected by the burden of a tenure-related severance cost. This, in turn, increases the compensation offered to recently trained workers by other firms, encouraging them to leave their current employment.

An important question is whether firms can devise ways to reduce the costs associated with mandated severance payments. Employers have two ways of doing this. First, they can maintain a very young work force with a high degree of turnover. Second, they can avoid, as much as possible, dismissing workers, especially older workers. These policies, however, have efficiency consequences. Concentrating on a young labor force distorts the choice of activities on the basis of age and largely ignores efficiency considerations and market prices.[7] Second, avoiding labor dismissals altogether amounts to treating labor as a *fixed* factor. In this case, hiring decisions are subject to delays, and if market conditions turn unfavorable, severance payments become an actual, realized loss for the employer and a bonus for the employee.

One of the most important reforms of labor regulations in Latin America would be to transform (part of) severance payments into a deferred compensation scheme. This, in fact, has been partially done in some countries. In Bolivia, for example, workers have access to the same severance payment in all cases of separation (quits and layoffs) after five years on the job. Other countries, including Brazil and more recently Peru and Colombia, have replaced the traditional mode of severance pay based on a month's pay times the number of years of service with a time of service fund. In Brazil, it is referred to as FGTS (Fondo de Garantia do Tempo de Servicio) and in Peru as CTS (Compensación por Tiempo de Servicio). In Brazil and in Peru, the time of service fund is accrued in case of separation (justified layoff and quits). A fraction of the salary (8 percent in Brazil, 8.33 percent in Peru) is accumulated in a fund in the name of the employee. Chilean law allows workers to choose this type of arrangement instead of the traditional severance payment after seven years on the job. In these cases, employers are required to deposit the equivalent of one-twelfth of the annual salary in a savings account in the employee's name.

Severance payments based on an accumulation of funds, as long as benefits are determined by contributions, do not interfere with an employer's decisions with respect to age-earnings profiles and do not discourage investments in training on the job. Unfortunately, in most cases, including Brazil and Chile, severance payments are not limited to the fund. Regardless of the methods designed by law to determine payments in case of separation, employers are often required to pay an additional severance in case of unjustified, including economic cause, dismissal.

Nicaragua and Venezuela impose the most stringent constraints on dismissals (table 8-15). Mexico appears to be the most liberal case. Argentina, Bolivia, and Peru have somewhat transparent systems. The Chilean law is the

Table 8-16. Basic Characteristics of Social Security Systems in Selected Countries of Latin America
(percentage unless otherwise noted)

Country	Decade of the first pension law	Total population covered	Economically active population covered	Statutory contribution rate[a]	Social security expedition as a percentage of GDP	Ratio of pensioners to contributors[b]	Population aged sixty-five or older[c]
Argentina	1920s	79	69	46	10	0.32	8.2
Bolivia	1950s	25	18	25	3	0.33	3.2
Brazil	1920s	96	96	26	5	0.18	4.0
Colombia	1940s	12	22	20	4	0.05	3.5
Chile	1920s	67	62	21	11	0.46	5.5
Ecuador	1930s	8	23	21	3	0.15	3.5
Mexico	1940s	53	42	18	3	0.08	3.6
Nicaragua	1950s	9	19	16	2	0.08	2.4
Peru	1930s	17	37	21	3	0.09	3.6
Venezuela	1960s	45	50	14	3	0.06	2.8

a. Total statutory percentage of payroll to be contributed by the insured person, the employer, and the state.
b. Dependency ratio, which is the number of pensioners divided by the number of contributors.
c. As a percentage of total population.
Source: Cox-Edwards 1992.

most clear and provides comprehensive legal protection to both employers and workers against breach of individual contracts.

Payroll Taxes

Payroll taxes increase the cost of labor, discouraging the creation of employment and reducing labor mobility. Whether particular levies, such as social security contributions, are perceived as pure taxes or as delayed compensations, it is important to determine the extent to which they distort the economy. In most Latin American countries, social security benefits—pensions and health care provision—are not related to contributions made to the system. This lack of balance results in (a large percentage of) contributions being considered a pure tax, while benefits are considered an entitlement (Cox-Edwards 1992; Mesa-Lago 1991).

Table 8-16 contains detailed data on social security and other payroll taxes and social security contributions in ten Latin American countries. In many of these countries, the social security system is financially insolvent, imposing increasing costs on the economy as a whole (Mesa-Lago 1991). There are several possible directions for improving the degree of efficiency of social security systems. From an efficiency point of view, the most important feature of any social security system is that participants perceive it as part (although a delayed part) of worker's compensation and not as a tax that increases the costs of hiring: in particular, it is a system that replaces pay-as-you-go regimes, which have no link between contributions and benefits, with a combination of individual capitalization accounts and minimum services assured by the government. This type of system has been operating in Chile since the early 1980s and is currently being imposed in Argentina, Mexico, and Peru.

From an efficiency and equity point of view, labor legislation should *not* be used either to protect the poor—because more often than not it works in the opposite direction—or to provide income transfers. In fact, most traditional regulations in the labor market—including minimum wages, high costs of dismissal, and pay-as-you-go social security regimes—tend to increase the cost of hiring and negatively affect employment, especially among persons with low skills and low net wages. The role of labor legislation, including social security, should be to promote the efficient use of labor and to protect workers from abusive practices. Social programs should be handled through alternative channels, including direct and focused transfers.

Labor–Management Relations

The existing labor legislation in most of Latin America predates the region's recent market-oriented reforms and encourages long and costly bargaining processes (table 8-17 highlights the most important features of conflict-dispute mechanisms in ten Latin American countries). With the exception of

Table 8-17. Dispute Resolution in Selected Countries of Latin America

Country	Right of employees				Right of employers		Maximum duration of a strike
	Basis of judicial procedure	To strike	To receive wages while on strike	To renounce union membership and return to work	To lock workers out	To hire temporary workers	
Argentina	Civil courts	Must be called by union; after conciliation channels are exhausted; Ministry of Labor pronounces legality	No, if workers fail to accept arbitration; yes, if the employer locks workers out	No	No, unless the strike is illegal	No	No maximum
Bolivia	Labor courts	Twenty-four days after presentation of petition to labor inspector; the majority of union or two-thirds of workers must agree	No, strike suspends contracts	No	Yes	Yes	No maximum; despite the law, many strikes begin before the tribunal's decision
Brazil	Labor courts	Yes, in the context of collective contract negotiations; quorum requirement to be decided by union; decided by head count vote	No	Yes, strike does not suspend contract	Requires prior authorization	No, unless the court declares the strike to be abusive	No maximum
Colombia	Labor courts; within two days of a declared strike, Ministry of Labor may call for arbitration	After period of direct negotiations; must be agreed through a secret ballot by an absolute majority of workers	No, strike suspends contracts	No	Not regulated	No, unless there is risk of serious damage to the facilities	Sixty days

Country	Authority						
Chile	Labor courts have jurisdiction over questions arising from application of the law	Yes, in the context of collective contract negotiations	No	Yes	Yes, if the strike affects more than half of workers; yes, if the strike stops essential work	Yes, from the first day of the strike if the last offer is equal to the previous contract-adjusted current price index; otherwise, only after fifteen days	When more than half of workers have returned to work, the strike ends
Ecuador	Labor Inspectorate	Yes, if direct negotiations fail, as long as the absolute majority of workers agree; solidarity strikes are permitted	Yes	No	No	Once the tribunal resolves, the strike ends	No maximum
Mexico	Labor courts	Tripartite Board must declare it existent or legal	No, unless the board decides the strike is imputable to the employer	No	No	Not regulated	No maximum
Nicaragua	Civil courts	Yes, if agreed by head count majority; does not have to occur in the context of collective bargaining	Yes	Workers can return to work, but wages are paid anyway	Yes, after conciliation, if authorized by Labor Inspectorate	Prohibited	No maximum
Peru	Ministry of Labor	Yes, if the majority approves; very few limitations	No, strike suspends labor contracts	Not regulated	No	Not regulated	No maximum
Venezuela	Labor Inspectorate	If direct negotiations fail, as long as the absolute majority of workers agree; solidarity strikes are permitted	No, strike suspends labor contracts	No	Not regulated	Not regulated	No maximum

Source: Cox-Edwards 1992.

Chile, where a labor reform was implemented in the early 1980s, the process is very similar across countries. Unions with legal representation propose a collective contract to which employers must respond. The state becomes part of the negotiations from the beginning, and the final agreement applies to all workers represented.

Traditionally, strikes are one of the most important mechanisms used to resolve disputes between unions and management (this, and the paragraphs that follow, are based on Cox-Edwards 1992). In general, strikes are mechanisms through which the seriousness of the workers' proposal is ascertained against the seriousness of the employer's disagreement. In theory, each party should risk something during the bargaining process; in this way, delays in reaching agreements are costly to both parties, encouraging a speedy and efficient resolution of the labor conflict. However, in most Latin American cases, the costs to employees of striking are relatively low compared with those incurred by employers. In fact, in most countries in table 8-17 the costs of striking to union members are lower than in other parts of the globe, including the United States and most of Europe. In a few cases, workers still receive wages when they are on strike. The most important cost to firms during a strike is that they cannot hire temporary replacements and thus are forced into stoppage.

A particularly negative consequence of current labor legislation in some Latin America countries is that the length and costs of strikes tend to increase during recessions. This is because during a recession—when sales are slow—the costs to the employer of stopping activities are relatively lower than during a boom period, when the firm's goal is to increase production and take advantage of the expansion in demand. Of course, to the extent that they lose their wages during strikes, workers may be less prone to strike during recessions. This system increases the social costs of negotiation, reducing output and social welfare.

Reforming legislation governing labor-management relations in Latin America is an important unfinished part of the recent structural reforms. In general, a modern and flexible legislation is characterized by incentives to resolve conflicts quickly and fairly. This requires clear rules of the game, modern institutions, an efficient judiciary, and a system in which both parties incur costs if the conflict becomes protracted. In most countries, however, the current situation is far from that: there are asymmetric costs for unions and employees that, in fact, do not penalize delaying agreements.

Addressing the Social Agenda: Policy Options and Priorities

Social problems in Latin America have deep historical roots and became especially urgent after the debt crisis. As argued at the outset of this chapter, the success of the reforms initiated during the 1980s ultimately depends on whether they significantly reduce the extent of poverty and inequality. If they do, countries will be able to move toward a phase of inclusive development in which the fruits of the reforms are distributed widely and political support for the transformation process is broad.

The design of human resources policy should recognize two basic dimensions of social problems. First, there are deep structural deficiencies in the delivery of social services, which have traditionally been provided in a centralized manner, with little involvement of the communities affected by them. Solving these problems requires substantial long-term policy initiatives, including major decentralization, an increase in the coverage and quality of education, and significant upgrading of nutritional and health programs. Tackling these structural problems not only requires abundant resources, but also takes significant time. The second key dimension of the region's social problems is the immediate need to provide, in the short run, relief to the poorest segments of society that traditionally have been neglected and were hit particularly hard during the adjustment period. In the aftermath of the debt crisis, a number of countries undertook programs aimed at strengthening the safety net.

Emergency Programs

Several countries designed social emergency programs in an effort to ameliorate consequences of the debt crisis and the subsequent adjustment efforts. Some of the programs were based on traditional public works efforts centralized by the government, while others opted for more decentralized models where the community itself took a central role in the design, administration, and supervision of the programs. Mexico's Solidarity Pact and Bolivia's emergency program are good examples of the second approach.

During the 1970s and 1980s, Chile implemented two emergency employment programs aimed at providing some minimal degree of support to those groups affected by the adjustment policies. The Minimum Employment Program (PEM) was created in 1975 at a time when unemployment had reached record levels. The program, administered by local governments and supervised by the National Planning Office, paid a reduced salary to unemployed workers who, for a small number of hours, performed menial public works. At first, the government severely restricted entry into the program. Slowly, however, most of these restrictions were lifted, allowing a larger number of unemployed to take part. This expansion in coverage explains why the proportion of the labor force employed by the program remained virtually constant between 1977 and 1981, in spite of the economic recovery and a reduction in the real value of PEM's compensation.

After the eruption of the debt crisis, the number of individuals employed by PEM in the Greater Santiago area increased from about 23,000 in May 1982 to 93,000 in May 1983. A new emergency program—the Employment Program for Heads of Households (POH), launched in October 1982—employed about 100,000 individuals in the Greater Santiago area in May 1983. The two programs combined absorbed more than 10 percent of the labor force of the Greater Santiago area in May 1983 (these programs were also implemented in other regions of the country; the PEM program was drastically reduced in February 1984, and by December 1988, only about 5,000 individuals were employed by the POH in the entire country; see Banco Central de Chile, *Boletín Mensual*, 1991). The two Chilean emergency programs had three main characteristics. First, the compensation paid to participants was intended to discourage people from considering it as a long-term solution to their poverty. Second, participants were required to work to obtain payments. At every moment, an effort was made to keep the program from becoming an unemployment insurance scheme. And third, the number of hours of work required was small enough to allow participants to search for permanent jobs (see Castañeda 1992; Edwards and Edwards 1991 for evaluation of the PEM program). As the economic divisions improved, their coverage was greatly reduced, until they were phased out in the late 1980s.

The Bolivian government established, with the help of a series of multilateral and bilateral agencies, an Emergency Social Fund (ESF) in 1986. Its main objective was to provide employment opportunities to individuals affected by the debt crisis, the stabilization program, and the collapse of the international tin market. In contrast with Chile's PEM, the Bolivian fund concentrated heavily on infrastructure projects and was demand driven: managers approved or rejected funding requests for small projects. These were implemented by private contractors hired by local governments and supervised by the central ESF administration. The Bolivian ESF Program funded projects in four areas (Newman, Jorgensen, and Pradhan 1991): (a) basic infrastructure, including road maintenance, irrigation, and drainage; (b) social infrastructure in health, education, and sanitation; (c) social assistance, including school feeding and vaccination programs; and (d) credit provision to microenterprises through nongovernmental organizations. As in the case of Chile, the ESF was designed as a temporary program with a three-year life span, 1986–89. The ESF was a success in several dimensions (Psacharopoulos 1992, box 4.2). First, it concentrated on individuals with the greatest need for jobs; workers were mostly unskilled heads of households. Second, participants increased their earnings 67 percent on average. However, in some of the poorest areas, the lack of institutional capacity to generate projects reduced the scope of the program (Newman, Jorgensen, and Pradhan 1991). Also, although most workers employed by the private subcontractors were poor, they were not the poorest of the poor.

After years of armed conflict and economic mismanagement, Nicaragua emerged from the 1980s with its economy in shambles. Income per capita had dropped two-thirds, hyperinflation had taken over, and exports were one-fourth of what they had been ten years earlier. The new government put together a comprehensive economic package aimed at eliminating inflation and ending the balance of payments crisis. As a way of dealing with poverty, the Chamorro administration developed a number of emergency programs. The most important was the Fondo de Inversión Social de Emergencia (FISE), sponsored by the World Bank and bilateral donors. This program was tailored after the Bolivian fund and had a budget of $66 million for 1993–94. As with ESF in Bolivia, FISE sought to provide temporary employment to the poor in a number of infrastructure projects. From early on, however, the program faced difficulties common to this type of scheme. First, the labor component was low, and the creation of employment was modest. It was, in fact, estimated that this program would create the equivalent of 4,000 full-time jobs, with a very high cost per new job. Second, the government lacked the administrative capacity to implement the number of projects required by the program.

In addition to FISE, two broad regional social emergency programs were implemented in Nicaragua: PRODERE and PMA. These programs, as a few smaller ones, were coordinated through the Programa de Reconciliación Nacional. A serious shortcoming of these programs was that they focused on the rural sector, without providing enough social support for cities. In particular, little effort was made to deal with the growing importance of the informal labor market.

As a response to the debt crisis, Mexico designed an innovative decentralized program aimed at combating poverty through a series of infrastructure projects. This program, which was part of the broader Programa Nacional de Solidaridad (PRONASOL), provided funds to the 1,300 poorest municipalities for small projects. This system differed in two respects from the programs implemented in Chile, Bolivia, and Nicaragua. First, in Mexico the local governments had a significant degree of autonomy, with authority and responsibilities over supervision and auditing. Second, to obtain funds, the local communities had to provide matching resources, including materials or labor (in Nicaragua's FISE, for example, services were not considered as matching resources). By going directly to the interested groups and skipping the central bureaucracy, Mexico was able to mobilize a large segment of the population.

The Mexican program had a major impact in poor rural areas and urban shanty towns. Approximately 40,000 small projects a year were implemented between 1989 and 1991: 12 million people were connected to potable water, and schools and hospitals were rehabilitated in a very cost-effective fashion (World Bank, *Financial Flows and the Developing Countries,* 1991). The decentralization in the selection and supervision of projects is at the heart of PRONASOL's success (Binswanger, Deininger, and Feder 1993). The peso crisis of 1994 has meant that Mexico will have to strengthen its social safety net to protect (at least partially) the poor from the required new austerity measures. El Salvador, Guatemala, and Honduras also experimented with these types of programs. It is too early, however, to know whether they will have the major impact they have had in Mexico.

Targeting Social Programs

One of the most serious shortcomings of traditional social programs in Latin America is that their beneficiaries were not the poor. Many of these programs were regressive. In the last decade, more and more policy analysts and experts argued that targeting social programs to the truly poor is an important feature of successful social policies. The fundamental step in designing targeted social programs is to identify the poor: Who are they? Where are they located? This is not an easy task in countries where information is limited. Experts have considered three alternative ways of facing this problem (Grosh 1993). The first is based on individual assessment, where the authorities use certain criteria to classify each member of the population as poor or nonpoor. Naturally, this procedure requires significant amounts of detailed information that is not always available in the poorer countries. A second criterion is based on group targeting in which complete groups of the population—identified by geographic location, gender, ethnicity, age, or other broad characteristics—are classified as poor and are targeted to receive benefits from the programs. Finally, self-targeting mechanisms are designed to encourage a process of self-selection in which the poor and nonpoor are separated on their own without the active participation of the authorities. These types of mechanisms are based on high transaction costs, low quality of the products distributed, and even stigma.

The difficulties of administering targeted programs, including the difficulty of identifying the poor, have prompted some authors to argue that the Latin American countries are not ready for this type of policy. However, in a recent study of thirty targeted programs throughout the region, Grosh (1992) discovers that in most cases the actual cost of running these programs was modest: in twenty-nine of the thirty cases, the administrative cost was below $25 a year per recipient, with a median administrative cost of about $10 a year per recipient. Along the same lines, Musgrove (1991) finds that the cost of targeting food supply programs had a range of between $30 and $50 per individual a year.

Since the late 1970s, Chile has relied more and more on targeted social programs. Although these programs ran into difficulties during the early years, as time passed the authorities improved them significantly. The Chilean approach to targeting has largely been a success. For example, Castañeda (1992) reports that 90 percent of the food distributed through the preschool nutrition programs went to the poorest three deciles of the population and 80 percent went to the rural sector. Also, after it was reformed in the early 1980s, the basic housing program was geared more toward the poor. While in 1969 only 20 percent of housing subsidies were received by the poorest three deciles, in 1983 this percentage had increased to 50 percent.

Often efforts to replace general subsidies with targeted programs run into political opposition. This is because those groups that tend to benefit the most from general subsidies—the middle and upper classes—are politically organized and, many times, very vocal. They strongly resent government efforts to take away what they consider an entitlement. This is particularly the case with the reduction (or elimination) of subsidies to university education in favor of primary education and the reduction of subsidies on gasoline. At the same time, the groups that are bound to benefit the most from targeted programs are usually politically weak. They include the marginalized, the disenfranchised, and the very poor in the rural sector. Although their political voices are small, they clearly constitute the groups most deserving of direct government assistance (in 1984, the Jamaican government replaced general food subsidies with a food stamp system geared at reaching the poor, especially school-age children; see Grosh 1993 for an evaluation of this program).

Policy Options for the Future

In the years to come, progress in poverty alleviation is likely to come from two mutually reinforcing sources. First, stronger growth will result in more employment and faster growing salaries, especially if growth occurs in labor-intensive sectors with a rapid growth in productivity. Second, governments will have to increase the provision of basic social services targeted to the poorest segments of the population. In Chile, the combination of fast growth and increased social expenditures dramatically reduced poverty in the early 1990s. Between 1989 and 1993, more than 1.3 million people left the poverty head count (Flaño and Ochoa 1993).

Politically, a fundamental challenge is to raise the availability of resources to fund social programs. In particular, there may be a temptation to slide back into populism, using the inflation tax as a way to fund these programs. History shows, however, that the inflation tax is one of the most regressive instruments. A second difficulty is the unwillingness of the middle class to contribute more resources for programs directed to the poor. In spite of these difficulties, additional resources could be raised through a combination of measurements. First, in most countries a more efficient tax administration, including a more severe tax enforcement system that heavily penalizes fraud and evasion, can still yield significant resources that would greatly affect the social sectors. For example, an increase in government revenue of 1 percent of GDP would mean quadrupling the amount of resources currently devoted to nutritional programs and effectively ending malnutrition in the region. Second, it is imperative that the authorities seriously consider cutting other programs in order to devote the idled resources to financing targeted social expenditure. An obvious candidate for significant cuts is the military budget. In most countries, a reduction in military outlays of 0.5 percent of GDP would be feasible and would go a long way toward expanding the provision of public services for the poor (it is important, however, not to exaggerate the potential of this source of resources; military budgets in Latin America are somewhat low compared with those in other developing areas; see UNDP 1992). And third, some countries may have to raise taxes in order to obtain the resources required to fund a minimal comprehensive attack on poverty.

From a political point of view, some countries may have to do more than expand programs aimed at alleviating poverty. This is particularly true in middle-income countries where the (relatively large) middle class has been severely squeezed by the crisis and adjustment programs. Unless some of their concerns are addressed, the middle class is not likely to continue supporting the reforms, thus placing them under political pressure.

PART III

Looking toward the Future

The Mexican Crisis of 1994 and the Future of the Latin American Reforms

FOR DECADES, THE STATE IN MOST LATIN AMERICAN COUNTRIES GREW at a rapid pace. Regulations were piled on top of regulations and, backed by promises of better economic conditions for the majority of the population, the public sector expanded continuously. After an auspicious beginning, this strategy began to falter in the 1970s. Contrary to its architect's expectations, this state-led development approach produced vulnerable and inefficient economies, macroeconomic instability, and an increasingly unequal distribution of income. The debt difficulties of 1982 unmasked the shortcomings of the traditional Latin American policies and generated a major crisis of the state. Suddenly, it became apparent that instead of isolating the region from foreign disturbances, decades of protectionism and heavy regulations had built weak economic structures that were unable to withstand the cyclical shocks of the late twentieth century. When compared to the resilient and rapidly growing economies of East Asia, the Latin American economic systems appeared particularly inadequate.

As the 1980s unfolded, an increasing number of Latin American leaders began to agree that the region was facing a serious crisis and that the transition to the twenty-first century required major economic reforms. Politicians who for decades had advocated an increased involvement of the state in everyday economic life began to argue in favor of competition, international openness, privatization, and a greater role for market forces. In the early 1990s it became apparent to leaders of a number of the region's countries that the market-oriented reforms had to be supplemented with strong and targeted social programs aimed at reducing poverty and providing a social safety net.

This book has provided a history of the market-oriented reforms that swept Latin America during the late 1980s and first half of the 1990s. The progress made in different sectors has been documented and the difficulties found in the path toward economic modernization have been discussed. The analysis focused on the period of 1982 to 1993 and shows that during this period the vast majority of the Latin American nations went through a true economic revolution. Countries that only a few years ago had been subject to an almost surrealistic array of controls and regulations began to experiment boldly with market-oriented solutions to decades-old problems.

Although in many countries the reform agenda advanced significantly between 1989 and 1993, by 1994 in a few of them the excitement of the initial years was subsiding. In others, interest groups negatively affected by the transformations stepped up their opposition to some of the market-oriented policies.[1] Moreover, in a few countries the implementation of social and poverty alleviation programs lagged behind, generating increased inequality, social tension, and political upheaval. And in some quarters, including the specialized international media, the December 1994 Mexican peso crisis generated some doubts about the long-term viability of the market-oriented reforms.

This chapter discusses how the Mexican crisis of 1994 is likely to affect the future of the Latin American modernization program. The two fundamental questions being addressed are what are the key lessons of the Mexican crisis—both for reformers worldwide and for other Latin countries—and whether the reforms are likely to be consolidated and sustained through time. The more important areas for future policy actions are singled out, and some of the constraints that the region is likely to face are analyzed. The forward-looking nature of the discussion means that the analysis is necessarily limited by the cutoff date for publishing this book. It reflects the prospects of reform sustainability at the time of this writing.

The Mexican Peso Crisis of 1994 and Its Lessons

On December 20 1994, barely ten days after the conclusion of the Summit of the Americas, Mexico devalued its currency. This event triggered a major crisis that threatened to engulf the region.[2] The authorities initially intended to widen the exchange rate band by (approximately) 15 percent. It soon became clear, however, that this was insufficient; after losing more than US$5 billion in international reserves in two days, the peso was freely floated on December 22. Foreign financiers reacted with panic to the news that Mexico could not maintain the announced parity and began to withdraw funds throughout Latin America. Suddenly, countries that had become the darlings of international investors during 1993–94 were considered high risks, as a number of analysts feared a repetition of the debt crisis of 1982.

The timing of the Mexican events was particularly ironic. During the Miami Summit of December 1994, U.S. president Bill Clinton had singled out Mexico as one of the best models of Latin America's progress in economic and political reform. He was not alone in his praise; almost since the inception of the reform process, Mexico had been considered by the specialized media and the international financial institutions as an exemplary—if not the exemplary—reformer. After the approval of NAFTA, many analysts, and especially Mexican officials, argued that Mexico was about to embark on a final takeoff that would allow it to join, in a relatively short period of time, the ranks of the most advanced nations.[3] This enthusiasm for Mexico's prospects was based on a combination of factors, including the breadth and depth of the reforms undertaken by the Salinas administration, the elimination of fiscal imbalances, the privatization process, and the opening of the economy were often cited as major achievements. However, these analyses failed to notice two important weaknesses in Mexico's development during the early 1990s: contrary to the case of other countries in the region, such as Chile and Colombia, Mexico had only experienced modest growth—GDP had grown at an average of 2.9 percent in 1990–94—and had developed an extraordinarily large current account deficit, which exceeded 7 percent of GDP in both 1993 and 1994 (recall the analysis in chapter 5).[4]

Many analysts were caught by surprise by the peso crisis of December 1994. At that time, a number of international investment firms were still recommending Mexican securities to their clients. Their persistent optimism was partially affected by the lack of availability of up-to-date financial information, especially on the evolution of the Bank of Mexico's stock of international reserves. When Secretary of Finance Jaime Serra Puche announced the devaluation on December 20, international financiers, and especially managers of mutual funds in New York, reacted first with disbelief and then with anger. During the next few weeks the financial world witnessed a remarkable spectacle of panics, mutual recriminations (Who lost Mexico? editorialists asked rhetorically), failed rescue packages, congressional hearings, and courageous efforts by policymakers in the rest of the region (especially in Argentina) to isolate their economies from what came to be known as "the tequila effect."

An immediate consequence of the crisis was that it raised, throughout the world, a number of questions regarding the sustainability—and even the merits—of the market-oriented reform process in Latin America and other regions. If Mexico was the best example of a successful reformer, observers asked, what could be expected of other cases? This section addresses some important questions related to the Mexican crisis and its consequences for the Latin American reform process. In particular, it deals with the following issues: (a) why (and how) did the crisis happen; (b) what are its main lessons, especially in terms of the strategy for market-oriented economic reform; and (c) what is the probability that it will spread to other countries in the region? The next section discusses how the Mexican crisis is likely to affect the long-term prospects for the reform movement in Latin America and the rest of the world.

Why Did the Crisis Happen?

The main cause behind the Mexican peso crisis was an unsustainable current account deficit that, starting in 1992, was financed by very large capital inflows (recall the discussion in chapter 5).[5] When, mostly as a result of political developments, capital inflows began to slow down in 1994, Mexico's economic authorities failed to react promptly and with sufficient energy.

In the aftermath of the crisis, many observers asked whether the main actors in this saga—Mexican politicians, U.S. policymakers, and experts from the international financial institutions—had been aware of the weaknesses of Mexico's macroeconomy. By and large, most analysts of the Mexican situation had recognized that the rapid inflow of foreign capital had generated a significant disequilibrium that called for corrective action. For instance, in September 1994, World Bank staff argued in *Trends in Developing Economies 1994* (World Bank 1994)—a publication available to libraries, scholars, analysts, and the public in general—that the excessive reliance on capital inflows had made Mexico vulnerable. According to the Bank in this book, Mexico's "current account deficit remains very high. . . . Underlying the large current account deficit has been a fall in private domestic saving, indicating that foreign capital inflows have in effect financed an increase in domestic consumption" (p. 331). From here it goes on to say that "productivity growth has so far been insufficient to offset the loss of external competitiveness implied by the peso appreciation . . ." and that "with current account deficits of over $20 billion supported by even higher levels of foreign capital inflows, Mexico is vulnerable to foreign capital volatility."

The Mexican authorities, in particular, acknowledged that the current account gap could not be maintained at the 1993–94 level in the long run, and they had planned to deal with the problem gradually, by slowly reducing the deficit to manageable levels. Broadly speaking, this plan was based on two key assumptions: first, improvements in productivity would increase export competitiveness, helping close the trade gap. Second, the approval of NAFTA would entice additional capital—especially in the form of direct foreign investment—to move into Mexico, providing space and time for the gradual adjustment to work. A number of developments, however, frustrated this plan. The political shocks of 1994—social unrest in Chiapas, the assassinations of presidential candidate Luis Donoldo Colosio and the PRI's secretary general Ruiz Massieu, the resignation of the attorney general, and the kidnapping of a prominent banker—scared foreign investors, who became particularly leery with respect to currency risk. Each of these negative political events translated into major declines in the stock of international reserves held by the Bank of Mexico. Under orthodox macroeconomic management, this situation would have called for the implementation of a defensive macroeconomic stance, resulting in higher interest rates and, under flexible exchange rate regimes, in a weakening of the domestic currency. This, however, was not an attractive option in an election year. In fact, in an effort to avoid rising peso interest rates, the Mexican authorities followed a two-pronged approach. First, they issued increasing amounts of peso-denominated, but dollar-indexed, short-maturity notes: *tesobonos*. Second, they followed a policy of targeting peso nominal interest rates, by determining a maximum yield on domestic currency treasury securities (CETES), above which the Treasury would not sell them. This strategy became known as "drawing the line" (in Spanish, *"tirar la rayita"*) and was in part the result of pressure by a group of U.S. mutual fund managers—the so-called Weston Forum—that threatened to reduce sharply their Mexican exposure if the Treasury raised peso interest rates (see Craig Torres, "Market Forces," *Wall Street Journal,* June 14, 1994, pp. A1, A6).

Higher interest rates in the United States during 1994 also contributed to the reduction in capital flows into Mexico, further frustrating the authorities' hope of a gradual adjustment. And, although productivity began to improve in 1993–94, it was not enough to generate the expected super boom in exports (on Mexico's low productivity growth and exports performance, see the discussion in chapter 5). As a result of these factors, and in spite of the rapid increase in outstanding *tesobonos*, capital inflows declined markedly during 1994—from almost US$30 billion in 1993 to only US$10.2 billion in 1994—and the current account deficit was financed largely through a reduction in international reserves, which dropped from approximately US$30 billion in February 1994 (immediately prior to the Colosio assassination) to US$5 billion by December 22.

The presidential elections affected the policy options, as the authorities ruled out implementing contractionary credit and fiscal policies as a way to reduce the deficit and put an end to the drainage of international reserves. In spite of the decline in international liquidity, the central bank decided to maintain its overall monetary program, sterilizing the reduction in international reserves (see Bank of Mexico 1995). Also, during 1993 and 1994 the fiscal stance became somewhat loose: the overall fiscal balance deteriorated by 2 percent of GDP while the primary balance deteriorated by almost 3 percentage points of GDP. Furthermore, because of the tripartite agreement with business and unions—the *pacto*—it was decided not to implement an early devaluation as a way to correct the accumulated overvaluation and help the adjustment. After the presidential elections were won by the PRI candidate, Ernesto Zedillo, the authorities still resisted putting in place a contractionary macroeconomic adjustment program. Some analysts have interpreted this as an effort by the Salinas administration—including Salinas himself—to leave office with an untarnished record.[6]

By mid-December speculators sensed that the Bank of Mexico was in a weak position, and Rosalind's whisper was heard with increasing insistence throughout certain circles—"I must tell you friendly in your ear, sell when you can, you are not for all markets."[7] Those who were better informed massively sold pesos and attacked the Bank of Mexico's international reserves. By then it was too late, as the very low level of international liquidity (approximately US$10 billion) had left Mexico with very little room for maneuvering.

The international financial community reacted to these events in disbelief and generated a chain-reaction financial panic. The lack of a comprehensive adjustment program—including supporting fiscal and credit policies—was seen as a particularly weak aspect of the devaluation package. The announcement by the U.S. Clinton administration of the provision of massive loan guarantees temporarily calmed the markets in mid-January. Soon, however, it became clear that the rescue package would not be approved by the U.S. Congress and that the Mexicans had badly underestimated the magnitude of the crisis, and new panic set in. It was not until April, and after the announcement on March 9 of an extremely strict adjustment program, that the markets began to settle down. At that time it had become clear that Mexico was facing a crisis of almost epic proportions and that its solution would require major and painful measures.

The abandonment of the parity on December 20 generated a major loss in confidence. Memories of 1982 hounded the market, and the public feared a forced debt rescheduling or, even worse, the imposition of capital and/or exchange controls. The demand for Mexican financial assets went into a free fall, and publicly and privately issued securities were redeemed as soon as they matured. This situation was greatly exacerbated by the very short maturity of treasury obligations (*tesobonos*); more than US$10 billion matured in the first three months of 1995. This sudden drop in the demand for Mexican financial assets provoked a devaluation of the peso that greatly exceeded most analysts' predictions; the exchange rate almost reached 8 pesos per dollar before the announcement of the March 9 program (compared to 3.3 before the eruption of the crisis). This overshooting of the exchange rate during the early months of 1995—greatly exceeding calculations based on simple purchasing power parity analyses—clearly indicated that in modern economies open to capital mobility the exchange rate plays two fundamental roles: on the one hand it determines (jointly with other variables) the current account balance, and on the other it helps clear the financial market. By missing this dual role of the exchange rate, the original January adjustment program fell short of what was required to calm the markets. In mid-April, however, some calm began to return to the financial markets, and the peso started a steady recovery process.

The March 9 Recovery Program

After the failure of early attempts at restoring market confidence, on March 9 the Mexican government unveiled a tight macroeconomic recovery program, backed by a major IMF standby agreement. The program's main objective was the restoration of stability and the rebuilding of international confidence. The plan also called for an aggressive effort to privatize infrastructure, decentralize governmental functions, reform the legal and judicial system, and improve the effectiveness of social programs. The program had four main elements.

The first was to adjust the prices of public sector goods, increase the value added tax from 10 to 15 percent, and reduce the real level of public expenditure. For 1995, tighter fiscal policy was expected to produce a primary budget surplus of 4.4 percent, twice as large as the one originally envisioned in January 1995.

Second, the authorities adopted a floating exchange rate regime, with monetary policy designed to help stabilize prices. To achieve an inflation target of 42 percent in 1995, the Bank of Mexico committed itself to an expansion of net domestic assets to 23 percent.

Third, to avoid banking problems—and in particular massive bankruptcies— the government embarked upon a program of intensive supervision and regulation, including increases in capital requirements and loan loss reserves and the removal of the ceiling for foreign ownership of Mexican banks. The government established a foreign currency line of credit to enable domestic banks to meet their international commitments and a subordinated convertible debt program to help banks experiencing a temporary fall in their capital requirement and gave FOBAPROA (Fondo Bancario de Protección al Ahorro) the right to convert into capital the subordinated debt of banks and to take them over. Mexico, with the assistance of a major World Bank operation, is engineering a program to strengthen the banking sector.

Fourth, notwithstanding a fiscal contraction, real expenditure for social and rural programs in 1995 was to increase by 2 percent, while other noninterest expenditure is expected to fall by almost 20 percent. An effort was made to fortify the social safety net by expanding the negative income tax, extending public health insurance for the unemployed, initiating a program of public works targeted to the poorest of the unemployed, and expanding the labor retraining program.

The fact that during May the exchange rate stabilized, and that the stock market has regained part of the lost ground, suggested that the adjustment program put in place was working.

Lessons of the Crisis

The 1994 peso crisis in Mexico teaches a number of important lessons. Some are broad and are related to the design of reform packages in economies throughout the world. Others are more specific to Latin America and refer to the future of the region's reform movement. In this section some of the general lessons—most of which have to do with economic transitional issues—are briefly discussed. In the next section, some lessons specific to Latin America are addressed, including those related to the sustainability of reforms.

The following five lessons, related mostly to the implementation phase of the reforms, emerge quite clearly from the Mexican crisis.

1. The current account is a key variable that should not get "out of line." Although current account sustainability cannot be defined mechanically, under most circumstances the current account deficit should rarely exceed 3 percent of GDP in the long run (see the appendix to this chapter for details). Since successful stabilization programs—and especially those based on a fixed nominal exchange rate—usually generate a private sector consumption boom, maintaining the current account under control will require a nontrivial public sector surplus.

2. The composition of capital inflows—short-term portfolio versus long-term direct investment funds—is extremely important. Short-term portfolio flows are very sensitive to short-term changes in interest rates and other political and macroeconomic variables. Long-term direct investment funds, conversely, are less volatile and do not respond to short-term speculative factors. Keeping short-term speculative capital under control while encouraging long-term investment—as Chile has done—makes eminent sense.

3. Productivity gains are a fundamentally important element in the way in which the overall external sector develops. Productivity growth is at the heart of export expansion and thus contributes to keeping the current account in balance. Countries that experience productivity gains early in their reform and adjustment program—before real exchange rate appreciation takes place—will generally be in a better position to handle external disturbances. As it was discussed in detail in chapter 5, Mexico's aggregate productivity growth performance was disappointing during the early years of the reforms.

4. There is an inherent danger in using fixed exchange rates as a stabilization device. Experience has shown that they tend to generate real exchange rate overvaluation and loss in external competitiveness. This is particularly the case in countries where contracts and other costs are subject to some inertia. Moreover, fixed nominal exchange rates tend to distract policymakers and the public from the need to maintain fiscal discipline.

5. The structure (and especially the maturity) of government debt is extremely important. Short-term debt represents a true danger under free capital mobility. In these circumstances rumors, "news," or (temporary) losses in confidence can result in very massive redemptions of government debt, generating serious liquidity problems. It was precisely because of the concentration of *tesobonos'* maturities in the short end of the spectrum that the Mexican situation got out of hand in January 1995. The failure of initial efforts to slow down the redemption of *tesobonos* resulted in the large overshooting of the peso-dollar rate during the first quarter of 1994.

These five lessons are very general and apply to any country embarked on a stabilization-cum-reform program. The Mexican crisis, however, also has important implications for the likely evolution of the reform process in Latin America. This is the subject of the next section.

Latin America after Mexico

The Mexican peso crisis made painfully clear that, in spite of the reforms, many of the Latin American economies remain vulnerable. A number of analysts have even questioned the sustainability of the Latin American reforms and have pointed out that the mismanagement of the Mexican macroeconomy during 1994—the piling up of short-term debt and the acute overvaluation of the currency—is an indication that Latin American countries are not yet ready for the rigors of a market-based system.[8] Although it is too early to know whether the reforms will be cemented, or whether, in some countries, disappointment and nostalgia will bring back populism, statism, and control, it is clear that the crisis has brought to the fore of the policy debate the need to consolidate the modernization process. Because of the crisis, all of a sudden it is clear to policymakers, intellectuals, and the public at large throughout the region that there are some urgent unfinished tasks. The complacency, self congratulation, and triumphalism observed toward mid-1994 have given way to a sense of urgency and an understanding that, indeed, the reform process never ends. The global economy of the late twentieth century is a bit like Alice's observation in *Through the Looking Glass* that "it takes all the running you can do to keep in the same place. If you want to go somewhere else, you must run at least twice as fast as that" (Carroll 1872). Leaders from a growing number of countries have concluded that deepening the reforms rapidly is the only way to counter skepticism, to deal with the doubts that have emerged among some international financial analysts, and, more important, to move firmly toward prosperity and social harmony.

How Is a Reform Process "Consolidated"?

Chapter 1 argued that the consolidation of the reform process requires the population at large—or at least a majority—to recognize that the modernization effort will generate, sooner rather than later, sustainable and solid results in the form of rapid growth and improved social conditions. Consolidation also requires the creation of new institutions that increase the transparency of the economic and political processes and shield the economy from the short-run effects of the political cycle. In most cases, this means that, in order to achieve consolidation, the reformist government has to form broad and stable political coalitions and convince a large proportion of the population on the merits of the new economic order. Obtaining voter support for sustaining the reforms generally requires maintaining the early achievement of the reforms—in most cases, macroeconomic stability—accelerating the rate of growth, ensuring that the fruits of progress accrue to all segments of society, and reducing inequality. Experiences in a number of countries also suggest that eliminating—or substantially reducing—corruption and reducing the extent of overall violence and crime are likely to increase political support for the reform process.

The consolidation of the reforms does not imply that every single policy measure will be maintained unaltered through time. It does mean, however, that the public debate begins to take place within well-specified boundaries that respect the fundamental pillars of the new economic approach: stability, openness, and a strong state that has a limited role as a producer and provides social services efficiently and fairly. In a democratic regime, specific policies are bound to be challenged and to change through time. However, although policies evolve in different directions, the broadly defined economic regime is stable.

By early 1994, only in Chile had the reform process entered the consolidation phase, with broad political support for the main pillars of the new economic regime—openness, market orientation, macroeconomic stability, and poverty alleviation—and where the probability of a policy reversal appeared to be very low. Chile has a third-generation "reformist" government, and the current political debate suggests that the candidates for office will continue to run on platforms that promote reform. Also, institutional reforms geared toward ensuring the durability of the new economic system, including a clear budgetary process and an independent central bank, have been implemented. Until the Chiapas uprising of January 1994, many analysts also thought that the Mexican reforms were consolidated. The Zapatistas' revolt and the assassination of the PRI candidate Luis Donaldo Colosio introduced, however, questions among some observers. These two events greatly affected Mexico and led to the crisis analyzed above. At the time of this writing, the reform process in the rest of Latin America is at different stages of implementation and enjoys different degrees of political popularity. The reelections of Alberto Fujimori in Peru and Carlos Menem in Argentina—both of which ran on platforms based on deepening the reforms—in 1995 suggest that these two nations may also be entering the consolidation phase.

From a policy perspective, the consolidation of the new economic system in Latin America will require action in three broad areas: first, maintaining prudent macroeconomic management; second, deepening the structural and institutional reforms in order to continue improving productivity and, ultimately, accelerate the rate of growth; and third, implementing decisive social programs aimed at reducing the extent of inequality and alleviating poverty. Underneath these actions is the need to rebuild the state. The new state that emerges in the years to come will have to be strong but very different from the state of the 1970s and early 1980s. As Latin America moves toward the twenty-first century, the state should stay away from those spheres where the private sector operates efficiently and act decisively in those where the private sector hesitates or fails. The state should provide social services for the poor, support quality education, contribute to the provision of basic infrastructure, provide a stable and credible regulatory system that encourages investment and protects consumers, ensure a macroeconomic environment conducive to export expansion, and develop rules and regulations that protect the environment.

The recent experience of the pioneer reforming country, Chile, suggests that in an economic system based on openness and competition and in a state active on the social front, productivity growth is one of the pillars of economic progress. In this context, the absorption and adaptation of technological progress become key elements of the development strategy. They ensure that the degree of international competitiveness is maintained, generating rapid real wage increases. The creation of a good-quality educational system (a task that is still incomplete in Chile), which provides the basis for successfully adopting new techniques, thus is fundamentally important.

A key lesson from the Chilean experience, and one that politicians and policymakers sometimes find difficult to accept, is that it takes substantial time for the reforms to generate full benefits in the form of sustained rapid growth, low and stable inflation, export booms, and permanent increases in wages. It takes time for resources to be reallocated, it takes time for new projects to come to fruition, and it takes time to open new international markets. Now that the urgencies of the debt crisis seem far in the past, impatience is taking over in some countries. However, as the experience of Brazil has shown, attempts to skip phases in the reform process—and in particular to bypass macroeconomic stabilization—are costly and ultimately unsuccessful. Multilateral and bilateral institutions should continue to support the reform process by providing funds and technical assistance that will help smooth the transition toward a modern economic system. In particular, the new emphasis on social projects is entirely appropriate and promises to be highly productive. At the same time, multilateral institutions should constantly monitor the evolution of the reforms and use their leverage fully to ensure that impatience, shortsightedness, and short-term political pressures do not derail this effort.

The three fundamental policy elements for the future—prudent macroeconomic management, further structural and institutional reforms, and poverty alleviation—often reinforce themselves. For instance, efforts to maintain macroeconomic balance, and thus avoid inflation and real exchange overvaluation, protect the purchasing power of the poor. Also, social security reforms increase the degree of efficiency of the labor market, which increases productivity, while at the same time improving public sector finances and the overall macroeconomic balance.

Prudent Macroeconomic Management

As Mexico showed so dramatically, in spite of significant progress during the last few years, in most countries the macroeconomic situation continues to be vulnerable. In many cases—Bolivia, the Dominican Republic, and El Salvador, for example—the public sector deficit has recently shown an upward trend. More important, with the return of democracy there are some indications that public finances may be subject to political cycle pressures. To safeguard the continuity of the reforms, the nostalgia for populist episodes should be avoided and prudent macroeconomic management maintained. Fiscal discipline will have to be intensified in order to generate higher public sector savings. Monetary policy should be cautious and real exchange rate overvaluation avoided—points made very clear by the Mexican crisis. More specifically, in the years to come, the following macroeconomic issues will be particularly important:

- In the short run it will be crucial to monitor capital movements and avoid overborrowing, unnecessary real exchange rate appreciation, a loss of competitiveness, and a decline in export dynamism.
- There will be a need to devise policies that encourage domestic savings, especially private savings.
- The authorities will have to make sure that investment in infrastructure recovers to levels compatible with rapid growth.
- A serious effort will have to be made to develop institutions that add transparency to macroeconomic policy and isolate macroeconomic management from short-run political pressures.

The theme that unifies these four policy areas is the need to maintain fiscal discipline. This message cannot be emphasized enough: as the region's history has repeatedly shown, fiscal imbalances often spawn serious crises that encourage speculation, retard growth, and increase poverty and frustration. Moreover, macroeconomic instability is often associated with political crises.

During 1992 and 1993 virtually every country in the region received large volumes of foreign portfolio capital. These inflows, which in some cases—Argentina, Chile, and Mexico, for example—constituted significant percentages of GDP, were the result of a number of factors, including the reduction in interest rates in the United States and a perception in international financial markets that the Latin American reforms have been largely successful. The increased availability of foreign resources affected countries' ability to manage monetary policy, pressured real exchange rates toward appreciation, and allowed these countries to run large current account deficits and accumulate sizable international reserves.

As the Mexican crisis evidenced, in most countries the volume of capital inflows observed in 1993–94 is not sustainable in the long run (current account deficits of 5–7 percent of GDP are, under most circumstances, not compatible with long-run solvency, when GDP is growing at 3–5percent, regardless of the level of interest rates). The experience of the early months of 1995 also suggests that in countries where public finances remain under control, adjustment to lower capital inflows is likely to be gradual and smooth. If macroeconomic management is less than prudent, it is possible that a sudden halt in capital inflows will occur, generating potentially serious macroeconomic dislocations.

In many countries, the reform of social security systems will be an important and, in some cases, urgent component of economic programs for the next few years. If adequately implemented, these reforms are likely to generate a series of four related positive effects. First, they will tend to reduce the fiscal burden on the central government, helping to achieve fiscal balance. Second, they will introduce choice in the health provision system, helping to improve its efficiency and fairness. Third, they will reduce labor market distortions, encouraging employment and productivity growth. And fourth, as is the case in Chile, they will encourage the development of local financial markets, providing a very important boost to private savings. Naturally, for the social security reforms to be fully effective and credible, it is necessary to implement an adequate regulatory system that closely monitors operations, avoiding corruption and reckless behavior.

The low level of domestic savings represents one of the most—if not *the* most—serious weaknesses in the region's macroeconomic position. In spite of significant progress in deregulating the financial sector, savings—and in particular private savings—continue to be low, which limits the pace of capital accumulation, slows down new investments in infrastructure, and curbs productivity growth. In 1993, the median ratio of gross domestic savings to GDP was 20 percent, more than 10 points below that of the East Asian economies (World Bank, *World Development Report 1995*). To achieve rapid growth in the years to come, Latin American countries have to raise domestic savings and investment to levels closer to those of the successful economies of East Asia.

Increases in public savings constitute the most rapid and reliable way of increasing domestic savings. Moreover, recent evidence from East Asia suggests that when higher public savings are accompanied with reforms that create safe and reliable financial institutions, especially banking sectors, increases in private savings are likely to follow (World Bank 1993a).[9] The need to implement efficient and effective regulatory and supervisory systems cannot be emphasized sufficiently; the recent history of the region is replete with major financial and banking crises that have had enormous costs.

In most countries, higher government savings should be achieved through a combination of higher revenues and reduced expenditures. On the revenue side, tax administration and tax compliance need to be improved. In particular, the prosecution of tax evaders should be stepped up and penalties for tax evasion increased (in many cases this will require a broad revision of tax legislation and a modernization of the judicial system). On the expenditure side, subsidies should be eliminated and government waste tackled. The reduction in military allocations also provides important possible sources of income, but its potential should not be overestimated. Recent figures from the United

Nations Development Programme show that, with the exception of Honduras and Nicaragua, military expenditures in Latin America are below the average in the developing countries. In that regard, however, a reduction in waste and (implicit and explicit) subsidies still provide the most promising source of increased savings. In many countries, accelerating the privatization process would also affect public savings. This would happen mostly through the reduction of subsidies and transfers made by central and regional governments to money-losing state-owned enterprises.

During the last decade or so, investment in infrastructure has been neglected in almost every country. Roads have not been maintained, power capacity has barely expanded, and ports have not been modernized. There is ample empirical evidence suggesting that infrastructure investment has positive externalities and a very high social rate of return (Aschauer 1989 and Uchimura and Gao 1993). Policies toward infrastructure investment will have to focus on two fundamental aspects. First, public investment should increase. However, to ensure high social rates of return, individual projects should be subject to rigorous economic evaluation. Second, a credible regulatory framework that ensures property rights and thus encourages private sector investment in infrastructure should be implemented. This is particularly important to ensure that newly privatized utilities will continue to expand their capacity (multilateral financial institutions will have an important role in helping these countries devise ways to increase long-term funding for privatized utilities and infrastructure projects).

Institutions play a fundamental role in determining the course of economic policy. At the macroeconomic level, the consolidation of the reforms that foster competition will be helped greatly by the creation of institutions that ensure the transparency of policymaking, avoid short-term political cycles, and allow the authorities to commit themselves credibly to a future course of action. Clearly defined and mandatory budgetary processes constitute a basic but extremely important institutional priority that has been often absent in Latin America. The national legislature should be required to approve a consolidated budget for the public sector as a whole before the initiation of the fiscal year, and the executive should be legally (and factually) constrained by it. (Surprisingly, a large number of Latin American countries lack a well-defined and mandatory budget process; the absence of this is closely related to the historical fiscal laxity in many countries of the region.) The implementation of independent central banks constitutes a second institutional reform that could add credibility to macroeconomic policy. This measure—recently implemented in Argentina, Chile, Colombia, Mexico, and Venezuela, among other countries—would (partially) isolate the monetary and, in some cases, exchange rate policy from partisan short-term political battles. As the Mexican crisis clearly indicates, however, the formal independence of the central bank is not a sufficient condition for avoiding monetary crises. In addition, appropriate policies should be promptly implemented. In an extensive comparative empirical study, Cukierman (1992) found that the degree of independence of the central bank is directly related to the long-term degree of macroeconomic stability. Naturally, for this reform to be truly effective it should have political legitimacy. This means that the notion, and practical implications, of a truly independent central bank have to have broad support among the population at large. The experience of Chile after 1989 suggests that even if the electorate initially has mixed views regarding this type of institution, it can, with the passage of time, come to support it strongly. However, the experience of Venezuela in April 1994, when the majority of the members of the Central Bank board resigned under pressure, indicates that when there are extreme differences of opinion between the executive branch and the central bank, the formal independence of the latter may not be that relevant in determining the course of monetary policy.

Deepening Structural and Institutional Reforms

In spite of significant progress, the modernization process is in its early stages in some countries. In some cases, such as the Dominican Republic, Ecuador, and Guatemala, the transformation process has just begun. In others, such as Colombia, Costa Rica, and Uruguay, the structural reform process is more advanced, but important institutional changes, including the creation of modern regulations and rules, are still lagging. In still other countries, the reform process has only affected the central (or federal) government and has not yet reached the provincial and municipal levels. In many countries, surrealistic regulations, red tape, and rampant corruption at the local government level greatly reduce the effectiveness of the reform effort. The historical evidence from Chile and Mexico strongly suggests that incomplete and partial reforms tend to stand in the way of a major economic takeoff. Broadly based reforms exhibit synergism and positive spillovers; partial reforms tend to generate credibility problems and encourage the postponement of investment and restructuring projects (Edwards 1993c).

During the next phase, the reform process will have to focus, in most countries, on two areas. First, measures geared toward increasing efficiency and productivity should be continued to ensure rigorous and sustainable growth. Second, the reform process should increasingly aim at creating institutions that strengthen the new Latin American state. This two-pronged approach toward deepening the reforms will not only accelerate the rate of growth but also strengthen the sustainability of the reforms. More specifically, the most important areas where the reforms have to be deepened include the labor market, education, privatization and deregulation, the civil service, and the consolidation of openness.

In virtually every country, the labor market is still a forgotten area in the reform process. As argued in chapter 8, labor market legislation is rigid in Latin America, and the use of labor is subject to substantial taxes that discourage employment creation. Also, the high costs of dismissal have introduced serious restrictions on economic restructuring and modernization, reducing the ability of local firms to respond aggressively to international challenges and opportunities. Moreover, in most countries existing labor legislation encourages the creation of massive informal sectors that, although functioning efficiently on the margins, have a negative effect on tax collection, modernization, and equity. International experience indicates that flexible and dynamic labor markets are a fundamental component of East Asia's success (World Bank 1993a). Also, consolidation of the region's nascent democracies requires defining modern and equitable bargaining processes, whereby unions truly and fairly represent the long-run interest of workers.

As pointed out in chapter 8, the provision of education in Latin America has long been plagued by serious problems. Net coverage at both the primary and secondary levels is low, and quality is dismal—one of the lowest in the world. And yet, education—or lack of it—is the main determinant of poverty and inequality. Moreover, investment in education, especially primary education, has very high rates of return, both private and social. Reforming the educational system requires creative initiatives that go beyond traditional formulas. There is little doubt that, to compete internationally, the teaching of science and technology has to be strengthened. Moreover, to incorporate traditionally neglected groups into the modern economic sectors, the education of the indigenous population has to be upgraded through bilingual programs.

To raise the quality of education, it is necessary to expand significantly the involvement of the community affected by the reforms. This means that in most countries decentralization should be a fundamental component of the modernization of education. The new system should combine public and private provision of education, and in some cases, the use of voucher systems is likely to induce competition, greater efficiency, and better results. In some cases, fiscal incentives should be considered as a way to encourage worker training programs.

Perhaps the first requirement for improving education is to upgrade teachers' skills and accountability. Eliminating the widespread practice of standardized pay—whereby teachers obtain (almost) the same salary independent of performance—would go a long way in this direction. This will allow schools to raise salaries as a teacher's commitment and involvement increase. In some countries, this type of reform may run into political opposition. Teachers' unions have proved to be among the most conservative groups in Latin America. In many countries they have opposed eminently reasonable reforms aimed at democratizing the educational system.

The evolution of Latin America's exports toward increased value added requires the implementation of policies that improve the technological capabilities of the export sector. Research and development activities often generate positive externalities and thus should be supported by the government. In addition to developing creative research and development policies, it is important to enact legislation that protects property rights in knowledge-based activities.

In a number of countries—including Bolivia, the Dominican Republic, and Ecuador—the state continues to play an important role in the productive process. Streamlining the size of the state through new rounds of privatization is likely to increase overall efficiency, allowing the public sector to strengthen its fundamental role of implementing social programs, providing education, and supporting investment in infrastructure.

As argued in chapter 7, it is important to recognize that the reform of the state, and especially privatization, should go hand in hand with the implementation of modern regulatory and supervisory frameworks. Particular emphasis should be given to the creation of truly professional and independent regulatory agencies, whose role is to ensure that the newly privatized public utilities do not abuse their power and that the authorities will not expropriate their assets. The implementation of regulatory institutions requires creating financing schemes that allow them to operate autonomously, without interference from political forces.

In some countries, such as Argentina and Brazil, government proceeds obtained from privatization have been used to finance current government expenditures. This is a dangerous practice that, under some circumstances, undermines fiscal responsibility and discipline. A preferred approach is to use privatization proceeds to reduce government liabilities, especially in social security. Indeed, a potentially serious danger in many privatization processes, such as in some of the Eastern European countries, is that the state divests itself of productive assets while it retains substantial liabilities. By using the proceeds from privatization to retire government debt, the magnitude of this problem can be reduced substantially.

In most countries, the administrative organization of the state responds to an era where dirigisme and planning were dominant. There are numerous ministries that are supposed to deal with economic issues in a command fashion, and few modern and autonomous supervisory agencies. There is a clear need to continue restructuring the public sector in order to increase efficiency and accountability. A recent study on the East Asian miracle (World Bank 1993) suggests that a very professional, efficient, and well-paid bureaucracy played an important role in the economic success of that region. In Latin America, there is an urgent need to modernize the judiciary system. The credible protection of property rights through a well-functioning and transparent court system is a key element for encouraging investment and ensuring the sustainability of the new economic regime. Additionally, in modern economies it is essential to have a lean and transparent conflict-resolution system that protects the rights of individuals and groups at the same time that it defuses costly confrontations. A deep reform of the judiciary is a fundamental requirement for truly consolidating the reforms. Justice is slow and ineffective in most of the region; corruption is common, and cases tend to drag for long periods of time.

Social Programs and Poverty Alleviation

As discussed in chapter 8, the Latin American countries historically neglected the social sectors. This resulted in staggering poverty indexes and in the most unequal income distribution in the world in the early 1980s. Today the poorest 20 percent of Latin Americans receive approximately 4 percent of GDP. As the Mexican crisis painfully shows, a fundamental task in the years to come is to address poverty and inequality with vigor and urgency. This would not only improve the living conditions of the population but also provide stability to the new economic system and to the region's new democracies. Failure to act aggressively in this area will exacerbate distributive conflicts and is likely to prompt discontent and, in some cases, even create the bases for a return to populism, dirigisme, and eventually chaos. As history has shown again and again, populist policies are often attractive in the short run, but their ultimate outcome is frustration and stagnation. Only to the extent that the region's development strategy becomes inclusive, allowing all segments of the population to benefit from growth, will the new system endure.

The new approach toward poverty and the social sectors should be based on three elements. First, policies that are conducive to growth and that create employment and generate higher wages should be fostered. Economic growth is the most important and durable path leading out of poverty. Consolidating the structural reforms along the lines discussed above should be the instrument through which higher growth is sustained. Second, government programs that raise the living standards of the poor should be vigorously implemented in the short run. This would allow government to tackle immediately the most serious consequences of poverty, including malnutrition, access to health services, and the provision of potable water. Directly involving the community in the design and implementation of many of these social programs is likely to increase their probability of success. Recent information from Chile suggests strongly that policies that emphasize higher growth and targeted programs can be highly successful. In little more than three years, the combination of strong growth and targeted social programs helped to reduce the number of people below the poverty line by 1.3 million, more than one-quarter of those in poverty in 1989. And third, policies that reduce inequality and provide efficient public services to the middle class should be undertaken. These policies should focus on areas that both have a positive effect on economic growth and are likely to generate a broader political support for the reform process. Improving the quality of the educational system and creating new institutions that strengthen the state—and, especially, reduce violence and crime—appear to be particularly appealing to the middle class.

Countries today must ask what additional steps they can take to increase the complementarity between the reforms required to recover growth and those required to improve long-run equity. Is it possible to reallocate public expenditure radically and quickly to eradicate the worst aspects of poverty in the short run without impairing public finances and the control of public deficits?

Reform programs based on market orientation are likely to increase the labor intensity of the growth process. Trade liberalization and reforms that reduce taxes on the use of labor and subsidies for the use of capital should be accelerated. Because schooling is one of the major determinants of income distribution in Latin America, investments in human capital and skills should be increased. To reduce inequality, an effort should be made to improve cost-recovery, making sure that the wealthy pay for their services. And, since in most countries the poor are concentrated among the indigenous population, programs especially targeted toward this segment of society should be undertaken.

Countries could be much more aggressive in reallocating public resources toward targeted social services, without impairing the fiscal adjustment or the pursuit of other efficiency objectives. With public expenditures usually accounting for 25 percent of GDP, a 10 percent reallocation of the budget can have a significant impact on the welfare of the poorest groups. Countries should aim at generating an increase equivalent to 2 to 3 percent of GDP by broadening the tax base, improving tax collection, and reducing evasion. Additional revenues can be obtained by eliminating subsidies, especially those that accrue mostly to the wealthier segments of society. In undertaking this kind of policy, however, an effort should be made to compensate the poor directly for the reduction of subsidies.

Historically, many Latin American countries have attempted to use labor legislation—including minimum wages, regulations on dismissals, and restrictions on temporary hiring—to improve income distribution and reduce poverty. These policies, however, failed badly. Instead of helping the poorest groups of society, they introduced serious distortions that discouraged employment creation and produced a small group of highly paid jobs in the protected sector. In addressing the needs of the poor, it will be important to avoid the mistakes of the past. Social policy concerns should be addressed using direct and well-focused instruments rather than distortions in the labor market. These instruments should be dynamic and flexible, stimulating the creation of jobs and allowing the economy to respond rapidly and productively to changes in international competitive conditions. This, indeed, is one of the fundamental lessons from the East Asian miracle.

Conclusions

The Latin American reforms have been broad and impressive. Few analysts would have predicted in 1984 that, merely a decade later, most of the region would be embarked on a sweeping transformation process that has significantly reduced the economic role of government and opened these economies to the rest of the world. In spite of their depth and scope, the transformation and modernization processes in Latin America are largely unfinished. Moreover, as the Mexican peso crisis of December 1994 clearly showed, macroeconomic equilibrium often continues to be fragile. In many countries, the results in terms of growth and social progress have not yet met expectations, and in almost every country there is a need to build new institutions that will help maintain the new economic order. Consolidating the reforms, making them a permanent feature of the Latin American economic and social landscape, is an enormous challenge facing the new democratic leaders.

Latin America is a tremendously diverse region. In the decades to come, we are likely to see the evolution of somewhat different modes of development across countries. There will be different emphases and priorities, including different economic roles for the state. History strongly suggests, however, that to generate sustained growth and prosperity while maintaining their idiosyncracies, national strategies should respect the fundamental pillars of what in this book I have called the new Latin American consensus: macroeconomic stability, outward orientation, and a state that stays away from production and efficiently provides public services and social programs aimed at effectively reducing poverty and inequality.

The economic history of Latin America has been compared to Gabriel García Márquez's classic novel *One Hundred Years of Solitude* (García Márquez 1970). Events seem to repeat themselves endlessly, following irregular and magical cycles of sorrow and frustration. The recent reforms that engulfed the region are beginning to break this melancholic circularity. After decades of timid performance and spiraling inequalities, and in spite of the Mexican crisis, there are rays of hope.

Appendix 9-1: The Simple Economics of Current Account Sustainability

The Mexican peso crisis of 1994 has raised questions about what is a "sustainable" level for the current account deficit in a particular country. Although there are no mechanical rules on this subject, there are some helpful guidelines that analysts can follow to detect departures from sustainability. This appendix develops a very simple approach for analyzing long-run current account behavior, and it briefly discusses which macroeconomic indicators are helpful to provide early warnings of an external crisis.

In general, there will be an "equilibrium" level of a country's liabilities that foreigners will be willing to hold in their portfolios. Naturally, this "equilibrium portfolio share" will not be constant and will depend on a number of conditions, including interest rate differentials, the perceived degrees of country and exchange risk, and the degree of openness of the economy. Moreover, when countries embark on (what is perceived to be) a successful reform program, the "equilibrium" level of the country's liabilities that will be willingly held by international investors is likely to increase as they will be eager to take part in the country's "takeoff."

Assume that in equilibrium international investors are willing to hold in their portfolios a ratio k^* of the home country's liabilities relative to its GDP.[10] Denoting liabilities by L and GDP by y:[11]

$$(9\text{-}1) \qquad\qquad k^* = L/y.$$

$k^* = k^*(...)$, in turn, depends on a number of variables, including interest rate differentials and perceived country risk. Equation 9-1 implies that the net accumulation of this country's liabilities will be, in equilibrium, equal to:

$$(9\text{-}2) \qquad\qquad \Delta L = g L,$$

where g is the "long-run" rate of growth of real GDP. Of course, if instead of the country's GDP, an alternative benchmark is used—say, exports—g should be interpreted as the rate of growth of that variable.

ΔL in equation 9-2 is this country's capital account surplus, and is equal to the current account deficit, plus the net accumulation of international reserves. The current account, in turn, is equal to the trade account deficit T plus the service account. The latter can be approximated by the product of the rate of return on liabilities r (for short, this will be referred to as the real rate of interest on the country's liabilities) times the stock of liabilities. Denoting the current account deficit by C, it is possible to write:

$$(9\text{-}3) \qquad\qquad \Delta L = \Delta R + C,$$

$$(9\text{-}4) \qquad\qquad C = T + r L,$$

$$(9\text{-}5) \qquad\qquad T = (M - X)$$

where M is total imports and X is exports. Assuming, as a first approximation, that the accumulation of reserves is equal to zero, equations 9-2 and 9-3 imply:

$$(9\text{-}2') \qquad\qquad C/y = g\, k^*.$$

This says that the "sustainable" current account to GDP ratio—that is, the current account deficit that can be maintained in the long run without violating the portfolio equilibrium condition (equation 9-1)—is equal to the desired liabilities to GDP ratio k^* times the long-run real GDP growth. Moreover, from equations 9-2´ and 9-4, it follows that:

(9-6) $T/y = (g - r) k^*.$

This is the well-known condition that states that in equilibrium the trade deficit (or resource transfer) can at most be equal to the difference between the real rate of growth in the economy and the real rate of interest on the country's liabilities, times k^*. What is particularly interesting about this equation is that it clearly states that a rate of growth in excess of "the" real interest rate is a requirement for a country to receive a positive resource transfer from the rest of the world. In rigor, equations 9-2′ and 9-6 establish upper limits for the current and trade account balances in the steady state.

A problem with this analysis is that even in the steady state it is very difficult to measure the desired ratio of the country's liabilities to GDP. However, some insight can be gained by looking at different hypothetical values of the equilibrium current account GDP ratio under alternative assumptions for k^*. This is done in table 9-1. These numbers are very revealing. They indicate, for instance, that if in equilibrium foreigners are willing to hold liabilities equal to one half of the country's GDP—that is $L/y = 0.5$—and the rate of real GDP growth is 5 percent, the long-run equilibrium current account ratio is 2.5 percent of GDP. Notice that even with a combination of a desired L/y of 1.0 and real growth of GDP of 7 percent a year, the equilibrium current account deficit is only 7 percent—below Mexico's ratio in 1994. The numbers in table 9-1, then, provide a first approximation to the issue of long-term current account sustainability. If a country's current account is very far from what according to these figures is reasonable, there are causes for concern and further analysis. In the case of Mexico, this analysis clearly indicates that in 1993 and 1994— when the current account balance exceeded 7 percent of GDP—the authorities' concern should have been how to adjust smoothly the external accounts to levels consistent with long-run equilibrium.

This simple framework is subject to some limitations, including the fact that it ignores international reserves and issues of transition. In what follows I address some of these questions, indicating ways in which they can be accommodated through revisions in the analysis.

Assume that the country in question (or more specifically its central bank) has a well-defined demand for international liquidity. In this case, as the economy expands, the desired level of reserves will also grow and a proportion of the capital inflows will be devoted to satisfying this higher demand for reserves. This means that the equation on the sustainable equilibrium current account will be given by:

(9-2″) $C/y = g \, k^* - (\Delta R/y),$

where ΔR is the desired increase in the stock of international reserves. Under the assumption that in equilibrium the authorities want to hold a certain number of months' worth of imports as reserves, this magnitude can be

*Table 9-1. Sustainability of Current Account Deficits: Hypothetical Values
of the Equilibrium Current Account Ratio under Alternative Assumptions
for the Ratio of a Country's Liabilities to Its GDP and for GDP Growth*

Ratio of liabili- ties to GDP (L/y)	Long-run rate of real GDP growth, in percent (g)				
	2	4	5	6	7
0.25	0.005	0.010	0.0125	0.015	0.0175
0.40	0.008	0.016	0.020	0.024	0.028
0.50	0.010	0.020	0.025	0.030	0.035
0.75	0.015	0.030	0.0375	0.045	0.0525
1.00	0.020	0.040	0.050	0.060	0.070

expressed in percentage form as $(R/y)^*$.[12] Denoting the (forward-looking equilibrium) rate of growth of imports as m, equation 9-2″ can be rewritten as:

$$(9\text{-}7) \qquad C/y = g\, k^* - m\, (R/y)^*\, \gamma,$$

where γ is the degree of openness of the economy and measured as the ratio of imports to GDP.

This analysis has concentrated on long-run equilibrium conditions and has ignored transitional issues. These, however, can be very important in cases when there are large shifts (positive or negative) in the portfolio demand for the country's liabilities. If, for example, due to changes in expectations or in external conditions (world interest rates, for example), there is an increase in the demand for the country's securities, it is possible for the current account balance to exceed, in the short run, the levels defined in table 9-1. Once portfolio equilibrium is regained, however, the current account balance will again revert to its long-run equilibrium level. A particularly serious case emerges when there is a decline in the portfolio demand for the country's securities—as was the case in Mexico after December 20, 1994. Under these circumstances, the current account balance will suffer a very severe contraction—and may even have to become positive—during the transitional period toward the new equilibrium.

1. Introduction: The Launching of the Reforms

1. Of course, performance varied significantly across countries. Brazil and Mexico grew particularly fast, while Chile tended to lag behind. In general, the great diversity of initial conditions and individual experiences make generalization difficult. In a way, it is not correct to refer to *the* Latin American experience. However, the region has experienced a series of similar problems and has shared, to some extent, a common fate. In this study, I have made an effort to deal both with systemic issues pertaining to a large number of countries and with case studies.

2. Once again, behind these averages, the records are remarkably diverse. In particular, many of the Caribbean economies experienced very low inflation rates during this period.

3. Fishlow (1991) argues that comparisons between Latin America and East Asia should be handled with care. His view is based on two facts. First, Latin America's inferior performance is concentrated in the years after the first oil shock. Second, and more important, in the period before the debt crisis, economic outcomes within Latin America were very uneven, with some countries—most notably Brazil—growing at a rate comparable to that of the East Asian economies and others—Chile—exhibiting increasing signs of stagnation. Fishlow's views on these matters are addressed in greater detail in chapter 3. See Maddison (1985) for a penetrating comparison of development strategies, as well as economic performance, in Latin America and East Asia.

4. Although the book concentrates on the 1982–93 period, in some instances information pertaining to 1994 is provided. In particular, chapter 9 briefly discusses the Mexican peso crisis of December 1994.

5. Throughout this book, the term "Latin America" refers to the economies of Latin America and the Caribbean.

6. As argued in chapter 5, these large inflows of capital generated problems for macroeconomic management by pressuring real exchange rates toward appreciation. For an analysis of the magnitude of these flows, including a comparison with East Asia, see Calvo, Leiderman, and Reinhart (1993).

7. In spite of recent growth, by 1991 only thirteen economies in the region had income per capita exceeding that of 1980: Antigua and Barbuda, the Bahamas, Barbados,

Belize, Chile, Colombia, Dominica, Jamaica, Paraguay, St. Kitts and Nevis, St. Lucia, and St. Vincent and the Grenadines.

8. This issue has become particularly important in the light of the Mexican crisis of 1994.

2. Muddling Through: Adjustment from 1982 to 1987

1. Throughout the book, a billion is 1,000 million, and all dollars are U.S. dollars.

2. Generally speaking, a country's ratio of debt to GDP cannot exceed a certain equilibrium level. When this level is achieved, the resource transfer is equal to the difference between the rate of growth of real GDP and the real interest rate times the stock of debt. Most Latin American countries systematically violated this basic solvency constraint in the late 1970s and early 1980s (see Edwards 1986a).

3. Folkerts-Landau (1985) and Edwards (1986a) discuss the differences between bank loans and bond premiums as predictors of country risk. They argue that due to a number of legal considerations, including syndicational and cross-default clauses, bank loan premiums do not capture fully the perceived probability of default.

4. These data refer to yields on U.S. dollar–denominated bonds of comparable maturities. For 1982 through 1985, the data were taken from Folkerts-Landau (1985). For 1980–81, the data obtained directly from the *International Herald Tribune*, which is the source used by Folkerts-Landau. The same bonds were followed through time. The following bonds were used: World Bank, 10¼, June 1987; Mexico, 8¼, March 1987; Brazil 8¼, December 1987. For all cases, except December 1984 and January 1985, the yields refer to the first Monday of each month. For December 1984 and January 1985, the second Monday was used. The fact that the yield differential is *negative* for the early months suggests that these data should be interpreted with some care. Kyle and Sachs (1984) also use yield differentials with respect to World Bank notes to illustrate changes in the valuation of the debt in developing countries. Gutentag and Herring (1985) look at the spread over LIBOR on Nafinsa floating rate notes. The discussion that follows draws partially on Edwards (1986b).

5. This interpretation is somewhat consistent with econometric results reported in Edwards (1986b), suggesting that liquidity considerations played no major role in the determination of risk premiums in the bond market.

6. A time-series regression analysis of Mexican bond spreads suggests that, although the spread responded to economic and financial variables (such as the price of oil and the evolution of international reserves), it did so rather slowly. This supports the view that the crisis was only anticipated by a few weeks.

7. In the early 1990s, capital inflows once again pressured real exchange rates toward appreciation in many countries (see chapters 5 and 9). There were, however, some exceptions in how the exchange rate was managed during the late 1970s. Colombia's pragmatic approach toward management—isolating the real exchange rate from inflation through a crawling peg—allowed it to avoid the deprotection effects of the coffee boom of 1975–79 and to maintain a reasonable macroeconomic equilibrium (Thomas 1986).

8. Korea, in contrast, experienced *negative* capital flight between 1980 and 1984 (Edwards 1989d).

9. Due to major and significant controls and regulations, investment in most of Latin America had, at that time, very low productivity.

10. In the majority of these countries, however, the share of private sector credit increased during 1987–91.

11. The ineffectiveness is particularly striking when analyzed in a historical perspective. Most episodes of successful devaluations in Latin America prior to the debt crisis were characterized by higher *effectiveness* indexes (Edwards 1989d). For some countries—Costa Rica, El Salvador, Nicaragua, Peru, and Trinidad and Tobago—the real devaluation effectiveness index was *negative*. In these cases, the ensuing inflation more than offset the nominal devaluation (Edwards 1989d).

3. The Emergence of a New Latin American Consensus

1. In a revealing book, Enrique Iglesias, a former secretary general of CEPAL and current president of the Inter-American Development Bank, discusses the convergence process and provides a list of the main policies similar to the one presented here (Iglesias 1992; see also Iglesias 1990). In the 1960s, the semiofficial Latin American view was that the training of Latin American economists in the industrial nations was detrimental to the region's development prospects (see, for example, Pinto and Sunkel 1966).

2. Raúl Prebisch was a remarkable intellectual force that greatly shaped early Latin American economic thinking. He was governor of the Argentine central bank in the 1930s and early 1940s, a period when he applied orthodox policies. In 1947, he published the first Spanish language guide to Keynes's *General Theory* (on the evolution of his thinking, see Prebisch 1984; Iglesias 1992, chap. 1; Solís 1988).

3. See, for example, the popular Paz and Sunkel (1971) textbook for discussion of economic policy in the context of the structuralist and protectionist view. See also the text on international economics by Ffrench-Davis and Griffin (1967). Castro and Lessa (1969) provided a popular, and widely used, text that discusses basic economic issues from a structuralist perspective.

4. This point was strongly made by Díaz-Alejandro (1970) in his monumental study on the external sector in Argentina. See also Díaz-Alejandro (1976) for work on Colombia. See Edwards (1988a, 1989d) for discussions of real exchange rate misalignment. It may be argued that, given the level of protectionism prevailing during this period, observed (and appreciated) real exchange rates were at an "equilibrium" level. However, under this interpretation, the highly appreciated real exchange rates still discouraged nontraditional exports.

5. See Fishlow (1987) for a discussion of these competing criticisms of import substitution. Edwards and Edwards (1991) discuss this problem from Chile's perspective. See also Sheahan (1987) and Cardoso and Helwege (1991). Vuskovic (1970) provides one of the most eloquent defenses of the *dependencista* position.

6. Some of the early East Asian "miracle" economies also relied on discriminatory export-promotion schemes. According to the World Bank (1993), however, these were largely ineffective.

7. Between 1960 and 1980, not one article dealing with the East Asian experiences was published in Latin America's most prestigious economics journal, *El Trimestre Económico*.

8. Rogelio Arellano (1990) finds that Korea has one of the least volatile real exchange rates in the developing countries. See Baum Oum (1989) for a description of the Korean exchange rate system. See Korean Development Institute (1989) for an analysis of some of the frictions between Korea and the United States.

9. The World Bank's book *The East Asian Miracle* has generated significant controversy. In particular, some analysts argue that the study's claim that selective industrial policies played no role in the success is not persuasive. See, in particular, Rodrik (1994) and Wade (1994). It is very likely that in the years to come, this will remain a highly controversial area of policy debate.

10. Sachs argues, in the context of the former U.S.S.R., that market-oriented reform should proceed rapidly and across-the-board. See Edwards (1992a, 1992b) for a general discussion of the sequencing of economic reform. See also the discussion in chapter 4 of this book.

11. Although the change in views in CEPAL is evident to any careful reader of its documents, some important differences of opinion remain within that institution.

12. See, for example, Arellano (1982), Cortázar (1982), Foxley (1982, 1983a, 1983b), and Meller, Livacich, and Arrau (1984). During the Pinochet regime, the military did not allow open political discussions. As a result, debates on economic policy became a substitute for political discussions. The CIEPLAN economists played an important and brave role in maintaining some sense of perspective in Chile during these years.

13. Foxley goes on to suggest that under democratic rule, import tariffs should be increased to an average of 30 percent, with a maximum effective rate of protection of 60 percent. He argues, however, that these policies would "not result in a return to the import-substitution model, as was known in Chile and Latin America during the 1950s and 1960s" (Foxley 1983b, p. 54).

14. The Aylwin government reduced import tariffs to a *uniform* 11 percent and has declined to participate in new regional integration efforts for fear that they will be "too protectionist."

15. Tariffs were reduced to 11 percent across-the-board in June 1991. The newly appointed independent central bank played an important role in further opening the economy during this period. In an incisive article, Fontaine (1992) notes that by 1989 the majority of Chilean voters were still skeptical about the merits of the market-oriented reforms. According to him, the process of convergence and synthesis began with the intellectual elites of the Socialist and Christian Democrat parties.

16. See Inter-American Dialogue (1992). This group includes leaders as diverse as Luis Inacio "Lula" da Silva from Brazil and Mario Varga Llosa from Peru.

17. Of course, the agreement is more clear for broad topics than for detailed policy. For example, CEPAL (1992b) suggests subsidizing research and development in certain sectors, a position that many mainstream observers consider conducive to serious distortions.

4. Macroeconomic Adjustment as a Priority

1. Analytically, it can be argued that Brazil is going through a "war of attrition" pre-stabilization process similar to the one analyzed by Alesina and Drazen (1991). Many of the insights generated formally by the new political economy literature were present in the early Latin American theories of inflation developed by Sunkel (1960), among

others. In early 1994, a new Brazilian stabilization plan was implemented. Contrary to previous efforts, this plan, designed under the leadership of Minister Fernando Henrique Cardoso, contemplated a fiscal adjustment as its central component.

2. The change in the official position on the debt crisis was influenced by a very important body of research undertaken in the Research Department of the IMF and at the World Bank. For a set of highly influential papers dealing with these issues, see Frenkel, Dooley, and Wickham (1989) and Selowsky and van der Tak (1986). See also Krugman (1988).

3. The regulations governing these operations are contained in chapters 18 and 19 of *Compendium of Rules on International Exchange* of the Central Bank of Chile (Banco Central de Chile 1993).

4. Obviously, in evaluating this program the usual considerations on the desirability of foreign investment should also be taken into account. See Ffrench-Davis (1990) for the opposite view.

5. I am grateful to Ricardo Martin for helping me to prepare this table.

6. In some countries, governments covered part of their deficit by floating domestic debt. However, given the poorly developed nature of the region's capital markets, this option was limited. Clearly, a vicious circle developed, where the lack of sophisticated capital markets precluded using domestic debt as a source of financing and, in turn, inflation discouraged the growth of the financial sector. See chapter 7 for a discussion of the reform of capital markets.

7. When the Allende government came to an end in 1973, Chile faced tremendous macroeconomic dislocation. Inflation surpassed 700 percent, and the fiscal deficit constituted 22 percent of GDP. During 1974, the new military government tackled the deficit through large cuts in expenditures and improvements in tax administration (see Edwards and Edwards 1991).

8. The original rate was 10,000 australes per dollar. After the currency reform of 1992, however, the rate became one Argentine peso per dollar.

9. The interpretation of "liquid" international reserves is somewhat lax since it includes government financial assets denominated in foreign currency (see Canavese 1991).

10. This view, or some variant of it, was adopted by a number of Latin American countries in the last two decades—for instance, the Southern Cone during the 1970s, Nicaragua in 1991, Argentina after 1991, and to some extent Mexico after 1988—with different degrees of success. History, however, unequivocally shows that, quite independent of other factors, if public finances are not tightly controlled, the adoption of an exchange rate anchors policy is doomed to fail. Remember the analysis of the heterodox programs in chapter 2.

11. These countries provide a unique opportunity to study the behavior of fixed exchange rates because they have the longest uninterrupted experience in the world with fixed parities (see Edwards 1993a for details; see also Edwards and Losada 1994).

12. Note that in Mexico exchange rate policy remains in the hands of the Ministry of Finance. Some observers have argued that this institutional arrangement contributed to the Mexican peso crisis of December 1994.

13. The presence of the expectations operator reflects the assumption that the domestic price of tradables is set before the rate of devaluation or of world inflation is observed.

14. This, however, is a somewhat misleading name since it is used to denote two quite different policies. While some authors refer to a strict purchasing-power-parity

rule as a "real target" policy, others define this "real target" as a policy aimed at accommodating changes in real exchange rate fundamentals (see Corden 1991b).

15. In this model, no explicit expression is included for the rate of growth of domestic credit. This responds to the assumption that the monetary authorities follow a passive credit policy that accommodates the inertial inflation.

16. In obtaining equation 4-6, I also assume that $E_{t-1}(P_t) = P_{-1}$.

17. Several authors discuss alternative ways of measuring the degree of persistence in the time series of GNP (Cochrane 1988). Much recent discussion centers on measuring persistence in nonstationary series.

18. This again assumes that aggregate demand measures have been eliminated ($t = 0$).

19. To test further whether the adoption of the fixed exchange rate in June 1979 had an effect on the inflation process, several tests on the structural stability of the inflation equations were computed. If the shift from an accommodating adjustable exchange rate regime to a rigidly predetermined one is credible, the inflation equation would be expected to capture a *change in regime*. These stability tests support the dummy variable results reported previously and show *no* structural break in the inflation equation. For example, in the case of equation 4-10, the chi-square statistic for structural stability has a value of $\chi^2(6) = 2.03$, indicating that there is no evidence of a change in the inflationary regime in mid-1979.

20. However, the adoption of incomes policies in Mexico took place two years after the fiscal accounts had been balanced (see Beristain and Trigueros 1990 for a useful description). This is, in fact, a critical difference between the Mexican program and the heterodox stabilization programs of Argentina, Brazil, and Peru.

21. One way to rationalize this is to think that the public interprets the adoption of the fixed rate as a *weak commitment* that can be abandoned under certain contingencies. If the private sector perceives that these contingencies are very permissive, the degree of commitment associated with the change in exchange rate regime will be very low or nonexistent.

5. The Opening of Latin America

1. Starting in the 1970s, a handful of countries—Brazil, Colombia, and Mexico—followed a trade strategy that combined import protection with active (selective) export promotion. In fact, the National Bureau of Economic Research study on trade policy in developing countries classifies Brazil and Colombia as having reached stage four of reduced anti-export bias (see Krueger 1978). I am grateful to Jaime Ros for calling this point to my attention.

2. Most authors agree that the import-substitution process rapidly ran into difficulties once low-technology consumer goods had been substituted. As countries tried to produce more sophisticated goods, capital goods, and machinery, they fought an increasingly uphill battle (see Fishlow 1985; Hirschman 1968). See also the discussion in chapter 8.

3. Of course, this amounts to the textbook notion that freer trade increases the level of domestic welfare. However, modern approaches go beyond this goal to consider the acceleration of growth as a goal of trade policy (see Edwards 1992c).

4. Traditional neoclassical growth models concentrate on the effect of national economic policies on the level of income per capita. The new generation of endogenous

growth models shifts attention to the relationship between different policies and the rate of growth of the economy (see Lucas 1988).

5. In chapter 17 of his *Principles of Political Economy* (1884), Mill states that "a country that produces for a larger market than its own can introduce a more extended division of labor, can make greater use of machinery, and is more likely to make inventions and improvements in the process of production." Arthur Lewis makes a similar proposition in his 1955 classic book on economic growth.

6. The procedure used compares employment before and after the trade reform, without controlling for the effect of other variables. However, during the second year (1967) of the liberalization effort, Yugoslavia experienced an increase in unemployment.

7. In spite of their before-and-after comparisons, almost every time unemployment increased after reform, the authors attribute it to causes other than the reform itself. For example, in the Argentine case, they talk about overvaluation; in the Israeli episode, they mention restrictive macroeconomic policies; in Korea, they talk about recession; and so on.

8. These are unweighted averages and thus are not comparable to those presented in table 5-1. There has been a long discussion in applied international trade theory on whether tariffs and nontariff barriers should be measured as weighted or unweighted averages. Both views have some merits and some limitations. An obvious problem of the weighted average approach (where the weights are the import shares) is that more restrictive distortions tend to have a very small weight. In the extreme case, prohibitive tariffs that effectively ban the importation of a particular item have no weight! Corden (1966) provides an early and still highly relevant discussion of these issues.

9. The issue of protecting local producers from dumping is important in the design of the new liberalized trade regimes. The crucial problem is to enact legislation that is able to distinguish true cases of unfair trade practices from simple cases of increased foreign competition stemming from more efficient productive processes. At this time, the approval of a dynamic and flexible antidumping legislation should be high on the region's agenda for legal and institutional reform.

10. This system with very low (or no) tariffs on intermediate inputs and high tariffs on final goods generated very high rates of effective protection to domestic value added. The use of effective protection is misleading, because effective rates of protection cannot provide much information on the general equilibrium consequences of tariff changes (Dixit 1986). In spite of this, they are still useful, because they indicate the degree of inefficiency a country is willing to accept for a particular sector.

11. However, tariff is sometimes a misleading term, since many countries traditionally relied on both import duties (that is, tariffs proper) and import duty surcharges or paratariffs (see Harberger 1992 for a discussion of the actual mechanics for reducing uneven tariffs).

12. Some countries, most notably Brazil, Chile, and Colombia, experimented with crawling pegs as early as the 1960s. However, only Colombia maintained a regime that avoided overvaluation of the real exchange rate.

13. The original data on growth of total factor productivity are from Martin's (1992) study on sources of growth in Latin America. The countries in table 5-4 initiated the reform before 1988. To compute a series on growth of total factor productivity, Martin analyzes the contributions of capital and labor and explicitly incorporates the role of changes in the degree of capital use. The countries considered in this study are Argentina, Bolivia, Chile, Colombia, Costa Rica, Dominican Republic, El Salvador,

Guatemala, Honduras, Mexico, Nicaragua, Panama, Peru, Uruguay, and Venezuela. Harberger (1992) presents data on growth of total factor productivity before and after a series of historical trade reform episodes. He finds that, in the majority of the cases, productivity growth increased after the liberalization process.

14. However, according to Harberger's data, growth of total factor productivity in 1986–90 exceeded the level of the years immediately after the crisis. The actual numbers calculated by Harberger are the following: 1950–60 = 3.8; 1960–75 = 3.9; 1975–82 = −2.5; 1982–86 = −2.8; 1986–90 = 0.8. An important difference between the Martin and Harberger computations is that Martin does not correct for different degrees of capacity use.

15. Naturally, exports can grow as a result of other policies, including an activist and selective industrial policy aimed at picking winners. The extent to which this is an efficient channel continues to be controversial. The recent World Bank study on the East Asian miracle argues that these types of policies were *not* important. For critiques of that study, see Wade (1994) and Rodrik (1994).

16. Trade liberalization aims at increasing a country's total volume of trade. Under textbook conditions, it is expected that, at the end of the reform, trade will be balanced. However, in a number of circumstances, including the need to pay the country's foreign debt, trade will not grow in a balanced way after a reform. This was the case in the majority of the Latin American countries.

17. The legal document that sets the basis for MERCOSUR is the Asunción Treaty, which had its origins in an integration act signed between Argentina and Brazil in 1986. New acts were signed between these two countries in 1989 and 1990 (for details, see Nogués and Quintanilla 1992).

18. The higher the common external tariff, the more likely it is that a customs union will have net negative welfare effects on its members because there will be additional diversion of trade. Commodities that, at the original tariff, were imported from the least expensive source will be imported from a less efficient regional member (on the creation and diversion of trade, see Dornbusch 1989a). Notice, however, that GATT does not allow for a common tariff exceeding the members' average before the union. It is unclear, however, whether this provision can actually be enforced.

19. It is assumed that not all inventions generated in the world can be freely appropriated. In that sense, A* could be interpreted as the accumulated stock of innovations in the more industrial countries that have spilled over to the rest of the world. Harberger (1959) provides an early discussion along these lines.

20. The instruments themselves do not have to be measured free of error. Of course, using instrumental variables is not the only way to deal with errors of measurement. Edwards (1992c) uses reversed regressions to construct intervals for a different proxy of openness in standard growth equations.

6. Privatization and Deregulation

1. The monthly journal *Latin Finance* provides useful and detailed information on the process of privatization in the region. The focus on massive privatization was developed rather late in the efforts to tackle the debt crisis. For example, the minor role assigned to privatization during the early debates on the debt crisis is reflected by the fact that in the pioneer volume edited by Jeffrey Sachs in 1989, which collected the

papers presented at a conference held in late 1987, the word "privatization" does not appear even once in the subject index (Sachs 1989b). Only three years later, the situation had changed dramatically, as is evidenced by the discussion in the volume edited by John Williamson in 1990 from a conference held in late 1989. In this book, issues related to privatization cover almost a full page in the subject index.

2. Not all of these ventures were successful. For instance, the acquisition of Aerolíneas Argentinas by a group led by Spain's Iberia ran into serious difficulties, forcing the government to buy back some of the shares from Iberia's local partner.

3. This assumes that in this game, the firms move first, deciding the level of investment made, and the government moves next, enacting rate adjustments. Since the firm has already moved, the government takes investment as a given. See Laffont and Tirole (1993) and Spulber (1989) for theoretical analyses of regulation based on strategic behavior by firms, politicians, and regulators.

4. In Jamaica, the majority party can alter any legislation at will. However, long-term contracts, or licenses, are traditionally honored. If conflicts regarding the interpretation of the contracts arise, the courts are called into action.

5. These firms were not nationalized. The Allende administration used an obscure piece of legislation from the 1930s to intervene in companies whose products were in short supply (see chapter 4 of Edwards and Edwards 1991 for details; also see Larraín and Meller 1991).

6. The actual price-setting procedure is quite sophisticated. First, long-run marginal costs are calculated; second, the capital asset-pricing model is used to determine the fair return of a hypothetical efficient firm. Tariffs are set for five years, with adjustments for inflation allowed every two months (Galal 1993).

7. Chile and Argentina made important progress toward increasing the efficiency of ports. Chile ended the unions' monopoly in 1981, when barriers to entry were virtually eliminated. According to Wisecarver (1985), the new legislation reduced the port operating costs by 50 percent in two years. In Argentina, the new port law greatly reduced the unions' monopoly power, allowing for the contract of service companies and replacing the system of charging per task with freely contracted salaries paid biweekly.

7. Capital Market Deregulation, Savings, and Investment

1. Institutional constraints and defects in legislation and regulations created an environment that weakened the supervisory authorities' ability to ensure financial stability. Some of the most serious institutional constraints were low wages for financial examiners, absence of computerized systems for off-site surveillance, information gathering, and auditing practices, and overlapping responsibilities across regulatory agencies. Legislation and regulation did not clearly define the process through which the distress of commercial banks was to be resolved or the rights of different parties. Thus, little incentive existed for the claimants on the bank (depositors, equity holders, and regulators) to resolve financial crises quickly. On these issues, see the important study by Glaessner and Mas (1991). This discussion draws on their work.

2. It is, in fact, possible to argue that if a gradual East Asian approach had been followed, deposit rates would be significantly lower. However, Rodríguez (1994) contends that, although *average* interest rates were very high, interest rates charged to prime borrowers were *not* significantly higher than international rates.

3. In the reformed system, the state plays a fundamental role in regulating and monitoring the operation of the management companies and guaranteeing "solidarity in the base" through a minimum pension. An important feature of the new social security system is that it requires every dependent worker (workers who are not self-employed) to make contributions equal to 10 percent of his or her disposable income.

4. For further details, see Edwards and Edwards (1991). In January 1993, the Chilean government announced that it was relaxing the restrictions for AFPs to invest in the stock market. Diamond and Valdés-Prieto (1994) persuasively argue that the current operating mode of Chile's AFPs generates sizable waste and point out that this is quite regressive.

5. In spite of the increase in capital flows discussed in chapters 4 and 5, the availability of foreign savings continues to be low from a historical perspective. Moreover, it is highly unlikely that foreign savings will continue in the steady state at their current levels.

6. The countries used in the regressions were chosen according to the availability of data and are listed in the appendix of Edwards (1994). The following instruments were used: constant, age dependency, average growth in 1970–82, ratio of money to GDP in 1970–82, private credit in 1970–82, real interest, government savings, social security, current account in 1970–82, income distribution, political instability, GNP per capita in 1988, and government consumption rate in 1983–92.

7. This is not necessarily the case for total savings during the transition from one regime to the other, because during the transition the government continues to have obligations to (older) retirees but receives no contributions from active workers. As a result, government savings tend to decline.

8. Poverty, Income Distribution, and Human Resources

1. Using a common poverty line across countries allows for meaningful cross-country comparisons (see *World Development Report 1993*, "World Development Indicators" [World Bank, various years] for a methodological discussion of the merits of common-basket poverty line computations). The purchasing-power-parity dollars were constructed by Summers and Heston as a way to avoid artificial data fluctuations due to changes in the exchange rate. If country-specific baskets are used to measure the evolution of poverty, five (rather than four) countries exhibit an improvement in the late 1980s. The additional country is Guatemala (Psacharopoulos 1992). However, this country-specific approach provides a very different picture of the *number* of poor people. For example, when the country-specific basket is used to measure poverty, the percentage of the population below the line in Venezuela in 1989 increases to 79 percent! In the case of Colombia, the poverty head count declines from more than 60 percent, when the Colombia basket is used, to less than 8 percent, when the common benchmark is used. These large variations illustrate strongly the difficulties associated with measuring and comparing poverty and social conditions across countries and time.

2. The strict question being asked is the probability of having income in the bottom 20 percent of the distribution. Naturally, as the data on poverty in tables 8-5 and 8-6 show, in most countries in the region, those in the bottom 20 percent actually have income below the poverty line.

3. Employment and unemployment statistics in the region are of doubtful quality. They have partial coverage and are not reliable. Most counties lack data on rural unemployment, forcing analysts to rely on urban data. These statistics should be interpreted with care.

4. As in most parts of the globe, AIDS has become a major public health problem in Latin America. In 1993, more than 1 million people, including 200,000 women of childbearing age, were HIV positive. HIV prevention programs will have to acquire a priority in Latin American health programs if an explosion of AIDS cases is to be avoided. A cost-effective way of dealing with the AIDS problem is to focus on preventing and treating sexually transmitted diseases, which usually facilitate transmission. Unfortunately, in many countries, cultural and religious views preclude more aggressive HIV prevention campaigns.

5. Recent evidence based on statistical analysis for a score of countries suggests that infrastructure investment is particularly productive and spills over to other sectors (De Long and Summers 1991). As argued in chapter 7, one should be careful, however, in interpreting this evidence for Latin American countries, whose history is replete with large and highly *un*productive investment projects. Having the adequate framework to determine the (social) return on public infrastructure projects is a necessary first step before expanding investment in this area.

6. High repetition rates reflect myriad factors, and a low level of repetition does not necessarily reflect high educational standards. In fact, the ideal situation is one where rates of repetition are low *and* standardized results are high.

7. Assembly-type activities that require limited training and operate in a satisfactory way with high turnover of personnel become relatively more attractive. Fine crafts and industrial activities that require a high degree of training and where personnel turn-over imposes a high cost become relatively less attractive, all other things remaining constant.

9. The Mexican Crisis of 1994 and the Future of the Latin American Reforms

1. The opposition to increasing the price of gasoline closer to world levels in Venezuela is a classic example of the middle class reaction to the reforms.

2. The Summit of the Americas took place in Miami, December 10–11, 1994, and brought together, for the first time in almost thirty years, all the democratically elected leaders of the hemisphere.

3. During 1993–94 the specialized financial media were full of stories praising Mexico. The book by Pedro Aspe (1993) offers a professional, and at the time highly influential, insider's assessment of the progress made by Mexico in the reform front.

4. A number of authors, however, began to point out as early as 1992 some of the weaknesses of the Mexican economy. See, for example, Dornbusch and Werner (1994) and Calvo (1994). See also Edwards (1994).

5. While large current account deficits can take place for a limited period of time, they cannot be maintained in the long run. This is a matter of arithmetic. A current account deficit of the magnitude of Mexico's would eventually require that the country devote 100 percent of its GNP to pay interest (and dividends) to foreign holders of Mexican securities. See the discussion in the appendix to this chapter.

6. See, for example, Rudiger Dornbusch's article "We Have Salinas to Blame for the Peso Debacle," *Business Week*, January 16, 1995, p. 20.

7. William Shakespeare, *As You Like It*, Act III, iv.

8. See, for example, "Latin America savours the tequila aftertaste," *The Economist*, May 20, 1995, pp. 41–42.

9. In this way, a virtuous circle can develop: higher public savings result in increases in capital accumulation and growth. In the presence of adequate institutions, higher growth results in higher private savings, further increases in capital accumulation, and even faster growth!

10. Ideally this should be a forward-looking measure of GDP.

11. Naturally, there is a problem of valuation here. For the time being, it will be assumed that L and y are measured in the same currency. Issues arising from exchange rate conversion will be tackled below, where some of the implications of this framework are discussed. The equilibrium level of the country's securities willingly held in the world portfolio can be measured relative to a number of benchmarks, including the country's GDP, its exports, or its wealth, or worldwide wealth. Each of these benchmarks has merits and drawbacks. In this appendix the discussion is presented in terms of the country's own GDP.

12. Nine months' worth of imports would be represented by a $(M/y)^*$ equal to 0.75.

References

Agacino, R., Gonzalo Rivas, and Enrique Román. 1992. "Apertura y eficiencia productiva: La experiencia chilena, 1975–1989." Working Paper 113. Inter-American Development Bank, Washington, D.C.

Agarwala, Ramgopal. 1983. *Price Distortions and Growth in Developing Countries.* World Bank Staff Working Paper 575. Washington, D.C.

Agenor, Pierre-Richard, and Mark P. Taylor. 1992. "Testing for Credibility Effects." *IMF Staff Papers* 39 (September): 545–71.

Aghevli, Bijan, James Boughton, Peter Montiel, Delano Villanueva, and Geoffrey Woglom. 1990. "The Role of National Saving in the World Economy: Recent Trends and Prospects." *IMF Occasional Paper No. 67.* Washington, D.C.

Aizenman, Joshua. 1990. "Trade Reforms, Credibility, and Development." Working Paper 3600. National Bureau of Economic Research, Cambridge, Mass.

Alesina, Alberto. 1988. "Macroeconomics and Politics." In Stanley Fischer, ed., *NBER Macroeconomics Annual.* Cambridge, Mass.: MIT Press.

Alesina, Alberto, and Allan Drazen. 1991. "Why Are Stabilizations Delayed?" *American Economic Review* 81 (5): 1170–88.

Alesina, Alberto, and Guido Tabellini. 1988. "Voting on the Budget Deficit." Working Paper 2759. National Bureau of Economic Research, Cambridge, Mass.

Alexander, Myrna, and Carlos Corti. 1993. "Privatization in Argentina." World Bank, Latin America and Caribbean Region, Washington, D.C.

Altimir, Oscar. 1982. *The Extent of Poverty in Latin America.* World Bank Staff Working Paper 522. Washington, D.C.

Altimir, Oscar, and Sebastian Piñera. 1979. "Análisis de descomposiciones de las desigualdades de ingreso en América Latina." In Oscar Muñoz, ed., *La desigualdad del ingreso en América Latina.* Buenos Aires: El Cid.

Arellano, José Pablo. 1982. *Modelo económico chileno: Trayectoria de una crítica.* Santiago: Editorial Aconcagua.

Arellano, Rogelio. 1990. "On the Causes and Consequences of Real Exchange Rate Variability: A Comparative Analysis of the East Asian and Latin American Experiences." Ph.D. diss. University of California, Los Angeles, Department of Economics.

Aschauer, David Allan. 1989. "Does Public Capital Crowd out Private Capital?" *Journal of Monetary Economics* 24 (2): 171–88.

Aspe, Pedro. 1993. *Economic Transformation the Mexican Way.* Cambridge, Mass.: MIT Press.

Azariadis, Costas, and Allan Drazen. 1990. "Threshold Externalities in Economic Development." *Quarterly Journal of Economics* 105 (May): 501–26.

Balassa, Bela and Associates. 1971. *The Structure of Protection in Developing Countries.* Baltimore, Md.: Johns Hopkins University Press.

———. 1982. *Development Strategies in Semi-Industrial Economies.* Baltimore, Md.: Johns Hopkins University Press.

———. 1985. "Exports, Policy Choices, and Economic Growth in Developing Countries after the 1973 Oil Shock." *Journal of Development Economics* 18 (2): 23–25.

———. 1988. "Outward Orientation." In Hollis Chenery and T. N. Srinivasan, eds., *Handbook of Development Economics.* Amsterdam: North-Holland.

Baldinelli, Elvio. 1991. "Armonización de políticas fiscales, crediticias, y de promoción de exportaciones." *Instituto para la Integración de América Latina* 16 (May): 3–17.

Baliño, Tomás. 1991. "The Argentine Banking Crisis of 1980." In Tomás Baliño and Vasudevan Sundararajan, eds., *Banking Crisis: Cases and Issues.* Washington, D.C.: International Monetary Fund.

Banco Central de Chile. 1993. *Compendium of Rules on International Exchange.* Santiago.

———. Various years. *Boletín Mensual.* Santiago.

Bank of Mexico. 1995. *Exposición sobre política monetaria: para el lapso de enero de 1995–31 de diciembre de 1995.* Mexico City.

Barro, Robert. 1974. "Are Government Bonds Net Wealth?" *Journal of Political Economy* 81 (December): 1095–1117.

———. 1991. "Economic Growth in a Cross-Section of Countries." *Quarterly Journal of Economics* 106 (May): [407]–43.

Barros, Ricardo. 1992. "Welfare, Inequality, Poverty, and Social Conditions in Brazil in the Last Three Decades." Paper presented at the conference Poverty and Inequality in Latin America, Brookings Institution, Washington, D.C., July.

Becker, Gary S. 1983. "A Theory of Competition among Pressure Groups for Political Influence." *Quarterly Journal of Economics* 98 (August): 371–400.

Beristain, Javier, and Ignacio Trigueros. 1990. "Mexico." In John Williamson, ed., *Latin American Adjustment: How Much Has Happened?* Washington, D.C.: Institute for International Economics.

Bhagwati, Jagdish. 1978. *Foreign Trade Regimes and Economic Development: Anatomy and Consequences of Exchange Control Regimes.* Cambridge, Mass.: National Bureau of Economic Research.

Bianchi, Andrés, Robert Devlin, and Joseph Ramos. 1987. "The Adjustment Process in Latin America, 1981–1986." Paper presented at the World Bank and International Monetary Fund Symposium on Growth-Oriented Adjustment Programs, Washington, D.C., February.

Bianchi, Andrés, and Takahashi Nohara, eds. 1988. *A Comparative Study on Economic Development between Asia and Latin America.* Tokyo: Institute of Developing Economies.

Binswanger, Hans P., Klaus Deininger, and Gershon Feder. 1993. "Agricultural Land Relations in the Developing World." *American Journal of Agricultural Economics* 75 (December): 1242–48.

Blanchard, Olivier, and Stanley Fischer. 1989. *Lectures on Macroeconomics*. Cambridge, Mass.: MIT Press.

Boeninger, Edgardo. 1992. "Governance and Development: Issues, Challenges, Opportunities, and Constraints." *Proceedings of the World Bank Annual Conference on Development Economics 1991*. Washington, D.C.: World Bank.

Bonelli, Regis. 1992. "Growth and Productivity in Brazilian Industries: Impacts of Trade Orientation." *Journal of Development Economics* 39 (1): 85–109.

Boskin, Michael. 1978. "Taxation, Savings, and the Rate of Interest." *Journal of Political Economy* 86 (supplement: S3–S27).

Bosworth, Barry. 1993. *Saving and Investment in the Open Economy*. Washington, D.C.: Brookings Institution.

Bruno, Michael. 1991. "High Inflation and the Nominal Anchors of an Open Economy." Princeton Essays in International Finance 183. International Finance Section, Department of Economics, Princeton University, Princeton, N.J.

Buffie, Edward, and Allen Sangines. 1988. "Economic Policy and Foreign Debt in Mexico." In Jeffrey Sachs, ed., *Developing Country Debt and Economic Performance*. Vol. 2: *Country Studies*. Chicago, Ill.: University of Chicago Press.

Bulow, Jeremy, and Kenneth Rogoff. 1988. "The Buyback Boondoggle." *Brookings Papers on Economic Activity* 2: 675–98.

Caballero, Ricardo, and Vittorio Corbo. 1989. "The Effect of Real Exchange Rate Uncertainty on Exports: Empirical Evidence." *World Bank Economic Review* 3 (May): 263–78.

Calvacati de Albuquerque, Marcos. 1992. "A situação social: O que diz o passado e o que promete o futuro." Instituto de Pesquisa Economica Aplicada, Brasília.

Calvo, Guillermo. 1978. "On the Time Consistency of Optimal Policy in a Monetary Economy." *Econometrica* 46 (November): 1411–28.

———. 1986. "Fractured Liberalism: Argentina under Martínez de Hoz." *Economic Development and Cultural Change* 34 (3): 511–33.

———. 1988. "Controlling Inflation: The Problem of Non-Indexed Debt." Working Paper 29. International Monetary Fund, Research Department, Washington, D.C.

———. 1989. "Controlling Inflation: The Problem of Non-Indexed Debt." In Sebastian Edwards and Felipe Larraín, eds., *Debt, Adjustment, and Recovery*. Oxford, Eng.: Basil Blackwell.

———. 1994. "Comments on Dornbusch and Werner." *Brookings Papers on Economic Activity*, No. 1.

Calvo, Guillermo, and Carlos A. Vegh Gramont. 1991. "Exchange Rate–Based Stabilization under Imperfect Credibility." Working Paper 77. International Monetary Fund, Washington, D.C.

Calvo, Guillermo, Leonardo Leiderman, and Carmen Reinhart. 1993. "Capital Inflows and Real Exchange Rate Appreciation in Latin America: The Role of External Factors." *IMF Staff Papers* 40 (March).

Canavese, Alfredo. 1991. "Hyperinflation and Convertibility-Based Stabilization in Argentina." Paper presented at the Conference on Stabilization and Growth, Instituto Torcuato Di Tella, Department of Economics, Buenos Aires, August.

Cárdenas, Mauricio, and Miguel Urrutia. 1992. "Macroeconomic Instability and Social Progress." Fedesarrollo, Bogotá, December.

Cardoso, Eliana A., and Rudiger Dornbusch. 1987. "Brazil's Tropical Plan." *American Economic Review* 77 (2): 288–92.

———. 1989. "Foreign Private Capital Flows." In Hollis Chenery and T. N. Srinivasan, eds., *Handbook of Development Economics*. Amsterdam: North-Holland.

Cardoso, Eliana A., and Ann Helwege. 1991. "Populism, Profligacy, and Redistribution." In Rudiger Dornbusch and Sebastian Edwards, eds., *The Macroeconomics of Populism in Latin America*. Chicago, Ill.: University of Chicago Press.

———. 1992. "Below the Line: Poverty in Latin America." *World Development* 20 (1): 19–37.

Cardoso, Eliana, Ricardo Barros, and Andre Urani. 1993. "Inflation and Unemployment as Determinants of Inequality in Brazil: The 1980s." In Rudiger Dornbusch and Sebastian Edwards, eds., *Stabilization, Economic Reform, and Growth Conference*. Cambridge Mass.: National Bureau of Economic Research.

Cariaga, Juan. 1990. "Bolivia." In John Williamson, ed., *Latin American Adjustment: How Much Has Happened?* Washington, D.C.: Institute for International Economics.

Carroll, Chris, and Lawrence Summers. 1991. "Consumption Growth Parallels Income Growth." In D. Bernheim and J. Shoven, eds., *National Saving and Economic Performance*. Chicago, Ill.: University of Chicago Press and the National Bureau of Economic Research.

Carroll, Chris, and David N. Weil. 1993. "Savings and Growth: A Reinterpretation." Working Paper 4470. National Bureau of Economic Research, Cambridge, Mass.

Carroll, Lewis. 1872. *Through the Looking Glass: And What Alice Found There*. London: Macmillan.

Castañeda, Tarsicio. 1992. *Combating Poverty: Innovative Social Reforms in Chile during the 1980s*. San Francisco, Calif.: ICS Press.

Castro, Antonio, and Carlos Lessa. 1969. *Introducción a la economía: Un enfoque estructuralista*. Santiago: Editorial Universitaria.

Cavallo, Domingo. 1985. *Volver a crecer*. Buenos Aires: Editorial Sudamericana.

CEPAL (Comisión Económica para América Latina). 1985. "La pobreza en América Latina: Dimensiones y políticas." *Estudios e Informes de la CEPAL* 54. Santiago.

———. 1988. *Balance preliminar de la economía de América Latina y el Caribe*. Santiago.

———. 1989. *Políticas macroeconómicas y brecha externa: América Latina en los años ochenta*. Santiago.

———. 1991. *Statistical Yearbook of Latin America*. Santiago: Comisión Económica para América Latina y el Caribe.

———. 1992a. *Balance preliminar de la economía de América Latina y el Caribe*. Santiago.

———. 1992b. *Equidad y transformación productiva: Un enfoque integrado*. Santiago.

———. 1993. "Directorio sobre inversión extranjera en América Latina y el Caribe 1993: Marco legal e información estadística." Santiago.

———. Various years. *Economic Survey of Latin America*. Santiago.

———. Various years. *Statistical Yearbook for Latin America and the Caribbean*. Santiago.

Cheyre, Hernando. 1991. *La reforma previsional en Chile*. Santiago: CEPAL.

Cline, William. 1989. "From the Baker Plan to the Brady Plan." In Ishrat Husain and Ishac Diwan, eds., *Dealing with the Debt Crisis*. World Bank Symposium. Washington, D.C.

Cochrane, J. 1988. "How Big Is the Random Walk of GNP?" *Journal of Political Economy* 96 (October): 893–920.

Coes, Donald. 1991. "Brazil." In Michael Michaely, Armeane Choksi, and Demetris Papageorgiou, eds., *Liberalizing Foreign Trade*. New York: Basil Blackwell.

Corbo, Vittorio, Timothy Condon, and Jaime de Melo. 1985. "Productivity Growth, External Shocks, and Capital Inflows in Chile: A General Equilibrium Analysis." *Journal of Policy Modeling* 7 (3): 379–405.

Corbo, Vittorio, Jaime de Melo, and James Tybout. 1986. "What Went Wrong in the Southern Cone?" *Economic Development and Cultural Change* 34 (3): 607–40.

Corbo, Vittorio, and Klaus Schmidt-Hebbel. 1991. "Public Policies and Saving in Developing Countries." *Journal of Development Economics* 36 (1): 89–115.

Corden, Warner Max. 1966. "The Structure of a Tariff System and the Effective Protection Rate." *Journal of Political Economy* 74 (3).

———. 1972. "Monetary Integration." Essays in International Finance 93. Princeton University, Princeton, N.J., April.

———. 1984. "The Normative Theory of International Trade." In R. Jones and P. Kenen, eds., *Handbook of International Economics*. Vol. 1. Amsterdam: North-Holland.

———. 1991a. "Exchange Rate Policy in Developing Countries." In Jaime de Melo and A. Sapir, eds., *Trade Theory and Economic Reform*. Cambridge, Mass.: Basil Blackwell.

———. 1991b. "Macroeconomic Policy and Growth: Some Lessons of Experience." *Proceedings of the World Bank Annual Conference on Development Economics 1990*. Washington, D.C.: World Bank.

Cortázar, René. 1982. "Precios y remuneraciones." In *Modelo económico chileno: Trayectoria de una crítica*. Santiago: Editorial Aconcagua.

Cox-Edwards, Alejandra. 1984. "Three Essays on Labor Markets in Developing Countries." Ph.D. diss., University of Chicago, Department of Economics, Chicago, Ill.

———. 1992. "Economic Reforms and Labor Market Legislation in Latin America." California State University, Long Beach, Department of Economics.

Cuddington, John. 1986. "Capital Flight: Estimates, Issues, and Explanations." Princeton Studies in International Finance 58. Princeton University, Princeton, N.J.

Cukierman, Alex. 1992. *Central Bank Strategy, Credibility, and Independence*. Cambridge, Mass.: MIT Press.

Cukierman, Alex, Sebastian Edwards, and Guido Tabellini. 1992. "Seignorage and Political Instability." *American Economic Review* 82 (June): 537–55.

Cumby, Robert, and Richard Levich. 1987. "On the Definition and Magnitude of Recent Capital Flight." Working Paper 2275. National Bureau of Economic Research, Cambridge, Mass.

de Gregorio, José. 1992. "Economic Growth in Latin America." *Journal of Development Economics* 39 (1): [59]–84.

———. 1994. "Inflation, Growth, and Central Banks: Theory and Evidence." Paper presented at the Latin American Seminar on Economic Growth, sponsored by the World Bank and the Inter-American Development Bank, Bogotá, Colombia, June.

De Long, Bradford, and Lawrence Summers. 1991. "Equipment Investment and Economic Growth." *Quarterly Journal of Economics* 106 (May): [445]–502.

De Soto, Hernando. 1986. *El otro sendero*. Lima: Instituto Libertad y Democracia.

Devarajan, Shantayanan, and Dani Rodrik. 1992. "Do the Benefits of Fixed Exchange Rates Outweigh Their Costs? The CFA Zone in Africa." In Ian Goldin and Alan Winters, eds., *Open Economies: Structural Adjustment and Agriculture*. Cambridge, Eng.: Center for Economic Policy Research and Cambridge University Press.

Diamond, Peter, and Salvador Valdés-Prieto. 1994. "Social Security Reforms." In Barry Bosworth, Rudiger Dornbusch, and Raúl Labán, eds., *The Chilean Economy: Policy Lessons and Challenges.* Washington, D.C.: Brookings Institution.

Dias Carneiro, Dionisio. 1987. "El plan cruzado: Una temprana evaluación despues de diez meses." In José Antonio Ocampo, ed., *Planes antiinflacionarios recientes en la América Latina.* Special issue of *El Trimestre Económico* 54 (September).

Díaz-Alejandro, Carlos. 1970. *Essays on the Economic History of the Argentine Republic.* New Haven, Conn.: Yale University Press.

———. 1976. *Foreign Trade Regimes and Economic Development: Colombia.* New York: National Bureau of Economic Research.

———. 1981. "Southern Cone Stabilization Plans." In William Cline and Sidney Weintraub, eds., *Economic Stabilization in Developing Countries.* Washington, D.C.: Brookings Institution.

Diwan, Ishac, and Dani Rodrik. 1992. "External Debt, Adjustment, and Burden Sharing: A Unified Framework." Princeton Studies in International Finance 73. Princeton University, Princeton, N.J.

Dixit, Avinash. 1986. "Tax Policy in Open Economies." In Alan Auerbach and Martin Feldstein, eds., *Handbook of Public Economics.* Amsterdam: North-Holland.

Dornbusch, Rudiger. 1986. "Special Exchange Rates for Capital Account Transactions." *World Bank Economic Review* 1 (September): 3–33.

———. 1989a. "Los costos y beneficios de la integración económica regional: Una revisión." *Pensamiento Iberoamericano* 15 (January–June): 25–53.

———. 1989b. "Debt Problems and the World Macroeconomy." In Jeffrey Sachs, ed., *Developing Country Debt and the World Economy.* Chicago, Ill.: University of Chicago Press.

———. 1991a. "Credibility and Stabilization." *Quarterly Journal of Economics* 106 (August): 837–50.

———. 1991b. "Policies to Move from Stabilization to Growth." *Proceedings of the World Bank Annual Conference on Development Economics 1990.* Washington, D.C.: World Bank.

———. 1992. "Lessons from Experiences with High Inflation." *World Bank Economic Review* 6 (January): 13–31.

Dornbusch, Rudiger, and Sebastian Edwards. 1990. "Macroeconomic Populism." *Journal of Development Economics* 32 (2): 247–77.

Dornbusch, Rudiger, and Sebastian Edwards, eds. 1991. *Macroeconomic Populism in Latin America.* Chicago, Ill.: University of Chicago Press.

Dornbusch, Rudiger, and Stanley Fischer. 1993. "Moderate Inflation." *World Bank Economic Review* 7, 1 (January): 1–44.

Dornbusch, Rudiger, and Alejandro Werner. 1994. "Mexico: Stabilization, Reform and No Growth." *Brookings Papers on Economic Activity*, No. 1.

Easterly, William. 1993. "Explaining Miracles: Growth Regressions Meet the Gang of Four." Paper presented at the East Asian Seminar on Economics, National Bureau of Economic Research, San Francisco, Calif., June.

Edwards, Sebastian. 1984. "The Order of Liberalization of the External Sector in Developing Countries." Princeton Essays in International Finance 156. Princeton University, Princeton, N.J.

———. 1985. "Stabilization with Liberalization: An Evaluation of Ten Years of Chile's Experiment with Free Market Policies, 1973–1983." *Economic Development and Cultural Change* 32 (January): 223–54.

————. 1986a. "Country Risk, Foreign Borrowing, and the Social Discount Rate in an Open Developing Economy." *Journal of International Money and Finance* 5 (March, supplement: S79–S96).

————. 1986b. "Pricing of Bonds and Bank Loans in International Markets: An Empirical Analysis of Developing Countries' Foreign Borrowing." *European Economic Review* 30 (June): 565–89.

————. 1986c. "Stabilization with Liberalization: An Evaluation of Ten Years of Chile's Experience with Free Market Policies, 1973–1983." In Armeane Choksi and Demetris Papageorgiou, eds., *Economic Liberalization in Developing Countries.* Oxford, Eng.: Basil Blackwell.

————. 1988a. *Exchange Rate Misalignment in Developing Countries.* World Bank Occasional Paper 2, New Series. Baltimore, Md.: Johns Hopkins University Press.

————. 1988b. "Financial Deregulation and Segmented Capital Markets: The Case of Korea." *World Development* 16 (January): 185–94.

————. 1989a. "The Debt Crisis and Macroeconomic Adjustment in Latin America." *Latin American Research Review* 24 (3): 172–86.

————. 1989b. "Exchange Rate Misalignment in Developing Countries." *World Bank Research Observer* 4 (1): 3–21.

————. 1989c. "The International Monetary Fund and the Developing Countries: A Critical Evaluation." *Carnegie-Rochester Conference Series on Public Policy* 31 (autumn): 7–68.

————. 1989d. *Real Exchange Rates, Devaluation, and Adjustment: Exchange Rate Policy in Developing Countries.* Cambridge, Mass.: MIT Press.

————. 1991. "Capital Flows, Foreign Direct Investment, and Debt-Equity Swaps in Developing Countries." In Horst Siebert, ed., *Capital Flows in the World Economy.* Symposium 1990. Tübingen, Ger.: JBC Mohr.

————. 1992a. "The Sequencing of Structural Adjustment and Stabilization." ICEG Occasional Paper 34. International Center for Economic Growth, San Francisco, Calif.

————. 1992b. "Sequencing and Welfare: Labor Markets and Agriculture." In Ian Goldin and Alan Winters, eds., *Open Economies: Structural Adjustment and Agriculture.* Cambridge, Eng.: Center for Economic Policy Research and Cambridge University Press.

————. 1992c. "Trade Orientations, Distortions, and Growth in Developing Countries." *Journal of Development Economics* 39 (July): 31–57.

————. 1993a. "Exchange Rates, Inflation, and Disinflation: Latin American Experiences." Working Paper 4320. National Bureau of Economic Research, Cambridge, Mass.

————. 1993b. "Exchange Rates as Nominal Anchors." *Weltwirtschaftliches Archiv* 129 (1): 1–32.

————. 1993c. "Openness, Trade Liberalization, and Growth in Developing Countries." *Journal of Economic Literature* 31 (3).

————. 1993d. "The Political Economy of Inflation and Stabilization in Developing Countries." Working Paper 4319. National Bureau of Economic Research, Cambridge, Mass.

————. 1994a. "Trade Liberalization Reforms in Latin America: Recent Experiences, Policy Issues and Future Prospects." In Graham Bird and Ann Helwege, eds., *Latin America's Economic Future.* San Diego: Academic Press.

———. 1994b. "Why Are Latin America's Saving Rates so Low?" Working Paper. Latin America and Caribbean Region, World Bank, Washington, D.C.

Edwards, Sebastian, and Alejandra Edwards. 1991. *Monetarism and Liberalization: The Chilean Experiment.* Chicago, Ill.: University of Chicago Press.

———. 1992. "Markets and Democracy: Lessons from Chile." *The World Economy* 15 (March): 203–19.

Edwards, Sebastian, and Fernando Losada. 1994. "Fixed Exchange Rates, Inflation, and Macroeconomic Discipline." Working Paper 4661. National Bureau of Economic Research, Cambridge, Mass.

Edwards, Sebastian, and Miguel Savastano. 1988. "Latin America's Intra-Regional Trade: Evolution and Future Prospects." Working Paper 2738. National Bureau of Economic Research, Cambridge, Mass.

Edwards, Sebastian, and F. Sturzenegger. 1992. "Inflationary Inertia and Endogenous Indexation." Department of Economics, University of California, Los Angeles.

Edwards, Sebastian, and Guido Tabellini. 1991. "Explaining Fiscal Policies and Inflation in Developing Countries." *Journal of International Money and Finance* 10 (March, supplement: S16–S48).

Elías, Víctor. 1992. *Sources of Growth: A Study of Seven Latin American Economies.* San Francisco, Calif.: ICS Press.

Erzan, Refik, Kiroaki Kuwahara, Saratino Marchese, and Rene Vossenar. 1989. "The Profile of Protection in Developing Countries." *UNCTAD Review* 1 (1): 1–22.

Fajnzylber, Fernando. 1990. *Unavoidable Industrial Restructuring in Latin America.* Durham, N.C.: Duke University Press.

Feder, Gershon. 1983. "On Exports and Economic Growth." *Journal of Development Economics* 12 (February–April): 59–73.

Feldstein, Martin. 1980. "International Differences in Social Security and Saving." *Journal of Public Economics* 14 (October): 225–44.

Fernández, Arturo. 1992. "Deregulation as a Source of Growth in Mexico." Working Paper. Instituto Tecnológico Autónomo de México, Tizapán, Mexico.

Ferretti, Martina. 1991. "Latin America Survey: Foreign Investment Regimes." *International Financial Law Review* 10 (July): 30–35.

Ffrench-Davis, Ricardo. 1973. *Políticas económicas en Chile, 1952–1970.* Santiago: Ediciones Nueva Universidad.

———. 1990. "Debt and Growth in Chile: Trends and Prospects." In David Felix, ed., *Debt and Transfiguration? Prospects for Latin America's Economic Revival.* New York: Sharpe.

Ffrench-Davis, Ricardo, and Thomas Griffin. 1967. *Teoría del comercio internacional.* Mexico City: Fondo de Cultura Económica.

Fischer, Stanley. 1985. *Indexing, Inflation, and Economic Policy.* Cambridge, Mass.: MIT Press.

———. 1988. "Recent Developments in Macroeconomics." *The Journal of the Royal Economic Society* 98 (June): 294–339.

Fishlow, Albert. 1985. "Revisiting the Great Debt Crisis of 1982." In Kwang Suk Kim and David Ruccio, eds., *Debt and Development in Latin America.* North Bend, Ind.: University of Notre Dame Press.

———. 1987. "The State of Latin American Economics." In *Economic and Social Progress in Latin America.* Washington, D.C.: Inter-American Development Bank.

————. 1989. "Lessons of the 1890s to the 1980s." In Guillermo Calvo, Ronald Findlay, Pentti Kouri, and Jorge Braga de Macedo, eds., *Debt, Stabilization, and Development: Essays in the Honor of Carlos Díaz-Alejandro.* Oxford, Eng.: Wider and Basil Blackwell.

————. 1990. "The Latin American State." *Journal of Economic Perspectives* 4 (summer): 61–74.

————. 1991. "Liberalization in Latin America." In Tariq Banuri, ed., *Economic Liberalization: No Panacea.* Oxford, Eng.: Oxford University Press.

Fiszbein, Ariel, and George Psacharopoulos. 1992. "Income Inequality Trends in Latin America in the Eighties: A Decomposition Analysis." Paper presented at the conference Poverty and Inequality in Latin America, Brookings Institution, Washington, D.C., July.

Flaño, Nicolás, and Francisco Ochoa. 1993. "The Chilean Path to Democratic Consolidation: Equitable Growth and Stability." Paper presented at the conference Chile: Model for Latin America, University of Wisconsin, Milwaukee, September.

Fleisig, Heywood. 1992. "Infrastructure and Economic Growth in Latin America." World Bank, Latin America and Caribbean Region, Washington, D.C.

Flood, Robert, and Peter Isard. 1988. "Monetary Policy Strategies." Research Dept., *International Monetary Fund Staff Papers* 36 (3).

Folkerts-Landau, D. 1985. "The Changing Role of International Bank Lending in Development Finance." *IMF Staff Papers* (June).

Fontaine, Arturo. 1992. "Sobre el pecado original de la transformación capitalista chilena." In Barry Levine, ed., *El desafío neoliberal: El fin del tercermundismo en América Latina.* Bogotá: Editorial Norma.

Fontaine, Juan. 1989. "The Chilean Economy in the Eighties: Adjustment and Recovery." In Sebastian Edwards and Felipe Larraín, eds., *Debt, Adjustment, and Recovery.* Oxford, Eng.: Basil Blackwell.

Foxley, Alejandro. 1982. "Resuelve el modelo económico los problemas de fondo?" In *Modelo económico chileno: Trayectoria de una crítica.* Santiago: Editorial Aconcagua.

————. 1983a. "Después del monetarismo." In Alejandro Foxley, René Cortázar, Patricio Meller, Andrés Solimano, José Pablo Arellano, Ricardo Ffrench-Davis, and Oscar Muñoz, eds., *Reconstrucción económica para la democracia.* Santiago: CIEPLAN.

————. 1983b. *Latin American Experiments in Neoconservative Economics.* Berkeley, Calif.: University of California Press.

Frenkel, Jacob, Michael Dooley, and Peter Wickham, eds. 1989. *Analytical Issues in Debt.* Washington, D.C.: International Monetary Fund.

Frenkel, Roberto, and José María Fanelli. 1987. "El Plan Austral: Un año y medio después." In José Antonio Ocampo, ed., *Planes antinflacionarios recientes en la América Latina.* Special issue of *El Trimestre Económico* 54 (September).

Fry, Maxwell. 1988. *Money, Interest, and Banking in Economic Development.* Baltimore, Md.: Johns Hopkins University Press.

Fukuda, Shinichi. 1993. "The Conditional Convergence in East Asian Countries." Paper presented at the East Asian Seminar on Economics, National Bureau of Economic Research, San Francisco, Calif., June.

Furtado, Celso. 1969. *La economía latinoamericana desde la conquista ibérica hasta la revolución cubana.* Santiago: Editorial Universitaria.

Galal, Ahmed. 1993. "Regulation and Commitment in the Development of Telecommunications in Chile." World Bank Policy Research Working Paper Series 1278. Washington, D.C.

Galal, Ahmed, Raúl Saez, and Clemencia Torres. 1992. "Welfare Consequences of Selling Public Enterprises: Chile." In Ahmed Galal, Leroy Jones, Pankaj Tandon, and Ingo Vogelsang, *Welfare Consequences of Selling Public Enterprises: An Empirical Analysis.* New York: Oxford University Press, 1994.

Gallagher, David. 1992. "Chile: La revolución pendiente." In Barry Levine, ed., *El desafío neoliberal: El fin del tercermundismo en América Latina.* Bogotá: Grupo Editorial Norma.

García Márquez, Gabriel. 1970. *One Hundred Years of Solitude.* New York: Harper & Row.

Gavito Mohar, Javier, Sergio Sánchez García, and Ignacio Trigueros Legarreta. 1992. "Los servicios financieros y el acuerdo de libre comercio: Bancos y casas de bolsa." In *México y el tratado trilateral de libre comercio.* Mexico City: ITAM and McGraw-Hill.

Gelb, Alan. 1989. "Financial Policies, Growth, and Efficiency." Policy Research Working Paper 202. World Bank, Washington, D.C.

Gersovitz, Mark. 1989. "Savings and Development." In Hollis Chenery and T. N. Srinivasan, eds., *Handbook of Development Economics.* Amsterdam: North-Holland.

Gil Díaz, Francisco. 1988. "Macroeconomic Policies, Crisis, and Growth in the Long Run: Mexico Country Study." World Bank, Latin America and Caribbean Region, Washington, D.C.

———. 1992. "Mexico's Recent Economic Policy." Paper presented at the Latin American Economics Workshop, University of California, Los Angeles, Department of Economics, April.

Giovannini, Alberto. 1983. "The Interest Elasticity of Savings in Developing Countries: The Existing Evidence." *World Development* 11 (July): 601–7.

Glade, William. 1991. *Privatization of Public Enterprises in Latin America.* San Francisco, Calif.: ICS Press.

Glaessner, Thomas C. 1992. "Colombia: Securities Market Development." World Bank, Latin America and Caribbean Region, Washington, D.C.

Glaessner, Thomas C., and Ignacio Mas. 1991. "Incentive Structure and Resolution of Financial Institution Distress: Latin American Experience." LAC Technical Department Report 12. World Bank, Latin America and Caribbean Region, Washington, D.C.

Griffith-Jones, Stefany, and Osvaldo Sunkel. 1986. *Debt and Development Crises in Latin America: The End of an Illusion.* Oxford, Eng.: Oxford University Press.

Grosh, Margaret E. 1990. *Social Spending in Latin America: The Story of the 1980s.* World Bank Discussion Paper 106. Washington, D.C.

———. 1992. "From Platitudes to Practice: Targeting Social Programs in Latin America." LAC Human Resource Division Report 10720. World Bank, Latin America and Caribbean Region, Washington, D.C.

———. 1993. "Five Criteria for Choosing among Poverty Programs." Paper presented at the conference Confronting the Challenge of Poverty and Inequality in Latin America, Brookings Institution, Washington, D.C., July.

Grossman, Gene M., and Elhanan Helpman. 1990. "Comparative Advantage and Long-Run Growth." *American Economic Review* 80 (September): 796–815.

———. 1991. *Innovation and Growth in the Global Economy.* Cambridge, Mass.: MIT Press.

Gutentag, Jack, and Richard Herring. 1985. *The Current Crisis of International Lending.* Washington, D.C.: Brookings Institution.

Gylfason, Thorvaldur. 1993. "Optimal Saving, Interest Rates, and Endogenous Growth." Seminar Paper 539. University of Stockholm.

Hachette, Dominique, and Rolf Luders. 1992. "Privatization in Argentina and Chile: Lessons from a Comparison." LAC Internal Discussion Paper 18. World Bank, Latin America and Caribbean Region, Washington, D.C.

Haggard, Stephan, and Robert Kaufman, eds. 1992. *The Politics of Economic Adjustment: International Constraints, Distributive Conflicts, and the State.* Princeton, N.J.: Princeton University Press.

Haggard, Stephan, and Steven Webb. 1993. "What Do We Know about the Political Economy of Economic Policy Reform?" *World Bank Research Observer* 8 (July): 143–68.

Hanson, James A. 1992. "Opening the Capital Account: A Survey of Issues and Results." Policy Research Working Paper 901. World Bank, Washington, D.C.

Hanson, James A., and Craig R. Neal. 1986. *Interest Rate Policies in Selected Developing Countries, 1970–1982.* World Bank Staff Working Paper 753. Washington, D.C.

Harberger, Arnold. 1959. "Using the Resources at Hand More Efficiently." *American Economic Review* 49 (May): 134–46.

———. 1971. "Three Basic Postulates of Applied Welfare Economics." *Journal of Economic Literature* 9 (September): 785–97.

———. 1972. "Investment in Men versus Investment in Machines: The Case of India." In Arnold Harberger, ed., *Project Evaluation: Collected Papers.* Chicago, Ill.: University of Chicago Press.

———. 1982. "The Chilean Economy in the 1970s: Crisis, Stabilization, Liberalization, Reform." In Karl Brunner and Allan Metzler, eds., *Economic Policy in a World of Change.* Carnegie-Rochester Conference Series on Public Policy 17. Amsterdam: North-Holland.

———. 1985a. "Lessons for Debtor-Country Managers and Policymakers." In Gordon Smith and John Cuddington, eds., *International Debt and the Developing Countries.* Washington, D.C.: World Bank.

———. 1985b. "Observations on the Chilean Economy, 1973–1983." *Economic Development and Cultural Change* 33 (April): 451–62.

———. 1990. "Towards a Uniform Tariff Structure." University of Chicago, Department of Economics, Chicago, Ill.

———. 1992. "The Sources of Economic Growth and Economic Liberalization, with Application to Mexico for the 1990s." University of California, Los Angeles, Department of Economics.

Hayashi, Fumio. 1986. "Why Is Japan's Saving Rate so Apparently High?" In NBER *Macroeconomics Annual 1986.* Cambridge, Mass.: MIT Press.

Heitger, Bernhard. 1987. "Import Protection and Export Performance: Their Impact on Economic Growth." *Weltwirtschaftliches Archiv* 132 (2).

Herrera, Alejandra. 1993. "The Privatization of Telecommunications Services: The Case of Argentina." *Columbia Journal of World Business* 28 (spring): 46–61 (reprint).

Hicks, Norman. 1992a. "The Role of the World Bank in the Latin American Reform Process." World Bank, Latin America and Caribbean Region, Washington, D.C.

———. 1992b. "Trends in Government Expenditures and Revenues in Latin America, 1975–1988." LAC Internal Discussion Paper. World Bank, Latin America and Caribbean Region, Washington, D.C.

Hill, Alice, and Manuel Abdala. 1993. "Regulation, Institutions, and Commitment: Privatization and Regulation in the Argentine Telecommunications Sector." World Bank, Policy Research Working Paper 1216. Washington, D.C.

Hirschman, Albert O. 1968. "The Political Economy of Import Substituting Industrialization in Latin America." *Quarterly Journal of Economics* 82 (February): 1–32.

———. 1987. "La economía política del desarrollo latinoamericano: Siete Ejercicios en Retrospectiva." *El Trimestre Económico* 54 (October–December): 769–804.

———. 1988. "How Keynes Was Spread from America." *Challenge* 31 (November): 4–7.

Ibarra, Luis. 1992. "Credibility of Trade Policy Reform: The Mexican Experience." Ph.D. diss., University of California, Los Angeles, Department of Economics.

IFC (International Finance Corporation). Various years. *Quarterly Review of Emerging Stock Markets.* Washington, D.C.

Iglesias, Enrique. 1990. "From Policy Consensus to Renewed Economic Growth." In John Williamson, ed., *Latin American Adjustment: How Much Has Happened?* Washington, D.C.: Institute for International Economics.

———. 1992. *Reflections on Economic Development: Toward a New Latin American Consensus.* Washington, D.C.: Inter-American Development Bank.

Iglesias, Enrique, and L. Emmerij, eds. 1991. *Restoring Financial Flows to Latin America.* Paris: Organization for Economic Cooperation and Development.

IMF (International Monetary Fund). Various years. *Annual Report (of the Board of Directors).* Washington, D.C.

———. Various years. *Annual Report on Exchange Rate Arrangements and Exchange Rate Restrictions.* Washington, D.C.

———. Various years. *Government Financial Statistics.* Washington, D.C.

———. Various years. *International Financial Statistics.* Washington, D.C.

———. Various years. *World Economic Outlook.* Washington, D.C.

Inter-American Dialogue. 1992. *Convergence and Community: The Americas in 1993.* Washington, D.C.

ITAM (Instituto Tecnológico Autónomo de México). 1992. *México y el tratado trilateral de libre comercio.* Mexico City: ITAM and McGraw-Hill.

———. 1994. *Lo negociado del tratado de libre comercio.* Mexico City: ITAM and McGraw-Hill.

Jappelli, Tulio, and Marco Pagano. 1994. "Saving, Growth, and Liquidity Constraints." *Quarterly Journal of Economics* 109 (February): 83–109.

Jaspersen, Frederick. 1992. "External Resource Flows to Latin America: Recent Developments and Prospects." Working Paper 116. Inter-American Development Bank, Washington, D.C.

Kamin, Steven. 1991. "Argentina's Experience with Parallel Exchange Markets: 1981–1990." International Finance Discussion Paper 407. Board of Governors of the Federal Reserve System, Washington, D.C., August.

Kessel, Georgina. 1992. "El sector petroquímico mexicano ante la integración del mercado norteamericano." In ITAM, *México y el tratado trilateral de libre comercio.* Mexico City: ITAM and McGraw-Hill.

Kiguel, Miguel Alberto. 1991. "Inflation in Argentina: Stop and Go since the Austral Plan." *World Development* 19 (8): 969–86.

Kiguel, Miguel Alberto, and Nissan Liviatan. 1992. "The Business Cycle Associated with Exchange Rate Stabilizations." *World Bank Economic Review* 6 (May): 279–305.

Kikeri, Sunita, John Nellis, and Mary Shirley. 1992. *Privatization: The Lessons of Experience.* Washington, D.C.: World Bank.

Kim, Kwang Suk. 1991. "Korea." In Michael Michaely, Armeane Choksi, and Demetris Papageorgiou, eds., *Liberalizing Foreign Trade.* New York: Basil Blackwell.

King, Robert, and Ross Levine. 1993a. "Finance and Growth: Schumpeter Might Be Right." *Quarterly Journal of Economics* 108 (August): 717–37.

————. 1993b. "Finance, Entrepreneurship, and Growth." Paper presented at the conference How Do National Policies Affect Long-Term Growth? World Bank, Washington, D.C., February.

Klaus, Václav. 1991. "A Perspective on Economic Transition in Czechoslovakia and Eastern Europe." Paper presented at the annual conference Development Economics 1990, World Bank, Washington, D.C.

Korean Development Institute. 1989. *Korea's Macroeconomic and Financial Policies.* KDI/11E Proceedings, Conference Series 89–3. Seoul.

Krueger, Ann. 1978. *Foreign Trade Regimes and Economic Development: Liberalization Attempts and Consequences.* Cambridge, Mass.: National Bureau of Economic Research.

————. 1980. "Trade Policy as an Input to Development." *American Economic Review* 70 (2).

————. 1981. *Trade and Employment in Developing Countries.* Chicago, Ill.: University of Chicago Press.

————. 1983. *Exchange Rate Determination.* Cambridge, Eng.: Cambridge University Press.

————. 1990. *Perspectives on Trade and Development.* Exeter, Eng.: Harvester Wheatsheaf.

————. 1993. "East Asian Experience and Endogenous Growth Theory." Paper presented at the East Asian Seminar on Economics, National Bureau of Economic Research, San Francisco, Calif., June.

Krugman, Paul R. 1979. "A Model of Balance of Payments Crises." *Journal of Money, Credit, and Banking* 11 (3): 311–25.

————. 1988. "Financing vs. Forgiving a Debt Overhang." Working Paper 2486. National Bureau of Economic Research, Cambridge, Mass.

Kydland, Finn, and Edward Prescott. 1977. "Rules Rather Than Discretion: The Inconsistency of Optimal Plans." *Journal of Political Economy* 85 (3): 473–92.

Kyle, J., and Jeffrey Sachs. 1984. "Developing Country Debt and the Market Value of Large Commercial Banks." Working Paper 1470. National Bureau of Economic Research, Cambridge, Mass.

Laffont, Jean-Jaques, and Jean Tirole. 1993. *A Theory of Incentives in Procurement and Regulation.* Cambridge, Mass.: MIT Press.

Lago, Ricardo. 1991. "The Illusion of Pursuing Redistribution through Macropolicy: Peru's Heterodox Experience, 1985–1990." In Rudiger Dornbusch and Sebastian Edwards, eds., *The Macroeconomics of Populism in Latin America.* Chicago, Ill.: University of Chicago Press.

Lal, Deepak. 1985. *The Real Aspects of Stabilization and Structural Adjustment Policies: An Extension of the Australian Adjustment Model.* World Bank Staff Working Paper 636. Washington, D.C.

Lamdany, Ruben. 1988. *Voluntary Debt-Reduction Operations: Bolivia, Mexico, and Beyond.* World Bank Discussion Paper 42. Washington, D.C.

Larraín, Felipe. 1988. "Debt Reduction and the Management of Chilean Debt." World Bank, Latin America and Caribbean Region, Washington, D.C.

Larraín, Felipe, and Patricio Meller. 1991. "The Socialist-Populist Chilean Experience: 1970–1973." In Rudiger Dornbusch and Sebastian Edwards, eds., *The Macroeconomics of Populism in Latin America.* Chicago, Ill.: University of Chicago Press.

Larraín, Felipe, and Andrés Velasco. 1990. "Can Swaps Solve the Debt Crisis? Lessons from the Chilean Experience." Princeton Studies in International Finance 69. Princeton University, Princeton, N.J.

Latin Finance. Various years. Miami, Fla.

Leamer, Edward. 1990. "Latin America as a Target of Trade Barriers Erected by the Major Developed Countries in 1983." *Journal of Development Economics* 32 (April): 337–68.

Leff, Nathaniel. 1968. *Economic Policy-making and Development in Brazil, 1947–1964.* New York: Wiley.

Lefort, Fernando, and Andrés Solimano. 1994. "Economic Growth after Market-Based Reform in Latin America: The Cases of Chile and Mexico." Working Paper. World Bank, Macroeconomics and Growth Division, Washington, D.C.

Leipziger, Danny, and Vinod Thomas. 1993. *The Lessons of East Asia: An Overview of Country Experience.* Washington, D.C.: World Bank.

Lewis, Arthur. 1955. *The Theory of Economic Growth.* London: Allen and Unwin.

Lin, Ching-Yuan. 1988. "East Asia and Latin America as Contrasting Models." *Economic Development and Cultural Change* 36 (S153–197, April).

Little, Ian, Tibor Scitovsky, and Maurice Scott. 1970. *Industry and Trade in Some Developing Countries.* Oxford, Eng.: Oxford University Press.

Losada, Fernando. 1993. "Partners, Neighbors, and Distant Cousins: Explaining Bilateral Trade Flows in Latin America." Working Paper. University of California, Los Angeles, Department of Economics.

————. 1994. "The Uruguay Round, GATT, and Regionalism." World Bank, Latin America and Caribbean Region, Washington, D.C.

Lucas, Robert E., Jr., 1988. "On the Mechanics of Economic Development." *Journal of Monetary Economics* 22 (July): 3–42.

————. 1993. "Making a Miracle." *Econometrica* 61 (March): 251–72.

Luders, Rolf. 1991. "Massive Divestiture and Privatization: Lessons from Chile." *Contemporary Policy Issues* 9 (October): 1–19.

Luders, Rolf, and Beatriz Arbildua. 1968. "Una evaluación comparada de tres programas anti-inflacionarios en Chile: una década de historia monetaria 1956–1966." *Cuadernos de Economía* 5 (April): 25–105.

Lustig, Nora. 1994. *The Future of Trade Policy in Latin America.* Washington, D.C.: Brookings Institution.

Maddison, Angus. 1985. *Two Crises: Latin America and Asia, 1929–38 and 1973–83.* Paris: Organization for Economic Cooperation and Development.

Marfán, Manuel, and Barry Bosworth. 1994. "Savings, Investment, and Economic Growth." In Barry Bosworth, Rudiger Dornbusch, and Raul Labán, eds., *The Chilean Economy: Policy Lessons and Challenges.* Washington, D.C.: Brookings Institution.

Márquez, Gustavo. 1992. "Poverty and Social Policies in Venezuela." Paper presented at the conference Poverty and Inequality in Latin America, Brookings Institution, Washington, D.C., July.

Martin, Ricardo D. 1992. "Sources of Growth in Latin America." World Bank, Latin America and Caribbean Region, Washington, D.C.

McGreevey, William Paul. 1990. *Social Security in Latin America: Issues and Options for the World Bank.* World Bank Discussion Paper 110. Washington, D.C.

McKinnon, Ronald. 1973. *Money and Capital in Economic Development.* Washington, D.C.: Brookings Institution.

———. 1982. "The Order of Economic Liberalization: Lessons from Chile and Argentina." *Carnegie-Rochester Conference Series on Public Policy* 17 (autumn).

———. 1991. *The Order of Economic Liberalization: Financial Control in the Transition to a Market Economy.* Baltimore, Md.: Johns Hopkins University Press.

Meller, Patricio, Ernesto Livacich, and Patricio Arrau. 1984. "Una Revision del Milagro Economico Chileno 1975–1981." *Coleccion Estudios CIEPLAN,* Santiago, Chile, Vol. 15 (December): 5–109.

Mesa-Lago, Carmelo. 1991. *Social Security and Prospects for Equity in Latin America.* World Bank Discussion Paper 140. Washington, D.C.

Michaely, Michael. 1985. "Demand for Protection against Exports of Newly Industrializing Countries." *Journal of Policy Modeling* 7 (spring): 123–32.

Michaely, Michael, Armeane Choksi, and Demetris Papageorgiou, eds. 1991. *Liberalizing Foreign Trade.* New York: Basil Blackwell.

Mill, John Stuart. 1884. *Principles of Political Economy.* New York: Appleton and Co.

Mincer, Jacob. 1965. "Investment in Human Capital and Personal Income Distribution." *Journal of Political Economy* 66 (3).

Modigliani, Franco. 1980. "The Life Cycle Hypothesis of Savings Twenty Years Later." In Michael Parkin, ed., *Contemporary Issues in Economics.* Manchester, Eng.: Manchester University Press.

Molina, Sergio. 1982. "Poverty: Description and Analysis of Policies for Overcoming It." Comisión Económica para América Latina, Santiago. CEPAL Review 18 (December): 87–110.

Montes-Negret, Fernando. 1988. "Colombia's Financial Sector." World Bank, Latin America and Caribbean Region, Washington, D.C.

Morales, Juan Antonio. 1987. "Estabilización y nueva política económica en Bolivia." In José Antonio Ocampo, ed., *Planes antiinflacionarios recientes en la América Latina.* Special issue of *El Trimestre Económico* 54 (September).

Morgan Guaranty and Trust Company. 1987. "World Financial Markets." Morgan Guaranty International Economics Department, New York.

Morley, Samuel. 1992. "Macroconditions and Poverty in Latin America." Inter-American Development Bank, Washington, D.C.

Morris, Felipe, Mark Dorfman, José Pedro Ortiz, and María Claudia Franco. 1990. *Latin America's Banking Systems in the 1980s: A Cross-Country Comparison.* World Bank Discussion Paper 81. Washington, D.C.

Musgrove, Philip. 1991. "Feeding Latin America's Children: An Analytical Survey of Food Programs." LAC Technical Department, Regional Studies Program Report 11. World Bank, Latin America and Caribbean Region, Washington, D.C.

Nam, Chon-Hyun. 1993. "The Role of Trade and Exchange Rate Policy in Korea's Growth." Paper prepared for East Asian Seminar on Economics, National Bureau of Economic Research, San Francisco, Calif., June.

Newfarmer, Richard. 1992. "Argentina: Fiscal Assessment." World Bank, Latin America and Caribbean Region, Washington, D.C.

Newman, John, Steen Jorgensen, and Menno Pradhan. 1991. "How Did Workers Benefit from Bolivia's Emergency Social Fund." *World Bank Economic Review* 2 (5): 367–93.

Nogués, Julio. 1990. "The Experience of Latin America with Export Subsidies." *Weltwirtschaftliches Archiv* 126 (1): 97–115.

Nogués, Julio, and Sunil Gulati. 1992. "Economic Policies and Performance under Alternative Trade Regimes: Latin America during the 1980s." LAC Technical Department Report 16. World Bank, Latin America and Caribbean Region, Washington, D.C.

Nogués, Julio, and Rosalinda Quintanilla. 1992. "Latin America's Integration and the Multilateral Trading System." Paper presented at the conference New Dimensions in Regional Integration, World Bank and CEPR, Washington, D.C.

North, Douglass. 1989. "Institutions and Economic Growth: An Historical Introduction." *World Development* 17 (9): 1319–332.

———. 1990. *Institutions, Institutional Change, and Economic Performance.* Cambridge, Eng.: Cambridge University Press.

OAS (Organization of American States). 1992. *Statistical Bulletin.* Washington, D.C.

Ocampo, José Antonio. 1989. "Colombia and the Latin American Debt Crisis." In Sebastian Edwards and Felipe Larraín, eds., *Debt, Adjustment, and Recovery: Latin America's Prospects for Growth and Development.* Oxford, Eng.: Basil Blackwell.

———. 1991a. "Determinants and Prospects for Medium-Term Growth in Colombia." Paper presented at the conference The Colombian Economy: Issues of Debt, Trade, and Development, Lehigh University, Department of Economics, Bethlehem, Penn., April.

———. 1991b. "Trade Policy and Industrialization in Colombia, 1967–1991." Paper presented at the conference Trade and Industrialization in LDCs, WIDER, Paris, September.

Ocampo, José Antonio, ed. 1987. *Planes antiinflacionarios recientes en la América Latina.* Special issue of *El Trimestre Económico* 54 (September).

Oks, Daniel. 1994. "Structural Reforms and Productivity Growth: Sectoral Analysis for Chile and Mexico." Paper presented at the Cross Fertilization Seminar Series, World Bank, Latin America and Caribbean Region, Washington, D.C.

Ortiz, Javier. 1993. "The Early History of Central Banking in Latin America: Legal Independence and Monetary Policies." Working Paper. University of California, Los Angeles, Department of Economics.

Oum, Baum. 1989. "Korea's Real Exchange Rate Policy in the 1980s: Evaluation and Prospects." In *Korea's Macroeconomic and Financial Policies.* Conference Series 89–3. Seoul: Korean Development Institute.

Paz, Pedro, and Osvaldo Sunkel. 1971. *El subdesarrollo latinoamericano y la teoría del desarrollo.* Madrid: Siglo Veintiuno de España.

Pérez-Campanero, Juan, and Alfredo Leone. 1991. "Liberalization and Financial Crisis in Uruguay, 1974–1987." In Tomás Baliño and Vasudevan Sundararajan, eds., *Banking Crisis: Causes and Issues.* Washington, D.C.: International Monetary Fund.

Persson, Torsten, and Guido Tabellini. 1990. *Macroeconomic Policy, Credibility, and Politics.* New York: Harwood Academic Publishers.

Philippe, Bernard. 1991. "The Chilean Electric Power Sector in the Last Decade: The Design and Implementation of New Policy." Universidad Católica de Chile, Department of Economics, Santiago.

Pinto, A., and Osvaldo Sunkel. 1966. "Latin American Economists in the United States." *Economic Development and Cultural Change* 15 (October): 79–86.

Prebisch, Raúl. 1947. *Introducción a Keynes.* Mexico City: Fondo de Cultura Económica.

———. 1950. "Commercial Policy in the Underdeveloped Countries." *American Economic Review* 40 (2).

———. 1984. "Five Stages in My Thinking on Development." In Dudley Seers, ed., *Pioneers in Development.* Oxford, Eng.: Oxford University Press.

Presidencia de la República del Perú. 1986. *Plan Nacional de Desarrollo.* Lima.

Psacharopoulos, George. 1992. "Poverty and Income Distribution in Latin America and the Caribbean." World Bank, Latin America and Caribbean Region, Washington, D.C.

———. 1993. "Human Resources in Latin America and the Caribbean: Priorities and Action." World Bank, Latin America and Caribbean Region, Washington, D.C.

Psacharopoulos, George, and Ariel Fiszbein. 1991. "A Cost-Benefit Analysis of Educational Investment in Venezuela, 1989." World Bank, Latin America and Caribbean Region, Washington, D.C.

Psacharopoulos, George, and Ying Ng. 1992. "Earnings and Education in Latin America: Assessing Priorities for Schooling Investments." Working Paper 1056. World Bank, Latin America and Caribbean Region, Washington, D.C.

Pyo, Hak. 1993. "A Time-Series Test on the Endogenous Growth Model with Human Capital." Paper presented at the East Asian Seminar on Economics, National Bureau of Economic Research, San Francisco, Calif., June.

Rabello de Castro, Paulo, and Mauricio Ronci. 1991. "Sixty Years of Populism in Brazil." In Rudiger Dornbusch and Sebastian Edwards, eds., *The Macroeconomics of Populism in Latin America.* Chicago, Ill.: University of Chicago Press.

Ramírez, G. G., and Francisco Rosende. 1992. "Responding to the Collapse: Chilean Banking Legislation after 1983." In Philip Brock, ed., *If Texas Were Chile: A Primer on Banking Reform.* San Francisco, Calif.: ICS Press.

Ramos, Joseph. 1986. *Neoconservative Economics in the Southern Cone of Latin America, 1973–1983.* Baltimore, Md.: Johns Hopkins University Press.

Rebelo, Sergio. 1991. "Long Run Policy Analysis and Long Run Growth." *Journal of Political Economy* 99 (June): 500–21.

Rodríguez, Carlos. 1982. "The Argentine Stabilization Plan of December 20th." *World Development* 10 (9): 801–11.

———. 1994. "Interest Rates in Latin America." Working Paper. World Bank, Latin America and Caribbean Region, Washington, D.C.

Rodrik, Dani. 1993. "Trade and Industrial Policy Reform in Developing Countries: A Review of Recent Theory and Evidence." Working Paper 4417. National Bureau of Economic Research, Cambridge, Mass.

———. 1994. "King Kong Meets Godzilla: The World Bank and the East Asian Miracle." Working Paper. Overseas Development Council, Washington, D.C.

Romer, Paul. 1986. "Increasing Returns and Long-Run Growth." *Journal of Political Economy* 94 (October): 1002–37.

———. 1989. "Capital Accumulation in the Theory of Long-Run Growth." In Robert Barro, ed., *Modern Business Cycle Theory.* Cambridge, Mass.: Harvard University Press.

Roubini, Nouriel, and Xavier Sala-i-Martin. 1992. "Financial Repression and Economic Growth." *Journal of Development Economics* 39 (July): 5–30.

Saborio, Sylvia, and Constantine Michalopoulos. 1992. "Central America at a Crossroads." Policy Research Working Paper 922. World Bank, Europe and Central Asia Country Department III, Washington, D.C.

Sachs, Jeffrey. 1981. "The Current Account and Macroeconomic Adjustment in the 1970s." *Brookings Papers on Economic Activity* 1: 201–68.

———. 1987. "Trade and Exchange Rate Policies in Trade-Oriented Adjustment Programs." In Vittorio Corbo, Morris Goldstein, and Mohsin Khan, eds., *Growth-Oriented Adjustment Programs.* Washington, D.C.: International Monetary Fund.

———. 1988. "Conditionality, Debt Relief, and the Developing Country Debt Crisis." Working Paper 2644. National Bureau of Economic Research, Cambridge, Mass.

———. 1989a. "The Debt Overhang of Developing Countries." In Guillermo Calvo, Ronald Findlay, Pentti Kouri, and Jorge Braga de Macedo, eds., *Debt, Stabilization, and Development: Essays in the Honor of Carlos Díaz-Alejandro.* Oxford, Eng.: Wider and Basil Blackwell.

———, ed. 1989b. *Developing Country Debt and the World Economy.* Chicago, Ill.: University of Chicago Press.

———. 1989c. "New Approaches to the Latin American Debt Crisis." Princeton Essays in International Finance 174. Princeton University, Princeton, N.J.

Sachs, Jeffrey, and D. Cohen. 1986. "Growth and External Debt under Risk of Potential Repudiation." *European Economic Review* 30 (3, June): 529–60.

Samuelson, Paul. 1954. "The Pure Theory of Public Expenditure." *Review of Economics and Statistics* 36 (November): 387–89.

Sánchez, Manuel. 1992. "Entorno macroeconómico frente al tratado de libre comercio." In *México y el tratado trilateral de libre comercio.* Mexico City: ITAM and McGraw-Hill.

Sargent, T. 1983. "Stopping Moderate Inflations: The Methods of Poincaré and Thatcher." In Rudiger Dornbusch and M. Simonsen, eds., *Inflation, Debt, and Indexation.* Cambridge, Mass.: MIT Press.

Schott, Jeffrey. 1991. "Trading Blocks and the World Trading System." *World Economy* 14 (March): 1–17.

Schultz, T. W. 1961. "Investment in Human Capital." *American Economic Review* 51 (March): 1–17.

———. 1980. "Nobel Prize Address." *Journal of Political Economy* 88 (August): 639–51.

Seabright, Paul. 1993. "Infrastructure and Industrial Policy in South Asia: Achieving the Transition to a New Regulatory Environment." South Asia Seminar Series, University of Cambridge, Department of Economics, Cambridge, Eng.

Selowsky, Marcelo. 1969. "On the Measurement of Education's Contribution to Growth." *Quarterly Journal of Economics* 83 (August): 449–63.

———. 1992. "Latin America: Protecting Children's Nutrition during the Adjustment." *Bank's World* 11 (February): 9–11, Washington, D.C.: World Bank.

Selowsky, Marcelo, and Herman van der Tak. 1986. "The Debt Problem and Growth." *World Development* 14 (9): 1107–24.

Shaw, Edward. 1973. *Financial Deepening in Economic Development.* New York: Oxford University Press.

Sheahan, John. 1987. *Patterns of Development in Latin America: Poverty, Repression, and Economic Strategy.* Princeton, N.J.: Princeton University Press.

Shome, Parthasarathi. 1994. "Recent Tax Policy Trends and Issues in Latin America." Working Paper. Fiscal Affairs Department, International Monetary Fund, Washington, D.C.

Singer, Hans. 1950. "The Distribution of Gains between Investing and Borrowing Countries." *American Economic Review* 40 (2): 473–85.

Solís, Leopoldo. 1988. "Raúl Prebisch at ECLA: Years of Creative Intellectual Effort." Occasional Paper 10. International Center for Economic Growth, San Francisco, Calif.

Spiller, Pablo. 1992. "Institutions and Regulatory Commitment in Utilities Privatization." Working Paper 51. Institute for Policy Reform, Washington, D.C.

Spulber, Daniel F. 1989. *Regulation and Markets.* Cambridge, Mass.: MIT Press.

Stigler, George. 1971. "The Theory of Economic Regulation." *Bell Journal of Economics* 2 (spring): 3–21.

Stiglitz, Joseph E. 1994. "The Role of the State in Financial Markets." *Proceedings of the World Bank Annual Conference on Development Economics 1993.* Washington, D.C.

Stiglitz, Joseph, and Andrew Weiss. 1981. "Credit Rationing in Markets with Imperfect Information." *American Economic Review* 71 (3): 393–410.

Sturzenegger, Federico. 1992. "Bolivia: Stabilization and Growth." University of California, Los Angeles, Department of Economics.

Summers, Robert, and Alan Heston. 1988. "A New Set of International Comparisons of Real Product and Price Level Estimates for 130 Countries." *Review of Income and Wealth* 34 (March).

Sunkel, Osvaldo. 1960. "Inflation in Chile: An Unorthodox Approach." *International Economic Papers* 10 (August).

Tandon, Pankaj. 1992. "World Bank Conference on the Welfare Consequences of Selling Public Enterprises: Case Studies from Chile, Malaysia, Mexico, and the U.K." World Bank, Washington, D.C., June.

Taylor, Lance. 1989. "Gap Disequilibria: Inflation, Investment, Saving, and Foreign Exchange." Working Paper (International) 76. United Nations University, World Institute for Development Economics Research, New York.

———. 1991. "Economic Openness: Problems to the Century's End." In Tariq Banuri, ed., *Economic Liberalization: No Panacea.* New York: Clarendon Press.

Thomas, Vinod. 1986. *Linking Macroeconomic and Agricultural Policies for Adjustment with Growth: The Colombian Experience.* Baltimore, Md.: Johns Hopkins University Press.

———. 1988. "Issues in Adjustment Lending." Policy, Planning, and Research Working Paper 2. Country Economics Dept., World Bank, Washington, D.C.

Thorp, Rosemary. 1992. "Reappraisal of the Origins of Import-Substituting Industrialization, 1930–1950." *Journal of Latin American Studies* 24: 181–95 (supplement).

Tironi, Ernesto. 1989. *Es posible reducir la pobreza.* Centro de Estudios del Desarrollo, Santiago.

El Trimestre Económico. Various issues. Fondo de Cultura Económica, Mexico City.

Tybout, James. 1992. "Linking Trade and Productivity: New Research Directions." *World Bank Economic Review* 6 (2): 189–211.

Uchimura, Kazuko, and Hong Gao. 1993. "The Impact of Infrastructure on Economic Development." World Bank, Latin America and Caribbean Region, Washington, D.C.

UNCTAD (United Nations Conference on Trade and Development). 1987. *Handbook of Trade Control Measures of Developing Countries.* Geneva.

UNDP (United Nations Development Programme). 1992. *Human Development Report, 1992.* New York: Oxford University Press.

UNICEF (United Nations Children's Fund). Various years. *The State of the World's Children.* New York: Oxford University Press.

Valdés, Alberto. 1992. "The Performance of the Agricultural Sector in Latin America." World Bank, Latin America and Caribbean Region, Washington, D.C.

Valdés, Jorge. 1989. *La Escuela de Chicago: Operación Chile.* Buenos Aires: Editorial Universitaria de Buenos Aires.

van Wijnbergen, Sweder. 1990. "Mexico in Transition: Toward a New Role for the Public Sector." World Bank, Latin America and Caribbean Region, Washington, D.C.

Velasco, Andrés. 1992. "Políticas de estabilización y teoría de juegos." *Colección Estudios CIEPLAN* 21 (May).

Velez, F., and G. Rubio. 1994. "El impacto del tratado de libre comercio en el campo mexicano." In Instituto Tecnológico Autónomo de México, *Lo negociado del tratado de libre comercio.* Mexico: McGraw-Hill.

Vuskovic, Pedro. 1970. "Distribución del ingreso y opciones de desarrollo." *Cuadernos de la Realidad Nacional* 7 (September).

Wade, Robert. 1994. "Is the Miracle Study Right That Selective Industrial Policies in Northeast Asia Are Unimportant?" Working Paper. Overseas Development Council, Washington, D.C.

Walton, Gary, ed. 1985. *The National Economic Policies of Chile.* Greenwich, Conn.: JAI Press.

Weiss, John. 1992. "Trade Policy Reform and Performance in Manufacturing: Mexico, 1975–1988." *Journal of Development Studies* 29 (October): 1–23.

WHO (World Health Organization). Various years. *Global Nutritional Status: Anthropometric Indicators.* Geneva: World Health Organization, Nutritional Unit, Division of Family Health.

Williamson, John. 1991. "Advice on the Choice of an Exchange Rate Policy." In Emil-Maria Claasen, ed., *Exchange Rate Policies in Developing and Post-Socialist Countries.* San Francisco, Calif.: ICS Press.

Williamson, John, ed. 1981. *Exchange Rate Rules: The Theory, Performance, and Prospects of the Crawling Peg.* New York: St. Martin's Press.

———. 1990. *Latin American Adjustment: How Much Has Happened?* Washington, D.C.: Institute for International Economics.

Willig, Robert. 1994. "Public versus Regulated Private Enterprise." *Proceedings of the World Bank Annual Conference on Development Economics 1993*. Washington, D.C., May.

Wisecarver, Daniel. 1985. "Economic Regulation and Deregulation in Chile, 1973–1983." In Gary Walton, ed., *National Economic Policies of Chile*. Greenwich, Conn.: JAI Press.

Wolff, Lawrence, Ernesto Schiefelbein, and Jorge Valenzuela. 1993. "Improving the Quality of Primary Education in Latin America: Towards the 21st Century." Regional Studies Program Report 28. World Bank, Latin America and Caribbean Region, Washington, D.C.

World Bank. 1993a. *The East Asian Miracle: Economic Growth and Public Policy*. New York: Oxford University Press.

———. 1993b. "Human Resources in Latin America and the Caribbean: Priorities and Action." Human Resource Division, Latin America and Caribbean Region, Washington, D.C.

———. 1994. *Trends in Developing Economies 1994*. Washington, D.C.

———. Various years. *Financial Flows to Developing Countries*. Washington, D.C.

———. Various years. *Social Indicators of Development*. Washington, D.C.

———. Various years. *World Debt Tables*. Washington, D.C.

———. Various years. *World Development Report*. New York: Oxford University Press.

———. Various years. *World Tables*. Baltimore, Md.: Johns Hopkins University Press.

Yepes, Guillermo, Luis Gutierrez, and Peter Gyamfi. 1992. "Infrastructure Maintenance in Latin America: The Costs of Neglect and Options for Improvement." LAC Technical Report 17. World Bank, Latin America and Caribbean Region, Washington, D.C.

Zuleta, Luis Alberto, Lino Jaramillo, Carlos Eduardo Bollén, Ana María Gómez, Juan Pablo Trujillo, Nubia Angarita, Tránsito Porras, and Gustavo Ramírez. 1992. "Privatización en Colombia: Experiencia y perspectivas." Working Paper 120. Inter-American Development Bank, Washington, D.C.

Index

Abnormal Importations Act (U.K., 1931), 43
Abortions, 267–68
Act of La Paz, 154, 155
Act of Barahona, 155–56
Administradoras de Fondos de Pensiones (AFP), 217
Aeroméxico, 193
Agacino, R., 133
Age structure of population, 270, 281
Agrarian reforms, 252
Agriculture, 45, 132, 159, 243; trade in, 135, 136, 159, 161
Alessandri, Jorge, 47, 170
Alfa Group, 20
Alfonsín administration, 36, 218
Allende Gossens, Salvador, 47, 173, 186
Altimir, Oscar, 258
Alvarez, Luis Echeverría, 18
Andean Pact, 11, 142, 154–56, 179, 246
APRA Plan, 5, 18, 37–39
Argentina, 24, 119, 179, 276; Austral Plan of, 5, 33–36; banking sector in, 106, 202, 203, 205, 207, 308; debt conversion programs of, 73, 79, 218, 219; financial reforms of, 211, 218–20; foreign debt in, 26, 90; heterodox stabilization attempts of, 33, 69; inflation in, 86, 97; market-oriented reforms in, 8, 9, 41, 42, 53; monetary policy in, 27, 35, 91; participation in MERCOSUR by, 149, 152; privatization in, 170, 176, 178, 194–99, 222, 311; regulatory framework in, 182, 197–98; social unrest in, 5; stock market in, 212, 213, 219–20; tax reform in, 97–99; trade liberalization in, 121–22, 128, 131
Aschauer, David Allan, 244–45
Aspe, Pedro, 42
Association of Southeast Asian Nations (ASEAN), 142
Asunción Treaty, 152
Austral Plan, 5, 33–36, 39–40
Automobiles, 159
Aylwin Azócar, Patricio, 53, 54, 86, 95, 191, 217
Azariadis, Costas, 273

Balassa, Bela, 56, 117
Banking sector: commercial, 73, 221, 223; failures or public bailouts of, 91, 202, 215, 216, 222; participation in debt-reduction agreements by, 70; privatization of publicly owned banks, 122, 175, 186, 215; publicly owned, 177, 204, 218, 219, 220–21; regulation or supervision of, 202–3, 215, 221; reserve requirements for,

Banking sector (*continued*)
208, 211, 216, 218, 219. *See also*
Central banks
Bankruptcy, 301
Barro, Robert, 166, 167, 240
Bianchi, Andrés, 48, 52
Bilateral assistance, 289, 305
Bilateral trade agreements, 142, 149,
159
Bilingual education, 310
Boeninger, Edgardo, 55
Bolivia, 142, 155, 203, 311; debt
buyback scheme of, 74–75; export
sector in, 134, 137; financial sector
in, 211, 220–22; inflation in, 220;
interest rates in, 221; labor market in,
280, 281; poverty and social
problems in, 260, 266, 267, 274, 275;
private investment in, 221;
privatization in, 170, 171; public
sector deficit in, 305–6; social
investment funds and, 58; social
programs in, 287, 288; trade
liberalization in, 125, 131, 155
Bonds: collateralized, 77, 79, 81, 107,
140; par, 81, 107; secondary market
for, 19–21, 26
Bosworth, Barry, 5, 133
Brady, Nicholas, 79
Brady Plan, 26, 32, 70, 84, 105;
agreements reached under, 73, 79–82
Brazil, 10, 21, 24, 105, 281; Cruzado
Plan of, 5, 18, 36–37; economy of, 8,
33, 47, 69, 136; financial sector in,
202, 204; foreign debt of, 17–18, 73,
79, 82; foreign ownership in, 179;
inflation in, 90–91; investment in,
24; participation in MERCOSUR by,
142, 152; poverty and social
problems in, 259–60, 261, 267, 270,
274; privatization in, 178, 311; social
security program of, 270; stock
market in, 213; trade policy of, 56–57
Budgets, fiscal, 99, 304, 308
Buenos Aires Stock Exchange, 219–21

Campos, Roberto, 47

Capital account adjustments, 122
Capital flight, 18, 23, 29, 31, 204
Capital gains tax, 87
Capital inflows, 141, 215, 298; halt in,
29, 254, 299; monetary pressures
accompanying, 28, 82, 92, 97, 137–
42, 306–7; short-term versus long-
term, 141–42, 302. *See also* Foreign
investment; Foreign lending
Capital markets, 12, 200, 201
Cárdenas, Mauricio, 260
Caribbean Community (CARICOM),
11, 71, 125, 158
Caribbean Free Trade Association
(CARIFTA), 157
Cartagena Accord, 246
Cavallo, Domingo, 42, 99, 196, 220
Central American Common Market
(CACM), 11, 156–57
Central banks, 75, 91, 103, 218; Bank
of Mexico, 297, 298, 299;
independence of, 96, 106, 308–9
CEPAL, 44, 45, 49, 200; shift in
perspective of, 41, 52–53
Chamorro, Violeta, 85, 289
Chiapas state uprising (Mexico), 5, 10,
159, 298, 304
Chile, 22–23, 24, 53, 81, 115, 245, 275,
281; debt-conversion schemes of, 75–
76; domestic savings in, 227–29;
economic policy and trade reform in,
128, 131, 134–36; exchange rate
policies in, 111–12, 141; export
sector in, 134–37, 141; financial
reforms of, 209, 211, 214–18, 308;
financial sector in, 106, 190, 202,
203, 207–8, 215; fiscal policies of, 86,
91; interest rates in, 27, 28;
investment in, 24, 248; market
orientation in, 41, 47, 56;
privatization in, 170, 171, 175, 176,
177, 178, 180, 183, 186–91; reform
process in, 9, 10, 53–55, 177, 178,
186–87, 304, 305; regulatory
framework in, 183, 187; socialist or
antimarket strategies in, 47, 54; social
programs in, 268, 287–88, 290–91;

social security system in, 178, 273;
tax reform in, 95–96; trade
liberalization in, 121–23
Choksi, Armeane, 120, 123
CIEPLAN, 53, 54
Civil service reform, 13, 309
Clinton, Bill, 245, 296
CODELCO copper mines, 171, 180
Collor de Melo, Fernando, 57, 86
Colombia, 23, 24, 142, 279, 281, 308;
export policies of, 118; foreign debt
of, 81, 82; domestic bonds (OMAs) of,
140; privatization in, 180; reforms in,
41, 92, 106; social issues in, 261, 266,
274, 276, 280; trade policy in, 57,
125, 128, 155
Colosio, Luis Donaldo, 298, 304
Commodity prices, 22
Competitiveness, 302, 310
Computerized tax collection, 97
Concertación coalition, 95
Conflict resolution, 283–86, 311
Conglomerates, local, 186, 187, 198
Construction, 89
Consumer welfare, 180, 305
Consumption, 32, 78
Convertibility Law (Argentina), 99,
198, 218, 219
Corruption, 173
Costa Rica, 10, 88; debt reduction
agreements of, 73, 79; education in,
274, 276; financial sector in, 204;
poverty and economic growth in,
131, 261; trade liberalization in, 131
Credit (domestic), 23, 24, 102;
constraints on, 105, 239; nonmarket
or direct, 205–6, 208, 211, 212, 219;
policies concerning, 26, 27–29, 36,
91–92, 99, 102, 105, 299; sectoral
allocation of, 205
Credit ratings, 202
Cruzado Plan (Brazil), 5, 18, 36–37,
39–40
Currency, 45; creation of, 38, 83, 111;
devaluation of, 24, 25, 38, 39, 43,
102, 123. See also Exchange rate
Current account balance, 225, 240;

deficit in, 4, 22, 24, 32, 123, 138;
importance of to Mexico's peso crisis,
298, 302; sustainability of, 314–17
Customs unions, 117
Debt crisis (1982), 5, 6, 9, 174, 254,
288, 295; economic effects of, 17, 53,
59, 69, 81–82, 207–8, 225, 254;
effect on employment and wages of,
262–63; market anticipation and
reaction to, 19, 21; origins of, 22–23;
underestimation of, 18–20, 69, 71–72
Debt (domestic), 69, 90, 199
Debt-equity swaps, 70, 73, 76, 106
Debt-for-development swaps, 107
Debt (foreign), 4, 17–18, 199, 302; and
debt-overhang problem, 11, 70, 105;
interest payments on, 26, 69, 81–82
Debt reduction, 69, 77, 78, 79, 81, 107;
agreements restructuring debt-service,
32, 71, 73, 106–7; buyback or
conversion schemes for, 74–76, 79, 107
Decentralization, 38, 98–99, 310
Declaration of San Salvador, 156
Deficits. *See* Current account balance;
Fiscal deficits or imbalances; Trade
deficits
Deindexation, 36, 104
Demand (aggregate), 36, 38, 70, 91
Democracy, 256, 306
Dependencistas, 47
Deregulation, 12, 40, 56, 58
Devaluation, currency, 24, 25, 38, 39,
43, 102, 109, 123, 300
Development strategies, 1–4, 59
Díaz-Alejandro, Carlos, 43
Dirigisme, 6, 12, 312
Dismissal, costs associated with, 278–
83, 309–10, 313
Dispute resolution, 283–86, 311
Distortions; economic, 9, 132; labor
market, 122, 130, 277–78; trade, 103,
166, 262
Divestiture. *See* Privatization
Domestic debt, 69, 90, 199
Domestic savings, 95, 208, 225, 228,
230–38, 239; and economic growth,
224, 225, 226; and investment, 225,

Domestic savings (*continued*)
227, 248; in Latin America and East
Asia compared, 229, 239–40, 298,
307; private, 238–40, 298; public,
240–42, 307
Dominican Republic, 266, 276, 311;
public sector deficit in, 305–6
Dooley, Michael, 78
Dornbusch, Rudiger, 120, 261, 264
Drazen, Allen, 273

East Asian economies: compared with
Latin American, 5, 52, 212, 229,
239–40, 252, 307; debt crisis of
compared with Latin American, 4–5,
42, 49–50, 51–53; education and,
273, 274, 277; exchange rate policies
of, 104; export policies of, 4–5, 49–
52; labor markets in, 310; as
"miracle" economies, 5, 51–52, 183,
243, 277, 313; state bureaucracy and,
311
Economic crises, 9, 187; debt crisis
(1982), 17, 53, 59, 69, 81–82, 207–8,
225, 254. *See also* Macroeconomic
instability
Economic growth, 56, 81, 105, 315;
and poverty, 255–56, 261–64, 291,
312, 313; infrastructure and, 105,
244; trade liberalization and, 119–20.
See also Productivity growth
Economic monitoring, 58
Economic policy: inward orientation in,
2, 44, 52; outward orientation in, 49,
50; traditional, 9, 43–48, 59
Ecuador, 9, 26, 134, 142, 155;
privatization in, 170, 171, 311; social
problems or issues in, 266, 279
Education, 12, 50, 179, 252, 267;
economic growth and, 274, 310;
income distribution and, 258–59,
260; in Latin America, 275–77, 304,
312; voucher systems of, 310
Edwards, Sebastian, 120, 261, 264
Ejido system, 132
Electricity, 179, 196
El Salvador; poverty and social

problems in, 260, 274; public sector
deficit in, 305–6; social programs in,
289
Employment, 261–62, 312, 313;
economic growth and, 262; effect of
debt crisis on, 262–63; layoffs, 178,
187; protective regulation regarding,
278–83, 309–10; trade liberalization
and, 121–22. *See also*
Unemployment; Wages
ENTEL (Argentina), 179
Entitlement programs, 291
Environmental protection, 159, 305
"Equilibrium portfolio share," 314–16
Ethnic factors, 266
European Economic Community
(EEC), 142
European Monetary System, 102
Exchange rate, 26, 49, 50, 57, 91, 104,
118; anchored or fixed nominal, 11,
38, 53, 99, 101–4, 302; anchors and
inflationary inertia, 107–14;
appreciation of real, 103–4, 122,
137–42, 302; depreciation or
devaluation of real, 29, 128, 133, 134;
flexible– or crawling peg, 29, 100–
101, 114, 128; flexible or floating, 22,
101, 105–6, 301; inflation and, 70,
97, 99–101, 104, 105, 137, 141, 218;
multiple, 26, 29, 31; overvaluation of
real, 22–23, 39, 52, 58, 103, 105,
117, 261, 302, 306; pressure of
capital inflows on, 11, 122, 300; trade
liberalization and, 120, 122–23, 128–
29, 140–41
Expenditure-reduction policies, 26–29,
89
Expenditure-switching policies, 29–32
Exports, 82, 118–20, 148, 276; and
anti-export bias, 117, 120; East
Asian policies on, 46, 49–52, 134,
156; industrial, 161, 310;
nontraditional, 124, 136, 137;
subsidies of, 140, 161, 206; trade
reform and, 133–37
Externalities, 171, 244–45
External shocks, 174, 298

Fajnzylber, Fernando, 52–53
Family planning, 266–68
Fertility rates, 267, 275
Financial deregulation, 200, 208, 212
Financial markets, 12, 307; barriers to entry into, 208, 211; productivity growth and, 249–51; regulation of, 202, 204–6, 208, 211, 212; repressive control of, 200–201, 203–8; risky behavior by, 206–7; supervisory requirements of, 221, 223. *See also* Banking sector; Investment
Financial reform, 55, 84, 86, 209–11
Financial shocks, 104
Financial uncertainty, 70–71, 219
Financieras (Chile), 215
Fiscal adjustments, 39, 69, 83, 92
Fiscal deficits or imbalances, 27, 69, 74, 174, 311; quasi-, 91
Fiscal policy, 34–36; austerity or reform in, 84–91, 105–6; budgetary process, 99, 304, 308; sustainability in, 105–6. *See also* Monetary policy
Fiscal surpluses, 95
Fiszbein, Ariel, 258, 259
Food subsidies, 268, 269
Foreign debt. *See* Debt (foreign)
Foreign investment, 6, 76, 87, 297; determinants of, 248; direct, 138, 149, 246–48; guaranteed, 219; portfolio, 138, 299, 314–16; regulation of, 161; restrictions on, 246
Foreign lending, 4, 17–18, 57
Foreign ownership, 179–80, 190
Foxley, Alejandro, 54–55
Franco, Itamar, 179
Frenkel, Jacob, 78
Fujimori, Alberto, 42, 155, 304

"Gang of Four," 274
García, Alán, 33, 37, 38, 173
GATT (General Agreement on Tariffs and Trade), 159, 160–61
Gaviria, César, 42, 223
Global markets or economy, 6, 300, 303

González, Felipe, 42
Government, 58–59, 170; credibility issues in, 101, 182–83; reducing role of, 48, 196. *See also* Institutional reform; Public finance; Public policy; State-building
Government control or intervention, 1, 4, 47–48, 49; in financial markets, 200–201, 202, 203–8. *See also* Regulatory framework
Great Depression, 43
Grossman, Gene M., 120
Growth (economic). *See* Economic growth
Grupos (local conglomerates), 186, 187, 215
Guatemala; health indicators in, 266; poverty and social problems in, 260, 266, 267, 274; social programs in, 289
Guyana, 158

Haggard, Stephan, 9
Haiti, 274
Health, 12, 179, 252, 260, 265–66, 312
Health services, 266, 269
Helpman, Elhaman, 120
Heterodox stabilization programs, 11, 33, 38; failure of, 40, 42, 48, 56, 69
Honduras, 203, 274, 307; poverty and social problems in, 260, 266, 267; social programs in, 289
Hong Kong, 274
Human development, 260, 264
Human resources, 43, 50, 167, 252, 262; policies regarding, 12, 58, 249, 262, 287
Hyperinflation, 39, 85, 86, 97, 194, 198, 220, 261

Iglesias, Enrique, 48
Illiteracy, 259, 260
IMF (International Monetary Fund), 1, 5, 26, 57, 86, 100; actions of in debt crisis, 17, 20, 21, 78; supporting reforms, 9, 55–58

Imports, 24, 158, 160, 317; duty-free, 134. *See also* Quotas; Tariffs

Import-substitution policies, 18, 44–46, 115

Income, real or per capita, 18, 260, 288

Income distribution, 26, 84, 252; efforts to improve, 37, 39, 86; inequities in, 1, 13, 45, 48, 119, 173, 256, 258, 264, 304; lack of data on, 256–57;

Income distribution (*continued*) in Latin America compared to East Asia, 5, 252; macroeconomic instability and, 260–61. *See also* Poverty

Income and Expenditures Commission (Mexico), 192, 193

Income tax, 87, 96

Indexation; inflation and, 36, 101, 108–11; in tax system, 95; of wages, 37, 53, 104, 114

Indigenous populations, 266, 310

Individual retirement accounts, 178, 273

Industrial exports, 161

Industrial production, 45, 130

Industrial subsidies, 44–45, 51, 54, 119

Inertia: economic, 97, 104; inflationary, 107–14

Infant mortality, 254, 260, 266

Inflation, 45, 138; policies against, 11, 22, 69, 70, 137; decline in, 9, 35, 37; deficit finance and, 55, 83–84, 90; exchange rate policy and, 70, 97, 99–101, 104, 106, 137, 141; high or variable rate of, 18, 27, 38, 69, 260; hyper-, 39, 85, 86, 97, 194, 198, 220, 261; in Latin America compared to East Asia, 5, 52; savings discouraged by, 203, 227

Inflationary inertia, and exchange rate anchors, 107–14

Inflation tax, 26, 167, 201, 291

Information processing, 201, 202

Infrastructure, 244, 245–46; deteriorated or inadequate, 6, 89, 244–45; investment in, 43, 58, 243–44, 304, 308; investment in reduced, 24, 105

Institute of Developing Economies, 52

Institutional reform, 57, 69, 96, 106, 304, 309–11

Intellectual property, 161, 310–11

Interest groups, 48, 118, 296

Interest payments, 26, 69, 81–82, 90

Interest rates, 12, 90, 239, 306, 315; ceilings on, 38, 200, 204, 208; domestic savings and, 225–27; deregulation of, 208, 211, 215; high or appreciation of, 122, 220, 221; negative real, 204–5, 212; regional increase of, 22, 27; worldwide decline of, 22

Internal debt. *See* Debt (domestic)

International markets or economy, 6, 300, 303

International media, 6, 20, 296

International reserves, 123, 139, 297, 300, 316. *See also* Reserve requirements

Intraregional trade, 142, 148, 149, 155

Investment, 304; domestic savings and, 224–25; infrastructural, 43, 58, 243–44, 304, 308; private, 24, 95, 243; public, 24, 26, 95, 105, 242–46. *See also* Foreign investment

Investment credits, 96

Jamaica, 58, 88, 158, 291

Japan, 142, 212, 239

Jobs. *See* Employment

Judiciary systems, 136, 182, 311

Jujuy province uprising (Argentina), 5

Kaufman, Robert, 9

Keynesian theory, 200

King, Robert, 201–2, 249

Korea, Republic of, 50, 212, 273, 274; trade policy of, 49–51, 121–22

Krueger, Anne, 118

Labor intensity, 313

Labor-management relations, 283–86

Labor market, 13, 39, 173, 178, 301; age structure of, 270, 281; costs associated with, 278–83, 309–10; distortions in, 122, 130, 132, 277–78,

309–10, 313; reform or deregulation of, 12, 55, 59, 123. *See also* Employment; Human resources; Unions

Land reforms, 252

Large enterprise divestiture, 175

Latin America: education in, 274–77; effects of 1982 debt crisis on, 49–50, 51–53; effects of 1994 peso crisis on, 297, 303; poverty in, 252–54, 312, 313; state-building for, 58–59, 304–5, 309. *See also* individual countries

Latin American Consensus, 40–43, 58–59, 65, 314

Law of Coparticipation (Argentina), 98

Law of Navigation and Maritime Trade (Mexico), 194

Lefort, Fernando 133

Legal systems, 136, 182, 311

Levine, Ross, 201–2, 249

Lewis, Arthur, 224

Life expectancy, 254, 260, 266

Liquidation, 222

Liquidity, 299, 300

Literacy, 259, 260

Loans, nonperforming, 211

Lobbying activities, 118, 119

López Portillo, José, 18, 20

Losada, Fernando, 218

Macroeconomic adjustment, 9, 48, 69, 70, 71, 105–6, 177, 300–301; prudent management policies of, 305–9

Macroeconomic equilibrium, 136, 256

Macroeconomic instability, 69, 84, 105, 118, 260, 295, 306–7

Madrid, Miguel de la, 21

Manufacturing sector, 1, 54, 118, 192; productivity of, 132–33, 136; subsidy of, 44–45, 51, 54, 119

Marfán, Manuel, 133

Market-oriented reforms, 5, 6–10, 67, 295–96; as condition for lending, 57–58; consolidation or deepening of, 303–5; credibility or sustainability of, 8, 13, 105–6, 211, 264, 297;

emerging consensus for, 40–43, 58–59, 65; factors behind, 42–43, 48, 55–56; readiness for, 303. *See also* Financial reform; Trade openness or liberalization

Markets. *See* Financial markets; Securities markets

Martínez de Hoz, 130

Marxist economics, 46, 47

McKinnon, Ronald, 122, 201

Media (international), 6, 20, 296

Menem, Carlos, 41, 86, 97, 196, 198, 218, 220

MERCOSUR (Mercado Común del Sur), 11, 142, 149–53

Mexicana Airlines, 193

Mexico, 20, 21, 24, 39–40, 248; central bank of, 106, 297, 298, 299, 308; Chiapas state uprising in, 5, 10, 159, 298, 304; debt and debt restructuring programs in, 26, 73, 77–78, 79; deregulation or regulatory reform in, 192, 193–94; domestic savings in, 227–29, 298; economic growth or productivity in, 132–33, 298, 302; exchange rate policy of, 112–14, 300–301; exports or export policy of, 118, 136, 137; financial sector in, 104, 206, 207, 301; fiscal policy of, 26, 91, 298–99; foreign ownership in, 179, 180; investment in, 24, 243, 296; market-oriented reforms in, 9, 42, 297; nontariff barriers in, 125, 127; oil reserves or production in, 18, 136, 243; Pacto de Solidaridad Social of, 39–40, 192, 299; privatization in, 57, 170, 176, 180, 191–94; social problems in, 256, 260, 261, 268, 279, 305; social programs in, 268, 287, 289, 301; stock market in, 212, 213, 214; tax reform in, 96–97; trade policy of, 26, 32, 125, 131–32, 297

Mexico's peso crisis (1994), 6, 10, 13, 42, 58, 92, 141, 295; adjustment program following, 300–301; anticipation of, 298, 299; capital inflows and, 298, 299, 302; causes of,

Mexico's peso crisis (1994) (*continued*)
82, 138–39, 214, 298–301; current
account balance and, 298, 302;
effects of, 297, 303; fixed exchange
rate and, 103; lessons of, 296, 301–3,
305, 309, 314
Michaely, Michael, 120, 123
Middle class, 291, 292
Military expenditures, 179, 243, 292,
307
Mill, John Stuart, 120
Minimum wage, 252, 278, 313
"Miracle" economies. *See* East Asian
economies
Monetary policy, 22, 24, 27, 45, 108,
306; expansionist, 38, 83, 102;
indirect instruments of, 91–92;
reform in, 35, 36, 104. *See also*
Exchange rate
Money creation, 38, 83, 111
Monopolies, 175, 196
Morley, Samuel, 260
Motor vehicles, 159
Multilateral institutions, 159, 160, 217,
305; reforms fostered by, 9, 42, 55–
58, 78. *See also* IMF (International
Monetary Fund); World Bank
Multilateral Investment Guarantee
Agency, 219
Mutual funds, 299

NAFTA (North American Free Trade
Agreement), 86, 158–60, 297, 298
National Bureau of Economic
Research, 50
Nationalization, 20, 47
NATO (North Atlantic Treaty
Organization), 86, 158–60, 297, 298
Natural gas, 196
Neostructuralism, 48
Neves, Trancredo, 21
New economic convergence, 11
Nicaragua, 9, 47, 267, 274, 281, 308;
economy of, 57, 288–89; financial
sector in, 177, 203, 204; social
investment in, 58, 289
Nogués, Julio, 159
Nohara, Takahashi, 48, 52

Nontariff barriers, 29, 31–32, 125–27,
160
Nutrition, 12, 252, 254, 268–69, 275,
312

OECD (Organization for Economic
Cooperation and Development), 159
Oil reserves or production: in
Argentina, 197; in Mexico, 18, 136,
243
Oil shock, 4, 17, 47, 173

Pacto de Solidaridad Social, 39–40,
192, 299
Papageorgiou, Demetris, 120, 123
Paraguay, 142
Par bonds, 81, 107
Payroll taxes, 283
Pension funds, 178, 217
Pérez, Carlos Andrés, 41
Peru, 9, 134, 142, 281; APRA Plan of, 5,
18, 37–39; economy of, 203, 243,
281; foreign debt in, 26; stabilization
attempts of, 33, 69; trade policy of,
125, 128, 155
Peso crisis. *See* Mexico's peso crisis
(1994)
Philippines, 121–22
Piñera, Sebastian, 258
Pinochet, Augusto, 53–54, 55
Plan Nacional de Desarrollo (Peru), 37–
38
Poincare, Raymond, 110
Political gridlock or polarization, 71,
83, 264
Political reform, 6, 9–10, 84
Political stability, 58
Political uncertainty or instability, 5, 8,
21, 59, 92, 187, 242, 243, 298
"Popular capitalism," 190
Population growth, 266–68
Populist policies, 6, 12, 39, 41, 45, 291,
303, 312
Portfolio investment, 138, 299;
"equilibrium portfolio share," 314–16
Poverty, 48, 59, 173, 252–54; debt crisis
and, 254; defining and identifying,
255, 256, 257–58, 290; economic

growth and, 261–64; factors related to, 258–60, 312. *See also* Income distribution

Poverty-alleviation programs. *See* Social programs

Prebisch, Raúl, 44, 200

Price controls or freezes, 18, 34, 36, 37, 38, 39, 41; release of, 39

Price inertia, 141

Primavera Plan (Argentina), 218

Privatization, 170–72, 174–76, 184–85, 245; of banks, 122, 175, 186, 215; effect on public finances, 177–80; efficiency of, 180–81, 198–99, 311; increasing public revenues through, 70, 86, 174, 175; programs toward, 5, 9, 12, 41, 45, 57, 58, 89, 96, 219; sequencing of, 176–77; of utilities, 89, 182, 308; welfare consequences of, 180–81

Productivity growth, 99, 124, 305; financial development and, 201–2, 249–51; trade policy and, 130–33, 164–66, 302

Property rights, 132, 136, 310, 311

Protectionism, 44, 56, 115–17, 159, 295; disguised, 161; economic consequences of, 117–19; outside Latin America, 43, 49

Psacharopoulos, George, 98, 256, 258–59, 274

Public finance: expenditures, 18, 22, 26, 244–45, 301; productivity and, 249; reform of, 55, 84, 86. *See also* Fiscal policy; Social security systems; Tax administration

Public goods theory, 202, 212

Public investment, 24, 26, 95, 105, 242–46. *See also* Infrastructure; Social programs

Public offerings, 197

Public policy; inward orientation of, 2, 44, 52; outward orientation of, 49, 50; political factors affecting, 52, 69–70, 83–84, 103, 106, 127, 243; populist, 6, 12, 39, 41, 45

Public savings, 240–41

Public service prices, 34, 86, 98–99

Public utilities, privatization of, 89

Public works programs, 301

Quasi-fiscal deficits, 91

Quintanilla, Rosalinda, 159

Quotas, 26, 32, 160

Ramos, Joseph, 48

Raw materials, demand for, 43

Rebelo, Sergio, 224

Recession, 140, 286

Reform Act of 1989 (Argentina), 196

Reform. *See* Market-oriented reforms

Regional trading blocs, 11, 46, 58, 142

Regulatory framework, 173, 181–83, 187, 190, 197–98; building of, 304–5, 307, 308; of financial markets, 202, 204–6, 208, 211, 212

Rent-seeking activities, 1, 44, 119

Reserve requirements, 208, 211, 216; public debt and, 218; rationalization of, 219, 220. *See also* International reserves

Resource transfers, negative, 11, 24, 78, 82, 138, 244, 316

Retraining, 301

Ricardian equivalence doctrine, 240

Risk, 315; agencies rating, 202, 216; risky behavior, 206–7

Rivas, Gonzalo, 133

Road construction, 89

Román, Enrique, 133

Romer, Paul, 119-20

Roubini, Nouriel, 166

Ruiz Massieu, José, 298

Rules of origin, 159

Sachs, Jeffrey, 18, 52

Sala-i-Martin, Xavier, 166

Sales tax, 95. *See also* Value-added tax

Salinas, Carlos, 191, 297

Sanitation, 266

Sarney, José, 36

Savings. *See* Domestic savings

School enrollment, 254, 275

School food programs, 269

Secondary bond market, 19–21, 26; debt-reduction schemes and, 73,

Secondary bond market (*continued*)
74–78; discounted bonds in, 79, 81;
sale of collateralized bonds in, 77;
sale of par bonds in, 81
Securities markets, 221, 222–23;
actions before and during debt crisis,
19, 21; stock markets and, 212–14,
219, 222–23. *See also* Investment;
Speculation
Securities transfer tax, 219
Seigniorage, 83, 84
Selowsky, Marcelo, 78
Serra Puche, Jaime, 297
Service sector, 132, 161
Severance pay, 178, 199, 278–81
Sewerage facilities, 266
Shares distribution, 174, 176, 190
Silva Herzog, Jesús, 20
Singapore, 274
Smoot-Hawley Tariff (1930), 43
Social agreement, 40
Social expenditures, 58, 245, 260
Social problems or issues, 12, 13, 286–
87; and health, 179, 252, 260, 265–
66, 312; nutrition, 252, 254, 268–69,
275, 312. *See also* Education; Poverty
Social programs, 5, 13, 41, 42, 48, 95,
289, 305; earlier de-emphasis of, 42–
43, 59, 86, 105, 296; emergency,
287–90; input/output relation in,
255; policy challenges regarding, 256,
291–92; targeting of, 41, 290–91,
312, 313
Social security systems, 216–17, 220,
240, 242, 243, 269–73, 282, 283, 307
Social unrest, 12, 39, 298
Solidarity Program (Mexico), 97
Solimano, Andrés, 133
Southern Cone: capital inflows and
inflation in, 139; debt problems
weakening financial sectors in, 29;
early reforms viewed as failed in, 115;
trade liberalization and labor market
adjustment in, 122. *See also*
Argentina; Chile; Uruguay
Soviet Union (former), 42

Spain, 42; effect of trade liberalization
on labor market in, 121–22
Speculation, 31, 99–100, 123, 200;
differentiated from longer-term
capital, 141–42
Stability in macroeconomic
environment, 52
State-building, 58–59, 304–5, 309
State-owned enterprise: importance of,
171, 173; public cost of, 173–74;
reform of, 57, 96, 178. *See also*
Privatization
Statism, 303
Stiglitz, Joseph E., 202
Stock markets, 212–14, 219, 222–23
Strikes, 286
Structuralism, 11, 45–46, 48, 171, 200
Structural reforms, 11, 69, 170, 252,
263, 304, 309–11
Subsidies, 26, 41, 99, 291, 308, 313;
export, 51; selective, 51, 54, 197;
tax, 96
Superintendency of Banks (Bolivia),
220, 221

Tablita, 26
Taiwan (China), 212, 274
Tariffs, 127, 128, 160; increases in, 29,
31, 140; reduction or elimination of,
50, 54–55, 152, 158
Tax administration, 13, 86, 96, 97, 291,
307; compliance problems and, 12,
26, 97, 98; means or systems of, 13,
87, 96, 97
Taxation. *See* Capital gains tax; Income
tax
Tax credits or exemptions, 134
Tax loopholes, 96
Tax reform, 55, 57, 69, 86, 92
Tax revenues, 55; inflation affecting, 26,
34, 38
Taylor, Lance, 115
Teachers, 310
Technocratic leadership, 42, 248
Technological capability, 51, 130–31,
248, 310

Telecommunications, 179, 182, 190, 196, 197
TELMEX, 179, 180, 191, 192
Temporary hiring, 313
Tesobonos, 299, 300
Thorp, Rosemary, 43
Trade, 254, 262; antidumping measures, 161; intraregional, 142, 148, 149, 155. *See also* Exports; Imports
Trade agreements, 159; bilateral, 142, 149, 159; customs unions, 117; regional, 11, 46, 142–45
Trade balance, 24
Trade deficits, 24, 124, 316
Trade distortions, 103, 166, 262
Trade openness or liberalization, 32, 43, 56, 57, 119, 123–25, 129, 158; economic effects of, 119–20 130–33, 249; exchange rate policy and, 120; export performance and, 50, 133–37; labor market effects of, 121–22; need or support for, 6, 48, 58, 309; pace of, 120–21, 128; sequencing of, 122–23; technological innovation and, 51, 130–31
Trade restrictions, 31, 56, 248
Trade shocks, 102, 103, 105, 140
TRADETAX variable, 166, 167, 169
Transition issues, 316; in privatization, 176–77; in trade liberalization, 122–23
Transparency: of court systems, 311; of transactions, 175–76
Transportation, 179, 193–94
2008 Bond (Mexican), 77

Underground economies, 173, 221
Unemployment, 18, 45, 262; programs to alleviate, 58, 301
Unidad Popular, 186, 215, 216
Uniform tariffs, 127
Unions, 193, 196, 310
United Nations Economic Commission for Latin America and the Caribbean. *See* CEPAL

United Nations human development index, 260
United States (U.S.), 43, 50, 158, 306; reaction to debt crisis, 71, 73. *See also* Brady Plan
Urrutia, Miguel, 260
Uruguay, 27, 47, 53, 142, 279; Brady Plan agreements of, 73, 79; financial sector in, 202, 203, 204, 206, 207; fiscal policies of, 26; privatization in, 170, 171; trade liberalization in, 124–25
Uruguay Round (GATT), 160–61
U.S.S.R. (former), 42
Utilities, 176, 179, 245; privatization of, 89, 182, 308

Value-added tax, 86–87, 88, 95, 96, 98
van der Tak, Herman, 78
Vegh Villegas, Alejandro, 47
Venezuela, 24, 36, 41, 88, 142, 155, 218; Brady Plan agreements of, 73, 79; exchange rate policy in, 26, 29, 31; expenditure-reducing policies of, 26; financial sector in, 106, 203, 208, 212, 308; foreign ownership in, 180; investment in, 24; labor market in, 279, 281; regulatory framework in, 182; social problems in, 266, 268, 276; trade policy in, 155
Villegas, Alejandro Vegh, 47
Violence, 298, 312

Wages, 26, 27, 124, 261, 279; control or freezing of, 34, 36; debt crisis affecting, 262–63; economic growth affecting, 261, 262, 263, 312; effect of debt crisis on, 262–63; indexation of, 53, 104; minimum, 252, 278, 313
Washington Consensus, 59
Water facilities, 266, 312
Weiss, John, 132
Weston Forum, 299
Wickham, Peter, 78
Women, 259, 260, 266, 267, 275
World Bank, 1, 5, 26, 49, 86, 100, 245,

World Bank (*continued*)
  264, 298; debt crisis and, 18, 78;
  reform or adjustment programs
  assisted by, 9, 55–58, 211, 217; social
  programs supported by, 58, 256, 289
World economic trends, 22, 110, 115, 140
World Trade Organization (WTO), 160

Yen Zone, 142
YPF (petroleum company), 197
Yugoslavia, 121–22

Zapatista revolt. *See* Chiapas state
  uprising
Zedilo, Ernesto, 171, 299